HIGH SPEED
DESIGN TECHNIQUES

PREFACE — **P**

HIGH SPEED OP AMPS — **1**

HIGH SPEED OP AMP APPLICATIONS — **2**

RF/IF SUBSYSTEMS — **3**

HIGH SPEED SAMPLING AND HIGH SPEED ADCs — **4**

HIGH SPEED ADC APPLICATIONS — **5**

HIGH SPEED DACs AND DDS SYSTEMS — **6**

HIGH SPEED HARDWARE DESIGN TECHNIQUES — **7**

INDEX — **I**

ANALOG DEVICES TECHNICAL REFERENCE BOOKS

PUBLISHED BY PRENTICE HALL

Analog-Digital Conversion Handbook
Digital Signal Processing Applications Using the ADSP-2100 Family
(Volume 1:1992, Volume 2:1994)
Digital Signal Processing in VLSI
DSP Laboratory Experiments Using the ADSP-2101
ADSP-2100 Family User's Manual

PUBLISHED BY ANALOG DEVICES

High Speed Design Techniques
Practical Analog Design Techniques
Linear Design Seminar
ADSP-21000 Family Applications Handbook
System Applications Guide
Applications Reference Manual
Amplifier Applications Guide
Mixed Signal Design Seminar Notes
High-Speed Design Seminar Notes
Nonlinear Circuits Handbook
Transducer Interfacing Handbook
Synchro & Resolver Conversion
THE BEST OF *Analog Dialogue*, 1967-1991

HOW TO GET INFORMATION FROM ANALOG DEVICES

Analog Devices publishes data sheets and a host of other technical literature supporting our products and technologies. Follow the instructions below for worldwide access to this information.

FOR DATA SHEETS

U.S.A. and Canada

■ Fax Retrieval. Telephone number 800-446-6212. Call this number and use a faxcode corresponding to the data sheet of your choice for a fax-on-demand through our automated AnalogFax™ system. Data sheets are available 7 days a week, 24 hours a day. Product/faxcode cross reference listings are available by calling the above number and following the prompts. There is a short index with just part numbers, faxcodes, page count and revision for each data sheet. There is also a longer index sorted by product type with short descriptions.

■ World Wide Web and Internet. Our address is http://www.analog.com. Use the browser of your choice and follow the prompts. We also provide extensive DSP literature support on an Internet FTP site. Type ftp ftp.analog.com or ftp 137.71.23.11. Log in as anonymous using your e-mail address for your password.

■ Analog Devices Literature Distribution Center. Call 800-262-5643 and select option two from the voice prompts, or call 617-461-3392 for direct access, or fax your request to 617-821-4273.

■ DSP Bulletin Board Service. For the latest updates, call 617-461-4258, 8 data bits, 1 stop bit, no parity, 300bps to 14.4kbps.

Europe and Israel

■ Fax Retrieval. Telephone number 49-8765-9300-xxxx, where xxxx is the faxcode. For a list of faxcodes dial 49-8765-9300-1000. (1000 is the code for the faxcode cross-reference listing.)

■ World Wide Web. Our address is http://www.analog.com. use the browser of your choice and follow the prompts.

■ Analog Devices Sales Offices. Call your local sales office and request a data sheet. A Worldwide Sales Directory including telephone listings is on pages 218 and 219 of the *1996 Short Form Designers' Guide*.

■ DSP Support Center. Fax requests to **49-89-57005-200 or e-mail dsp.europe@analog.com. The Bulletin Board Service is at **43-1-8887656.

Australia and New Zealand

■ Fax Retrieval. Telephone number 61-59-864377. Follow the voice prompts.

India

■ Call 91-80-526-3606 or fax 91-80-526-3713 and request the data sheet of interest.

Other Locations

■ World Wide Web. Our address is http://www.analog.com. Use the browser of your choice and follow the prompts.

■ Analog Devices Sales Offices. Call your local sales office and request a data sheet. A Worldwide Sales Directory including telephone numbers is listed on pages 218 and 219 of the *1996 Short Form Designers' Guide.*

TECHNICAL SUPPORT AND CUSTOMER SERVICE

■ In the U.S.A. and Canada, call 800-ANALOGD, (800-262-5643). For technical support on all products, select option one, then select the product area of interest. For price and delivery, select option three. For literature and samples, select option two.
Non-800 Number: 617-937-1428

HIGH SPEED
DESIGN TECHNIQUES

ACKNOWLEDGMENTS

Thanks are due the many technical staff members of Analog Devices in Engineering and Marketing who provided invaluable inputs during this project. Particular credit is due the individual authors whose names appear at the beginning of their material.

Special thanks go to Adolfo Garcia, Walter G. Jung, and Ed Grokulsky for thoroughly reviewing the material for content and accuracy.

Linda Grimes Brandon of Brandon's WordService prepared the new illustrations and typeset the text. Ernie Lehtonen of the Analog Devices' art department supplied many camera-ready drawings. Judith Douville compiled the index, and printing was done by R. R. Donnelley and Sons, Inc.

Walt Kester
1996

ISBN-0-916550-17-6

HIGH SPEED
DESIGN TECHNIQUES

PREFACE

SECTION 1
HIGH SPEED OP AMPS

- ■ Voltage Feedback Op Amps

- ■ Current Feedback Op Amps

- ■ Effects of Feedback Capacitance

- ■ High-Speed Current-to-Voltage Converters, and the Effects of Inverting Input Capacitance

- ■ Noise Comparisons between Voltage Feedback Op Amps and Current Feedback Op Amps

- ■ DC Characteristics of High Speed Op Amps

SECTION 2
HIGH SPEED OP AMP APPLICATIONS

- ■ Optimizing the Feedback Network for Maximum Bandwidth Flatness in Wideband CFB Op Amps

- ■ Driving Capacitive Loads

- ■ Cable Drivers and Receivers

- ■ A High Performance Video Line Driver

- ■ Differential Line Drivers/Receivers

- High Speed Clamping Amplifiers

- Single-Supply/Rail-to-Rail Considerations

- High Speed Video Multiplexing with Op Amps Using Disable Function

- Video Programmable Gain Amplifier

- Video Multiplexers and Crosspoint Switches

- High Power Line Drivers and ADSL

- High Speed Photodiode Preamps

SECTION 3
RF/IF SUBSYSTEMS

- Dynamic Range Compression

- Linear VCAs

- Log/Limiting Amplifiers

- Receiver Overview

- Multipliers, Modulators, and Mixers

- Modulation / Demodulation

- Receiver Subsystems

SECTION 4
HIGH SPEED SAMPLING AND HIGH SPEED ADCs

- Fundamentals of High Speed Sampling

- Baseband Antialiasing Filters

- Undersampling

- Antialiasing Filters in Undersampling Applications

- Distortion and Noise in an Ideal N-bit ADC

- Distortion and Noise in Practical ADCs

- High Speed ADC Architectures

SECTION 5
HIGH SPEED ADC APPLICATIONS

- Driving ADC Inputs for Low Distortion and Wide Dynamic Range

- Applications of High Speed ADCs in CCD Imaging

- High Speed ADC Applications in Digital Receivers

SECTION 6
HIGH SPEED DACs AND DDS SYSTEMS

- Introduction to DDS

- Aliasing in DDS Systems

- 125MSPS DDS System (AD9850)

- DDS Systems as ADC Clock Drivers

- Amplitude Modulation in a DDS System

- The AD9831/AD9832 Complete DDS System

- Spurious Free Dynamic Range Considerations in DDS Systems

- High Speed Low Distortion DAC Architectures

- Improving SFDR Using Sample-and-Hold Deglitchers

- High Speed Interpolating DACs

- QPSK Signal Generation Using DDS (AD9853)

SECTION 7
HIGH SPEED HARDWARE DESIGN TECHNIQUES

- Analog Circuit Simulation

- Prototyping Analog Circuits

- Evaluation Boards

- Grounding in High Speed Systems

- Power Supply Noise Reduction and Filtering

- Power Supply Regulation/Conditioning

- Thermal Management

- EMI/RFI Considerations

- Shielding Concepts

INDEX

HIGH SPEED
DESIGN TECHNIQUES

PREFACE   **P**

HIGH SPEED OP AMPS   **1**

HIGH SPEED OP AMP APPLICATIONS   **2**

RF/IF SUBSYSTEMS   **3**

HIGH SPEED SAMPLING AND HIGH SPEED ADCs   **4**

HIGH SPEED ADC APPLICATIONS   **5**

HIGH SPEED DACs AND DDS SYSTEMS   **6**

HIGH SPEED HARDWARE DESIGN TECHNIQUES   **7**

INDEX   **I**

PREFACE

P

P

PREFACE:
HIGH SPEED DESIGN TECHNIQUES

High speed integrated circuits, both analog, digital, and mixed-signal are used in all types of electronic equipment today. This book examines high speed *linear* ICs both from the theoretical and practical application point of view.

Figure P.1 shows some of the typical applications for high speed integrated circuits by market segment. Many applications can be filled using standard linear IC products, while others may be better served with specially designed chipsets (see Figure P.2).

All of these high speed linear ICs depend upon a broad base of high speed core competencies shown in Figure P.3. Analog Devices has been a leader in real-world signal processing for over 30 years and has the required expertise in each critical competency area. Regardless of how complex or highly integrated mixed-signal ICs may become, there is no escaping the requirement for these basic building blocks.

An understanding of these building blocks is required for the customer to successfully specify, select, and apply new high speed products at the system level. While a detailed knowledge of the internal circuits is not required, an overall understanding of the operation of the devices is critical to success.

This book is not intended to be a system design manual. Instead, it covers the theory and application of many high speed analog signal processing building blocks such as amplifiers, ADCs, DACs, etc. System applications are presented when they are of broad general interest or illustrate emerging market trends.

The proper application of high speed devices also requires a thorough knowledge of good hardware design techniques, such as simulation, prototyping, layout, decoupling, and grounding. The last section in the book focuses on these issues as well as EMI and RFI design considerations.

HIGH SPEED PRODUCTS: TYPICAL APPLICATIONS

VIDEO	IMAGING	COMMUNICATIONS	INSTRUMENTATION

◆ Cameras	◆ Medical	◆ Cellular:
		   Broadband
		   Narrowband
			◆ Oscilloscopes

◆ Mixing	◆ Scanners	◆ Direct Broadcast
		   Satellite
			◆ Spectrum
			   Analyzers

◆ Distribution	◆ Copiers	◆ Hybrid Fiber Coax
		   (HFC)
			◆ Frequency
			   Synthesizers

◆ Video
   Conferencing
	◆ Lasers	◆ CATV	◆ Automatic Test
			   Equipment

◆ Displays	◆ CCD	◆ ADSL/HDSL	◆ Data Acquisition
◆ MPEG Systems	◆ Radar/Sonar	◆ Data Recovery and Retiming	

Figure P.1

ADI HIGH SPEED INTEGRATED / CHIPSET SOLUTIONS

■ Cellular Communications: GSM, DECT,
   AMPS, PCS, etc. (Handsets and Basestations)

■ ADSL/HDSL

■ CCD Imaging

■ Video Signal Processing (MPEG, etc.)

■ Fiber Optic and Disk Drive Data Recovery

■ Direct Broadcast Satellite Receivers

■ High Speed Modems

■ Multimedia Sound and Video Processing

Figure P.2

CORE COMPETENCIES: "DC TO LIGHT"

- **Amplifiers:**
  Op Amps, VCAs, PGAs, Log Amps,
  Sample-and-Hold Amplifiers

- **Switches and Multiplexers**

- **Analog-to-Digital Converters (ADCs)**

- **Digital-to-Analog Converters (DACs)**

- **Analog Signal Processing**
  Multipliers, RMS-DC Converters, etc.

- **RF/IF Signal Processing**

- **DSP**

Figure P.3

SECTION 1

HIGH SPEED OP AMPS

- Voltage Feedback Op Amps

- Current Feedback Op Amps

- Effects of Feedback Capacitance

- High-Speed Current-to-Voltage Converters, and the Effects of Inverting Input Capacitance

- Noise Comparisons between Voltage Feedback Op Amps and Current Feedback Op Amps

- DC Characteristics of High Speed Op Amps

1

SECTION 1
HIGH SPEED OPERATIONAL AMPLIFIERS
Walt Kester

INTRODUCTION

High speed analog signal processing applications, such as video and communications, require op amps which have wide bandwidth, fast settling time, low distortion and noise, high output current, good DC performance, and operate at low supply voltages. These devices are widely used as gain blocks, cable drivers, ADC pre-amps, current-to-voltage converters, etc. Achieving higher bandwidths for less power is extremely critical in today's portable and battery-operated communications equipment. The rapid progress made over the last few years in high-speed linear circuits has hinged not only on the development of IC processes but also on innovative circuit topologies.

The evolution of high speed processes by using amplifier bandwidth as a function of supply current as a figure of merit is shown in Figure 1.1. (In the case of duals, triples, and quads, the current per amplifier is used). Analog Devices BiFET process, which produced the AD712 and OP249 (3MHz bandwidth, 3mA current), yields about 1MHz per mA. The CB (Complementary Bipolar) process (AD817, AD847, AD811, etc.) yields about 10MHz/mA of supply current. Ft's of the CB process PNP transistors are about 700MHz, and the NPN's about 900MHz.

The latest generation complementary bipolar process from Analog Devices is a high speed dielectrically isolated process called XFCB (eXtra Fast Complementary Bipolar). This process (2-4 GHz Ft matching PNP and NPN transistors), coupled with innovative circuit topologies allow op amps to achieve new levels of cost-effective performance at astonishing low quiescent currents. The approximate figure of merit for this process is typically 100MHz/mA, although the AD8011 op amp is capable of 300MHz bandwidth on 1mA of supply current due to its unique two-stage current-feedback architecture.

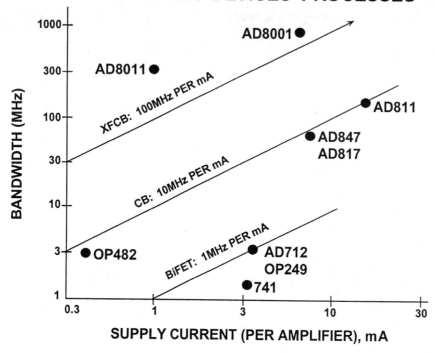

Figure 1.1

In order to select intelligently the correct op amp for a given application, an understanding of the various op amp topologies as well as the tradeoffs between them is required. The two most widely used topologies are voltage feedback (VFB) and current feedback (CFB). The following discussion treats each in detail and discusses the similarities and differences.

VOLTAGE FEEDBACK (VFB) OP AMPS

A voltage feedback (VFB) op amp is distinguished from a current feedback (CFB) op amp by circuit topology. The VFB op amp is certainly the most popular in low frequency applications, but the CFB op amp has some advantages at high frequencies. We will discuss CFB in detail later, but first the more traditional VFB architecture.

Early IC voltage feedback op amps were made on "all NPN" processes.

These processes were optimized for NPN transistors, and the "lateral" PNP transistors had relatively poor performance. Lateral PNPs were generally only used as current sources, level shifters, or for other non-critical functions. A simplified diagram of a typical VFB op amp manufactured on such a process is shown in Figure 1.2.

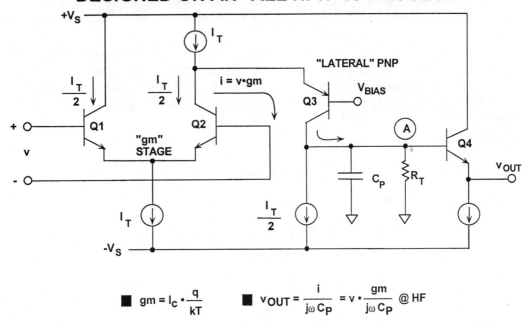

VOLTAGE FEEDBACK (VFB) OP AMP DESIGNED ON AN "ALL NPN" IC PROCESS

$$gm = I_C \cdot \frac{q}{kT}$$

$$v_{OUT} = \frac{i}{j\omega C_P} = v \cdot \frac{gm}{j\omega C_P} \text{ @ HF}$$

Figure 1.2

The input stage is a differential pair consisting of either a bipolar pair (Q1, Q2) or a FET pair. This "g_m" (transconductance) stage converts the small-signal differential input voltage, v, into a current, i, i.e., it's transfer function is measured in units of conductance, $1/\Omega$, (or mhos). The small signal emitter resistance, r_e, is approximately equal to the reciprocal of the small-signal g_m. The formula for the small-signal g_m of a single bipolar transistor is given by the following equation:

$$g_m = \frac{1}{r_e} = \frac{q}{kT}(I_C) = \frac{q}{kT}\left(\frac{I_T}{2}\right), \text{ or}$$

$$g_m \approx \left(\frac{1}{26mV}\right)\left(\frac{I_T}{2}\right)$$

I_T is the differential pair tail current, I_C is the collector bias current ($I_C = I_T/2$), q is the electron charge, k is Boltzmann's constant, and T is abso-

lute temperature. At +25°C, V_T = kT/q= 26mV (often called the Thermal Voltage, V_T).

As we will see shortly, the amplifier unity gain-bandwidth product, f_u, is equal to $g_m/2\pi Cp$, where the capacitance Cp is used to set the dominant pole frequency. For this reason, the tail current, I_T, is made proportional to absolute temperature (PTAT). This current tracks the variation in r_e with temperature thereby making g_m independent of temperature. It is relatively easy to make Cp reasonably constant over temperature.

The output of one side of the g_m stage drives the emitter of a lateral PNP transistor (Q3). It is important to note that Q3 is not used to amplify the signal, only to level shift, i.e., the signal current variation in the collector of Q2 appears at the collector of Q3. The output collector current of Q3 develops a voltage across high impedance node A. Cp sets the dominant pole of the frequency response. Emitter follower Q4 provides a low impedance output.

The effective load at the high impedance node A can be represented by a resistance, R_T, in parallel with the dominant pole capacitance, Cp. The small-signal output voltage, v_{out}, is

equal to the small-signal current, i, multiplied by the impedance of the parallel combination of R_T and Cp.

Figure 1.3 shows a simple model for the single-stage amplifier and the corresponding Bode plot. The Bode plot is constructed on a log-log scale for convenience.

MODEL AND BODE PLOT FOR A VFB OP AMP

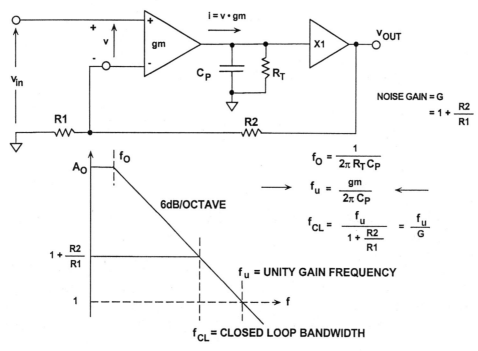

Figure 1.3

The low frequency breakpoint, f_0, is given by:

$$f_0 = \frac{1}{2\pi R_T Cp}.$$

Note that the high frequency response is determined solely by g_m and Cp:

$$v_{out} = v \cdot \frac{g_m}{j\omega Cp}.$$

The unity gain-bandwidth frequency, f_u, occurs where $|v_{out}| = |v|$. Solving

the above equation for f_u, assuming $|v_{out}| = |v|$:

$$f_u = \frac{g_m}{2\pi Cp}.$$

We can use feedback theory to derive the closed-loop relationship between the circuit's signal input voltage, v_{in}, and it's output voltage, v_{out}:

$$\frac{v_{out}}{v_{in}} = \frac{1 + \dfrac{R2}{R1}}{1 + \dfrac{j\omega Cp}{g_m}\left(1 + \dfrac{R2}{R1}\right)}$$

At the op amp 3dB closed-loop bandwidth frequency, f_{cl}, the following is true:

$$\frac{2\pi f_{cl} Cp}{g_m}\left(1+\frac{R2}{R1}\right)=1\text{, and hence}$$

$$f_{cl} = \frac{g_m}{2\pi Cp}\left(\frac{1}{1+\frac{R2}{R1}}\right)\text{, or}$$

$$f_{cl} = \frac{f_u}{1+\frac{R2}{R1}}.$$

This demonstrates a fundamental property of VFB op amps: *The closed-loop bandwidth multiplied by the closed-loop gain is a constant*, i.e., the VFB op amp exhibits a constant gain-bandwidth product over most of the usable frequency range.

Some VFB op amps (called *de-compensated*) are unstable at unity gain and are designed to be operated at some minimum amount of closed-loop gain. For these op amps, the gain-bandwidth product is still relatively constant over the region of allowable gain.

Now, consider the following typical example: $I_T = 100\mu A$, $Cp = 2pF$. We find that:

$$g_m = \frac{I_T/2}{V_T} = \frac{50\mu A}{26mV} = \frac{1}{520\Omega}$$

$$f_u = \frac{g_m}{2\pi Cp} = \frac{1}{2\pi(520)(2\cdot10^{-12})} = 153MHz$$

Now, we must consider the large-signal response of the circuit. The slew-rate, SR, is simply the total available charging current, $I_T/2$, divided by the dominant pole capacitance, Cp. For the example under consideration,

$$I = C\frac{dv}{dt},\ \frac{dv}{dt} = SR,\ SR = \frac{I}{C}$$

$$SR = \frac{I_T/2}{Cp} = \frac{50\mu A}{2pF} = 25V/\mu s.$$

The full-power bandwidth (FPBW) of the op amp can now be calculated from the formula:

$$FPBW = \frac{SR}{2\pi A} = \frac{25V/\mu s}{2\pi\cdot1V} = 4MHz,,$$

where A is the peak amplitude of the output signal. If we assume a 2V peak-to-peak output sinewave (certainly a reasonable assumption for high speed applications), then we obtain a FPBW of only 4MHz, even though the small-signal unity gain-bandwidth product is 153MHz! For a 2V p-p output sinewave, distortion will begin to occur much lower than the actual FPBW frequency. We must increase the SR by a factor of about 40 in order for the FPBW to equal 153MHz. The only way to do this is to increase the tail current, I_T, of the input differential pair by the same factor. This implies a bias current of 4mA in order to achieve a FPBW of 160MHz. We are assuming that Cp is a fixed value of 2pF and cannot be lowered by design.

VFB OP AMP BANDWIDTH AND SLEW RATE CALCULATION

■ Assume that $I_T = 100\mu A$, $Cp = 2pF$

■ $g_m = \dfrac{I_C}{V_T} = \dfrac{50\mu A}{26mV} = \dfrac{1}{520\Omega}$

■ $f_u = \dfrac{g_m}{2\pi\, Cp} = 153MHz$

■ Slew Rate = SR = $\dfrac{I_T/2}{Cp} = 25V/\mu s$

BUT FOR 2V PEAK-PEAK OUTPUT (A = 1V)

■ $FPBW = \dfrac{SR}{2\pi\, A} = 4MHz$

■ Must increase I_T to 4mA to get FPBW = 160MHz!!

■ Reduce g_m by adding emitter degeneration resistors

Figure 1.4

In practice, the FPBW of the op amp should be approximately 5 to 10 times the maximum output frequency in order to achieve acceptable distortion performance (typically 55-80dBc @ 5 to 20MHz, but actual system requirements vary widely).

Notice, however, that increasing the tail current causes a proportional increase in g_m and hence f_u. In order to prevent possible instability due to the large increase in f_u, g_m can be reduced by inserting resistors in series with the emitters of Q1 and Q2 (this technique, called *emitter degeneration*, also serves to linearize the g_m transfer function and lower distortion).

A major inefficiency of conventional bipolar voltage feedback op amps is their inability to achieve high slew rates without proportional increases in quiescent current (assuming that Cp is fixed, and has a reasonable minimum value of 2 or 3pF). This of course is not meant to say that high speed op amps designed using this architecture are deficient, it's just that there are circuit design techniques available which allow equivalent performance at lower quiescent currents. This is extremely important in portable battery operated equipment where every milliwatt of power dissipation is critical.

VFB OP AMPS DESIGNED ON COMPLEMENTARY BIPOLAR PROCESSES

With the advent of complementary bipolar (CB) processes having high quality PNP transistors as well as NPNs, VFB op amp configurations such as the one shown in the simplified diagram (Figure 1.5) became popular.

VFB OP AMP USING TWO GAIN STAGES

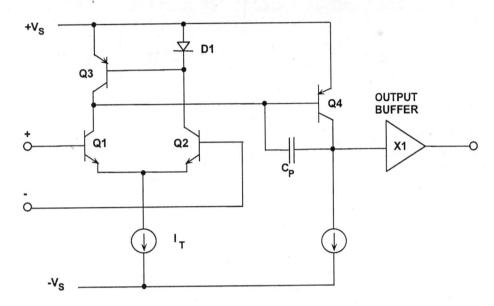

Figure 1.5

Notice that the input differential pair (Q1, Q2) is loaded by a current mirror (Q3 and D1). We show D1 as a diode for simplicity, but it is actually a diode-connected PNP transistor (matched to Q3) with the base and collector connected to each other. This simplification will be used in many of the circuit diagrams to follow in this section. The common emitter transistor, Q4, provides a *second* voltage gain stage. Since the PNP transistors are fabricated on a complementary bipolar process, they are high quality and matched to the NPNs and suitable for voltage gain. The dominant pole of the amplifier is set by Cp, and the combination of the gain stage, Q4, and Cp is often referred to as a *Miller Integrator*. The unity-gain output buffer is usually a complementary emitter follower.

The model for this two-stage VFB op amp is shown in Figure 1.6. Notice that the unity gain-bandwidth frequency, f_u, is still determined by the gm of the input stage and the dominant pole capacitance, Cp. The second gain stage increases the DC open-loop gain, but the maximum slew rate is still limited by the input stage tail current: $SR = I_T/Cp$.

MODEL FOR TWO STAGE VFB OP AMP

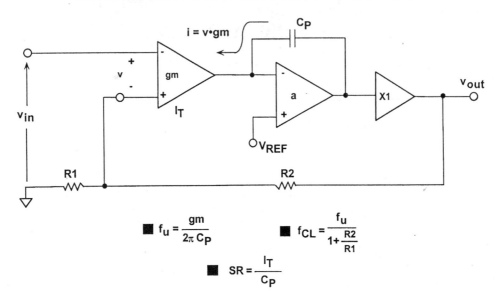

$$f_u = \frac{gm}{2\pi\, C_P}$$

$$f_{CL} = \frac{f_u}{1 + \dfrac{R2}{R1}}$$

$$SR = \frac{I_T}{C_P}$$

Figure 1.6

The two-stage topology is widely used throughout the IC industry in VFB op amps, both precision and high speed.

Another popular VFB op amp architecture is the *folded cascode* as shown in Figure 1.7. An industry-standard video amplifier family (the AD847) is based on this architecture. This circuit takes advantage of the fast PNPs available on a CB process. The differential signal currents in the collectors of Q1 and Q2 are fed to the emitters of a PNP cascode transistor pair (hence the term *folded cascode*). The collectors of Q3 and Q4 are loaded with the current mirror, D1 and Q5, and Q4 provides voltage gain. This single-stage architecture uses the junction capacitance at the high-impedance node for compensation (and some variations of the design bring this node to an external pin so that additional external capacitance can be added).

AD847-FAMILY FOLDED CASCODE SIMPLIFIED CIRCUIT

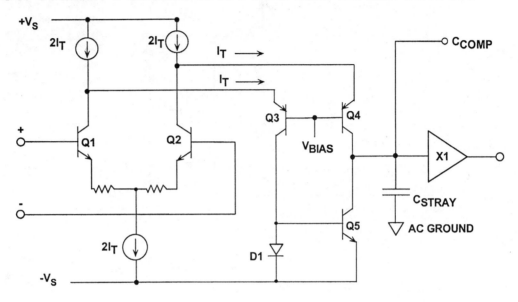

Figure 1.7

With no emitter degeneration resistors in Q1 and Q2, and no additional external compensating capacitance, this circuit is only stable for high closed-loop gains. However, unity-gain compensated versions of this family are available which have the appropriate amount of emitter degeneration.

The availability of JFETs on a CB process allows not only low input bias current but also improvements in the tradeoff which must be made between g_m and I_T found in bipolar input stages. Figure 1.8 shows a simplified diagram of the AD845 16MHz op amp.

JFETs have a much lower g_m per mA of tail current than a bipolar transistor. This allows the input tail current (hence the slew rate) to be increased without having to increase Cp to maintain stability. The unusual thing about this seemingly poor performance of the JFET is that it is exactly what is needed on the input stage. For a typical JFET, the value of g_m is approximately $I_s/1V$ (I_s is the source current), rather than $I_c/26mV$ for a bipolar transistor, i.e., about 40 times lower. This allows much higher tail currents (and higher slew rates) for a given g_m when JFETs are used as the input stage.

AD845 BiFET 16MHz OP AMP SIMPLIFIED CIRCUIT

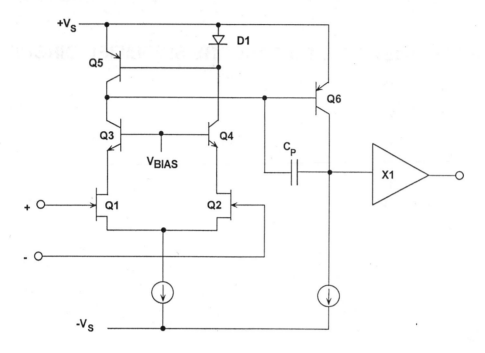

Figure 1.8

A New VFB Op Amp Architecture for "Current-on-Demand" Performance, Lower Power, and Improved Slew Rate

Until now, op amp designers had to make the above tradeoffs between the input gm stage quiescent current and the slew-rate and distortion performance. Analog Devices' has patented a new circuit core which supplies *current-on-demand* to charge and discharge the dominant pole capacitor, Cp, while allowing the quiescent current to be small. The additional current is proportional to the fast slewing input signal and adds to the quiescent current. A simplified diagram of the basic core cell is shown in Figure 1.9.

"QUAD-CORE" VFB gm STAGE FOR CURRENT-ON-DEMAND

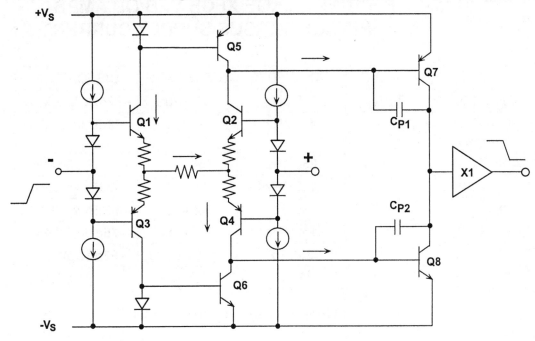

Figure 1.9

The *quad-core* (g_m stage) consists of transistors Q1, Q2, Q3, and Q4 with their emitters connected together as shown. Consider a positive step voltage on the inverting input. This voltage produces a proportional current in Q1 which is mirrored into Cp1 by Q5. The current through Q1 also flows through Q4 and Cp2. At the dynamic range limit, Q2 and Q3 are correspondingly turned off. Notice that the charging and discharging current for Cp1 and Cp2 is not limited by the quad core bias current. In practice, however, small current-limiting resistors are required forming an "H" resistor network as shown. Q7 and Q8 form the second gain stage (driven differentially from the collectors of Q5 and Q6), and the output is buffered by a unity-gain complementary emitter follower.

The quad core configuration is patented (Roy Gosser, U.S. Patent 5,150,074 and

others pending), as well as the circuits which establish the quiescent bias currents (not shown in the diagram). A number of new VFB op amps using this proprietary configuration have been released and have unsurpassed high frequency low distortion performance, bandwidth, and slew rate at the indicated quiescent current levels (see Figure 1.10). The AD9631, AD8036, and AD8047 are optimized for a gain of +1, while the AD9632, AD8037, and AD8048 for a gain of +2. The same quad-core architecture is used as the *second* stage of the AD8041 rail-to-rail output, zero-volt input single-supply op amp. The input stage is a differential PNP pair which allows the input common-mode signal to go about 200mV below the negative supply rail. The AD8042 and AD8044 are dual and quad versions of the AD8041.

"QUAD-CORE" TWO STAGE XFCB VFB OP AMPS
AC CHARACTERISTICS VERSUS SUPPLY CURRENT

PART #	I_{SY} / AMP	BANDWIDTH	SLEW RATE	DISTORTION
AD9631/32	17mA	320MHz	1300V/µs	−72dBc@20MHz
AD8036/37 Clamped	20mA	240MHz	1200V/µs	−72dBc@20MHz
AD8047/48	5.8mA	250MHz	750V/µs	−66dBc@5MHz
AD8041 (1)	5.2mA	160MHz	160V/µs	−69dBc@10MHz
AD8042 (2)	5.2mA	160MHz	200V/µs	−64dBc@10MHz
AD8044 (4)	2.75mA	150MHz	170V/µs	−75dBc@5MHz
AD8031 (1)	0.75mA	80MHz	30V/µs	−62dBc@1MHz
AD8032 (2)	0.75mA	80MHz	30V/µs	−62dBc@1MHz

Number in ( ) indicates single, dual, or quad

Figure 1.10

CURRENT FEEDBACK (CFB) OP AMPS

We will now examine the current feedback (CFB) op amp topology which has recently become popular in high speed op amps. The circuit concepts were introduced many years ago, however modern high speed complementary bipolar processes are required to take full advantage of the architecture.

It has long been known that in bipolar transistor circuits, currents can be switched faster than voltages, other things being equal. This forms the basis of non-saturating emitter-coupled logic (ECL) and devices such as current-output DACs. Maintaining low impedances at the current switching nodes helps to minimize the effects of stray capacitance, one of the largest detriments to high speed operation. The

current mirror is a good example of how currents can be switched with a minimum amount of delay.

The current feedback op amp topology is simply an application of these fundamental principles of current steering. A simplified CFB op amp is shown in Figure 1.11. The non-inverting input is high impedance and is buffered directly to the inverting input through the complementary emitter follower buffers Q1 and Q2. Note that the inverting input impedance is very low (typically 10 to 100Ω), because of the low emitter resistance. In the ideal case, it would be zero. This is a fundamental difference between a CFB and a VFB op amp, and also a feature which gives the CFB op amp some unique advantages.

SIMPLIFIED CURRENT FEEDBACK (CFB) OP AMP

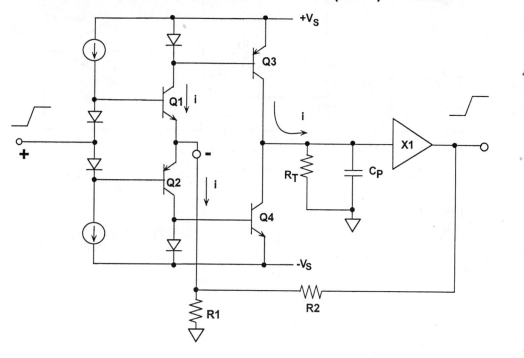

Figure 1.11

The collectors of Q1 and Q2 drive current mirrors which mirror the inverting input current to the high impedance node, modeled by RT and Cp. The high impedance node is buffered by a complementary unity gain emitter follower. Feedback from the output to the inverting input acts to force the inverting input *current* to zero, hence the term *Current Feedback*. (In the ideal case, for zero inverting input impedance, no small signal voltage can exist at this node, only small signal current).

Consider a positive step voltage applied to the non-inverting input of the CFB op amp. Q1 immediately sources a proportional current into the external feedback resistors creating an *error current* which is mirrored to the high impedance node by Q3. The voltage developed at the high impedance node is equal to this current multiplied by

the equivalent impedance. This is where the term *transimpedance op amp* originated, since the transfer function is an impedance, rather than a unitless voltage ratio as in a traditional VFB op amp.

Note that the error current is not limited by the input stage bias current, i.e., *there is no slew-rate limitation in an ideal CFB op amp*. The current mirrors supply *current-on-demand* from the power supplies. The negative feedback loop then forces the output voltage to a value which reduces the inverting input error current to zero.

The model for a CFB op amp is shown in Figure 1.12 along with the corresponding Bode plot. The Bode plot is plotted on a log-log scale, and the open-loop gain is expressed as a transimpedance, T(s), with units of ohms.

CFB OP AMP MODEL AND BODE PLOT

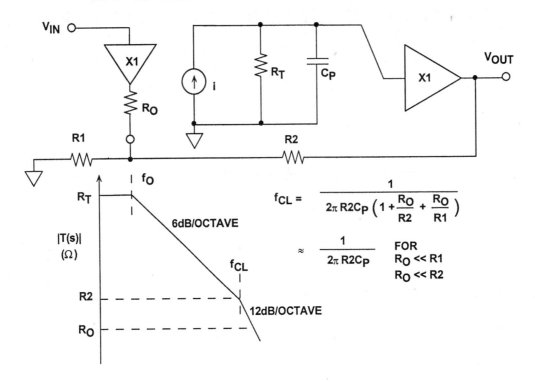

Figure 1.12

The finite output impedance of the input buffer is modeled by Ro. The input error current is *i*. By applying the principles of negative feedback, we can derive the expression for the op amp transfer function:

$$\frac{v_{out}}{v_{in}} = \frac{1 + \dfrac{R2}{R1}}{1 + j\omega C p R2\left(1 + \dfrac{Ro}{R2} + \dfrac{Ro}{R1}\right)}.$$

At the op amp 3db closed-loop bandwidth frequency, f_{cl}, the following is true:

$$2\pi f_{cl} C p R2\left(1 + \frac{Ro}{R2} + \frac{Ro}{R1}\right) = 1.$$

Solving for f_{cl}:

$$f_{cl} = \frac{1}{2\pi C p R2\left(1 + \dfrac{Ro}{R2} + \dfrac{Ro}{R1}\right)}.$$

For the condition Ro << R2 and R1, the equation simply reduces to:

$$f_{cl} = \frac{1}{2\pi C p R2}$$

Examination of this equation quickly reveals that *the closed-loop bandwidth of a CFB op amp is determined by the internal dominant pole capacitor, Cp, and the external feedback resistor R2, and is independent of the gain-setting resistor, R1.* This ability to maintain constant bandwidth independent of gain makes CFB op amps ideally suited for wideband programmable gain amplifiers.

1

Because the closed-loop bandwidth is inversely proportional to the external feedback resistor, R2, a CFB op amp is usually optimized for a specific R2. Increasing R2 from it's optimum value lowers the bandwidth, and decreasing it may lead to oscillation and instability because of high frequency parasitic poles.

The frequency response of the AD8011 CFB op amp is shown in Figure 1.13 for various closed-loop values of gain (+1, +2, and +10). Note that even at a gain of +10, the closed loop bandwidth is still greater than 100MHz. The peaking which occurs at a gain of +1 is typical of wideband CFB op amps when used in the non-inverting mode and is due primarily to stray capacitance at the inverting input. The peaking can be reduced by sacrificing bandwidth and using a slightly larger feedback resistor. The AD8011 CFB op amp represents state-of-the-art performance, and key specifications are shown in Figure 1.14.

AD8011 FREQUENCY RESPONSE
G = +1, +2, +10

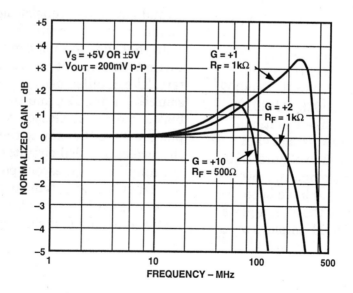

Figure 1.13

AD8011 CFB OP AMP KEY SPECIFICATIONS

- ■ 1mA Power Supply Current (+5V or ±5V)

- ■ 300MHz Bandwidth (G = +1)

- ■ 2000 V/µs Slew Rate

- ■ 29ns Settling Time to 0.1%

- ■ Video Specifications (G = +2)
  Differential Gain Error 0.02%
  Differential Phase Error 0.06°
  25MHz 0.1dB Bandwidth

- ■ Distortion
  –70dBc @ 5MHz
  –62dBc @ 20MHz

- ■ Fully Specified for ±5V or +5V Operation

Figure 1.14

Traditional current feedback op amps have been limited to a single gain stage, using current-mirrors as previously described. The AD8011 (and also others in this family: AD8001, AD8002, AD8004, AD8005, AD8009, AD8013, AD8072, AD8073), unlike traditional CFB op amps uses a two-stage gain configuration as shown in Figure 1.15. Until now, fully complementary two-gain stage CFB op amps have been impractical because of their high power dissipation. The AD8011 employs a second gain stage consisting of a pair of complementary amplifiers (Q3 and Q4). Note that they are not connected as current mirrors but as grounded-emitters. The detailed design of current sources (I1 and I2), and their respective bias circuits (Roy Gosser, patent-applied-for) are the key to the success of the two-stage CFB circuit; they keep the amplifier's quiescent power low, yet are capable of supplying *current-on-demand* for wide current excursions required during fast slewing.

SIMPLIFIED TWO-STAGE CFB OP AMP

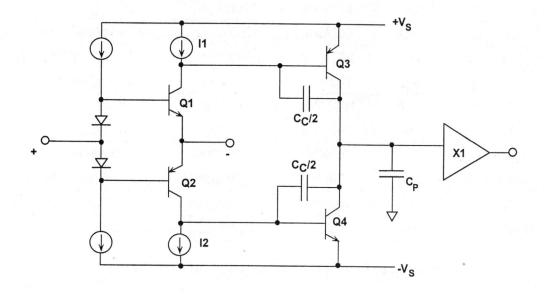

Figure 1.15

A further advantage of the two-stage amplifier is the higher overall bandwidth (for the same power), which means lower signal distortion and the ability to drive heavier external loads.

Thus far, we have learned several key features of CFB op amps. The most important is that for a given complementary bipolar IC process, *CFB generally always yields higher FPBW (hence lower distortion) than VFB for the same amount of quiescent supply current.* This is because there is practically no slew-rate limiting in CFB. Because of this, the full power bandwidth and the small signal bandwidth are approximately the same.

The second important feature is that the *inverting input impedance of a CFB op amp is very low.* This can be advantageous when using the op amp in the inverting mode as an I/V converter, because there is much less sensitivity to inverting input capacitance than with VFB.

The third feature is that *the closed-loop bandwidth of a CFB op amp is determined by the value of the internal Cp capacitor and the external feedback resistor R2 and is relatively independent of the gain-setting resistor R1.* We will now examine some typical applications issues and make further comparisons between CFBs and VFBs.

CURRENT FEEDBACK OP AMP FAMILY

PART	I$_{SY}$/AMP	BANDWIDTH	SLEW RATE	DISTORTION
AD8001 (1)	5.5mA	880MHz	1200V/μs	−65dBc@5MHz
AD8002 (2)	5.0mA	600MHz	1200 V/μs	−65dBc@5MHz
AD8004 (4)	3.5mA	250MHz	3000 V/μs	−78dBc@5MHz
AD8005 (1)	0.4mA	180MHz	500 V/μs	−53dBc@5MHz
AD8009 (1)	11mA	1000MHz	7000 V/μs	−80dBc@5MHz
AD8011 (1)	1mA	300MHz	2000 V/μs	−70dBc@5MHz
AD8012 (2)	1mA	300MHz	1200 V/μs	−66dBc@5MHz
AD8013 (3)	4mA	140MHz	1000 V/μs	ΔG=0.02%, Δφ=0.06 °
AD8072 (2)	5mA	100MHz	500 V/μs	ΔG=0.05%, Δφ=0.1 °
AD8073 (3)	5mA	100MHz	500 V/μs	ΔG=0.05%, Δφ=0.1 °

Number in ( ) Indicates Single, Dual, Triple, or Quad

Figure 1.16

SUMMARY: CURRENT FEEDBACK OP AMPS

- CFB yields higher FPBW and lower distortion than VFB for the same process and power dissipation

- Inverting input impedance of a CFB op amp is low, non-inverting input impedance is high

- Closed-loop bandwidth of a CFB op amp is determined by the internal dominant-pole capacitance and the external feedback resistor, independent of the gain-setting resistor

Figure 1.17

EFFECTS OF FEEDBACK CAPACITANCE IN OP AMPS

At this point, the term *noise gain* needs some clarification. Noise gain is the amount by which a small amplitude noise voltage source in series with an input terminal of an op amp is amplified when measured at the output. The input voltage noise of an op amp is modeled in this way. It should be noted that the DC noise gain can also be used to reflect the input offset voltage (and other op amp input error sources) to the output.

Noise gain must be distinguished from *signal gain*. Figure 1.18 shows an op amp in the inverting and non-inverting mode. In the non-inverting mode, notice that noise gain is equal to signal gain. However, in the inverting mode, the noise gain doesn't change, but the signal gain is now –R2/R1. Resistors are shown as feedback elements, however, the networks may also be reactive.

NOISE GAIN AND SIGNAL GAIN COMPARISON

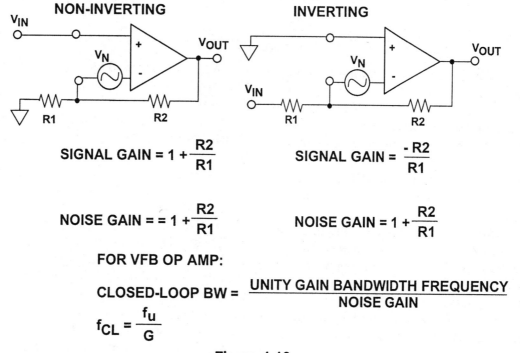

NON-INVERTING

$$\text{SIGNAL GAIN} = 1 + \frac{R2}{R1}$$

$$\text{NOISE GAIN} = = 1 + \frac{R2}{R1}$$

INVERTING

$$\text{SIGNAL GAIN} = \frac{-R2}{R1}$$

$$\text{NOISE GAIN} = 1 + \frac{R2}{R1}$$

FOR VFB OP AMP:

$$\text{CLOSED-LOOP BW} = \frac{\text{UNITY GAIN BANDWIDTH FREQUENCY}}{\text{NOISE GAIN}}$$

$$f_{CL} = \frac{f_u}{G}$$

Figure 1.18

Two other configurations are shown in Figure 1.19 where the noise gain has been increased independent of signal gain by the addition of R3 across the input terminals of the op amp. This technique can be used to stabilize decompensated op amps which are unstable for low values of noise gain. However, the sensitivity to input noise and offset voltage is correspondingly increased.

INCREASING THE NOISE GAIN
WITHOUT AFFECTING SIGNAL GAIN

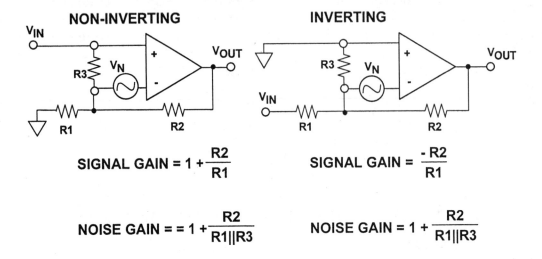

NON-INVERTING

$$\text{SIGNAL GAIN} = 1 + \frac{R2}{R1}$$

$$\text{NOISE GAIN} = = 1 + \frac{R2}{R1\|R3}$$

INVERTING

$$\text{SIGNAL GAIN} = \frac{-R2}{R1}$$

$$\text{NOISE GAIN} = 1 + \frac{R2}{R1\|R3}$$

Figure 1.19

Noise gain is often plotted as a function of frequency on a Bode plot to determine the op amp stability. If the feedback is purely resistive, the noise gain is constant with frequency. However, reactive elements in the feedback loop will cause it to change with frequency. Using a log-log scale for the Bode plot allows the noise gain to be easily drawn by simply calculating the breakpoints determined by the frequencies of the various poles and zeros. The point of intersection of the noise gain with the open-loop gain not only determines the op amp *closed-loop bandwidth*, but also can be used to analyze stability.

An excellent explanation of how to make simplifying approximations using Bode plots to analyze gain and phase performance of a feedback networks is given in Reference 4.

Just as signal gain and noise gain can be different, so can the *signal bandwidth* and the *closed-loop bandwidth*. The op amp closed-loop bandwidth, f_{cl},

is always determined by the intersection of the noise gain with the open-loop frequency response. The signal bandwidth is equal to the closed-loop bandwidth only if the feedback network is purely resistive.

It is quite common to use a capacitor in the feedback loop of a VFB op amp to shape the frequency response as in a simple single-pole lowpass filter (see Figure 1.20a). The resulting noise gain is plotted on a Bode plot to analyze stability and phase margin. Stability of the system is determined by the net slope of the noise gain and the open loop gain where they intersect. For unconditional stability, the noise gain plot must intersect the open loop response with a net slope of less than 12dB/octave. In this case, the net slope where they intersect is 6dB/octave, indicating a stable condition. Notice for the case drawn in Figure 1.20a, the second pole in the frequency response occurs at a considerably higher frequency than f_u.

NOISE GAIN STABILITY ANALYSIS FOR VFB AND CFB OP AMPS WITH FEEDBACK CAPACITOR

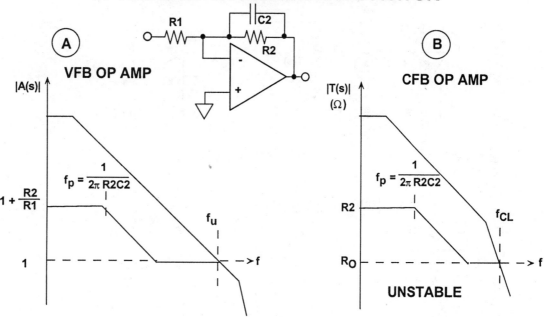

Figure 1.20

In the case of the CFB op amp (Figure 1.20b), the same analysis is used, except that the open-loop transimpedance gain, T(s), is used to construct the Bode plot. The definition of *noise gain* (for the purposes of stability analysis) for a CFB op amp, however, must be redefined in terms of a *current* noise source attached to the inverting input (see Figure 1.21). This current is re-flected to the output by an impedance which we define to be the "current noise gain" of a CFB op amp:

"CURRENT NOISE GAIN"

$$\equiv Ro + Z2\left(1 + \frac{Ro}{Z1}\right)$$

CURRENT "NOISE GAIN" DEFINITION
FOR CFB OP AMP FOR USE IN STABILITY ANALYSIS

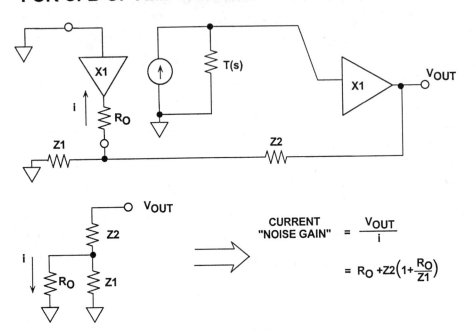

$$\text{CURRENT "NOISE GAIN"} = \frac{V_{OUT}}{i}$$

$$= R_O + Z2\left(1+\frac{R_O}{Z1}\right)$$

Figure 1.21

Now, return to Figure 1.20b, and observe the CFB *current noise gain* plot. At low frequencies, the CFB current noise gain is simply R2 (making the assumption that Ro is much less than Z1 or Z2. The first pole is determined by R2 and C2. As the frequency continues to increase, C2 becomes a short circuit, and all the invertng input current flows through Ro (refer back to Figure 1.21).

The CFB op amp is normally optimized for best performance for a fixed feedback resistor, R2. Additional poles in the transimpedance gain, T(s), occur at frequencies above the closed loop bandwidth, f_{cl}, (set by R2). Note that the intersection of the CFB current noise

gain with the open-loop T(s) occurs where the slope of the T(s) function is 12dB/octave. This indicates instability and possible oscillation.

It is for this reason that *CFB op amps are not suitable in configurations which require capacitance in the feedback loop,* such as simple active integrators or lowpass filters. They can, however, be used in certain active filters such as the Sallen-Key configuration shown in Figure 1.22 which do not require capacitance in the feedback network.

VFB op amps, on the other hand, make very flexible active filters. A multiple feedback 20MHz lowpass filter using the AD8048 is shown in Figure 1.23.

EITHER CFB OR VFB OP AMPS CAN BE USED IN
THE SALLEN-KEY FILTER CONFIGURATION

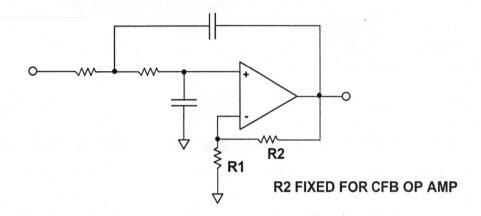

R2 FIXED FOR CFB OP AMP

Figure 1.22

MULTIPLE FEEDBACK 20MHz LOWPASS FILTER
USING THE AD8048 VFB OP AMP

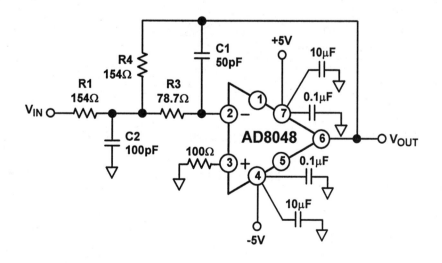

Figure 1.23

In general, the amplifier should have a bandwidth which is at least ten times the bandwidth of the filter if problems due to phase shift of the amplifier are to be avoided. (The AD8048 has a bandwidth of over 200MHz in this configuration). The filter is designed as follows:
Choose:

Fo = Cutoff Frequency = 20MHz
$\propto$ = Damping Ratio = 1/Q = 2
H = Absolute Value of Circuit Gain
   = $|-R4/R1|$ = 1
k = $2\pi FoC1$

$$C2 = \frac{4C1(H+1)}{\alpha^2} = 100pF, \text{ for C1} = 50pF$$

$$R1 = \frac{\alpha}{2Hk} = 159.2\Omega, \text{ use } 154\Omega$$

$$R3 = \frac{\alpha}{2k(H+1)} = 79.6\Omega, \text{ use } 78.7\Omega$$

$$R4 = H \cdot R1 = 159.2\Omega, \text{ use } 154\Omega$$

HIGH SPEED CURRENT-TO-VOLTAGE CONVERTERS, AND THE EFFECTS OF INVERTING INPUT CAPACITANCE

Fast op amps are useful as current-to-voltage converters in such applications as high speed photodiode preamplifiers and current-output DAC buffers. A

typical application using a VFB op amp as an I/V converter is shown in Figure 1.24.

COMPENSATING FOR INPUT CAPACITANCE IN A CURRENT-TO-VOLTAGE CONVERTER USING VFB OP AMP

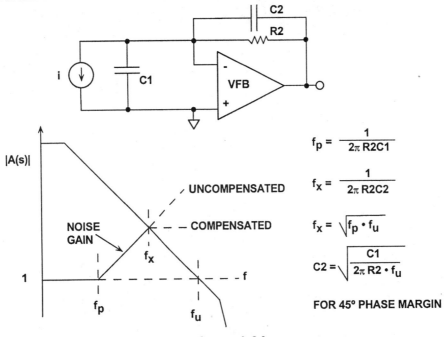

$$f_p = \frac{1}{2\pi R2C1}$$

$$f_x = \frac{1}{2\pi R2C2}$$

$$f_x = \sqrt{f_p \cdot f_u}$$

$$C2 = \sqrt{\frac{C1}{2\pi R2 \cdot f_u}}$$

FOR 45° PHASE MARGIN

Figure 1.24

The net input capacitance, C1, forms a pole at a frequency f_p in the noise gain transfer function as shown in the Bode plot, and is given by:

$$f_p = \frac{1}{2\pi R2 C1} .$$

If left uncompensated, the phase shift at the frequency of intersection, f_x, will cause instability and oscillation. Introducing a zero at f_x by adding feedback capacitor C2 stabilizes the circuit and yields a phase margin of about 45 degrees. The location of the zero is given by:

$$f_x = \frac{1}{2\pi R2 C2} .$$

Although the addition of C2 actually decreases the pole frequency slightly, this effect is negligible if C2 << C1. The frequency f_x is the geometric mean of f_p and the unity-gain bandwidth frequency of the op amp, f_u,

$$f_x = \sqrt{f_p \cdot f_u} .$$

These equations can be solved for C2:

$$C2 = \sqrt{\frac{C1}{2\pi R2 \cdot f_u}} .$$

This value of C2 will yield a phase margin of about 45 degrees. Increasing the capacitor by a factor of 2 increases the phase margin to about 65 degrees (see References 4 and 5).

In practice, the optimum value of C2 may be optimized experimentally by varying it slightly to optimize the output pulse response.

A similar analysis can be applied to a CFB op amp as shown in Figure 1.25. In this case, however, the low inverting input impedance, Ro, greatly reduces the sensitivity to input capacitance. In fact, an ideal CFB with zero input impedance would be totally insensitive to any amount of input capacitance!

COMPENSATING FOR INPUT CAPACITANCE IN A CURRENT-TO-VOLTAGE CONVERTER USING CFB OP AMP

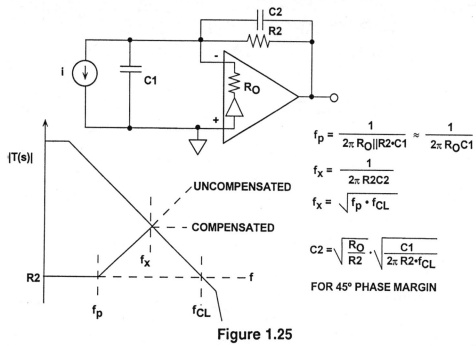

$$f_p = \frac{1}{2\pi\, R_O || R2 \cdot C1} \approx \frac{1}{2\pi\, R_O C1}$$

$$f_x = \frac{1}{2\pi\, R2 C2}$$

$$f_x = \sqrt{f_p \cdot f_{CL}}$$

$$C2 = \sqrt{\frac{R_O}{R2}} \cdot \sqrt{\frac{C1}{2\pi\, R2 \cdot f_{CL}}}$$

FOR 45° PHASE MARGIN

Figure 1.25

The pole caused by C1 occurs at a frequency fp:

$$f_p = \frac{1}{2\pi(Ro\|R2)C1} \approx \frac{1}{2\pi RoC1}.$$

This pole frequency will be generally be much higher than the case for a VFB op amp, and the pole can be ignored completely if it occurs at a frequency greater than the closed-loop bandwidth of the op amp.

We next introduce a compensating zero at the frequency f_x by inserting the capacitor C2:

$$f_x = \frac{1}{2\pi R2C2}.$$

As in the case for VFB, f_x is the geometric mean of f_p and f_{cl}:

$$f_x = \sqrt{f_p \cdot f_u}.$$

Solving the equations for C2 and rearranging it yields:

$$C2 = \sqrt{\frac{Ro}{R2}} \cdot \sqrt{\frac{C1}{2\pi R2 \cdot f_{cl}}}.$$

There is a significant advantage in using a CFB op amp in this configuration as can be seen by comparing the similar equation for C2 required for a VFB op amp. If the unity-gain bandwidth product of the VFB is equal to the closed-loop bandwidth of the CFB (at the optimum R2), then the size of the CFB compensation capacitor, C2, is reduced by a factor of $\sqrt{R2/Ro}$.

A comparison in an actual application is shown in Figure 1.26. The full scale output current of the DAC is 4mA, the net capacitance at the inverting input of the op amp is 20pF, and the feedback resistor is 500Ω. In the case of the VFB op amp, the pole due to C1 occurs at 16MHz. A compensating capacitor of 5.6pF is required for 45 degrees of phase margin, and the signal bandwidth is 57MHz.

LOW INVERTING INPUT IMPEDANCE OF CBF OP AMP MAKES IT RELATIVELY INSENSITIVE TO INPUT CAPACITANCE WHEN USED AS A CURRENT-TO-VOLTAGE CONVERTER

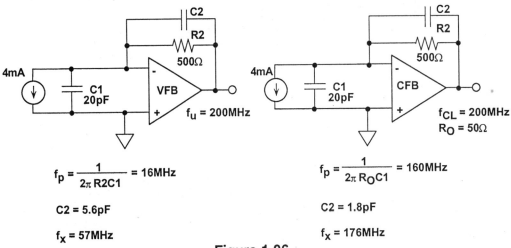

Figure 1.26

For the CFB op amp, however, because of the low inverting input impedance (Ro = 50Ω), the pole occurs at 160MHz, the required compensation capacitor is about 1.8pF, and the corresponding signal bandwidth is 176MHz. In actual practice, the pole frequency is so close to the closed-loop bandwidth of the op amp that it could probably be left uncompensated.

It should be noted that a CFB op amp's relative insensitivity to inverting input capacitance is when it is used in the inverting mode. In the non-inverting mode, even a few picofarads of stray capacitance on the inverting input can cause significant gain-peaking and potential instability.

Another advantage of the low inverting input impedance of the CFB op amp is when it is used as an I/V converter to buffer the output of a high speed current output DAC. When a step function current (or DAC switching glitch) is applied to the inverting input of a VFB op amp, it can produce a large voltage transient until the signal can propagate through the op amp to its output and negative feedback is regained. Back-to-back Schottky diodes are often used to limit this voltage swing as shown in Figure 1.27. These diodes must be low capacitance, small geometry devices because their capacitance adds to the total input capacitance.

A CFB op amp, on the other hand, presents a low impedance (Ro) to fast switching currents even before the feedback loop is closed, thereby limiting the voltage excursion without the requirement of the external diodes. This greatly improves the settling time of the I/V converter.

LOW INVERTING INPUT IMPEDANCE OF CFB OP AMP HELPS REDUCE AMPLITUDE OF FAST DAC TRANSIENTS

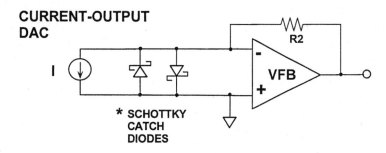

Figure 1.27

NOISE COMPARISONS BETWEEN VFB AND CFB OP AMPS

Op amp noise has two components: low frequency noise whose spectral density is inversely proportional to the square root of the frequency and white noise at medium and high frequencies. The low-frequency noise is known as 1/f noise (the noise *power* obeys a 1/f law - the noise voltage or noise current is proportional to $1/\sqrt{f}$). The frequency at which the 1/f noise spectral density equals the white noise is known as the "1/f Corner Frequency" and is a figure of merit for the op amp, with the low values indicating better performance. Values of 1/f corner frequency vary from a few Hz for the most modern low noise low frequency amplifiers to several hundreds, or even thousands of Hz for high-speed op amps.

In most applications of high speed op amps, it is the total output rms noise that is generally of interest. Because of the high bandwidths, the chief contributor to the output rms noise is the white noise, and that of the 1/f noise is negligible.

In order to better understand the effects of noise in high speed op amps, we use the classical noise model shown in Figure 1.28. This diagram identifies all possible white noise sources, including the external noise in the source and the feedback resistors. The equation allows you to calculate the total output rms noise over the closed-loop bandwidth of the amplifier. This formula works quite well when the frequency response of the op amp is relatively flat. If there is more than a few dB of high frequency peaking, however, the actual noise will be greater than the predicted because the contribution over the last octave before the 3db cutoff frequency will dominate. In most applications, the op amp feedback network is designed so that the bandwidth is relatively flat, and the formula provides a good estimate. Note that BW in the equation is the equivalent noise bandwidth which, for a single-pole system, is obtained by multiplying the closed-loop bandwidth by 1.57.

Figure 1.29 shows a table which indicates how the individual noise contributors are referred to the output. After calculating the individual noise spectral densities in this table, they can be squared, added, and then the square root of the sum of the squares yields the RSS value of the output noise spectral density since all the sources are uncorrelated. This value is multiplied by the square root of the noise bandwidth (noise bandwidth = closed-loop bandwidth multiplied by a correction factor of 1.57) to obtain the final value for the output rms noise.

OP AMP NOISE MODEL FOR A
FIRST-ORDER CIRCUIT WITH RESISTIVE FEEDBACK

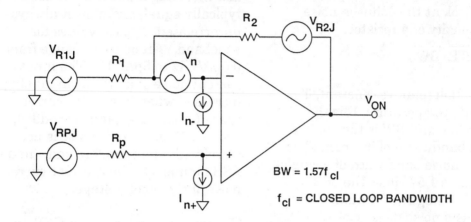

$$V_{ON} = \sqrt{BW} \sqrt{I_{n-}^2 R_2^2 + I_{n+}^2 R_p^2 \left[1 + \frac{R_2}{R_1}\right]^2 + V_n^2 \left[1 + \frac{R_2}{R_1}\right]^2 + 4kTR_2 + 4kTR_1 \left[\frac{R_2}{R_1}\right]^2 + 4kTR_p \left[1 + \frac{R_2}{R_1}\right]^2}$$

Figure 1.28

REFERRING ALL NOISE SOURCES TO THE OUTPUT

NOISE SOURCE EXPRESSED AS A VOLTAGE	MULTIPLY BY THIS FACTOR TO REFER TO THE OP AMP OUTPUT
Johnson Noise in R_p: $\sqrt{4kTR_p}$	Noise Gain $= 1 + \dfrac{R2}{R1}$
Non-Inverting Input Current Noise Flowing in R_p: $I_{n+}R_p$	Noise Gain $= 1 + \dfrac{R2}{R1}$
Input Voltage Noise: V_n	Noise Gain $= 1 + \dfrac{R2}{R1}$
Johnson Noise in R1: $\sqrt{4kTR1}$	$-R2/R1$ (Gain from input of R1 to Output)
Johnson Noise in R2: $\sqrt{4kTR2}$	1
Inverting Input Current Noise Flowing in R2: $I_{n-}R2$	1

Figure 1.29

Typical high speed op amps with bandwidths greater than 150MHz or so, and bipolar input stages have input voltage noises ranging from about 2 to 20nV/√Hz. To put voltage noise in perspective, let's look at the Johnson noise spectral density of a resistor:

$$v_n = \sqrt{4kTR \cdot BW} \, ,$$

where k is Boltzmann's constant, T is the absolute temperature, R is the resistor value, and BW is the equivalent noise bandwidth of interest. (The equivalent noise bandwidth of a single-pole system is 1.57 times the 3dB frequency). Using the formula, a 100Ω resistor has a noise density of 1.3nV/√Hz, and a 1000Ω resistor about 4nV/√Hz (values are at room temperature: 27°C, or 300K).

The base-emitter in a bipolar transistor has an equivalent noise voltage source which is due to the "shot noise" of the collector current flowing in the transistor's (noiseless) incremental emitter resistance, re. The current noise is proportional to the square root of the collector current, Ic. The emitter resistance, on the other hand, is inversely proportional to the collector current, so *the shot-noise voltage is inversely proportional to the square root of the collector current*. (Reference 5, Section 9).

Voltage noise in FET-input op amps tends to be larger than for bipolar ones, but current noise is extremely low (generally only a few tens of fA/√Hz) because of the low input bias currents. However, FET-inputs are not generally required for op amp applications requiring bandwidths greater than 100MHz.

Op amps also have input current noise on each input. For high-speed FET-input op amps, the gate currents are so low that input current noise is almost always negligible (measured in fA/√Hz).

For a VFB op amp, the inverting and non-inverting input current noise are typically equal, and almost always uncorrelated. Typical values for wideband VFB op amps range from 0.5pA/√Hz to 5pA/√Hz. The input current noise of a bipolar input stage is increased when input bias-current cancellation generators are added, because their current noise is not correlated, and therefore adds (in an RSS manner) to the intrinsic current noise of the bipolar stage.

The input voltage noise in CFB op amps tends to be lower than for VFB op amps having the same approximate bandwidth. This is because the input stage in a CFB op amp is usually operated at a higher current, thereby reducing the emitter resistance and hence the voltage noise. Typical values for CFB op amps range from about 1 to 5nV/√Hz.

The input current noise of CFB op amps tends to be larger than for VFB op amps because of the generally higher bias current levels. The inverting and non-inverting current noise of a CFB is usually different because of the unique input architecture, and are specified separately. In most cases, the inverting input current noise is the larger of the two. Typical input current noise for CFB op amps ranges from 5 to 40pA/√Hz.

The general principle of noise calculation is that uncorrelated noise sources add in a root-sum-squares manner, which means that if a noise source has a contribution to the output noise of a system which is less than 20% of the amplitude of the noise from other noise source in the system, then its contribution to the total system noise will be less than 2% of the total, and that noise source can almost invariably be ignored - in many cases, noise sources smaller than 33% of the largest can be ignored. This can simplify the calculations using the formula, assuming the correct decisions are made regarding the sources to be included and those to be neglected.

The sources which dominate the output noise are highly dependent on the closed-loop gain of the op amp. Notice that for high values of closed loop gain, the op amp voltage noise will tend be the chief contributor to the output noise. At low gains, the effects of the input current noise must also be considered, and may dominate, especially in the case of a CFB op amp.

Feedforward/feedback resistors in high speed op amp circuits may range from less than 100Ω to more than 1kΩ, so it

is difficult to generalize about their contribution to the total output noise without knowing the specific values and the closed loop gain. The best way to make the calculations is to write a simple computer program which performs the calculations automatically and include all noise sources. In most high speed applications, the source impedance noise can be neglected for source impedances of 100Ω or less.

Figure 1.30 shows an example calculation of total output noise for the AD8011 (300MHz, 1mA) CFB op amp. All six possible sources are included in the calculation. The appropriate multiplying factors which reflect the sources to the output are also shown on the diagram. For G=2, the close-loop bandwidth of the AD8011 is 180MHz. The correction factor of 1.57 in the final calculation converts this single-pole bandwidth into the circuits equivalent noise bandwidth.

AD8011 OUTPUT NOISE ANALYSIS

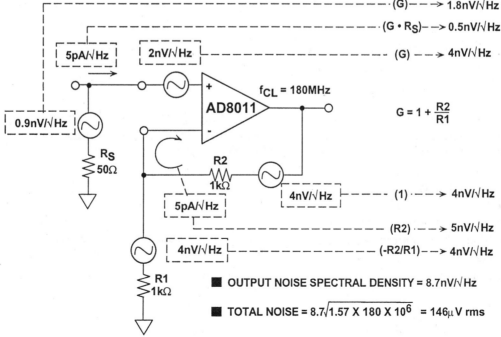

Figure 1.30

In communications applications, it is common to specify the *noise figure* (NF) of an amplifier. Figure 1.31 shows the definition. NF is the ratio of the total integrated output noise from all sources to the total output noise which would result if the op amp were "noiseless" (this noise would be that of the source resistance multiplied by the gain of the op amp using the closed-loop bandwidth of the op amp to make the calculation).

Noise figure is expressed in dB. The value of the source resistance must be specified, and in most RF systems, it is 50Ω. Noise figure is useful in communications receiver design, since it can be used to measure the decrease in signal-to-noise ratio. For instance, an amplifier with a noise figure of 10dB following a stage with a signal-to-noise ratio of 50dB reduces the signal-to-noise ratio to 40dB.

NOISE FIGURE OF AN OP AMP

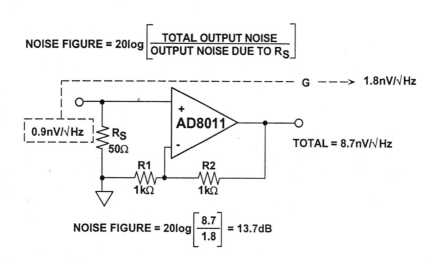

Figure 1.31

The ratio is commonly expressed in dB and is useful in signal chain analysis. In the previous example, the total output voltage noise was 8.7nV/√Hz. Integrated over the closed loop bandwidth of the op amp (180MHz), this yielded an output noise of 146µV rms. The noise of the 50Ω source resistance is 0.9nV/√Hz. If the op amp were noiseless (with noiseless feedback resistors), this noise would appear at the output multiplied by the noise gain (G=2) of the op amp, or 1.8nV/√Hz. The total output rms noise just due to the source

resistor integrated over the same bandwidth is 30.3µV rms. The noise figure is calculated as:

$$NF = 20\log_{10}\left(\frac{146}{30.3}\right) = 13.7dB.$$

The same result can be obtained by working with spectral densities, since the bandwidths used for the integration are the same and cancel each other in the equation.

$$NF = 20\log_{10}\left(\frac{8.7}{1.8}\right) = 13.7dB.$$

HIGH SPEED OP AMP NOISE SUMMARY

- ■ **Voltage Feedback Op Amps:**

  - ◆ **Voltage Noise: 2 to 20nV/√Hz**
  - ◆ **Current Noise: 0.5 to 5pA/√Hz**

- ■ **Current Feedback Op Amps:**

  - ◆ **Voltage Noise: 1 to 5nV/√Hz**
  - ◆ **Current Noise: 5 to 40pA/√Hz**

- ■ **Noise Contribution from Source Negligible if < 100Ω**

- ■ **Voltage Noise Usually Dominates at High Gains**

- ■ **Reflect Noise Sources to Output and Combine (RSS)**

- ■ **Errors Will Result if there is Significant High Frequency Peaking**

Figure 1.32

DC Characteristics of High Speed Op Amps

High speed op amps are optimized for bandwidth and settling time, not for precision DC characteristics as found in lower frequency op amps such as the industry standard OP27. In spite of this, however, high speed op amps do have reasonably good DC performance. The model shown in Figure 1.33 shows how to reflect the input offset voltage and the offset currents to the output.

MODEL FOR CALCULATING TOTAL OP AMP OUTPUT VOLTAGE OFFSET

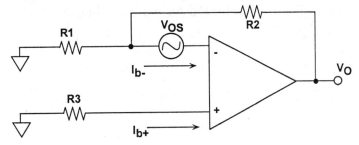

- ■ $V_O = \pm V_{OS} \left[1 + \dfrac{R2}{R1} \right] + I_{b+}R3 \left[1 + \dfrac{R2}{R1} \right] - I_{b-}R2$

- ■ IF $I_{b+} = I_{b-}$ AND $R3 = R1\|R2$

$$V_O = \pm V_{OS} \left[1 + \frac{R2}{R1} \right]$$

Figure 1.33

Input offset voltages of high speed bipolar input op amps are rarely trimmed, since offset voltage matching of the input stage is excellent, typically ranging from 1 to 3mV, with offset temperature coefficients of 5 to 15μV/°C.

Input bias currents on VFB op amps (with no input bias current compensation circuits) are approximately equal for (+) and (–) inputs, and can range from 1 to 5μA. The output offset voltage due to the input bias currents can be nulled by making the effective source resistance, R3, equal to the parallel combination of R1 and R2.

This scheme will not work, however, with bias-current compensated VFB op amps which have additional current generators on their inputs. In this case, the net input bias currents are not necessarily equal or of the same polarity. Op amps designed for rail-to-rail input operation (parallel PNP and NPN differential stages as described later in this section) have bias currents which are also a function of the common-mode input voltage. External bias current cancellation schemes are ineffective with these op amps also. It should be noted, however, that it is often desirable to match the source impedance seen by the (+) and (–) inputs of VFB op amps to minimize distortion.

CFB op amps generally have unequal and uncorrelated input bias currents because the (+) and (–) inputs have completely different architectures. For this reason, external bias current cancellation schemes are also ineffective. CFB input bias currents range from 5 to 15μA, being generally higher at the inverting input

OUTPUT OFFSET VOLTAGE SUMMARY

- ■ High Speed Bipolar Op Amp Input Offset Voltage:
    - ◆ Ranges from 1 to 3mV for VFB and CFB
    - ◆ Offset TC Ranges from 5 to 15μV/°C
- ■ High Speed Bipolar Op Amp Input Bias Current:
    - ◆ For VFB Ranges from 1 to 5μA
    - ◆ For CFB Ranges from 5 to 15μA
- ■ Bias Current Cancellation Doesn't Work for:
    - ◆ Bias Current Compensated Op Amps
    - ◆ Current Feedback Op Amps

Figure 1.34

PSRR CHARACTERISTICS OF HIGH SPEED OP AMPS

As with most op amps, the power supply rejection ratio (PSRR) of high speed op amps falls off rapidly at higher frequencies. Figure 1.35 shows the PSRR for the AD8011 CFB 300MHz CFB op amp. Notice that at DC, the PSRR is nearly 60dB, however, at

10MHz, it falls to only 20dB, indicating the need for excellent external LF and HF decoupling. These numbers are fairly typical of most high speed VFB or CFB op amps, although the DC PSRR may range from 55 to 80dB depending on the op amp.

AD8011 POWER SUPPLY REJECTION RATIO

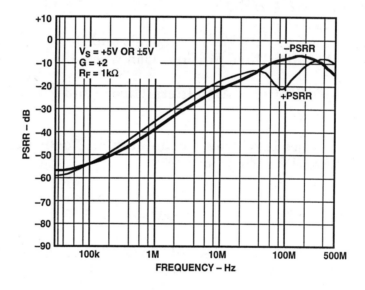

Figure 1.35

The power pins of op amps must be decoupled directly to a large-area ground plane with capacitors which have minimal lead length. It is generally recommended that a low-inductance ceramic surface mount capacitor

(0.01µF to 0.1µF) be used for the high frequency noise. The lower frequency noise can be decoupled with low-inductance tantalum electrolytic capacitors (1 to 10µF).

REFERENCES

1. Thomas M. Frederiksen, **Intuitive Operational Amplifiers**, McGraw-Hill, 1988.

2. Sergio Franco, *Current Feedback Amplifiers*, **EDN**, Jan.5, 1989.

3. Roy Gosser, U.S Patent 5,150,074.

4. James L. Melsa and Donald G. Schultz, **Linear Control Systems**, McGraw-Hill, 1969, pp. 196-220.

5. **Amplifier Applications Guide**, Analog Devices, Inc., 1992, Section 3.

6. Walter G. Jung, **IC Op amp Cookbook, Third Edition**, Howard Sams & Co., 1986, ISBN: 0-672-22453-4.

7. Paul R. Gray and Robert G. Meyer, **Analysis and Design of Analog Integrated Circuits, Third Edition**, John Wiley, 1993.

8. J. K. Roberge, **Operational Amplifiers-Theory and Practice**, John Wiley, 1975.

9. Henry W. Ott, **Noise Reduction Techniques in Electronic Systems, Second Edition**, John Wiley, Inc., 1988.

10. Lewis Smith and Dan Sheingold, *Noise and Operational Amplifier Circuits*, **Analog Dialogue 25th Anniversary Issue**, pp. 19-31, 1991.

11. D. Stout, M. Kaufman, **Handbook of Operational Amplifier Circuit Design**, New York, McGraw-Hill, 1976.

12. Joe Buxton, *Careful Design Tames High-Speed Op Amps*, **Electronic Design**, April 11, 1991.

13. J. Dostal, **Operational Amplifiers**, Elsevier Scientific Publishing, New York, 1981.

14. Barrie Gilbert, *Contemporary Feedback Amplifier Design*,

15. Sergio Franco, **Design with Operational Amplifiers and Analog ICs**, McGraw-Hill Book Company, 1988.

16. Jerald Graeme, **Photodiode Amplifiers-Op Amp Solutions**, Gain Technology Corporation, 2700 W. Broadway Blvd., Tucson, AZ 85745, 1996.

SECTION 2

HIGH SPEED OP AMP APPLICATIONS

■ Optimizing the Feedback Network for Maximum Bandwidth Flatness in Wideband CFB Op Amps

■ Driving Capacitive Loads

■ Cable Drivers and Receivers

■ A High Performance Video Line Driver

■ Differential Line Drivers/Receivers

■ High Speed Clamping Amplifiers

■ Single-Supply/Rail-to-Rail Considerations

■ High Speed Video Multiplexing with Op Amps Using Disable Function

■ Video Programmable Gain Amplifier

■ Video Multiplexers and Crosspoint Switches

■ High Power Line Drivers and ADSL

■ High Speed Photodiode Preamps

2

SECTION 2
HIGH SPEED OP AMP APPLICATIONS
Walt Kester, Walt Jung

OPTIMIZING THE FEEDBACK NETWORK FOR MAXIMUM BANDWIDTH FLATNESS IN WIDEBAND CFB OP AMPS

Achieving the highest 0.1dB bandwidth flatness is important in many video applications. Because of the critical relationship between the feedback resistor and the bandwidth of a CFB op amp, optimum bandwidth flatness is highly dependent on the feedback resistor value, the resistor parasitics, as well as the op amp package and PCB parasitics. Figure 2.1 shows the fine scale (0.1dB/division) flatness plotted versus the feedback resistance for the AD8001 in a non-inverting gain of 2. These plots were made using the AD8001 evaluation board with surface mount resistors.

AD8001 CFB OP AMP BANDWIDTH FLATNESS OPTIMIZED BY PROPER SELECTION OF FEEDBACK RESISTOR

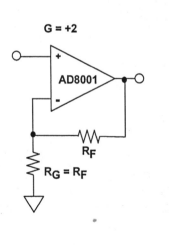
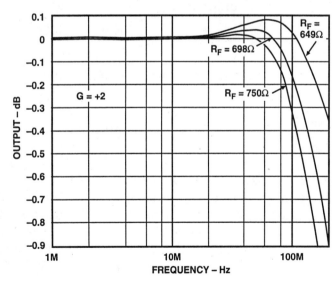

Figure 2.1

It is recommended that once the optimum resistor values have been determined, 1% tolerance values should be used. In addition, resistors of different construction have different associated parasitic capacitance and inductance.

Surface mount resistors are the optimum choice, and it is not recommended that leaded components be used with high speed op amps at these frequencies because of their parasitics.

Slightly different resistor values may be required to achieve optimum performance in the DIP versus the SOIC packages (see Figure 2.2). The SOIC package exhibits slightly lower parasitic capacitance and inductance than the DIP. The data shows the optimum feedback (R_G) and feedforward (R_F) resistors for highest 0.1dB bandwidth for the AD8001 in the DIP and the SOIC packages. As you might suspect, the SOIC package can be optimized for slightly higher 0.1dB bandwidth because of its lower parasitics.

OPTIMUM VALUES OF R_F AND R_G FOR AD8001 DIP AND SOIC PACKAGES (MAXIMUM 0.1dB BANDWIDTH)

AD8001AN (DIP) GAIN			
Component	−1	+1	+2
R_F	649Ω	1050Ω	750Ω
R_G	649Ω	-	750Ω
0.1dB Flatness	105MHz	70MHz	105MHz

AD8001AR (SOIC) GAIN			
Component	−1	+1	+2
R_F	604Ω	953Ω	681Ω
R_G	604Ω	-	681Ω
0.1dB Flatness	130MHz	100MHz	120MHz

Figure 2.2

As has been discussed, the CFB op amp is relatively insensitive to capacitance on the inverting input when it is used in the inverting mode (as in an I/V application). This is because the low inverting input impedance is in parallel with the external capacitance and tends to minimize its effect. In the non-inverting mode, however, even a few picofarads of stray inverting input capacitance may cause peaking and instability. Figure 2.3 shows the effects of adding summing junction capacitance to the inverting input of the AD8004 (SOIC package) for G = +2. Note that only 1pF of added inverting input capacitance (C_J) causes a significant increase in bandwidth and an increase in peaking. For G = −2, however, 5pF of additional inverting input capacitance causes only a small increase in bandwidth and no significant increase in peaking.

High speed VFB op amps are sensitive to stray inverting input capacitance when used in either the inverting or non-inverting mode.

AD8004 CFB OP AMP SENSITIVITY TO INVERTING INPUT CAPACITANCE FOR G = +2, G = – 2

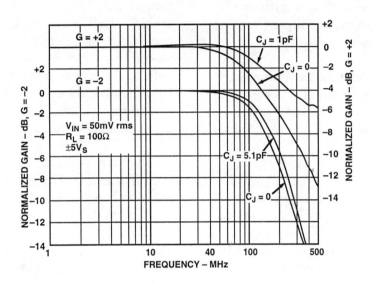

Figure 2.3

DRIVING CAPACITIVE LOADS

From system and signal fidelity points of view, transmission line coupling between stages is best, and is described in some detail in the next section. However, complete transmission line system design may not always be possible or practical. In addition, various other parasitic issues need careful consideration in high performance designs. One such problem parasitic is amplifier load capacitance, which potentially comes into play for all wide bandwidth situations which do not use transmission line signal coupling.

A general design rule for wideband linear drivers is that capacitive loading (cap loading) effects should *always* be considered. This is because PC board capacitance can build up quickly, especially for wide and long signal runs

over ground planes insulated by a thin, higher K dielectric. For example, a 0.025" PC trace using a G-10 dielectric of 0.03" over a ground plane will run about 22pF/foot (Reference 1). Even relatively small load capacitance (i.e., <100 pF) can be troublesome, since while not causing outright oscillation, it can still stretch amplifier settling time to greater than desirable levels for a given accuracy.

The effects of cap loading on high speed amplifier outputs are not simply detrimental, they are actually an anathema to high quality signals. However, before-the-fact designer knowledge still allows high circuit performance by employing various tricks of the trade to combat the capacitive loading. If it is not driven via a transmission line, remote signal circuitry should be checked for capacitive loading very carefully, and characterized as best possible. Drivers which face poorly defined load capacitance should be bullet-proofed accordingly with an appropriate design technique from the options list below.

Short of a true matched transmission line system, a number of ways exist to drive a load which is capacitive in nature while maintaining amplifier stability.

Custom capacitive load (cap load) compensation includes two possible options, namely a); overcompensation, and b); an intentionally forced-high loop noise gain allowing crossover in a stable region. Both of these steps can be effective in special situations, as they reduce the amplifier's effective closed loop bandwidth, so as to restore stability in the presence of cap loading.

Overcompensation of the amplifier, when possible, reduces amplifier bandwidth so that the additional load capacitance no longer represents a danger to phase margin. As a practical matter however, amplifier compensation nodes to allow this are available on few high speed amplifiers. One such useful example is the AD829, compensated by a single capacitor at pin 5. In general, almost any amplifier using external compensation can always be over compensated to reduce bandwidth. This will restore stability against cap loads, by lowering the amplifier's unity gain frequency.

Forcing a high noise gain, is shown in Figure 2.4, where the capacitively loaded amplifier with a noise gain of unity at the left is seen to be unstable, due to a $1/\beta$ - open loop rolloff intersection on the Bode diagram in an unstable −12dB/octave region. For such a case, quite often stability can be restored by introducing a higher noise gain to the stage, so that the intersection then occurs in a stable −6dB/octave region, as depicted at the diagram right Bode plot.

To enable a higher noise gain (which does not necessarily need to be the same as the stage's *signal gain*), use is made of resistive or RC pads at the amplifier input, as in Figure 2.5. This trick is more broad in scope than overcompensation, and has the advantage of not requiring access to any internal amplifier nodes. This generally allows use with any amplifier setup, even voltage followers. The technique adds an extra resistor R_D, which works against R_F to force the noise gain of the stage to a level appreciably higher than the signal gain (which is unity in both cases here). Assuming that C_L is a value which produces a parasitic pole near the amplifier's natural crossover, this loading combination would likely lead to oscillation due to the excessive phase lag. However with R_D connected, the higher amplifier noise gain produces a new $1/\beta$ - open loop rolloff intersection, about a decade lower in frequency. This is set low enough that the extra phase lag from C_L is no longer a problem, and amplifier stability is restored.

CAPACITIVE LOADING ON OP AMP GENERALLY REDUCES PHASE MARGIN AND MAY CAUSE INSTABILITY, BUT INCREASING THE NOISE GAIN OF THE CIRCUIT IMPROVES STABILITY

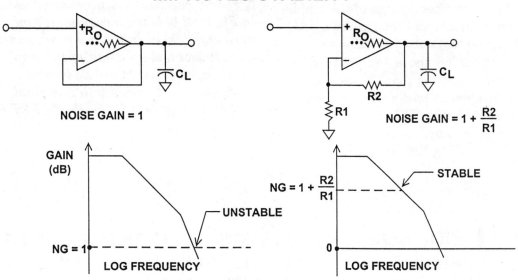

Figure 2.4

RAISING NOISE GAIN (DC OR AC) FOR FOLLOWER OR INVERTER STABILITY

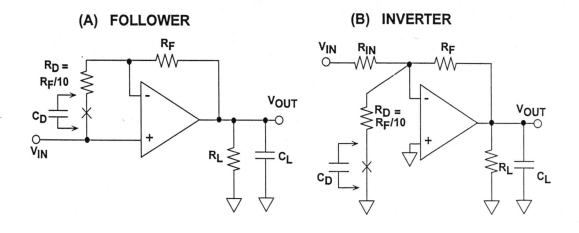

Figure 2.5

A drawback to this trick is that the DC offset and input noise of the amplifier are raised by the value of the noise gain, when the optional C_D is *not* present. But, when C_D is used in series with R_D, the offset voltage of the amplifier is not raised, and the gained-up AC noise components are confined to a frequency region above $1/(2\pi \cdot R_D \cdot C_D)$. A further caution is that the technique can be somewhat tricky when separating these operating DC and AC regions, and should be applied carefully with regard to settling time (Reference 2).

Note that these simplified examples are generic, and in practice the absolute component values should be matched to a specific amplifier.

"Passive" cap load compensation, shown in Figure 2.6, is the most simple (and most popular) isolation technique available. It uses a simple "out-of-the-loop" series resistor R_X to isolate the cap load, and can be used with any amplifier, current or voltage feedback, FET or bipolar input.

OPEN-LOOP SERIES RESISTANCE ISOLATES CAPACITIVE LOAD FOR AD811 CURRENT FEEDBACK OP AMP (CIRCUIT BANDWIDTH = 13.5MHz)

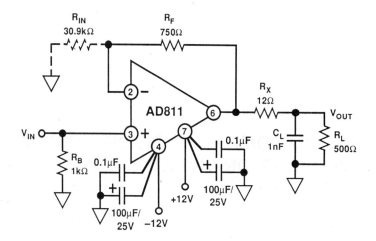

Figure 2.6

As noted, this technique can be applied to virtually any amplifier, which is a major reason why it is so useful. It is shown here with a current feedback amplifier suitable for high current line driving, the AD811, and it consists of just the simple (passive) series isolation resistor, R_X. This resistor's minimum value for stability will vary from device

to device, so the amplifier data sheet should be consulted for other ICs. Generally, information will be provided as to the amount of load capacitance tolerated, and a suggested minimum resistor value for stability purposes.

Drawbacks of this approach are the loss of bandwidth as R_X works against C_L, the loss of voltage swing, a possible lower slew rate limit due to I_{MAX} and C_L, and a gain error due to the R_X-R_L division. The gain error can be optionally compensated with R_{IN}, which is ratioed to R_F as R_L is to R_X. In this example, a $\pm 100mA$ output from the op amp into C_L can slew V_{OUT} at a rate of $100V/\mu s$, far below the intrinsic AD811 slew rate of $2500V/\mu s$. Although the drawbacks are serious, this form of cap load compensation is nevertheless useful because of its simplicity. If the amplifier is not otherwise protected, then an R_X resistor of 50-100Ω should be used with virtually any amplifier facing capacitive loading. Although a non-inverting amplifier is shown, the technique is equally applicable to inverter stages.

With very high speed amplifiers, or in applications where lowest settling time is critical, even small values of load capacitance can be disruptive to frequency response, but are nevertheless sometimes inescapable. One case in point is an amplifier used for driving ADC inputs. Since high speed ADC inputs quite often look capacitive in nature, this presents an oil/water type problem. In such cases the amplifier *must* be stable driving the capacitance, but it must also preserve its best bandwidth and settling time characteristics. To address this type of cap load case, R_S and C_L performance data for a specified settling time is most appropriate.

Some applications, in particular those that require driving the relatively high impedance of an ADC, do not have a convenient back termination resistor to dampen the effects of capacitive loading. At high frequencies, an amplifier's output impedance is rising with frequency and acts like an inductance, which in combination with C_L causes peaking or even worse, oscillation. When the bandwidth of an amplifier is an appreciable percentage of device F_t, the situation is complicated by the fact that the loading effects are reflected back into its internal stages. In spite of this, the basic behavior of most very wide bandwidth amplifiers such as the AD8001 is very similar.

In general, a small damping resistor (R_s) placed in series with C_L will help restore the desired response (see Figure 2.7). The best choice for this resistor's value will depend upon the criterion used in determining the desired response. Traditionally, simply stability or an acceptable amount of peaking has been used, but a more strict measure such as 0.1% (or even 0.01%) settling will yield different values. For a given amplifier, a family of R_s - C_L curves exists, such as those of Figure 2.7. These data will aid in selecting R_s for a given application.

AD8001 R$_S$ REQUIRED FOR VARIOUS C$_L$ VALUES

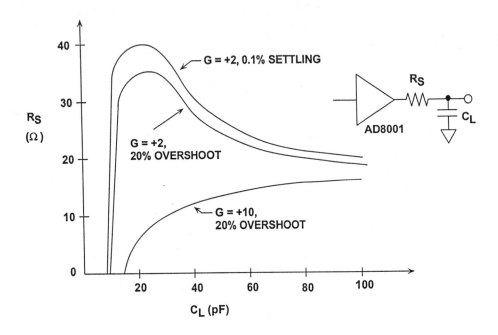

Figure 2.7

The basic shape of this curve can be easily explained. When C_L is very small, no resistor is necessary. When C_L increases to some threshold value an R_S becomes necessary. Since the frequency at which the damping is required is related to the $R_S \bullet C_L$ time constant, the R_S needed will initially increase rapidly from zero, and then will decrease as C_L is increased further. A relatively strict requirement, such as for 0.1%, settling will generally require a larger R_S for a given C_L, giving a curve falling higher (in terms of R_S) than that for a less stringent requirement, such as 20% overshoot. For the common gain configuration of +2, these two curves are plotted in the figure for 0.1% settling (upper-most curve) and 20% overshoot (middle curve). It is also worth mentioning that higher closed loop gains lessen the problem dramatically, and will require less R_S for the

same performance. The third (lower-most) curve illustrates this, demonstrating a closed loop gain of 10 R_S requirement for 20% overshoot for the AD8001 amplifier. This can be related to the earlier discussion associated with Figure 2.5.

The recommended values for R_S will optimize response, but it is important to note that generally C_L will degrade the maximum bandwidth and settling time performance which is achievable. In the limit, a large $R_S \bullet C_L$ time constant will dominate the response. In any given application, the value for R_S should be taken as a starting point in an optimization process which accounts for board parasitics and other secondary effects.

Active or "in-the-loop" cap load compensation can also be used as shown in Figure 2.8, and this scheme modifies the *passive configuration to provide feed-back correction for the DC & low frequency gain error associated with R_X. In contrast to the passive form, active*

compensation can only be used with voltage feedback amplifiers, because current feedback amplifiers don't allow the integrating connection of C_F.

ACTIVE "IN-LOOP" CAPACITIVE LOAD COMPENSATION CORRECTS FOR DC AND LF GAIN ERRORS

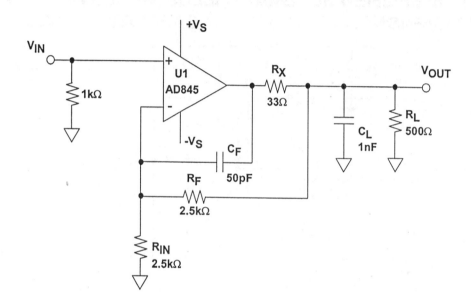

Figure 2.8

This circuit returns the DC feedback from the output side of isolation resistor R_X, thus correcting for errors. AC feedback is returned via C_F, which bypasses R_X/R_F at high frequencies. With an appropriate value of C_F (which varies with C_L, for fixed resistances) this stage can be adjusted for a well damped transient response (Reference 2,3). There is still a bandwidth reduction, a headroom loss, and also (usually) a slew rate reduction, but the DC errors can be very low. A drawback is the need to tune C_F to C_L, as even if this is done well initially, any change to C_L will alter the response away from flat. The circuit as shown is useful for voltage feedback amplifiers only, be-

cause capacitor C_F provides integration around U1. It also can be implemented in inverting fashion, by driving the bottom end of R_{IN}.

Internal cap load compensation involves the use of an amplifier which has topological provisions for the effects of external cap loading. To the user, this is the most transparent of the various techniques, as it works for any feedback situation, for any value of load capacitance. Drawbacks are that it produces higher distortion than does an otherwise similar amplifier without the network, and the compensation against cap loading is somewhat signal level dependent.

The internal cap load compensated amplifier sounds at first like the best of all possible worlds, since the user need do nothing at all to set it up. Figure 2.9, a simplified diagram of an AD817 amplifier with internal cap load compensation, shows how it works. The cap load compensation is the C_F-resistor network shown around the unity gain output stage of the amplifier - note that the dotted connection of this network underscores the fact that it only makes its presence felt for certain load conditions.

AD817 SIMPLIFIED SCHEMATIC ILLUSTRATES INTERNAL COMPENSATION FOR DRIVING CAPACITIVE LOADS

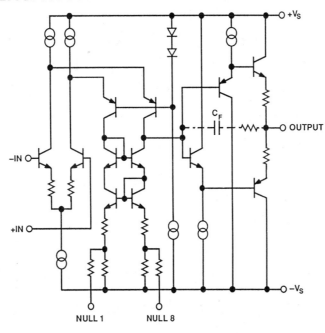

Figure 2.9

Under normal (non-capacitive or light resistive) loading, there is limited input/output voltage error across the output stage, so the C_F network then sees a relatively small voltage drop, and has little or no effect on the AD817s high impedance compensation node. However when a capacitor (or other heavy) load is present, the high currents in the output stage produce a voltage difference across the C_F network, which effectively adds capacitance to the compensation node. With this relatively heavy loading, a net larger compensation capacitance results, and reduces the amplifier speed in a manner which is adaptive to the external capacitance, C_L. *As a point of reference, note that it requires 6.3mA peak current to support a 2Vp-p swing across a 100pF load at 10MHz.*

Since this mechanism is resident in the amplifier output stage and it affects the overall compensation characteristics dynamically, it acts independent of the specific feedback hookup, as well as size of the external cap loading. In other words, it can be transparent to the user in the sense that no specific design conditions need be set to make it work (other than selecting an IC which employs it). Some amplifiers using internal cap load compensation are the AD847 and the AD817, and their dual equivalents, AD827 and AD826.

There are, however, some caveats also associated with this internal compensation scheme. As with the passive compensation techniques, bandwidth decreases as the device slows down to prevent oscillation with higher load currents. Also, this adaptive compensation network has its greatest effect when enough output current flows to

produce significant voltage drop across the C_F network. Conversely, at small signal levels, the effect of the network on speed is less, so greater ringing may actually be possible for some circuits for lower-level outputs.

The dynamic nature of this internal cap load compensation is illustrated in Figure 2.10, which shows an AD817 unity gain inverter being exercised at both high and low output levels, with common conditions of $V_S = \pm15V$, $R_L = 1k\Omega$, $C_L = 1nF$, and using $1k\Omega$ input/feedback resistors. In both photos the input signal is on the top trace and the output signal is on the bottom trace, and the time scale is fixed. In the 10V p-p output (A) photo at the left, the output has slowed down appreciably to accommodate the capacitive load, but settling is still relatively clean, with a small percentage of overshoot. This indicates that for this high level case,

RESPONSE OF INTERNAL CAP LOAD COMPENSATED AMPLIFIER VARIES WITH SIGNAL LEVEL

(A) V_{OUT} = 10V p-p   (B) V_{OUT} = 200mV p-p

Vertical Scale: 5V/div   Vertical Scale, 100mV/div

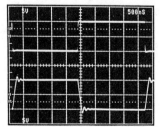   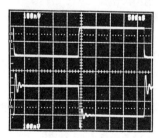

Horizontal Scale: 500ns/div

AD817 INVERTER
$R_F = R_{IN} = 1k\Omega$
$R_L = 1k\Omega$, $C_L = 1nF$, Vs = $\pm15V$

Figure 2.10

the bandwidth reduction due to C_L is most effective. However, in the (B) photo at the right, the 200mVp-p output shows greater overshoot and ringing, for the lower level signal. The point is that the performance of the cap load compensated amplifier is signal dependent, but is always stable with any cap load.

Finally, because the circuit is based on a nonlinear principle, the internal network affects distortion performance and load drive ability, and these factors influence amplifier performance in video applications. Though the network's presence does not by any means make devices like the AD847 or AD817 unusable for video, it does not permit the very lowest levels of distortion and differential gain and phase which are achievable with otherwise comparable amplifiers (for example, the AD818 which is an AD817 without the internal compensating network).

While the individual techniques for countering cap loading outlined above have various specific tradeoffs as noted, all of the techniques have a common drawback of reducing speed (both bandwidth and slew rate). If these parameters cannot be sacrificed, then a matched transmission line system is the solution, and is discussed in more detail later in the chapter. As for choosing among the cap load compensation schemes, it would seem on the surface

that amplifiers using the internal form offer the best possible solution to the problem- just pick the right amplifier and forget about it. And indeed, that would seem the "panacea" solution for all cap load situations - if you use the "right" amplifier you never need to think about cap loading again. Could there be more to it?

Yes! The "gotcha" of internal cap load compensation is subtle, and lies in the fact that the dynamic adaptive nature of the compensation mechanism actually can produce higher levels of distortion, vis-à-vis an otherwise similar amplifier, *without* the C_F -resistor network. Like the old saying about no free lunches, if you care about attaining top-notch levels of high frequency AC performance, you should give the issue of whether to use an internally compensated cap load amplifier more serious thought than simply picking a trendy device.

On the other hand, if you have no requirements for the lowest levels of distortion, then such an amplifier could be a good choice. Such amplifiers are certainly easier to use, and relatively forgiving about loading issues. Some applications of this chapter illustrate the distortion point specifically, quoting performance in a driver circuit with/ without the use of an internal cap load compensated amplifiers.

CABLE DRIVERS AND RECEIVERS

High quality video signals are best transmitted over terminated coaxial cable having a controlled characteristic impedance. The characteristic impedance is given by the equation Zo = $\sqrt{(L/C)}$ where L is the distributed inductance per foot, and C is the distributed capacitance per foot. Popular values are 50, 75, and 93 or 100Ω.

If a length of coaxial cable is terminated, it presents a *resistive* load to the driver. If left unterminated, however, it may present a predominately capacitive load to the driver depending on the output frequency. If the length of an unterminated cable is much less than the wavelength of the output frequency of the driver, then the load appears approximately as a lumped capacitance. For instance, at the audio frequency of 20kHz (wavelength ≈ 50,000 feet, or 9.5miles), a 5 foot length of unterminated 50Ω coaxial cable would appear as a lumped capacitance of approximately 150pF (the distributed capacitance of coaxial cable is about 30pF/ft). At 100MHz (wavelength ≈ 10 feet), however, the unterminated coax must be treated as a transmission line in order to calculate the standing wave pattern and the voltage at the unterminated cable output.

Because of skin effect and wire resistance, coaxial cable exhibits a loss which is a function of frequency. This varies considerably between cable types. For instance the attenuation in at 100MHz of RG188A/U is 8dB/100ft, RG58/U is 5.5dB/100ft, and RG59/U 3.6dB/100ft (Reference 4).

Skin effect also affects the pulse response of long coaxial cables. The response to a fast pulse will rise sharply for the first 50% of the output swing, then taper off during the remaining portion of the edge. Calculations show that the 10 to 90% waveform risetime is 30 times greater than the 0 to 50% risetime when the cable is skin effect limited (see Reference 5).

DRIVING CABLES

- All Interconnections are Really Transmission Lines Which Have a Characteristic Impedance (Even if Not Controlled)

- The Characteristic Impedance is Equal to $\sqrt{L/C}$, where L and C are the Distributed Inductance and Capacitance

- Correctly Terminated Transmission Lines Have Impedances Equal to Their Characteristic Impedance

- Unterminated Transmission Lines Behave Approximately as Lumped Capacitance if the Wavelength of the Output Frequency is Much Greater than the Length of the Cable

  - Example: At 20kHz (Wavelength = 9.5 miles), 5 feet of Unterminated 50Ω Cable (30pF/ft) Appears Like 150pF Load

  - Example: At 100MHz (Wavelength = 10 feet), 5 feet of 50Ω Cable Must be Properly Terminated to Prevent Reflections and Standing Waves!!!!

Figure 2.11

It is useful to examine what happens for conditions of proper and improper cable source/load terminations. To illustrate the behavior of a high speed op amp driving a coaxial cable, consider the circuit of Figure 2.12. The AD8001 drives 5 feet of 50Ω coaxial cable which is load-end terminated in the characteristic impedance of 50Ω. No termination is used at the amplifier (driving) end. The pulse response is also shown in the figure.

The output of the cable was measured by connecting it directly to the 50Ω input of a 500MHz Tektronix 644A digitizing oscilloscope. The 50Ω resistor termination is actually the input of the scope. The 50Ω load is not a perfect termination (the scope input capacitance is about 10pF), so some of the pulse is reflected out of phase back to the source. When the reflection reaches the op amp output, it sees the closed-loop output impedance of the op amp which, at 100MHz, is approximately 100Ω. Thus, it is reflected back to the load with no phase reversal, accounting for the negative-going "blip" which occurs approximately 16ns after the leading edge. This is equal to the round-trip delay of the cable (2•5ft•1.6 ns/ft=16ns). In the frequency domain (not shown), the cable mismatch will cause a loss of bandwidth flatness at the load.

PULSE RESPONSE OF AD8001 DRIVING
5 FEET OF LOAD-TERMINATED 50Ω COAXIAL CABLE

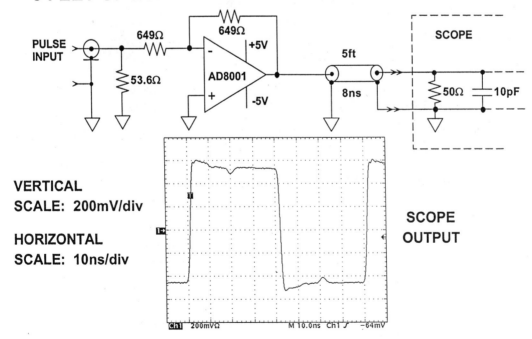

Figure 2.12

Figure 2.13 shows a second case, the results of driving the same coaxial cable, but now used with both a 50Ω source-end as well as a 50Ω load-end termination. This case is the preferred way to drive a transmission line, because a portion of the reflection from the load impedance mismatch is absorbed by the amplifier's source termination resistor. The disadvantage is that there is a 2x gain reduction, be-

cause of the voltage division between the equal value source/load terminations. However, a major positive attribute of this configuration, with matched source and load terminations in conjunction with a low-loss cable, is that the best bandwidth flatness is ensured, especially at lower operating frequencies. In addition, the amplifier is operated under near optimum loading conditions, i.e., a resistive load.

PULSE RESPONSE OF AD8001 DRIVING 5 FEET OF SOURCE AND LOAD-TERMINATED 50Ω COAXIAL CABLE

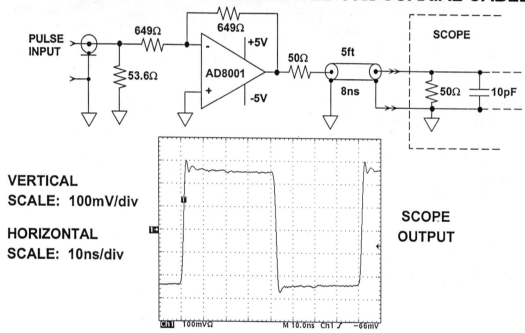

VERTICAL
SCALE: 100mV/div

HORIZONTAL
SCALE: 10ns/div

SCOPE
OUTPUT

Figure 2.13

Source-end (only) terminations can also be used as shown in Figure 2.14, where the op amp is source terminated by the 50Ω resistor which drives the cable. The scope is set for 1MΩ input impedance, representing an approximate open circuit. The initial leading edge of the pulse at the op amp output sees a 100Ω load (the 50Ω source resistor in series with the 50Ω coax impedance.

When the pulse reaches the load, a large portion is reflected in phase because of the high load impedance, resulting in a full-amplitude pulse at the load. When the reflection reaches the source-end of the cable, it sees the 50Ω source resistance in series with the op amp closed loop output impedance (approximately 100Ω at the frequency represented by the 2ns risetime pulse edge). The reflected portion remains in phase, and appears at the scope input as the positive-going "blip" approximately 16ns after the leading edge.

PULSE RESPONSE OF AD8001 DRIVING 5 FEET OF SOURCE-TERMINATED 50Ω COAXIAL CABLE

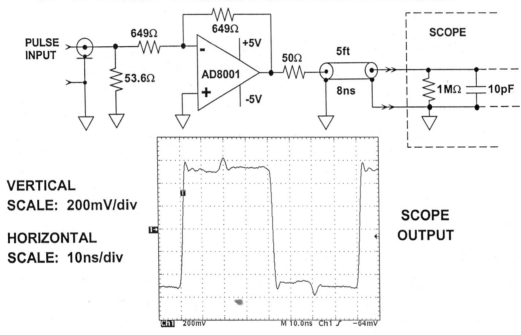

VERTICAL SCALE: 200mV/div

HORIZONTAL SCALE: 10ns/div

SCOPE OUTPUT

Figure 2.14

From these experiments, one can easily see that the preferred method for minimum reflections (and therefore maximum bandwidth flatness) is to use both source and load terminations and try to minimize any reactance associated with the load. The experiments represent a worst-case condition, where the frequencies contained in the fast edges are greater than 100MHz. (Using the rule-of-thumb that bandwidth = 0.35/risetime). At video frequencies, either load-only, or source-only termi-

nations may give acceptable results, but the data sheet should always be consulted to determine the op amp's closed-loop output impedance at the maximum frequency of interest. A major disadvantage of the source-only termination is that it requires a truly high impedance load (high resistance and minimal parasitic capacitance) for minimum absorption of energy. It also places a burden on this amplifier to maintain a low output impedance at high frequencies.

Now, for a truly worst case, let us replace the 5 feet of coaxial cable with an uncontrolled-impedance cable (one that is largely capacitive with little inductance). Let us use a capacitance of 150pF to simulate the cable (corresponding to the total capacitance of 5 feet of coaxial cable whose distributed capacitance is about 30pF/foot). Figure 2.15 shows the output of the AD8001

driving a lumped 160pF capacitance (including the scope input capacitance of 10pF). Notice the overshoot and ringing on the pulse waveform due to the capacitive loading. This example illustrates the need to use good quality controlled-impedance coaxial cable in the transmission of high frequency signals.

PULSE RESPONSE OF AD8001 DRIVING 160pF ∥ 50Ω LOAD

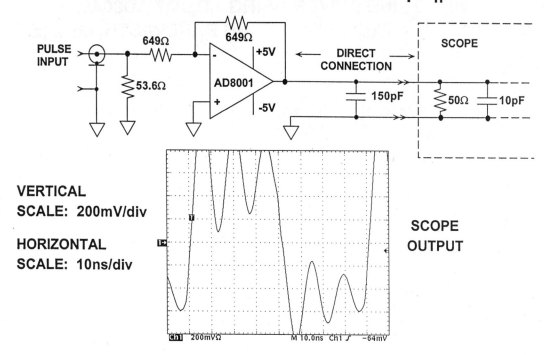

Figure 2.15

A HIGH PERFORMANCE VIDEO LINE DRIVER

The AD8047 and AD8048 VFB op amps have been optimized to offer outstanding performance as video line drivers. They utilized the "quad core" g_m stage as previously described for high slew rate and low distortion. The AD8048 (optimized for G = +2) has a differential gain of 0.01% and a differential phase of 0.02°, making it suitable for HDTV applications. In the configuration shown in Figure 2.16, the 0.1dB bandwidth is 50MHz for ±5V supplies, slew rate is 1000V/µs, and 0.1% settling time is 13ns. Total quiescent current is 6mA (±5V), and quiescent power dissipation 60mW.

VIDEO LINE DRIVER USING AD8047/AD8048: ΔG = 0.01%, Δφ = 0.02°, 50MHz 0.1dB BANDWIDTH, 6mA (±5V)

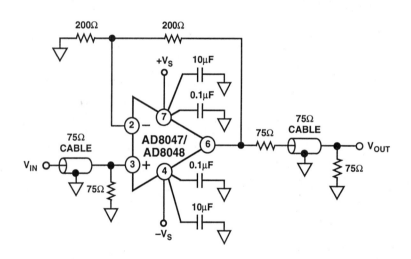

Figure 2.16

DIFFERENTIAL LINE DRIVERS/RECEIVERS

Many applications require gain/phase matched complementary or differential signals. Among these are analog-digital-converter (ADC) input buffers, where differential operation can provide lower levels of 2nd harmonic distortion for certain converters. Other uses include high frequency bridge excitation, and drivers for balanced transmission twisted pair lines such as in ADSL and HDSL.

The transmission of high quality signals across noisy interfaces (either between individual PC boards or between racks) has always been a challenge to design engineers. Differential techniques using high common-mode-rejection-ratio (CMRR) instrumentation amplifiers largely solves the problem at low frequencies.

At audio frequencies, transformers, or products such as the SSM-2142 balanced line driver and SSM-2141/SSM-2143 line receiver offer outstanding CMRRs and the ability to transmit low-level signals in the presence of large amounts of noise. At high frequencies, small toroid transformers using bifilar windings are effective.

The problem of signal transmission at video frequencies is complex. Transformers are not effective, because the baseband video signal has low-frequency components down to a few tens of Hz. Video signals are generally single-ended, and therefore don't adapt easily to balanced transmission line techniques. In addition, shielded twin-conductor coaxial cable with good bandwidth is usually somewhat bulky and expensive. Finally, designing high bandwidth, low distortion differential video drivers and receivers with high

CMRRs at high frequencies is an extremely difficult task.

Even with the above problems, there are differential techniques available now which offer distinct advantages over single-ended methods. Some of these techniques make use of discrete components, while others utilize the latest in state-of-the-art video differential amplifiers.

Two solutions to the problem of differential transmission and reception are shown in Figure 2.17. The first represents the ideal case, where a balanced differential line driver drives a balanced twin-conductor coaxial cable which in turn drives a differential line receiver. This circuit, however, is difficult to implement fully at video frequencies for the reasons previously discussed.

TWO APPROACHES FOR
DIFFERENTIAL LINE DRIVING/RECEIVING

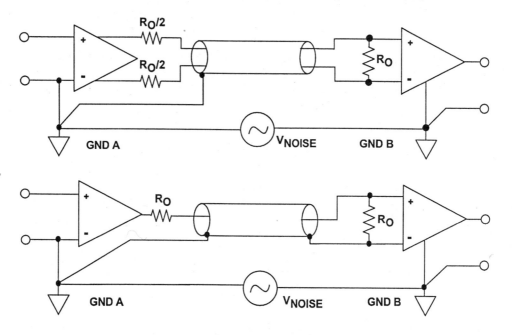

Figure 2.17

The second and most often used approach makes use of a single-ended driver which drives a source-terminated coaxial cable. The shield of the coaxial cable is grounded at the transmitting end. At the receiving end, the coaxial cable is terminated in its characteristic impedance, but the shield is left float-ing in order to prevent a ground loop between the two systems. The common mode ground noise is rejected by the CMRR of the differential line receiver. The success of this approach depends upon the characteristics of the line receiver.

Inverter-Follower Differential Driver

The circuit of Figure 2.18 is useful as a high speed differential driver for driving high speed 10-12 bit ADCs, differential video lines, and other balanced loads at levels of 1-4Vrms. As shown it operates from ±5V supplies, but it can also be adapted to supplies in the range of ±5 to ±15V. When operated directly from ±5V as here, it minimizes potential for destructive ADC overdrive when higher supply voltage buffers drive a ±5V powered ADC, in addition to minimizing driver power.

DIFFERENTIAL DRIVER USING INVERTER/FOLLOWER

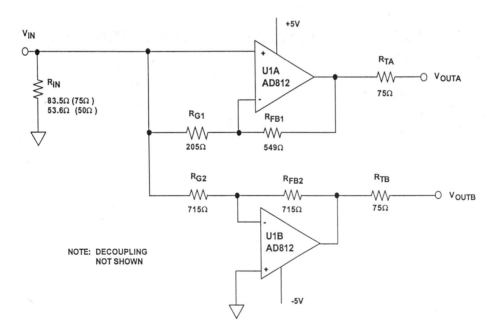

Figure 2.18

In many of these differential drivers the performance criteria is high. In addition to low output distortion, the two signals should maintain gain/phase flatness. In this topology, two sections of an AD812 dual current feedback amplifier are used for the channel A & B buffers, U1A & U1B. This can provide inherently better open-loop bandwidth matching than the use of two singles (where bandwidth varies between devices from different manufacturing lots).

The two buffers here operate with precise gains of ±1, as defined by their respective feedback and input resistances. Channel B buffer U1B is conventional, and uses a matched pair of 715Ω resistors- the value for using the AD812 on ±5V supplies.

In channel A, non-inverting buffer U1A has an inherent signal gain of 1, by virtue of the bootstrapped feedback network R_{FB1} and R_{G1}(Reference 5). It also has a higher noise gain, for phase matching. Normally a current feedback amplifier operating as a simple unity gain follower would use one (optimum) resistor R_{FB1}, and no gain resistor at all. Here, with input resistor R_{G1} added, a U1A noise gain like that of U1B results. Due to the bootstrap connection of R_{FB1}-R_{G1}, the signal gain is maintained at unity. Given the matched open loop bandwidths of U1A and U1B, similar noise gains in the A-B channels provide closely matched output bandwidths between the driver sides, a distinction which greatly impacts overall matching performance.

In setting up a design for the driver, the effects of resistor gain errors should be considered for R_{G2}-R_{FB2}. Here a worst case 2% mis-match will result in less than 0.2dB gain error between channels A and B. This error can be improved simply by specifying tighter resistor ratio matching, avoiding trimming.

If desired, phase matching is trimmed via R_{G1}, so that the phase of channel A closely matches that of B. This can be done for new circuit conditions, by using a pair of closely matched (0.1% or better) resistors to sum the A and B channels, as R_{G1} is adjusted for the best null conditions at the sum node. The A-B gain/phase matching is quite effective in this driver, with test results of the circuit as shown 0.04dB and 0.1° between the A and B output signals at 10MHz, when operated into dual 150Ω loads. The 3dB bandwidth of the driver is about 60MHz.

Net input impedance of the circuit is set to a standard line termination value such as 75Ω (or 50Ω), by choosing R_{IN} so that the desired value results with R_{IN} in parallel with R_{G2}. In this example, an R_{IN} value of 83.5Ω provides a standard input impedance of 75Ω when paralleled with 715Ω. For the circuit just as shown, dual voltage feedback amplifier types with sufficiently high speed and low distortion can also be used. This allows greater freedom with regard to resistor values using such devices as the AD826 and AD828.

Gain of the circuit can be changed if desired, but this is not totally straightforward. An easy step to satisfy diverse gain requirements is to simply use a triple amplifier such as the AD813, with the third channel as a variable gain input buffer.

Cross-Coupled Differential Driver

Another differential driver approach uses cross-coupled feedback to get very high CMR and complementary outputs at the same time. In Figure 2.19, by connecting AD8002 dual current feed-back amplifier sections as cross-coupled inverters, their outputs are forced equal and opposite, assuring zero output common mode voltage.

CROSS-COUPLED DIFFERENTIAL DRIVER
PROVIDES BALANCED OUTPUTS AND 250MHz BANDWIDTH

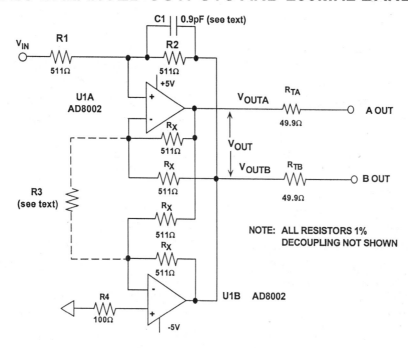

Figure 2.19

The gain cell which results, U1A and U1B plus cross-coupling resistances R_X, is fundamentally a differential input and output topology, but it behaves as a voltage feedback amplifier with regard to the feedback port at the U1A (+) node. The gain of the stage from V_{IN} to V_{OUT} is:

$$G = \frac{V_{OUT}}{V_{IN}} = \frac{2R2}{R1}$$

where V_{OUT} is the differential output, equal to $V_{OUTA} - V_{OUTB}$.

This relationship may not be obvious, so it can be derived as follows:

Using the conventional inverting op amp gain equation, the input voltage V_{IN} develops an output voltage V_{OUTB} given by:

$$V_{OUTB} = -V_{IN}\frac{R2}{R1}.$$

Also, $V_{OUTA} = -V_{OUTB}$,

because V_{OUTA} is inverted by U1B.

However, $V_{OUT} = V_{OUTA} - V_{OUTB} = -2V_{OUTB}$.

Therefore,

$$V_{OUT} = -2\left(-V_{IN}\frac{R2}{R1}\right) = 2V_{IN}\frac{R2}{R1},$$

and

$$\frac{V_{OUT}}{V_{IN}} = \frac{2R2}{R1}.$$

This circuit has some unique benefits. First, differential gain is set by a single resistor ratio, so there is no necessity for side-side resistor matching with gain changes, as is the case for conventional differential amplifiers (see line receivers, below). Second, because the (overall) circuit emulates a voltage feedback amplifier, these gain resistances are not as restrictive as in the case of a conventional current feedback amplifier. Thus, they are not highly critical as to value as long as the equivalent resistance seen by U1A is reasonably low ($\leq 1k\Omega$ in this case). Third, the cell bandwidth can be optimized to the desired gain by a single optional resistor, R3, as follows. If for instance, a net gain of 20 is desired (R2/R1=10), the bandwidth would otherwise be reduced by roughly this amount, since without R3, the cell operates with a constant gain-bandwidth product (working in the voltage feedback mode). With R3 present however, advantage can be taken of the AD8002 current feedback amplifier characteristics. Additional internal gain is added by the connection of R3, which, given an appropriate value, effectively raises gain-bandwidth to a level so as to restore the bandwidth which would

otherwise be lost by the higher closed loop gain.

In the circuit as shown, no R3 is necessary at the low working gain of 2 times differential, since the 511Ω R_X resistors are already optimized for maximum bandwidth. Note that these four matched R_X resistances are somewhat critical, and will change in absolute value with the use of another current feedback amplifier. At higher gain closed loop gains as set by R2/R1, R3 can be chosen to optimize the working transconductance in the input stages of U1A and U1B, as follows:

$$R3 \cong \frac{Rx}{(R2/R1)-1}$$

As in any high speed inverting feedback amplifier, a small high-Q chip type feedback capacitance, C1, may be needed to optimize flatness of frequency response. In this example, a 0.9pF value was found optimum for minimizing peaking. In general, provision should be made on the PC layout for an NPO chip capacitor in the range of 0.5-2pF. This capacitor is then value selected at board characterization for optimum frequency response.

For the dual trace, 1-500MHz swept frequency response plot of Figure 2.20, output levels were 0dBm into matched 50Ω loads, through back termination resistances R_{TA} and R_{TB}, at V_{OUTA} and V_{OUTB}. In this plot the vertical scale is 2dB/div, and it shows the 3dB bandwidth of the driver measuring about 250MHz, with peaking about 0.1dB. The four R_X resistors along with R_{TA} and R_{TB} control low frequency amplitude matching, which was within 0.1dB in the lab tests, using 511Ω 1% resistor types. For tightest amplitude matching, these resistor ratios can be more closely controlled.

FREQUENCY RESPONSE OF AD8002 CROSS-COUPLED DRIVER IS > 250MHz (C1 = 0.9pF ± 0.1pF)

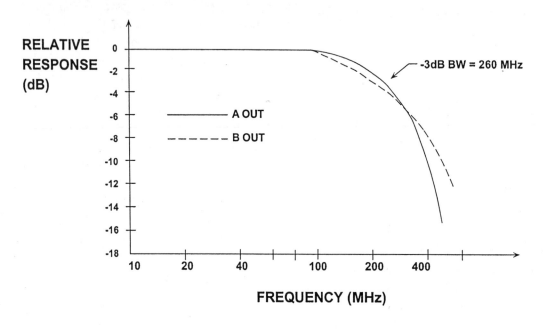

Figure 2.20

Due to the high gain-bandwidths involved with the AD8002, the construction of this circuit should follow RF rules, with the use of a ground plane, chip bypass capacitors of zero lead length at the ±5V supply pins, and surface mount resistors for lowest inductance.

4 Resistor Differential Line Receiver

Figure 2.21 shows a low cost, medium performance line receiver using a high speed op amp rated for video use. It is actually a standard 4 resistor difference amplifier optimized for high speed, with a differential to single-ended gain of R2/R1. Using low value, DC accurate/AC trimmed resistances for R1-R4 and a high speed, high CMR op amp provides the good performance.

SIMPLE VIDEO LINE RECEIVER USING THE AD818 OP AMP

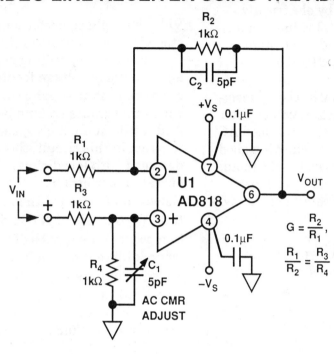

Figure 2.21

Practically speaking however, at low frequencies resistor matching can be more critical to overall CMR than the rated CMR of the op amp. For example, the worst case CMR (in dB) of this circuit due to resistor mismatch is:

$$CMR = 20\log_{10}\left(\frac{1 + \dfrac{R2}{R1}}{4Kr}\right).$$

In this expression the term "Kr" is a single resistor tolerance in fractional form (1%=0.01, etc.), and it is assumed the amplifier has significantly higher CMR ($\geq$100dB). Using discrete 1% metal films for R1/R2 and R3/R4 yields a worst case CMR of 34dB, 0.1% types 54dB, etc. Of course 4 random 1% resistors will on the average yield a CMR better than 34dB, but not dramatically so. A single substrate dual matched pair thin film network is preferred, for reasons of best noise rejection and simplicity. One type suitable is the Ohmtek 1005, (Reference 6) which has a ratio match of 0.1%, which will provide a worst case low frequency CMR of 66 dB.

This circuit has an interesting and desirable side property. Because of the resistors it divides down the input voltage, and the amplifier is protected against overvoltage. This allows CM voltages to exceed ±5V supply rails in some cases without hazard. For operation with ±15V supplies, inputs should not exceed the supply rails.

At frequencies above 1MHz, the bridge balance is dominated by AC effects, and a C1-C2 capacitive balance trim should be used for best performance. The C1 adjustment is intended to allow this, providing for the cancellation of stray layout capacitance(s) by electrically matching the net C1-C2 values. In a given PC layout with low and stable parasitic capacitance, C1 is best adjusted once in 0.5pF increments, for best high frequency CMR. Using designated PC pads, production values then would use the trimmed value. Good AC matching is essential to achieving good CMR at high frequencies. C1-C2 should be types similar physically, such as NPO (or other stable) ceramic chip style capacitors.

While the circuit as shown has unity gain, it can be gain-scaled in discrete steps, as long as the noted resistor ratios are maintained. In practice, this means using taps on a multi-ratio network for gain change, so as to raise both R2 and R4, in identical proportions. There is no other simple way to change gain in this receiver circuit. Alternately, a scheme for continuous gain control without interaction with CMR is to follow this receiver with a scaling amplifier/driver with adjustable gain. The similar AD828 dual amplifier allows this with the addition of only two resistors.

Video gain/phase performance of this stage is dependent upon the device used for U1 and the operating supply voltages. Suitable voltage feedback amplifiers work best at supplies of ± 10 - ± 15V, which maximizes op amp bandwidth. And, while many high speed amplifiers function in this circuit, those expressly designed with low distortion video operation perform best. The circuit as shown can be used with supplies of ± 5 to ± 15V, but lowest NTSC video distortion occurs for supplies of ± 10V or more, where differential gain/differential phase errors are less than 0.01%/0.05°. Operating at ± 5V supplies, the distortion rises somewhat, but the lowest power drain of 70mW occurs.

One drawback to this circuit is that it does load a 75Ω video line to some extent, and so should be used with this loading taken into account. On the plus side, it has wide dynamic range for both signal and CM voltages, plus the inherent overvoltage protection.

Active Feedback Differential Line Receiver

Fully integrating the line receiver function eliminates the resistor-related drawbacks of the 4 resistor line receiver, improving CMR performance, ease of use, and overall circuit flexibil-ity. An IC designed for this function is the AD830 active feedback amplifier (Reference 7,8). Its use as a differential line receiver with gain is illustrated in Figure 2.22.

VIDEO LOOP-THROUGH CONNECTION USING THE AD830

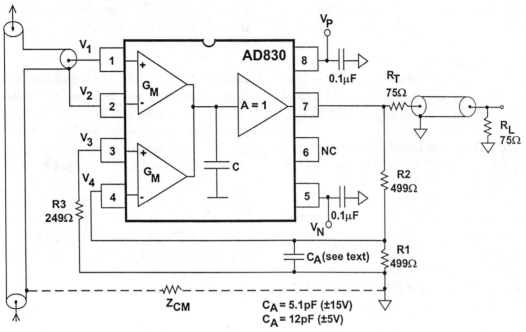

Figure 2.22

The AD830 operates as a feedback amplifier with two sets of fully differential inputs, available at pins 1-2 and 3-4, respectively. Internally, the outputs of the two stages are summed and drive a buffer output stage. Both input stages have high CMR, and can handle differential signals up to ±2V, and CM voltages can range up to $-V_S+3V$ or $+V_S-2.1V$, with a ±1V differential input applied. While the AD830 does not normally need protection against CM voltages, if sustained transient voltage beyond the rails is encountered, an optional pair of equal value ($\cong 200\Omega$) resistances can be used in series with pins 1-2.

In this device the overall feedback loop operates so that the differential voltages V_{1-2} and V_{3-4} are forced to be equal. Feedback is taken from the output back to one input differential

pair, while the other pair is driven by a differential input signal. An important point of this architecture is that high CM rejection is provided by the two differential input pairs, so CMR isn't dependent on resistor bridges and their associated matching problems. The inherently wideband balanced circuit and the quasi-floating operation of the driven input provide the high CMR, which is typically 100dB at DC.

The general expression for the U1 stage's gain "G" is like a non-inverting op amp, or:

$$G = \frac{V_{OUT}}{V_{IN}} = 1 + \frac{R2}{R1}$$

For lowest DC offset, balancing resistor R3 is used (equal to R1 ∥ R2).

In this example of a video "loop-through" connection, the input signal tapped from a coax line and applied to one input stage at pins 1-2, with the scaled output signal tied to the second input stage between pins 3-4. With the R1-R2 feedback attenuation of 2/1, the net result is that the output of U1, is then equal to $2 \cdot V_{IN}$, i.e., a gain of 2.

Functionally, the input and local grounds are isolated by the CMR of the AD830, which is typically 75dB at frequencies below 1MHz, 60dB at 4.43MHz, and relatively supply independent.

With the addition of an output source termination resistor R_T, this circuit has an overall loaded gain of unity at the load termination, R_L. It is a ground isolating video repeater, driving the terminated 75Ω output line, delivering a final output equal to the original input, V_{IN}.

NTSC video performance will be dependent upon supplies. Driving a terminated line as shown, the circuit has optimum video distortion levels for $V_s = \pm 15V$, where differential gain is typically 0.06%, and differential phase 0.08°. Bandwidth can be optimized by the optional 5.1pF (or 12pF) capacitor, C_A, which allows a 0.1dB bandwidth of 10MHz with ±15V operation. The differential gain and phase errors are about 2× at ±5V.

HIGH SPEED CLAMPING AMPLIFIERS

There are many situations where it is desirable to clamp the output of an op amp to prevent overdriving the circuitry which follows. Specially designed high speed, fast recovery clamping amplifiers offer an attractive alternative to designing external clamping/protection circuits. The AD8036/AD8037 low distortion, wide bandwidth clamp amplifiers represent a significant breakthrough in this technology. These devices allow the designer to specify a high (V_H) and low (V_L) clamp voltage. The output of the device clamps when the input exceeds either of these two levels. The AD8036/AD8037 offer superior clamping performance compared to competing devices that use output-clamping. Recovery time from overdrive is less than 5ns.

The key to the AD8036 and AD8037's fast, accurate clamp and amplifier performance is their proprietary input clamp architecture. This new design reduces clamp errors by more than 10×

over previous output clamp based circuits, as well as substantially increasing the bandwidth, precision, and versatility of the clamp inputs.

Figure 2.23 is an idealized block diagram of the AD8036 connected as a unity gain voltage follower. The primary signal path comprises A1 (a 1200V/μs, 240MHz high voltage gain, differential to single-ended amplifier) and A2 (a G=+1 high current gain output buffer). The AD8037 differs from the AD8036 only in that A1 is optimized for closed-loop gains of two or greater.

The input clamp section is comprised of comparators C_H and C_L, which drive switch S1 through a decoder. The unity-gain buffers in series with the $+V_{IN}$, V_H, and V_L inputs isolate the input pins from the comparators and S1 without reducing bandwidth or precision.

AD8036/AD8037 CLAMP AMPLIFIER EQUIVALENT CIRCUIT

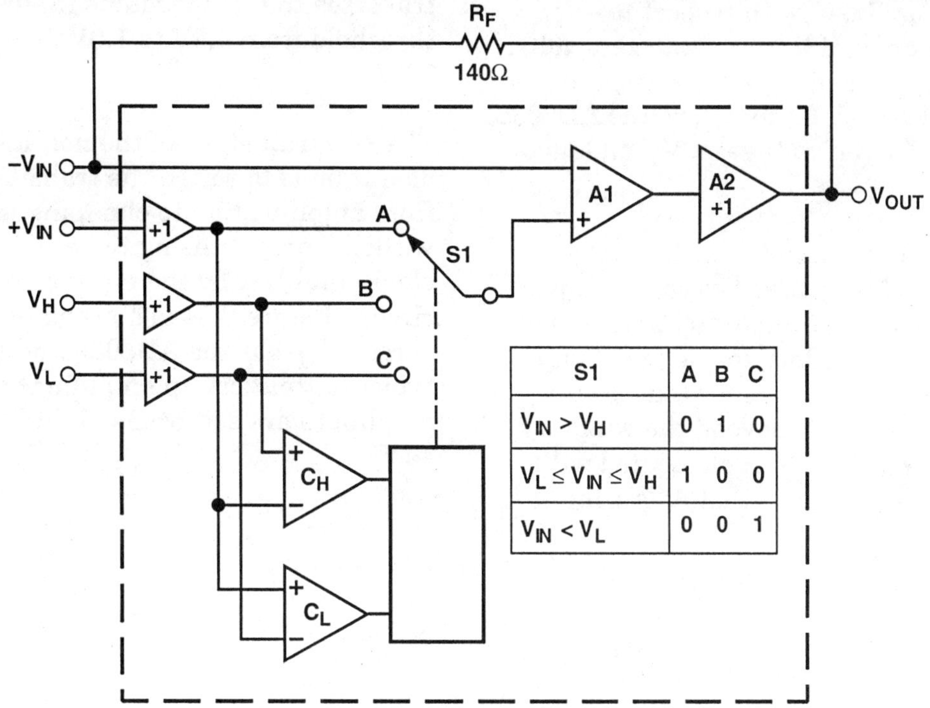

S1	A B C
$V_{IN} > V_H$	0 1 0
$V_L \leq V_{IN} \leq V_H$	1 0 0
$V_{IN} < V_L$	0 0 1

Figure 2.23

The two comparators have about the same bandwidth as A1 (240MHz), so they can keep up with signals within the useful bandwidth of the AD8036. To illustrate the operation of the input clamp circuit, consider the case where V_H is referenced to +1V, V_L is open, and the AD8036 is set for a gain of +1 by connecting its output back to its inverting input through the recommended 140Ω feedback resistor. Note that the main signal path always operates closed loop, since the clamping circuit only affects A1's noninverting input.

If a 0V to +2V voltage ramp is applied to the AD8036's $+V_{IN}$ for the connection just described, V_{OUT} should track $+V_{IN}$ perfectly up to +1V, then should limit at exactly +1V as $+V_{IN}$ continues to +2V.

In practice, the AD8036 comes close to this ideal behavior. As the $+V_{IN}$ input voltage ramps from zero to 1V, the output of the high limit comparator C_H starts in the off state, as does the output of C_L. When $+V_{IN}$ just exceeds V_H (practically, by about 18mV), C_H changes state, switching S1 from "A" to "B" reference level. Since the + input of A1 is now connected to V_H, further increases in $+V_{IN}$ have no effect on the AD8036's output voltage. The AD8036 is now operating as a unity-gain buffer for the V_H input, as any variation in V_H, for V_H > 1V, will be faithfully produced at V_{OUT}.

Operation of the AD8036 for negative input voltages and negative clamp levels on V_L is similar, with comparator C_L controlling S1. Since the comparators see the voltage on the $+V_{IN}$ pin as their common reference level, the voltage V_H and V_L are defined as "High" or "Low" with respect to $+V_{IN}$. For example, if V_{IN} is set to zero volts, V_H is open, and V_L is $+1V$, comparator C_L will switch S1 to "C", so the AD8036 will buffer the voltage on V_L and ignore $+V_{IN}$.

The performance of the AD8036/ AD8037 closely matches the ideal just described. The comparator's threshold extends from 60mV inside the clamp window defined by the voltages on V_L and V_H to 60mV beyond the window's edge. Switch S1 is implemented with current steering, so that A1's + input

makes a continuous transition from say, V_{IN} to V_H as the input voltage traverses the comparator's input threshold from 0.9V to 1.0V for V_H = 1.0V.

The practical effect of the non-ideal operation is to soften the transition from amplification to clamping modes, without compromising the absolute clamp limit set by the input clamping circuit. Figure 2.24 is a graph of V_{OUT} versus V_{IN} for the AD8036 and a typical *output* clamp amplifier. Both amplifiers are set for G=+1 and V_H = +1V.

COMPARISON BETWEEN INPUT AND OUTPUT CLAMPING

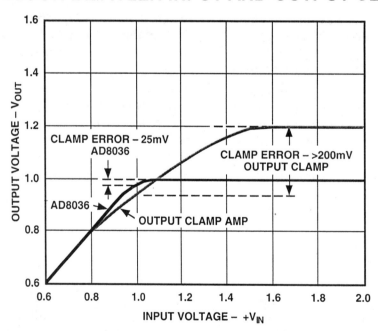

Figure 2.24

2

The worst case error between V_{OUT} (ideally clamped) and V_{OUT} (actual) is typically 18mV times the amplifier closed-loop gain. This occurs when V_{IN} equals V_H (or V_L). As V_{IN} goes above and/or below this limit, V_{OUT} will stay within 5mV of the ideal value.

In contrast, the output clamp amplifier's transfer curve typically will show some compression starting at an input of 0.8V, and can have an output voltage as far as 200mV over the clamp limit. In addition, since the output clamp causes the amplifier to operate open-loop in the clamp mode, the amplifier's output impedance will increase, potentially causing additional errors, and the recovery time is significantly longer.

It is important that a clamped amplifier such as the AD8036/AD8037 maintain

low levels of distortion when the input signals approach the clamping voltages. Figure 2.25 shows the second and third harmonic distortion for the amplifiers as the output approaches the clamp voltages. The input signal is 20MHz, the output signal is 2V peak-to-peak, and the output load is 100Ω.

Recovery from step voltage which is two times over the clamping voltage is shown in Figure 2.26. The input step voltage starts at +2V and goes to 0V (left-hand traces on scope photo). The input clamp voltage (V_H) is set at +1V. The right-hand trace shows the output waveform. The key specifications for the AD8036/AD8037 clamped amplifiers are summarized in Figure 2.27.

AD8036/AD8037 DISTORTION NEAR CLAMPING REGION, OUTPUT = 2V p-p, LOAD = 100Ω, F = 20MHz

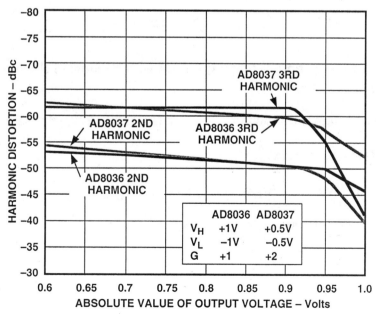

Figure 2.25

AD8036 / AD8037 OVERDRIVE (2x) RECOVERY

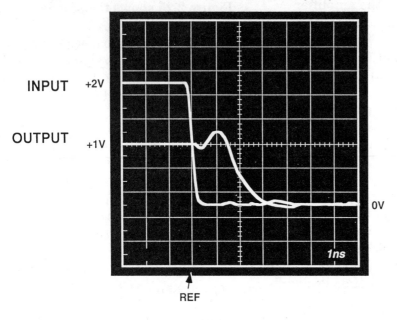

HORIZONTAL SCALE: 1ns/div

Figure 2.26

AD8036/AD8037 SUMMARY SPECIFICATIONS

- ■ Proprietary Input Clamping Circuit with Minimized Nonlinear Clamping Region

- ■ Small Signal Bandwidth: 240MHz (AD8036), 270MHz (AD8037)

- ■ Slew Rate: 1500V/µs

- ■ 1.5ns Overdrive Recovery

- ■ Low Distortion: -72dBc @ 20MHz (500Ω load)

- ■ Low Noise: 4.5nv/√Hz, 2pA/√Hz

- ■ 20mA Supply Current on ±5V

Figure 2.27

Figure 2.28 shows the AD9002 8-bit, 125MSPS flash converter driven by the AD8037 (240MHz bandwidth) clamping amplifier. The clamp voltages on the AD8037 are set to +0.55 and −0.55V, referenced to the ±0.5V input signal, with the external resistive dividers. The AD8037 also supplies a gain of two, and an offset of −1V (using the AD780 voltage reference), to match the 0 to −2V input range of the AD9002

flash converter. The output signal is clamped at +0.1V and −2.1V. This multi-function clamping circuit therefore performs several important functions as well as preventing damage to the flash converter which occurs if its input exceeds +0.5V, thereby forward biasing the substrate diode. The 1N5712 Schottky diode adds further protection during power-up.

AD9002 8-BIT, 125MSPS FLASH CONVERTER DRIVEN BY AD8037 CLAMP AMPLIFIER

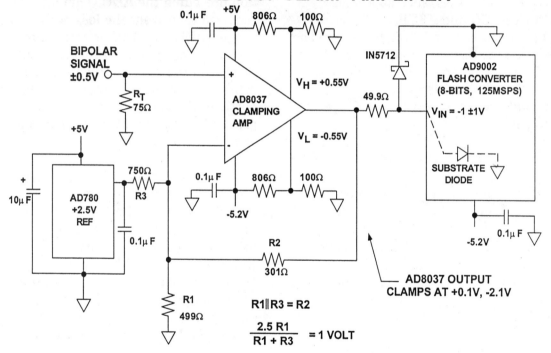

Figure 2.28

The feedback resistor, R2 = 301Ω, is selected for optimum bandwidth per the data sheet recommendation. For a gain of two, the parallel combination of R1 and R3 must also equal R2:

$$\frac{R1 \cdot R3}{R1 + R3} = R2 = 301\Omega$$

(nearest 1% standard resistor value).

In addition, the Thevenin equivalent output voltage of the AD780 +2.5V reference and the R3/R1 divider must be +1V to provide the −1V offset at the output of the AD8037.

$$\frac{2.5 \cdot R1}{R1 + R3} = 1 volt$$

Solving the equations yields R1 = 499Ω, R3 = 750Ω (using the nearest 1% standard resistor values).

Other input and output voltages ranges can be accommodated by appropriate changes in the external resistors.

Further examples of applications of these fast clamping op amps are given in Reference 9.

SINGLE-SUPPLY/RAIL-TO-RAIL CONSIDERATIONS

The market is driving high speed amplifiers to operate at lower power on lower supply voltages. High speed bipolar processes, such as Analog Devices' CB and XFCB, are basically 12V processes, and circuits designed on these processes are generally limited to ±5V power supplies (or less). This is ideal for high speed video, IF, and RF signals, which rarely exceed 5V peak-to-peak.

The emphasis on low power, battery-operated portable communications and instrumentation equipment has brought about the need for ICs which operate on single +5V, and +3V, and lower supplies. The term *single-supply* has various implications, some of which are often further confused by marketing hype.

There are many obvious reasons for lower power dissipation, such as the ability to function without fans, reliability issues, etc. There are, therefore, many applications for single-supply devices other than in systems which have only one supply voltage. For example, the lower power dissipation of a single-supply ADC may be the reason for its selection, rather than the fact that it requires just one supply.

There are also systems which truly operate on a single power supply. In such cases, it can often be difficult to maintain DC coupling from a trans-ducer all the way through to the ADC. In fact, AC coupling is often used in single-supply systems, with DC restoration preceding the ADC. This may be required to prevent the loss of dynamic range which would otherwise occur because of the need to provide adequate headroom to an AC coupled signal of arbitrary duty cycle. In the AC-coupled portions of such systems, a "false-ground" is often created, usually centered between the rails.

There are other disadvantages associated with lower power supply voltages. Signal swings are limited, therefore high-speed single-supply circuits tend to be more sensitive to corruption by wideband noise, etc. The single-supply op amp and ADC usually utilize the same power bus that supplies the digital circuits, making proper filtering and decoupling extremely critical.

In order to maximize the signal swing in single-supply circuits, it is desirable that a high speed op amp utilize as much of the supply range as possible on both the input and output. Ideally, a true *rail-to-rail* input op amp has an input common-mode range that includes both supply rails, and an output range which does likewise. This makes for some interesting tradeoffs and compromises in the circuit design of the op amp.

In many cases, an op amp may be fully specified for both dual ±5V and single-supply operation but neither its input nor its output can actually swing closer than about 1V to either supply rail. Such devices must be used in applications where the input and output common-mode restrictions are not violated. This generally involves offsetting the inputs using a false ground reference scheme.

To summarize, there are many tradeoffs involved in single-supply high-speed designs. In many cases, using devices specified for operation on +5V, but without true rail inclusive input/output operation can give good performance. Amplifiers are also becoming available that are true single supply rail-to-rail devices. Understanding single-supply rail-to-rail input and output limitations is easy if you understand a few basics about the circuitry inside the op amp. We shall consider input and output stages separately.

HIGH SPEED SINGLE SUPPLY AMPLIFIERS

- ■ Single Supply Offers:
  - ◆ Lower Power
  - ◆ Battery Operated Portable Equipment
  - ◆ Simplifies Power Supply Requirements (one voltage)

- ■ Design Tradeoffs:
  - ◆ Limited Signal Swings Increase Sensitivity to Noise
  - ◆ Usually Share Noisy Digital Power Supply
  - ◆ DC Coupling Throughout is Difficult
  - ◆ Rail-to-Rail Input and Output Increases Signal Swing, but not Required in All Applications
  - ◆ Many Op Amps Specified for Single Supply, but do not have Rail-to-Rail Inputs or Outputs

Figure 2.29

There is some demand for high-speed op amps whose input common-mode voltage includes both supply rails. Such a feature is undoubtedly useful in some applications, but engineers should recognize that there are relatively few applications where it is absolutely essential. These should be carefully distinguished from the many applications where common-mode range *close* to the supplies or one that includes one of the supplies is necessary, but input rail-to-rail operation is not.

In many single-supply applications, it is required that the input go to only one of the supply rails (usually ground).

Amplifiers which will handle zero-volt inputs are relatively easily designed using PNP differential pairs (or N-channel JFET pairs) as shown in Figure 2.30 (circuit used in the AD8041, AD8042, AD8044). The input common-mode range of such an op amp extends from about 200mV below the negative supply to within about 1V of the positive supply. If the stage is designed with N-channel JFETs (AD820/AD822/AD823/AD824), the input common-mode range would also include the negative rail.

PNP INPUT STAGE ALLOWS
INPUT TO GO TO THE NEGATIVE RAIL

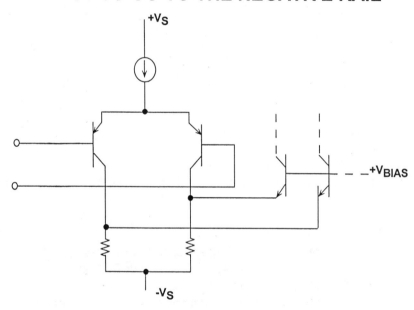

Figure 2.30

The input stage could also be designed with NPN transistors (or P-channel JFETs), in which case the input common-mode range would include the positive rail and to within about 1V of the negative rail; however, this requirement typically occurs in applications such as high-side current sensing, a low-frequency measurement application. The OP282/OP482 input stage uses the P-channel JFET input pair whose input common-mode range includes the positive rail.

True rail-to-rail input stages require two long-tailed pairs (see Figure 2.31), one of NPN bipolar transistors (or N-channel JFETs), the other of PNP transistors (or N-channel JFETs). These two pairs exhibit *different* offsets and bias currents, so when the applied input common-mode voltage changes, the amplifier input offset voltage and input bias current does also. In fact, when both current sources (I1 and I2) remain active throughout the entire input common-mode range, amplifier

2

input offset voltage is the *average* offset voltage of the NPN pair and the PNP pair. In those designs where the current sources are alternatively switched off at some point along the input common-mode voltage, amplifier input offset

voltage is dominated by the PNP pair offset voltage for signals near the negative supply, and by the NPN pair offset voltage for signals near the positive supply.

RAIL-TO-RAIL INPUT STAGE TOPOLOGY

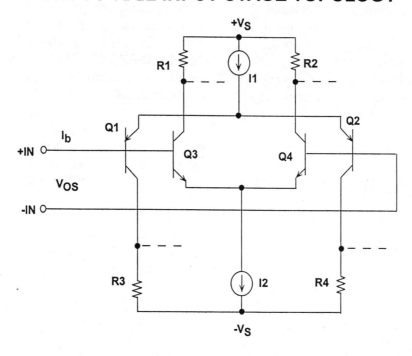

Figure 2.31

Amplifier input bias current, a function of transistor current gain, is also a function of the applied input common-mode voltage. The result is relatively poor common-mode rejection (CMR), and a changing common-mode input impedance over the common-mode input voltage range, compared to famil-iar dual-supply devices. These specifica-tions should be considered carefully when choosing a rail-rail input op amp, especially for a non-inverting configura-tion. Input offset voltage, input bias

current, and even CMR may be quite good over *part* of the common-mode range, but much worse in the region where operation shifts between the NPN and PNP devices and vice versa.

True rail-to-rail amplifier input stage designs must transition from one differ-ential pair to the other differential pair somewhere along the input common-mode voltage range. Devices like the AD8031/AD8032 (specified for ±5V, +5V, +3V, and +2.5V) have a common-mode crossover threshold at approximately 1V below the positive supply. The PNP differential input stage is active from about 200mV below the negative supply to within about 1V of the positive supply. Over this common-mode range, amplifier input offset voltage, input bias current, CMR, input noise voltage/current are primarily determined by the characteristics of the PNP differential pair. At the crossover threshold, however, amplifier input offset voltage becomes the average offset voltage of the NPN/PNP pairs and can change rapidly. Also, amplifier bias currents, dominated by the PNP differential pair over most of the input common-mode range, change polarity and magnitude at the crossover threshold when the NPN differential pair becomes active.

Applications which require true rail-rail inputs should therefore be carefully evaluated, and the amplifier chosen to ensure that its input offset voltage, input bias current, common-mode rejection, and noise (voltage and current) are suitable.

Figure 2.32 shows two typical high-speed op amp output stages. The emitter-follower stage is widely used, but its output voltage range is limited to within about 1V of either supply voltage. This is sufficient for many applications, but the common-emitter stage (used in the AD8041/8042/8044/8031/8032 and others) allows the output to swing to within the transistor saturation voltage, $V_{CE(SAT)}$, of the rails. For small amounts of load current (less than 100µA), the saturation voltage may be as low as 5 to 20mV, but for higher load currents, the saturation voltage can increase to several hundred millivolts (for example, 500mV at 50mA). This is illustrated in Figure 2.33 for the AD8042 (zero-volts in, rail-to-rail output). The solid curves show the output saturation voltage of the PNP transistor (output sourcing current), and the dotted curves the NPN transistor (sinking current). The saturation voltage increases with increasing temperature as would be expected.

An output stage constructed of CMOS FETs can provide true rail-to-rail performance, but only under no-load conditions, and in much lower frequency amplifiers. If the output must source or sink current, the output swing is reduced by the voltage dropped across the FETs internal "on" resistance (typically 100Ω).

HIGH SPEED SINGLE SUPPLY OP AMP OUTPUT STAGES

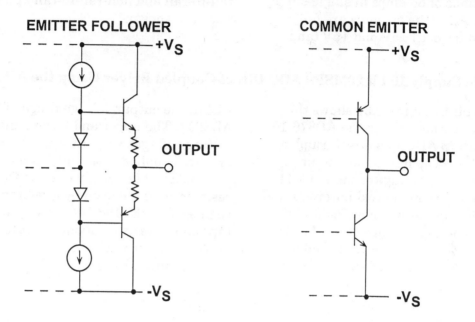

Figure 2.32

AD8042 OUTPUT SATURATION VOLTAGE VERSUS LOAD CURRENT

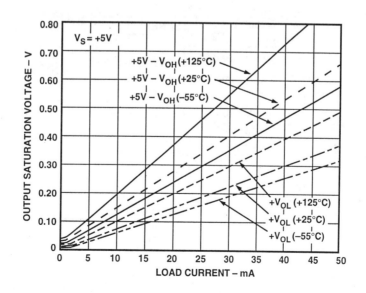

Figure 2.33

SINGLE SUPPLY OP AMP APPLICATIONS

The following section illustrates a few applications of op amps in single-supply circuits. All of the op amps are fully specified for both ±5V and +5V (and +3V where the design supports it). Both rail-to-rail and non-rail-to-rail applications are shown.

A Single-Supply 10-bit 20MSPS ADC Direct-Coupled Driver Using the AD8011

The circuit in Figure 2.34 shows the AD8011 op amp driving the AD876 10-bit, 20MSPS ADC in a direct-coupled application. The input and output common-mode voltage of the AD8011 must lie between approximately +1 and +4V when operating on a single +5V supply. The input range of the AD876 is 2V peak-to-peak centered around a common-mode value of +2.6V, well within the output voltage range of the AD8011. The upper and lower range setting voltages are +1.6V and +3.6V and are supplied externally to the AD876. They are easily derived from a resistor divider driven by a reference such as the REF198 (+4.096V). The two taps on the resistor divider should be buffered using precision single-supply op amps such as the AD822 (dual).

DC COUPLED SINGLE SUPPLY DRIVER FOR
AD876 10-BIT, 20MSPS ADC

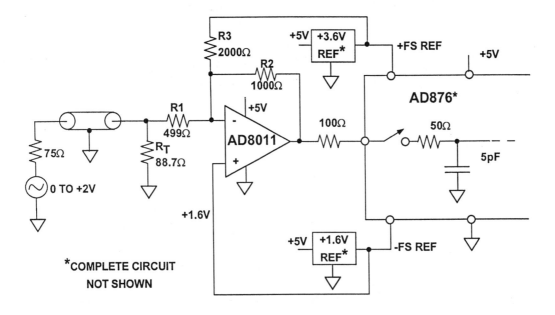

Figure 2.34

The source is represented as a 2V video signal referenced to ground. (The equivalent of a current generator of 0 to 27mA in parallel with the 75Ω source resistor. The termination resistor, R_T, is selected such that the parallel combination of R_T and R1 is 75Ω. The peak-to-peak swing at the termination resistor is 1V, so the AD8011 must supply a gain of two.

The non-inverting input of the AD8011 is biased to a common-mode voltage of +1.6V (well within it's allowable common-mode range). R3 is calculated as follows:

When the source voltage is zero-volts, there is a current of 3.0mA flowing through R1 (499Ω) and into 40.6Ω to ground (the equivalent parallel combination of the 75Ω source and the 88.7Ω termination resistor is 40.6Ω). The output of the AD8011 should be +3.6V under these conditions. This means that 2mA must flow through R2. Therefore R3 (connected to the +3.6V source) must supply 1.0mA into the summing junction (+1.6V), and therefore its value must be 2000Ω.

The input of the AD876 has a series MOSFET switch that turns on and off at the sampling frequency. This MOSFET is connected to a hold capacitor internal to the device. The on im-

pedance of the MOSFET is about 50Ω, while the hold capacitor is about 5pF.

In a worst case condition, the input voltage to the AD876 will change by a full-scale value (2V) in one sampling cycle. When the input MOSFET turns on, the output of the op amp will be connected to the charged hold capacitor through the series resistance of the MOSFET. Without any other series resistance, the instantaneous current that flows would be 40mA. This causes settling problems for the op amp.

The series 100Ω resistor limits the instantaneous current to about 13mA. This resistor cannot be made too large, or the high frequency performance will be affected. In practice, the optimum value is often determined experimentally.

The sampling MOSFET of the AD876 is closed for half of each cycle (25ns when sampling at 20MSPS). Approximately 7 time constants are required for settling to 10 bits. The series 100Ω resistor along with the 50Ω on resistance and the 5pF hold capacitor form a time constant of about 750ps. These values leave a comfortable margin for settling. Overall, the AD8011 provides adequate buffering for the AD876 ADC without introducing distortion greater than that of the ADC itself.

A 10-Bit, 40MSPS ADC Low-Distortion Single-Supply ADC Driver Using the AD8041 Op Amp

A DC coupled application which requires the rail-to-rail output capability of the AD8041 is shown in Figure 2.35 as a driver for the AD9050 10-bit, 40MSPS single-supply ADC. The input range of the AD9050 is 1V p-p centered around +3.3V. The maximum input signal is therefore +3.8V. The non-inverting input of the AD8041 is driven with a common-mode voltage of +1.65V which is derived from the unused differential input of the AD9050. This allows the op amp to act as a level shifter for the ground-referenced bipolar input 1V p-p signal, with unity gain

as determined by the 1kΩ resistors, R1 and R2.

Op amps with complementary emitter follower outputs such as the AD8011 (operating on +5V) generally will exhibit high frequency distortion for sinewaves with full-scale amplitudes of 1V p-p centered at +3.3V. Because of its common emitter output stage, however, the AD8041 is capable of driving the AD9050, while maintaining a distortion floor of greater than 66dB with a 4.9MHz fullscale input (see Figure 2.36).

DC COUPLED SINGLE-SUPPLY DRIVER FOR AD9050 10-BIT, 40MSPS ADC

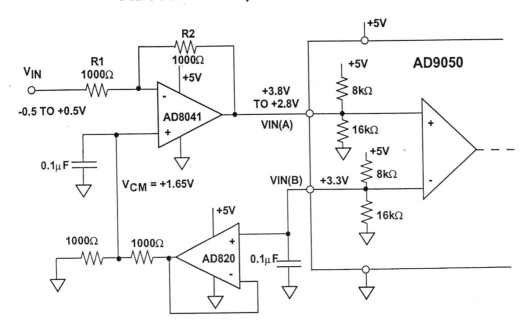

Figure 2.35

FFT OUTPUT OF AD9050 CIRCUIT WITH 4.9MHz INPUT AND 40MSPS SAMPLING FREQUENCY

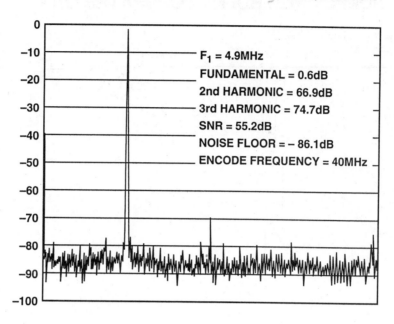

F_1 = 4.9MHz

FUNDAMENTAL = 0.6dB

2nd HARMONIC = 66.9dB

3rd HARMONIC = 74.7dB

SNR = 55.2dB

NOISE FLOOR = – 86.1dB

ENCODE FREQUENCY = 40MHz

Figure 2.36

Single-Supply RGB Buffer

Op amps such as the AD8041/AD8042/ and AD8044 can provide buffering of RGB signals that include ground while operating from a single +3V or +5V supply. The signals that drive an RGB monitor are usually supplied by current output DACs that operate from a single +5V supply. Examples of such are triple video DACs like the ADV7120/21/22 from Analog Devices.

During the horizontal blanking interval, the current output of the DACs goes to zero, and the RGB signals are pulled to ground by the termination resistors. If more than one RGB monitor is desired, it cannot simply be connected in parallel because it will provide an additional termination. Therefore, buffering must be provided before connecting a second monitor.

Since the RGB signals include ground as part of their dynamic output range, it has previously been required to use a dual supply op amp to provide this buffering. In some systems, this is the only component that requires a negative supply, so it can be quite inconvenient to incorporate this multiple monitor feature.

Figure 2.37 shows a diagram of one channel of a single supply gain-of-two buffer for driving a second RGB monitor. No current is required when the amplifier output is at ground. The termination resistor at the monitor helps pull the output down at low voltage levels.

SINGLE SUPPLY RGB BUFFER OPERATES ON +3V OR +5V

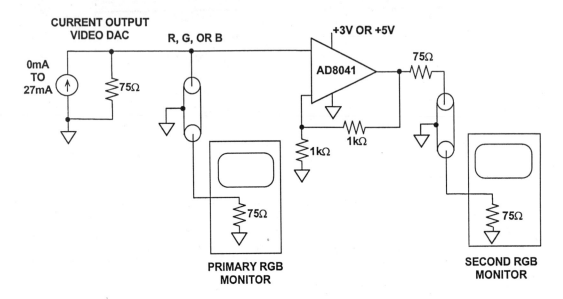

Figure 2.37

Figure 2.38 shows the output of such a buffer operating from a single +3V supply and driven by the Blue signal of a color bar pattern. Note that the input and output are at ground during the horizontal blanking interval. The RGB signals are specified to output a maximum of 700mV peak. The output of the AD8041 is +1.4V with the termination resistors providing a divide-by-two. The Red and Green signals can be buffered in the same manner with a duplication of this circuit. Another possibility is to use the quad AD8044 single-supply op amp.

Single-Supply Sync Stripper

Some RGB monitors use only three cables total and carry the synchronizing signals and the Green (G) signal on the same cable. The sync signals are pulses that go in the negative direction from the blanking level of the G signal.

In some applications, such as prior to digitizing component video signals with ADCs, it is desirable to remove or strip the sync portion from the G signal. Figure 2.39 is a circuit using the AD8041 running on a single +5V supply that performs this function.

INPUT / OUTPUT OF SINGLE SUPPLY RGB BUFFER OPERATING ON +3V

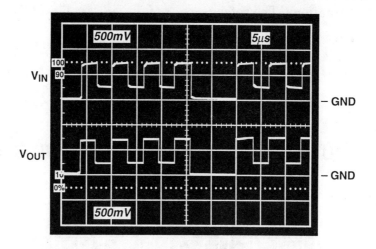

Figure 2.38

SINGLE SUPPLY VIDEO SYNC STRIPPER

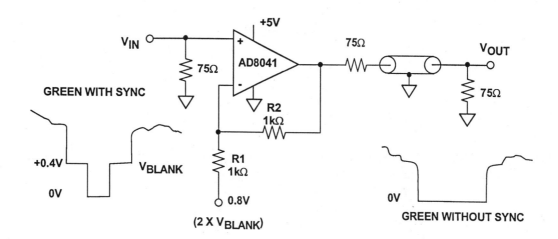

Figure 2.39

The upper waveform in Figure 2.40 shows the Green plus sync signal that is output from an ADV7120, a single supply triple video DAC. Because the DAC is single supply, the lowest level of the sync tip is at ground or slightly above. The AD8041 is set from a gain of two to compensate for the divide-by-two of the output terminations. The refer-ence voltage for R1 should be twice the DC blanking level of the G signal. If the blanking level is at ground and the sync tip is negative, as in some dual supply systems, then R1 can be tied to ground. In either case, the output will have the sync removed and have the blanking level at ground.

INPUT / OUTPUT OF SINGLE SUPPLY SYNC STRIPPER

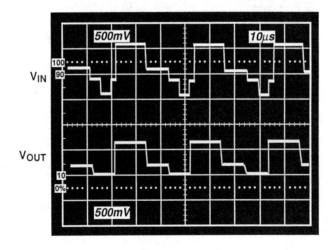

Figure 2.40

A Single-Supply Video Line Driver with Zero-Volt Output,
Eamon Nash

When operated with a single supply, the AD8031 80MHz rail-to-rail voltage feedback op amp has optimum distor-tion performance when the signal has a common mode level of Vs/2, and when there is about 500mV of headroom to each rail. If low distortion is required for signals which swing close to ground, an emitter follower can be used at the op amp output.

Figure 2.41 shows the AD8031 config-ured as a single supply gain-of-two line driver. With the output driving a back terminated 50Ω line, the overall gain is unity from Vin to Vout. In addition to minimizing reflections, the 50Ω back termination resistor protects the transistor from damage if the cable is short circuited. The emitter follower, which is inside the feedback loop, ensures that the output voltage from the AD8031 stays about 700mV above ground. Using this circuit excellent distortion is obtained even when the output signal swings to within 50mV of ground. The circuit was tested at 500kHz and 2MHz using a single +5V supply. For the 500kHz signal, THD was 68dBc with a peak-to-peak swing at Vout of 1.85V (50mV to +1.9V). This corresponds to a signal at the emitter follower output of

3.7V p-p (100mV to 3.8V). Data was taken with an output signal of 2MHz, and a THD of 55dBc was measured with a Vout of 1.55V p-p (50mV to 1.6V).

This circuit can also be used to drive the analog input of a single supply high speed ADC whose input voltage range is ground-referenced. In this case, the emitter of the external transistor is connected directly to the ADC input. A peak positive voltage swing of approximately 3.8V is possible before significant distortion begins to occur.

LOW DISTORTION ZERO-VOLT OUTPUT
SINGLE SUPPLY LINE DRIVER USING AD8031

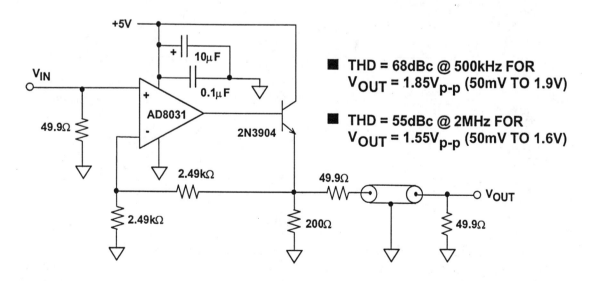

Figure 2.41

Headroom Considerations in AC-Coupled Single-Supply Circuits

The AC coupling of arbitrary wave-forms can actually introduce problems which don't exist at all in DC coupled or DC restored systems. These problems have to do with the waveform duty cycle, and are particularly acute with signals which approach the rails, as they can in low supply voltage systems which are AC coupled.

In Figure 2.42 (A), an example of a 50% duty cycle square wave of about 2Vp-p level is shown, with the signal swing biased symmetrically between the

upper and lower clip points of a 5V supply amplifier. Assume that the amplifier has a complementary emitter follower output and can only swing to the limited DC levels as marked, about 1V from either rail. In cases (B) and (C), the duty cycle of the input wave-form is adjusted to both low and high duty cycle extremes *while maintaining the same peak-to-peak input level.* At the amplifier output, the waveform is seen to clip either negative or positive, in (B) and (C), respectively.

WAVEFORM DUTY CYCLE TAXES
HEADROOM IN AC COUPLED SINGLE SUPPLY AMPLIFIERS

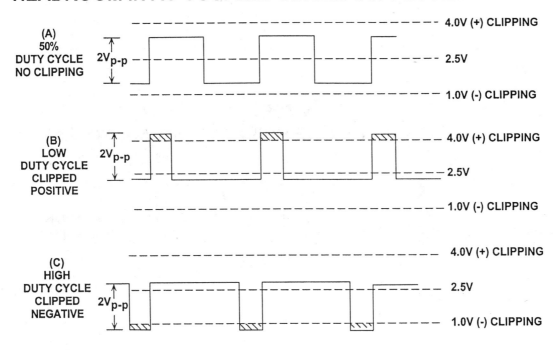

Figure 2.42

Since standard video waveforms *do* vary in duty cycle as the scene changes, the point is made that low distortion operation on AC coupled single supply stages must take the duty cycle headroom degradation effect into account. If a stage has a 3Vp-p output swing avail-

able before clipping, and it must cleanly reproduce an *arbitrary* waveform, then the maximum allowable amplitude is less than 1/2 of this 3Vp-p swing, that is <1.5Vp-p. An example of violating this criteria is the 2Vp-p waveform of Figure 2.42, which is clipping for both the high and low duty cycles. Note that the criteria set down above is based on avoiding hard clipping, while subtle distortion increases may in fact take place at lower levels. This suggests an even more conservative criteria for lowest distortion operation such as composite NTSC video amplifiers.

Figure 2.43 shows a single supply gain-of-two composite video line driver using the AD8041. Since the sync tips of a composite video signal extend below ground, the input must be AC coupled and shifted positively to prevent clipping during negative excursions. The input is terminated in 75Ω and AC coupled via the 47µF to a voltage divider that provides the DC bias point to the input. Setting the optimal common-mode bias voltage requires some understanding of the nature of composite video signals and the video performance of the AD8041.

SINGLE SUPPLY AC COUPLED COMPOSITE VIDEO LINE DRIVER HAS $\Delta G = 0.06\%$ AND $\Delta \phi = 0.06°$

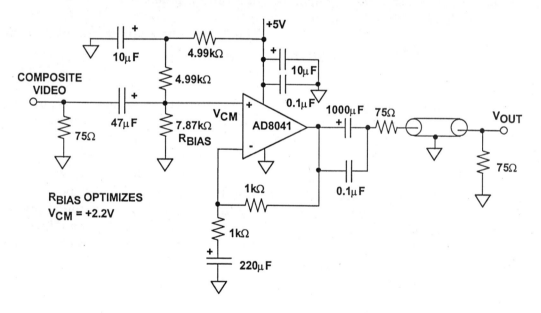

Figure 2.43

As discussed above, signals of bounded peak-to-peak amplitude that vary in duty cycle require larger dynamic swing capability than their peak-to-peak amplitude after AC coupling. As a worst case, the dynamic signal swing required will approach twice the peak-to-peak value. The two bounding cases are for a duty cycle that is mostly low, but occasionally goes high at a fraction of a percent duty cycle, and vice versa.

Composite video is not quite this demanding. One bounding extreme is for a signal that is mostly black for an entire frame, but occasionally has a white (full intensity), minimum width spike at least once per frame.

The other extreme is for a video signal that is full white everywhere. The blanking intervals and sync tips of such a signal will have negative going excursions in compliance with composite video specifications. The combination of horizontal and vertical blanking intervals limit such a signal to being at its highest level (white) for only about 75% of the time.

As a result of the duty cycle variations between the two extremes presented above, a 1V p-p composite video signal that is multiplied by a gain-of-two requires about 3.2V p-p of dynamic voltage swing at the output for the op amp to pass a composite video signal of arbitrary duty cycle without distortion.

The AD8041 not only has ample signal swing capability to handle the dynamic range required, but also has excellent differential gain and phase when buffering these signals in an AC coupled configuration.

To test this, the differential gain and phase were measured for the AD8041 while the supplies were varied. As the lower supply is raised to approach the video signal, the first effect is that the sync tips become compressed before the differential gain and phase are adversely affected. Thus, there must be adequate swing in the negative direction to pass the sync tips without compression.

As the upper supply is lowered to approach the video, the differential gain and phase were not significantly adversely affected until the difference between the peak video output and the supply reached 0.6V. Thus, the highest video level should be kept at least 0.6V below the positive supply rail.

Taking the above into account, it was found that the optimal point to bias the non-inverting input was at +2.2V DC. Operating at this point, the worst case differential gain was 0.06% and the differential phase 0.06°.

The AC coupling capacitors used in the circuit at first glance appear quite large. A composite video signal has a lower frequency band edge of 30Hz. The resistances at the various AC coupling points - especially at the output - are quite small. In order to minimize phase shifts and baseline tilt, the large value capacitors are required. For video system performance that is not to be of the highest quality, the value of these capacitors can be reduced by a factor of up to five with only a slight observable change in the picture quality.

Single-Supply AC Coupled Single-Ended-to-Differential Driver

The circuit shown in Figure 2.44 provides a flexible solution to differential line driving in a single-supply application and utilizes the dual AD8042. The basic operation of the cross-coupled configuration has been described earlier in this section. The input, V_{IN}, is a single-ended signal that is capacitively coupled into the feedforward resistor, R1. The non-inverting inputs of each half of the AD8042 are biased at +2.5V. The gain from single-ended input to differential output is equal to 2R2/R1. The gain can be varied by changing one resistor (either R1 or R2).

SINGLE SUPPLY AC COUPLED DIFFERENTIAL DRIVER

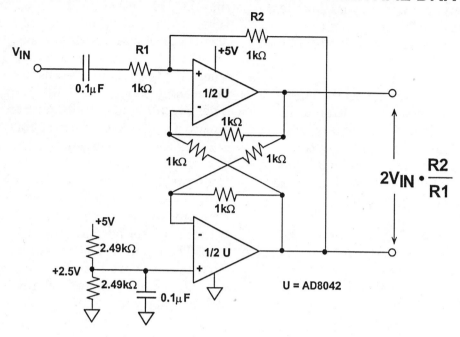

Figure 2.44

HIGH SPEED VIDEO MULTIPLEXING WITH OP AMPS UTILIZING DISABLE FUNCTION

A common video circuit function is the multiplexer, a stage which selects one of "N" video inputs and transmits a buffered version of the selected signal to the output. A number of video op amps (AD810, AD813, AD8013) have a *disable* mode which, when activated by applying the appropriate level to a pin on the package, disables the op amp output stage and drops the power to a lower value.

In the case of the AD8013 (triple current-feedback op amp), asserting any one of the disable pins about 1.6V from the negative supply will put the corresponding amplifier into a disabled, powered-down state. In this condition, the amplifier's quiescent current drops to about 0.3mA, its output becomes a high impedance, and there is a high

level of isolation from the input to the output. In the case of the gain-of-two line driver, for example, the impedance at the output node will be about equal to the sum of the feedback and feedforward resistors (1.6kΩ) in parallel with about 12pF capacitance. Input-to-output isolation is about 66dB at 5MHz.

Leaving the disable pin disconnected (floating) will leave the corresponding amplifier operational, in the enabled state. The input impedance of the disable pin is about 40kΩ in parallel with 5pF. When driven to 0V, with the negative supply at –5V, about 100µA flows into the disable pin.

When the disable pins are driven by CMOS logic, on a single +5V supply, the disable and enable times are about 50ns. When operated on dual supplies, level shifting will be required from standard logic outputs to the disable pins.

The AD8013's input stages include protection from the large differential voltages that may be applied when disabled. Internal clamps limit this voltage to about ±3V. The high input-to-output isolation will be maintained for voltages below this limit.

Wiring the amplifier outputs together as shown in Figure 2.45 will form a 3:1 multiplexer with about 50ns switching time between channels. The 0.1dB bandwidth of the circuit is 35MHz, and the OFF channel isolation is 60dB at 10MHz. The simple logic level-shifting circuit shown on the diagram does not significantly affect switching time.

The resistors were chosen as follows. The feedback resistor R2 of 845Ω was

chosen first for optimum bandwidth of the AD8013 current feedback op amp. When any given channel is ON, it must drive both the termination resistor R_L, and the net dummy resistance, $R_X/2$, where R_X is an equivalent series resistance equal to R1 + R2 + R3. To provide a net overall gain of unity plus an effective source resistance of 75Ω, the other resistor values must be as shown.

Configuring two amplifiers as unity gain followers and using the third to set the gain results in a high performance 2:1 multiplexer as shown in Figure 2.46. The circuit takes advantage of the very low crosstalk between the amplifiers and achieves the OFF channel isolation shown in Figure 2.47. The differential gain and phase performance of the circuit is 0.03% and 0.07°, respectively.

3:1 VIDEO MULTIPLEXER SWITCHES IN 50ns

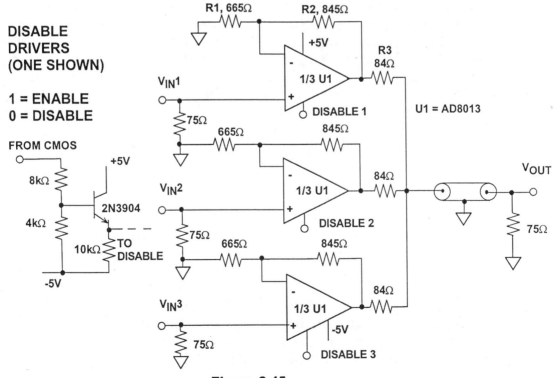

Figure 2.45

2:1 VIDEO MULTIPLEXER

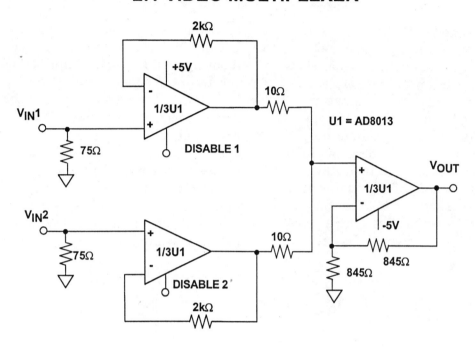

Figure 2.46

2:1 MULTIPLEXER ON-CHANNEL GAIN AND MUX OFF-CHANNEL FEEDTHROUGH VS. FREQUENCY

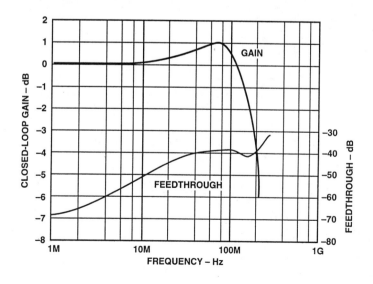

Figure 2.47

VIDEO PROGRAMMABLE GAIN AMPLIFIER USING THE AD813 TRIPLE CURRENT FEEDBACK OP AMP

Closely related to the multiplexers described above is a programmable gain video amplifier, or PGA, as shown in Figure 2.48. In the case of the AD813, the individual op amps are disabled by pulling the disable pin about 2.5V below the positive supply. This puts the corresponding amplifier in its powered down state. In this condition, the amplifier's quiescent supply current drops to about 0.5mA, its output becomes a high impedance, and there is a high level of isolation

between the input and the output. Leaving the disable pin disconnected (floating) will leave the amplifier operational, in the enabled state. The input impedance of the disable pins is about 35kΩ in parallel with 5pF. When grounded, about 50µA flows out of a disable pin when operating on ±5V supplies. The switching threshold is such that the disable pins can be driven directly from +5V CMOS logic with no level shifting (as was required in the previous example).

PROGRAMMABLE GAIN AMPLIFIER USING AD813 TRIPLE CFB OP AMP

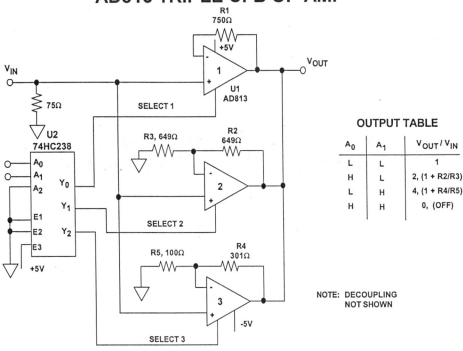

A_0	A_1	V_{OUT}/V_{IN}
L	L	1
H	L	2, (1 + R2/R3)
L	H	4, (1 + R4/R5)
H	H	0, (OFF)

Figure 2.48

With a two-line digital control input, this circuit can be set up to provide 3 different gain settings. This makes it a useful circuit in various systems which can employ signal normalization or gain ranging prior to A/D conversion, such as

CCD systems, ultrasound, etc. The gains can be binary related as here, or they can be arbitrary. An extremely useful feature of the AD813 CFB current feedback amplifier is the fact that the bandwidth does not reduce as gain is increased. Instead, it stays relatively constant as gain is raised. Thus more useful bandwidth is available at the higher programmed gains than would be true for a fixed gain-bandwidth product VFB amplifier type.

In the circuit, channel 1 of the AD813 is a unity gain channel, channel 2 has a gain of 2, and channel 3 a gain of 4, while the fourth control state is OFF. As is indicated by the table, these gains can varied by adjustment of the R2/R3 or R4/R5 ratios. For the gain range and values shown, the PGA will be able to maintain a 3dB bandwidth of about 50MHz or more for loading as shown (a high impedance load of 1kΩ or more is assumed). Fine tuning the bandwidth for a given gain setting can be accomplished by lowering the resistor values at the higher gains, as shown in the circuit, where for G=1, R1=750Ω, for G=2, R2=649Ω, and for G=4, R4=301Ω.

VIDEO MULTIPLEXERS AND CROSSPOINT SWITCHES

Traditional CMOS switches and multiplexers suffer from several disadvantages at video frequencies. Their switching time (typically 100ns or so) is not fast enough for today's applications, and they require external buffering in order to drive typical video loads. In addition, the small variation of the CMOS switch "on" resistance with signal level (called R_{on} *modulation*) introduces unwanted distortion and degradation in differential gain and phase. Multiplexers based on complementary bipolar technology offer a better solution at video frequencies.

Functional block diagrams of the AD8170/8174/8180/8182 bipolar video multiplexer are shown in Figure 2.49. These devices offer a high degree of flexibility and are ideally suited to video applications, with excellent differential gain and phase specifications. Switching time for all devices in the family is 10ns to 0.1%. The AD8170/8174 muxes include an on-chip current feedback op amp output buffer whose gain can be set externally. Off channel isolation and crosstalk are typically greater than 80dB for the entire family. Key specifications are shown in Figure 2.50.

Figure 2.51 shows an application circuit for three AD8170 2:1 muxes where the RGB monitor can be switched between two computers. The AD8174 4:1 mux is used in Figure 2.52 to allow a single high speed ADC to digitize the RGB outputs of a scanner. Figure 2.53 shows two AD8174 4:1 muxes expanded into an 8:1 mux.

AD8170/8174/8180/8182 BIPOLAR VIDEO MULTIPLEXERS

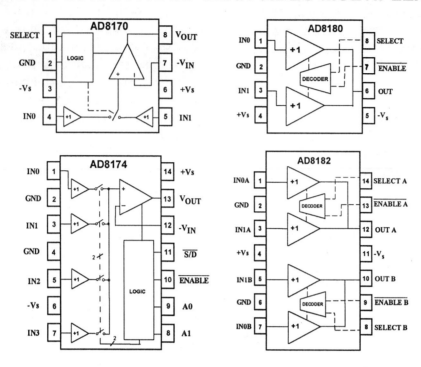

Figure 2.49

AD817X AND AD818X MULTIPLEXER KEY SPECIFICATIONS

- ■ 10ns Switching Time

- ■ Wide Bandwidth (-3dB BW):
    - ◆ 200MHz (AD817X)
    - ◆ 600MHz (AD818X)

- ■ Gain Flatness (0.1dB):
    - ◆ 80MHz (AD817X)
    - ◆ 150MHz (AD818X)

- ■ 0.02% / 0.02° Differential Gain and Phase (AD817X, R_L = 150Ω)
- ■ 0.02% / 0.03° Differential Gain and Phase (AD818X, R_L = 1kΩ)

- ■ Off-Channel Isolation and Crosstalk > –80dB @ 10MHz

- ■ Low Power (±5V Supplies):

    - ◆ AD8170 - 65mW   ◆ AD8174 - 85mW
    - ◆ AD8180 - 35mW   ◆ AD8182 - 70mW

Figure 2.50

DUAL SOURCE RGB MULTIPLEXER USING THREE 2:1 MUXES

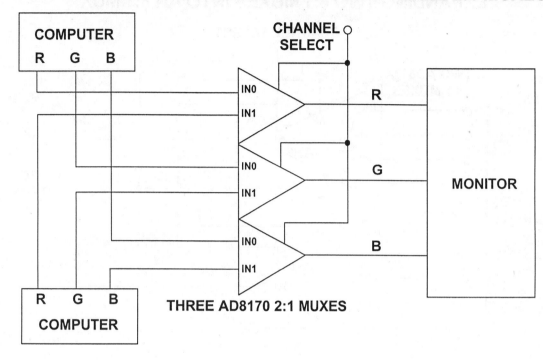

Figure 2.51

2

DIGITIZING RGB SIGNALS WITH ONE ADC AND A 4:1 MUX

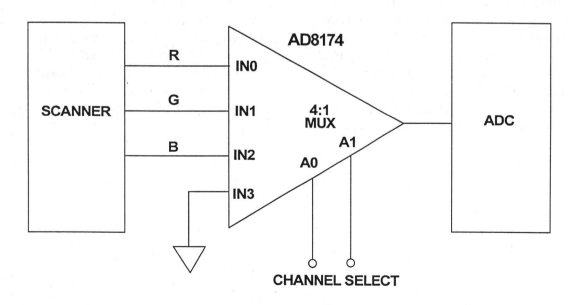

Figure 2.52

EXPANDING TWO 4:1 MUXES INTO AN 8:1 MUX

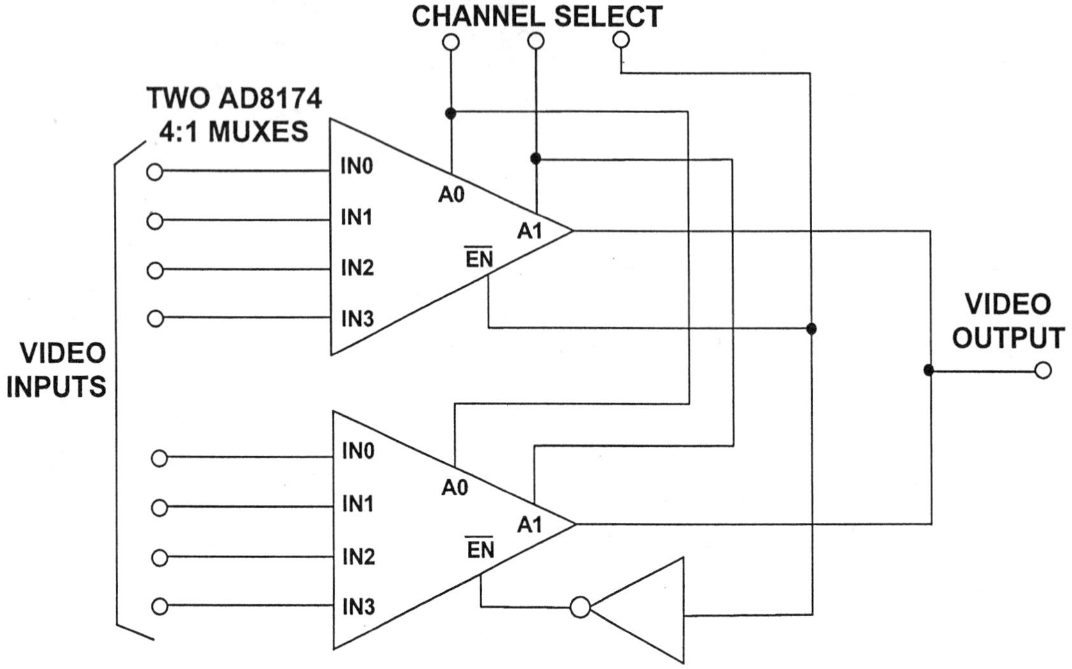

Figure 2.53

The AD8116 extends the concepts above to yield a 16×16 buffered video crosspoint switch matrix (Figure 2.54). The 3dB bandwidth is greater than 200MHz, and the 0.1dB gain flatness extends to greater than 40MHz. Channel switching time is less than 30ns to 0.1%. Crosstalk is 70dB and isolation is 90dB (both measured at 10MHz). Differential gain and phase is 0.01% and 0.01° for a 150Ω load. Total power dissipation is 900mW on ±5V supplies.

The AD8116 includes output buffers which can be put into a high impedance state for paralleling crosspoint stages so that the off channels do not load the output bus. The channel switching is performed via a serial digital control which can accommodate "daisy chaining" of several devices. The AD8116 is packaged in a 128-pin TQFP package. Key specifications for the device are summarized in Figure 2.55.

AD8116 16×16 BUFFERED VIDEO CROSSPOINT SWITCH

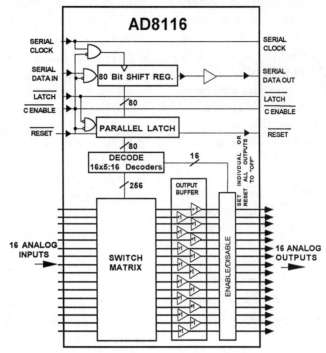

Figure 2.54

AD8116 CROSSPOINT SWITCH KEY SPECIFICATIONS

■ 16×16 Buffered Inputs and Outputs

■ Output Buffer Disable Feature Allows Expansion

■ 3dB Bandwidth 200MHz, 0.1dB Bandwidth 40MHz

■ 30ns Switching to 0.1%

■ Differential Gain 0.01%, Differential Phase 0.01°

■ Power Dissipation: 900mW (±5V Supplies)

■ 128-pin TQFP, 0.36 Square Inches Area

Figure 2.55

HIGH POWER LINE DRIVERS AND ADSL

ADSL (Asymmetric Digital Subscriber Line) uses the current subscriber line connection to the central office to transmit data as high as 8Mbps, almost 300 times the speed of the fastest traditional modem. ADSL uses the entire bandwidth (approximately 1MHz) of the connection in addition for the modulation scheme called Discrete Multi Tone (DMT).

Although high-speed fiber links already exist, it is still too difficult and expensive to bring them directly to every residence. ADSL uses the existing infrastructure for "the last mile" connecting the home and the local central office (which already has a high-speed fiber link to the national network).

Many applications are uneven (asymmetric) in their bandwidth needs - sending more information in one direction than the other. Typically, a user will request a video channel, ask for information from a central database, or view complex graphical images on a web page. All of these applications require considerable bandwidth. In contrast, the user may only send commands or files back up to the server. Realizing this, ADSL was designed to deliver a bigger downstream capacity to the home, while having a smaller two-way capacity.

Key to the ADSL system is the requirement for a low-distortion differential drive amplifier which delivers approximately 40V p-p into a 60Ω differential load impedance. The AD815 dual high current driver can deliver 40V p-p differential into a 50Ω load (corresponding to 400mA peak current!) using the application circuit shown in Figure 2.56. Low harmonic distortion is also required for ADSL applications, since it affects system bit error rates. The typical distortion of the device is shown in Figure 2.57 for 50Ω and 200Ω differential loads.

There are three AD815 models, two are available in a 15-pin power package, and the third as a 24-pin thermally enhanced SOIC. The 15-pin power package (AD815AY-through hole and AD815AVR-surface mount) has a low thermal resistance (θ_{JA} = 41°C/W) which can be reduced considerably (to θ_{JA} = 16 °C/W) by connecting the package to an area of copper which acts as a heat sink. The AD815 incorporates a thermal shutdown circuit to protect the die from thermal overload.

The AD815 also has applications as a general purpose high current coil, transformer, or twisted pair cable driver, a CRT convergence adjustment control, or a video signal distribution amplifier. Each amplifier in the AD815 is capable of driving 6 back-terminated 75Ω video loads with a differential gain and phase of 0.05% and 0.45° respectively.

ADSL DIFFERENTIAL LINE DRIVER USING THE AD815

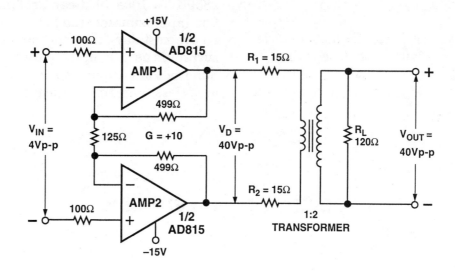

Figure 2.56

THD VS. FREQUENCY FOR AD815 DIFFERENTIAL DRIVER

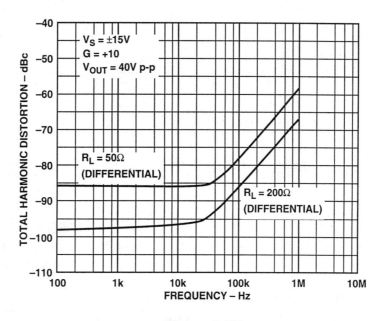

Figure 2.57

HIGH SPEED PHOTODIODE PREAMPS

Photodiodes generate a small current which is proportional to the level of illumination. They have many applications ranging from precision light meters to high-speed fiber optic receivers.

The equivalent circuit for a photodiode is shown in Figure 2.58. One of the standard methods for specifying the sensitivity of a photodiode is to state its short circuit photocurrent (I_{sc}) at a given light level from a well defined light source. The most commonly used source is an incandescent tungsten lamp running at a color temperature of 2850K. At 100fc (foot-candles) illumination (approximately the light level on an overcast day), the short circuit current is usually in the picoamps to hundreds of microamps range for small area (less than 1mm^2) diodes.

PHOTODIODE EQUIVALENT CIRCUIT

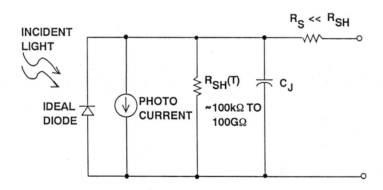

Figure 2.58

The short circuit current is very linear over 6 to 9 decades of light intensity, and is therefore often used as a measure of absolute light levels. The open circuit forward voltage drop across the photodiode varies logarithmically with light level, but, because of its large temperature coefficient, the diode voltage is seldom used as an accurate measure of light intensity.

The shunt resistance is usually in the order of several hundred kΩ to more than 1GΩ at room temperature, and decreases by a factor of two for every 10°C rise in temperature. Diode capacitance is a function of junction area and the diode bias voltage. A value of 10 to 50pF at zero bias is typical for small area diodes.

Photodiodes may either be operated with zero bias (*photovoltaic* mode) or reverse bias (*photoconductive* mode) as shown in Figure 2.59. The most precise linear operation is obtained in the photovoltaic mode, while higher switching speeds are realizable when the diode is operated in the photoconductive mode. Under reverse bias conditions, a small amount of current called *dark current* will flow even when there is no illumination. There is no dark current

in the photovoltaic mode. In the photovoltaic mode, the diode noise is basically the thermal noise generated by the shunt resistance. In the photoconductive mode, shot noise due to conduction is an additional source of noise. Photodiodes are usually optimized during the design process for use in either the photovoltaic mode or the photoconductive mode, but not both.

Optimizing photodiode preamplifiers is probably one of the most challenging of design problems, especially if high bandwidth and direct coupling is required. Figure 2.60 shows a basic photodiode preamp designed with an op amp connected as a current-to-voltage converter.

PHOTODIODE MODES OF OPERATION

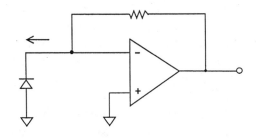

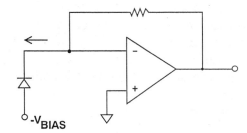

PHOTOVOLTAIC

· **Zero Bias**
· **No Dark Current**
· **Precision Applications**
· **Low Noise (Johnson)**

PHOTOCONDUCTIVE

· **Reverse Bias**
· **Dark Current Exists**
· **High Speed Applications**
· **Higher Noise (Johnson + Shot)**

Figure 2.59

HIGH BANDWIDTH PHOTODIODE PREAMP EQUIVALENT CIRCUIT

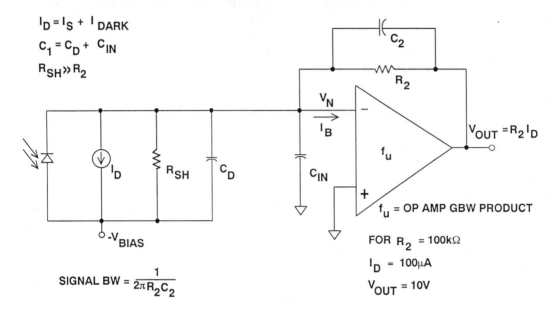

Figure 2.60

The sensitivity of the circuit is determined by the amount of photodiode current multiplied by the feedback resistor R2. The key parameters of the diode (see Figure 2.61) are its sensitivity (output current as a function of illumination level), dark current (the amount of current which flows due to the reverse bias voltage when the diode is not illuminated), risetime, shunt capacitance, and shunt resistance.

The key parameters of the op amp are its input voltage and current noise, bias current, unity gain-bandwidth product, f_u, and input capacitance, C_{in}.

The Motorola 5082-4204 PIN Photodiode will be used as an example for our discussion. Its characteristics are given in Figure 2.61. It is typical of many commercially available PIN photodiodes. As in most high-speed photo-

diode applications, the diode is operated in the reverse-biased or *photoconductive* mode. This greatly lowers the diode junction capacitance, but causes a small amount of *dark current* to flow even when the diode is not illuminated (we will show a circuit which compensates for the dark current error later in the section).

This photodiode is linear with illumination up to approximately 50 to 100µA of output current. The dynamic range is limited by the total circuit noise and the diode dark current (assuming no dark current compensation).

Using the simple circuit shown in Figure 2.60, assume that we wish to have a full scale output of 10V for a diode current of 100µA. This determines the value of the feedback resistor R2 to be 10V/100µA = 100kΩ.

MOTOROLA 5082-4204 PHOTODIODE

- ■ Sensitivity: 350µA @ 1mW, 900nm

- ■ Maximum Linear Output Current: 100µA

- ■ Area: 0.002cm^2 (0.2mm^2)

- ■ Capacitance: 4pF @ 10V reverse bias

- ■ Shunt Resistance: $10^{11}\Omega$

- ■ Risetime: 10ns

- ■ Dark Current: 600pA @ 10V reverse bias

Figure 2.61

Analysis of Frequency Response and Stability

The photodiode preamp model is the classical second-order system shown in Figure 2.62, where the I/V converter has a total input capacitance C1 (the sum of the diode capacitance and the op amp input capacitance). The shunt resistance of the photodiode is neglected since it is much greater than R2, the feedback resistor.

The net input capacitance, C1, forms a pole at a frequency f_p in the noise gain transfer function as shown in the Bode plot.

$$f_p = \frac{1}{2\pi R2C1} \cdot$$

Note that we are neglecting the effects of the compensation capacitor C2 and are assuming that it is small relative to C1 and will not significantly affect the pole frequency f_p when it is added to the circuit. In most cases, this approximation yields results which are close enough, considering the other variables in the circuit.

If left uncompensated, the phase shift at the frequency of intersection, f_x, will cause instability and oscillation. Introducing a zero at f_x by adding the feedback capacitor C2 stabilizes the circuit and yields a phase margin of about 45 degrees.

COMPENSATING FOR INPUT CAPACITANCE IN A CURRENT-TO-VOLTAGE CONVERTER USING VFB OP AMP

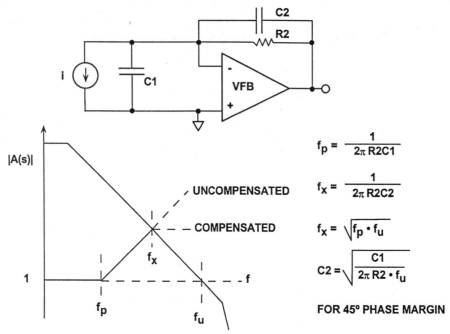

$$f_p = \frac{1}{2\pi R2C1}$$

$$f_x = \frac{1}{2\pi R2C2}$$

$$f_x = \sqrt{f_p \cdot f_u}$$

$$C2 = \sqrt{\frac{C1}{2\pi R2 \cdot f_u}}$$

FOR 45° PHASE MARGIN

Figure 2.62

$$f_x = \frac{1}{2\pi R2C2}$$

Since f_x is the geometric mean of f_p and the unity-gain bandwidth frequency of the op amp, f_u,

$$f_x = \sqrt{f_p \cdot f_u} \ .$$

These equations can be solved for C2:

$$C2 = \sqrt{\frac{C1}{2\pi R2 \cdot f_u}} \ .$$

This value of C2 will yield a phase margin of about 45 degrees. Increasing the capacitor by a factor of 2 increases the phase margin to about 65 degrees (see References 4 and 5).

In practice, the optimum value of C2 should be optimized experimentally by varying it slightly to optimize the output pulse response.

Selection of the Op Amp

The photodiode preamp should be a wideband FET-input one in order to minimize the effects of input bias current and allow low values of photo-currents to be detected. In addition, if the equation for the 3dB bandwidth, f_x, is rearranged in terms of f_u, R2, and C1, then

$$f_x = \sqrt{\frac{f_u}{2\pi R2 C1}},$$

where $C1 = C_D + C_{in}$

By inspection of this equation, it is clear that in order to maximize f_x, the FET-input op amp should have both a high unity gain-bandwidth product, f_u, and a low input capacitance, C_{in}. In fact, the ratio of f_u to C_{in} is a good figure-of-merit when evaluating different op amps for this application. Figure 2.63 compares a number of FET-input op amps suitable for photodiode preamps.

By inspection, the AD823 op amp has the highest ratio of unity gain-bandwidth product to input capacitance, in addition to relatively low input bias current. For these reasons, it was chosen for the wideband photodiode preamp design.

FET-INPUT OP AMP COMPARISON TABLE FOR WIDE BANDWIDTH PHOTODIODE PREAMPS

	Unity GBW Product, f_u (MHz)	Input Capacitance C_{in} (pF)	f_u/C_{in} (MHz/pF)	Input Bias Current I_b (pA)	Voltage Noise @10kHz (nV/√Hz)
AD823	16	1.8	8.9	3	16
AD843	34	6	5.7	600	19
AD744	13	5.5	2.4	100	16
AD845	16	8	2	500	18
AD745[*]	20	20	1	250	2.9
AD645	1	1	1	1.5	8
AD820	1.9	2.8	0.7	2	13
AD743	4.5	20	0.2	250	2.9

[*] Stable for Noise Gains ≥ 5, Usually the Case, Since
High Frequency Noise Gain = $1 + C_1/C_2$, and C_1 Usually ≥ $4C_2$.

Figure 2.63

Using the diode capacitance, C_D=4pF, and the AD823 input capacitance, C_{in}=1.8pF, the value of C1 = C_D+C_{in} = 5.8pF. Solving the above equations using C1=5.8pF, R2=100kΩ, and f_u=16MHz, we find that:

$$f_p = 274\text{kHz}$$
$$C2 = 0.76\text{pF}$$
$$f_x = 2.1\text{MHz}.$$

In the final design (Figure 2.64), note that the 100kΩ resistor is replaced with three 33.2kΩ film resistors to minimize stray capacitance. The feedback capaci-

tor, C2, is a variable 1.5pF ceramic and is adjusted in the final circuit for best bandwidth/pulse response. The overall circuit bandwidth is approximately 2MHz.

The full scale output voltage of the preamp for 100µA diode current is 10V, and the error (RTO) due to the photo-diode dark current of 600pA is 60mV. The dark current error can be canceled using a second photodiode of the same type in the non-inverting input of the op amp as shown in Figure 2.64.

2MHz BANDWIDTH PHOTODIODE PREAMP
WITH DARK CURRENT COMPENSATION

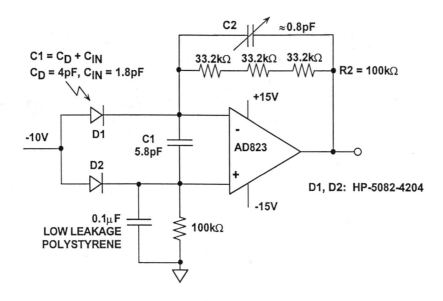

Figure 2.64

Photodiode Preamp Noise Analysis

As in most noise analyses, only the key contributors need be identified. Because the noise sources combine in an RSS manner, any single noise source that is at least three or four times as large as any of the others will dominate.

In the case of the wideband photodiode preamp, the dominant sources of output noise are the input voltage noise of the op amp, V_{ni}, and the resistor noise due to R2, V_{nR2}. The input current noise of the FET-input op amp is negligible. The shot noise of the photodiode (caused by the reverse bias) is negligible because of the filtering effect of the shunt capacitance C1. The resistor noise is easily calculated by knowing that a 1kΩ resistor generates about 4nV/√Hz, therefore, a 100kΩ resistor generates 40nV/√Hz. The bandwidth for integration is the signal bandwidth, 2.1MHz, yielding a total output rms noise of:

$$V_{nR2(OUT)} = 40\sqrt{1.57 \cdot 2.1 \cdot 10^6} = 73\mu Vrms.$$

The factor of 1.57 converts the approximate single-pole bandwidth of 2.1MHz into the *equivalent noise bandwidth*.

The output noise due to the input voltage noise is obtained by multiplying the noise gain by the voltage noise and integrating the entire function over frequency. This would be tedious if done rigorously, but a few reasonable approximations can be made which greatly simplify the math. Obviously, the low frequency 1/f noise can be neglected in the case of the wideband circuit. The primary source of output noise is due to the high-frequency noise-gain peaking which occurs between f_p and f_u. If we simply assume that the output noise is constant over the entire range of frequencies and use the maximum value for AC noise gain [1+(C1/C2)], then

$$V_{ni(OUT)} \approx V_{ni}\left(1 + \frac{C1}{C2}\right)\sqrt{1.57f_x} = 250\mu Vrms.$$

The total rms noise referred to the output is then the RSS value of the two components:

$$V_{n(TOTAL)} = \sqrt{(73)^2 + (250)^2} = 260\mu Vrms.$$

The total output dynamic range can be calculated by dividing the full scale output signal (10V) by the total output rms noise, 260μVrms, and converting to dB, yielding approximately 92dB.

EQUIVALENT CIRCUIT FOR OUTPUT NOISE ANALYSIS

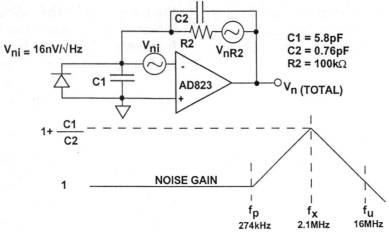

$V_{ni} = 16nV/\sqrt{Hz}$

V_{ni}

C2

R2

V_{nR2}

C1

AD823

V_n (TOTAL)

C1 = 5.8pF
C2 = 0.76pF
R2 = 100kΩ

$1 + \dfrac{C1}{C2}$

1

NOISE GAIN

f_p
274kHz

f_x
2.1MHz

f_u
16MHz

- ■ $V_{ni(out)} \approx V_{ni} \left(1 + \dfrac{C1}{C2}\right) \sqrt{1.57 f_x}$ = 250μV rms

- ■ $V_{nR2(out)} \approx \sqrt{4kTR2 \cdot 1.57 f_x}$ = 73μV rms

- ■ $V_{n(TOTAL)} = \sqrt{250^2 + 73^2}$ = 260μV rms

- ■ DYNAMIC RANGE = 20 log $\left[\dfrac{10V}{260\mu V}\right]$ = 92dB

Figure 2.65

REFERENCES

1. Walt Kester, *Maintaining Transmission Line Impedances on the PC Board*, within Chapter 11 of **System Applications Guide**, Analog Devices, 1993.

2. Joe Buxton, *Careful Design Tames High-Speed Op Amps*, **Electronic Design**, April 11, 1991.

3. Walt Jung, *Op Amps in Line-Driver and Receiver Circuits, Part1* **Analog Dialogue**, Vol. 26-2, 1992.

4. William R. Blood, Jr., **MECL System Design Handbook** (HB205, Rev.1), Motorola Semiconductor Products, Inc., 1988.

5. Dave Whitney, Walt Jung, *Applying a High-Performance Video Operational Amplifier*, **Analog Dialogue**, 26-1, 1992.

6. Ohmtek, Niagara Falls, NY, (716) 283-4025.

7. Walt Kester, *Video Line Receiver Applications Using the AD830 Active Feedback Amplifier Topology*, within Chapter 11 of **System Applications Guide**, Analog Devices, 1993.

8. Walt Jung, *Analog-Signal-Processing Concepts Get More Efficient*, **Electronic Design Analog Applications Issue**, June 24, 1993.

9. Peter Checkovich, *Understanding and Using High-Speed Clamping Amplifiers*, **Analog Dialogue**, Vol. 29-1, 1995.

10. Walt Jung, Scott Wurcer, *Design Video Circuits Using High-Speed Op-Amp Systems*, **Electronic Design Analog Applications Issue**, November 7, 1994.

11. W. A. Kester, *PCM Signal Codecs for Video Applications*, **SMPTE Journal**, No. 88, November 1979, pp. 770-778.

12. *IEEE Standard for Performance Measurements of A/D and D/A Converters for PCM Television Circuits*, **IEEE Standard 746-1984**.

13. **Practical Analog Design Techniques**, Chapters 1, 2, and 4, 1995, Analog Devices.

14. **Amplifier Applications Guide**, 1992, Analog Devices.

15. Jerald G. Graeme, **Photodiode Amplifiers: Op Amp Solutions**, McGraw Hill, 1995.

2

SECTION 3

RF/IF SUBSYSTEMS

- Dynamic Range Compression

- Linear VCAs

- Log/Limiting Amplifiers

- Receiver Overview

- Multipliers, Modulators, and Mixers

- Modulation / Demodulation

- Receiver Subsystems

3

SECTION 3
RF/IF SUBSYSTEMS
Walt Kester, James Bryant, Bob Clarke, Barrie Gilbert

DYNAMIC RANGE COMPRESSION

In many cases, a wide dynamic range is an essential aspect of a signal, something to be preserved at all costs. This is true, for example, in the high-quality reproduction of music and in communications systems. However, it is often necessary to compress the signal to a smaller range without any significant loss of information. Compression is often used in magnetic recording, where the upper end of the dynamic range is limited by tape saturation, and the lower end by the granularity of the medium. In professional noise-reduction systems, compression is "undone" by precisely-matched nonlinear expansion during reproduction. Similar techniques are often used in conveying speech over noisy channels, where the performance is more likely to be measured in terms of word-intelligibility than audio fidelity. The reciprocal processes of compressing and expanding are implemented using "compandors", and many schemes have been devised to achieve this function.

There is a class of *linear* dynamic range compression systems where the gain of the amplifiers in the signal processing chain is independent of the instantaneous amplitude of the signal, but is controlled by a closed loop system in such a way as to render the output (that is the peak, or rms value) essentially constant. The harmonic distortion is relatively low. These systems use what are often called *variable-gain amplifiers*. While correct, this lacks precision, because *nonlinear* amplifiers (such as log amps) also exhibit variable gain, but in direct response to the signal magnitude. The term *voltage controlled amplifier* (VCA) is preferred in this context; it clearly describes the way in which the gain control is implemented, while allowing latitude in regard to the actual circuit means used to achieve the function. The gain may be controlled by a *current* within the circuit, but usually a voltage. Analog multipliers may be used as VCAs, but there are other topologies which will be discussed later in this section.

Logarithmic amps find applications where signals having wide dynamic ranges (perhaps greater than 100dB) must be processed by elements, such as ADCs, which may have limited dynamic ranges. Log amps have maximum incremental gain for small signals; the gain decreases in inverse proportion to the magnitude of the input. This permits the amplifier to accept signals with a wide input dynamic range and compress them substantially.

Log amps provide nonlinear dynamic range compression and are used in applications where low harmonic distortion is not a requirement. All types of log amps produce a low dynamic range output without the need to first acquire some measure of the signal amplitude for use in controlling gain.

We will first examine *linear* compression techniques using voltage-controlled amplifiers within automatic-gain-control (AGC) loops. *Nonlinear* signal compression using log amps is then discussed.

Both AGC loops using VCAs and log amps make excellent building blocks for highly integrated RF/IF subsystems for signal processing in communications systems as will be demonstrated.

RF / IF SUBSYSTEM BUILDING BLOCKS

■ Signal Dynamic Range Compression Techniques

◆ Linear: Automatic Gain Control Loop (AGC) using Voltage Controlled Amplifier (VCA) and Detector

◆ Non-Linear: Demodulating / Limiting Logarithmic Amplifiers

■ Modulation / Demodulation: In-Phase and Quadrature (I/Q) and Polar (Amplitude and Phase)

◆ Dynamic Range Compression Required

◆ IF Subsystems: AGC, Log / Limiting, RSSI, Mixers

Figure 3.1

AUTOMATIC GAIN CONTROL (AGC) AND VOLTAGE-CONTROLLED AMPLIFIERS (VCAs)

In radio systems, the received energy exhibits a large dynamic range due to the variability of the propagation path, requiring dynamic-range compression in the receiver. In this case, the wanted information is in the modulation envelope (whatever the modulation mode), not in the absolute magnitude of the carrier. For example, a 1MHz carrier modulated at 1kHz to a 30% modulation depth would convey the same information, whether the received carrier level is at 0dBm or −120dBm. Some type of automatic gain control (AGC) in the receiver is generally utilized to restore the carrier amplitude to some normalized reference level, in the presence of large input fluctuations.

AGC circuits are dynamic-range compressors which respond to some metric of the signal – often its mean amplitude – acquired over an interval corresponding to many periods of the carrier. Consequently, they require time to adjust to variations in received signal level. The time required to respond to a sudden increase in signal level can be reduced by using peak detection methods, but with some loss of robustness, since transient noise peaks can now activate the AGC detection circuits. Nonlinear filtering and the concept of "delayed AGC" can be useful in optimizing an AGC system. Many tradeoffs are found in practice; Figure 3.2 shows a basic system.

A TYPICAL AUTOMATIC GAIN CONTROL (AGC) SYSTEM

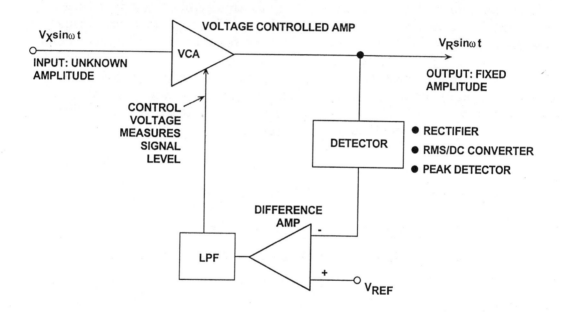

Figure 3.2

It is interesting to note that in an AGC loop actually has two outputs. The obvious output is the amplitude-stabilized signal. The less obvious output is the control voltage to the VCA, which is in reality, a measure of the average amplitude of the input signal. If the system is precisely scaled, the control voltage may be used as a measure of the input signal, sometimes referred to as a *received signal strength indicator* (RSSI).

VOLTAGE CONTROLLED AMPLIFIERS (VCAs)

An analog multiplier can be used as a variable-gain amplifier as shown in Figure 3.3. The control voltage is applied to one input, and the signal to the other. In this configuration, the gain is directly proportional to the control voltage.

Most VCAs made with analog multipliers have gain which is *linear in volts* with respect to the control voltage, and they tend to be noisy. There is a demand, however, for a VCA which combines a wide gain range with constant bandwidth and phase, low noise with large signal-handling capabilities, and low distortion with low power consumption, while providing accurate, stable, *linear-in-dB* gain. The AD600, AD602, and AD603 achieve these demanding

and conflicting objectives with a unique and elegant solution - the X-AMP™ (for *exponential amplifier*). The concept is simple: a fixed-gain amplifier follows a passive, broadband attenuator equipped with special means to alter its attenuation under the control of a voltage (see Figure 3.4). The amplifier is optimized for low input noise, and negative feedback is used to accurately define its moderately high gain (about 30 to 40dB) and minimize distortion. Since this amplifier's gain is fixed, so also are its ac and transient response characteristics, including distortion and group delay; since its gain is high, its input is never driven beyond a few millivolts. Therefore, it is always operating within its small signal response range.

USING A MULTIPLIER AS A
VOLTAGE-CONTROLLED AMPLIFIER (VCA)

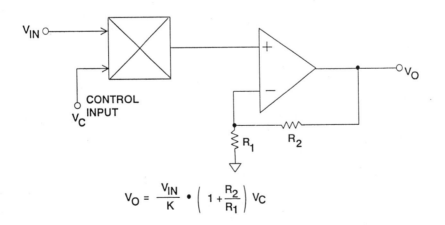

$$V_O = \frac{V_{IN}}{K} \cdot \left(1 + \frac{R_2}{R_1} \right) V_C$$

Figure 3.3

SINGLE CHANNEL OF THE DUAL 30MHz AD600/AD602 X-AMP

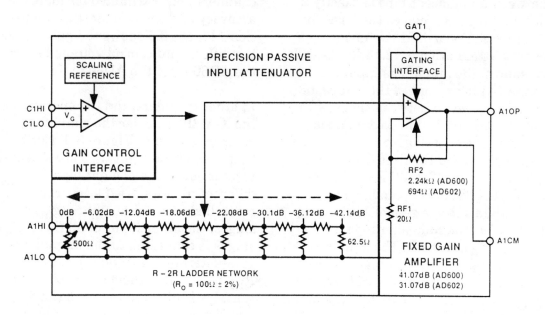

Figure 3.4

GAIN OF THE AD600/AD602
AS A FUNCTION OF CONTROL VOLTAGE

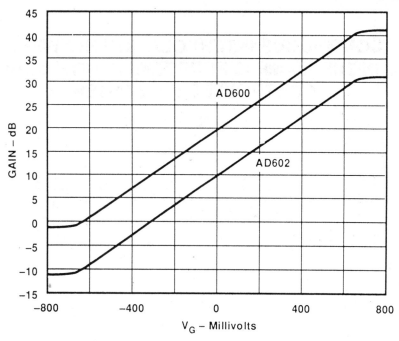

Figure 3.5

The attenuator is a 7-section (8-tap) R-2R ladder network. The voltage ratio between all adjacent taps is exactly 2, or 6.02dB. This provides the basis for the precise linear-in-dB behavior. The overall attenuation is 42.14dB. As will be shown, the amplifier's input can be connected to any one of these taps, or even *interpolated* between them, with only a small deviation error of about ±0.2dB. The overall gain can be varied all the way from the fixed (maximum) gain to a value 42.14dB less. For example, in the AD600, the fixed gain is 41.07dB (a voltage gain of 113); using this choice, the full gain range is −1.07dB to +41.07dB. The gain is related to the control voltage by the relationship $G_{dB} = 32V_G + 20$ where V_G is in volts. For the AD602, the fixed gain is 31.07dB (a voltage gain of 35.8), and the gain is given by $G_{dB} = 32V_G + 10$.

The gain at $V_G = 0$ is laser trimmed to an absolute accuracy of ±0.2dB. The gain scaling is determined by an on-chip bandgap reference (shared by both channels), laser trimmed for high accuracy and low temperature coefficient. Figure 3.5 shows the gain versus the differential control voltage for both the AD600 and the AD602.

In order to understand the operation of the X-AMP, consider the simplified diagram shown in Figure 3.6. Notice that each of the eight taps is connected to an input of one of eight bipolar differential pairs, used as current-controlled transconductance (g_m) stages; the other input of all these g_m stages is connected to the amplifier's gain-determining feedback network, R_{F1}/R_{F2}. When the emitter bias current, I_E, is directed to one of the 8 transistor pairs (by means not shown here), it becomes the input stage for the complete amplifier.

CONTINUOUS INTERPOLATION BETWEEN TAPS IN THE X-AMP IS PERFORMED WITH CURRENT-CONTROLLED gm STAGES

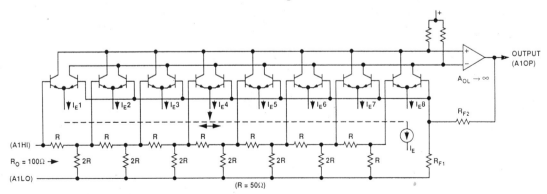

Figure 3.6

When I_E is connected to the pair on the left-hand side, the signal input is connected directly to the amplifier, giving the maximum gain. The distortion is very low, even at high frequencies, due to the careful open-loop design, aided by the negative feedback. If I_E were now to be abruptly switched to the second pair, the overall gain would drop by exactly 6.02dB, and the distortion would remain low, because only one g_m stage remains active.

In reality, the bias current is *gradually* transferred from the first pair to the second. When I_E is equally divided between two gm stages, both are active, and the situation arises where we have an op amp with two input stages fighting for control of the loop, one getting the full signal, and the other getting a signal exactly half as large.

Analysis shows that the effective gain is reduced, not by 3dB, as one might first expect, but rather by 20log1.5, or 3.52dB. This error, when divided equally over the whole range, would amount to a gain ripple of ±0.25dB; however, the interpolation circuit actually generates a Gaussian distribution of bias currents, and a significant fraction of I_E always flows in adjacent stages. This smoothes the gain function

and actually lowers the ripple (see Reference 12). As I_E moves further to the right, the overall gain progressively drops.

The total input-referred noise of the X-AMP™ is 1.4nV/√Hz; only slightly more than the thermal noise of a 100Ω resistor which is 1.29nV/√Hz at 25°C. The input-referred noise is constant regardless of the attenuator setting, therefore the output noise is always constant and independent of gain. For the AD600, the amplifier gain is 113 and the output noise spectral density is therefore 1.4nV/√Hz×113, or 158nV/√Hz. Referred to its maximum output of 2V rms, the signal-to-noise ratio would be 82dB in a 1MHz bandwidth. The corresponding signal-to-noise ratio of the AD602 is 10dB greater, or 92dB. Key features of the AD600/AD602 are summarized in Figure 3.7

The AD603 X-AMP is a single version of the AD600/AD602 which provides 90MHz bandwidth. There are two pin-programmable gain ranges: −11dB to +31dB with 90MHz bandwidth, and +9dB to +51dB with 9MHz bandwidth. Key specifications for the AD603 are summarized in Figure 3.8.

KEY FEATURES OF THE AD600/AD602 X-AMPS

- Precise Decibel-Scaled Gain Control

- Accurate Absolute Gain Calibration

- Low Input-Referred Noise (1.4nV/√Hz)

- Constant Bandwidth (dc to 35MHz)

- Low Distortion: −60dBc THD at ±1V Output

- Stable Group Delay (±2ns Over Gain Range)

- Response Time: Less than 1μs for 40dB Gain Change

- Low Power (125mW per channel maximum)

- Differential Control Inputs

Figure 3.7

KEY FEATURES OF THE AD603 X-AMP

- Precise "Linear in dB" Gain Control

- Pin Programmable Gain Ranges:

    −11dB to +31dB with 90MHz Bandwidth

    +9dB to + 51dB with 9MHz Bandwidth

- Bandwidth Independent of Variable Gain

- Low Input-Referred Noise (1.3nV/√Hz)

- ±0.5dB Typical Gain Accuracy

- Low Distortion: −60dBc, 1V rms Output @ 10MHz

- Low Power (125mW)

- 8-pin Plastic SOIC or Ceramic DIP

Figure 3.8

A COMPLETE 80dB RMS-LINEAR-dB MEASUREMENT SYSTEM

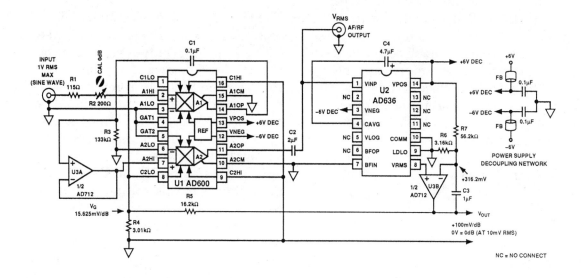

Figure 3.9

AN 80 dB RMS-LINEAR-dB MEASUREMENT SYSTEM

RMS/DC converters provide a means to measure the rms value of an arbitrary waveform. They also may provide a low-accuracy logarithmic ("decibel-scaled") output. However, they have a fairly small dynamic range – typically only 50dB. More troublesome is that the bandwidth is roughly proportional to the signal level; for example, the AD636 provides a 3dB bandwidth of 900kHz for an input of 100mV rms, but only a 100kHz bandwidth for an input of 10mV rms. Its "raw" logarithmic output is unbuffered, uncalibrated, and not stable over temperature, requiring considerable support circuitry, including at least two adjustments and a special high-TC resistor.

All of these problems can be eliminated using an RMS/DC converter (i.e., AD636) merely as *the detector element* in an AGC loop, in which the difference between the rms output of the AD636 and a fixed DC reference is nulled in a loop integrator. The dynamic range and the accuracy with which the signal can be determined are now entirely dependent on the amplifier used in the AGC system. Since the input to the RMS/DC converter is forced to a constant amplitude, close to its maximum input capability, the bandwidth is no longer signal-dependent. If the amplifier has a precise exponential ("linear-dB") gain-control law, its control voltage is forced by the AGC loop to have the general form

$$V_{LOG} = V_S \log_{10} \frac{V_{IN(RMS)}}{V_Z}$$

where V_S is the logarithmic slope and V_Z is the logarithmic intercept, that is, the value of V_{IN} for which V_{LOG} is zero.

Figure 3.9 shows a practical wide-dynamic-range rms measurement system using the AD600. It can handle inputs from 100µV to 1V rms (4 decades) with a constant measurement bandwidth of 20Hz to 2MHz, limited primarily by the AD636 RMS/DC converter. Its logarithmic output is a buffered voltage, accurately-calibrated to 100mV/dB, or 2V per decade, which simplifies the interpretation of the reading when using a DVM, and is arranged to be –4V for an input of 100µV rms input, zero for 10mV, and +4V for a 1V rms input. In terms of the above equation, V_S is 2V and V_Z is 10mV.

Note that the peak "log-output" of ±4V requires the use of ±6V supplies for the dual op-amp U3 (AD712), although lower supplies would suffice for the AD600 and AD636. If only ±5V supplies are available, it will either be necessary to use a reduced value for V_S (say, 1V, in which case the peak output would be only ±2V), or to restrict the dynamic range of the signal to about 60dB.

The two amplifiers of the AD600 are used in cascade. The modest bandwidth of the unity-gain buffer U3A acts as a low pass filter, thus eliminating the risk of instability at the highest gains. The buffer also allows the use of a high-impedance coupling network (C1/R3) which introduces a high-pass corner at about 12Hz. An input attenuator of 10dB (x 0.316) is now provided by R1 + R2 operating in conjunction with the AD600's input resistance of 100Ω. The adjustment provides exact calibration of V_Z in critical applications, but R1 and R2 may be replaced by a fixed resistor of 215Ω if very close calibration is not needed, since the input resistance of the AD600 (and all the other key parameters of it and the AD636) are already laser-trimmed for accurate

operation. This attenuator allows inputs as large as ±4V to be accepted, that is, signals with an rms value of 1V combined with a crest-factor of up to 4.

The output of A2 is AC-coupled via another 12Hz high-pass filter formed by C2 and the 6.7kΩ input resistance of the AD636. The averaging time-constant for the RMS/DC converter is determined by C4. The unbuffered output of the AD636 (at pin 8) is compared with a fixed voltage of +316mV set by the positive supply voltage of +6V and resistors R6 and R7. (V_Z is proportional to this voltage, and systems requiring greater calibration accuracy should replace the supply-dependent reference with a more stable source. However, V_S is independent of the supply voltages, being determined by the band-gap reference in the X-AMP.) Any difference in these voltages is integrated by the op-amp U3B, with a time-constant of 3ms formed by the parallel sum of R6/R7 and C3.

If the gain of the AD600 is too high, V_{OUT} will be greater than the "set-point" of 316mV, causing the output of U3B – that is, V_{LOG} – to ramp up (note that the integrator is non-inverting). A fraction of V_{LOG} is connected to the *inverting* gain-control inputs of the AD600, causing the gain to be reduced, as required, until V_{OUT} is equal to 316mV (DC), at which time the AC voltage at the output of A2 is forced to exactly 316mV (rms). This fraction is set by R4 and R5 such that a 15.625mV change in the control voltages of A1 and A2 – which would change the gain of the two cascaded amplifiers by 1 dB – requires a change of 100mV at V_{LOG}. Since A2 is forced to operate well below its limiting level, waveforms of high crest-factor can be tolerated throughout the amplifier.

To verify the operation, assume an input of 10mV rms is applied to the input, resulting in a voltage of 3.16mV rms at the input to A1 (due to the 10dB attenuator). If the system performs as claimed, V_{LOG} (and hence V_G) should be zero. This being the case, the gain of both A1 and A2 will be 20dB and the output of the AD600 will be 100 times (40dB) greater than its input, 316mV rms. This is the input required at the AD636 to balance the loop, confirming the basic operation. Note that unlike most AGC circuits, (which often have a high gain/temperature coefficient due to the internal "kT/q" scaling), the voltages and thus the output of this measurement system are very stable over temperature. This behavior arises directly from the exact exponential calibration of the ladder attenuator.

Typical results are shown for a sinewave input at 100kHz. Figure 3.10 shows that the output is held very close to the set-point of 316mV rms over an input range in excess of 80dB.

SIGNAL OUTPUT V_{out} VERSUS INPUT LEVEL

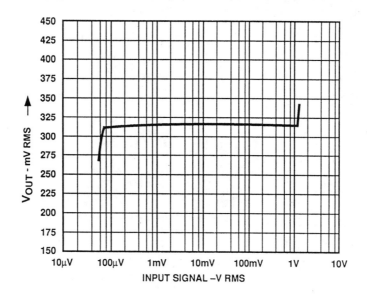

Figure 3.10

Figure 3.11 shows the "decibel" output voltage, V_{LOG}, and Figure 3.12 shows that the *deviation* from the ideal output logarithmic output is within ±1 dB for the 80dB range from 80μV to 800mV.

THE LOGARITHMIC OUTPUT V_{LOG} VERSUS INPUT SIGNAL LEVEL

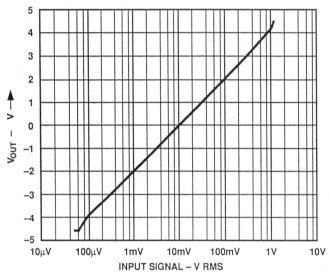

Figure 3.11

DEVIATION FROM THE IDEAL LOGARITHMIC OUTPUT

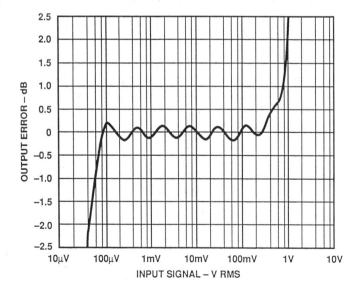

Figure 3.12

By suitable choice of the input attenuator, R1+R2, this could be centered to cover any range from 25µV to 250mV to, say, 1mV to 10V, with appropriate correction to the value of V_Z. (Note that V_S is not affected by the changes in the range). The gain ripple of ±0.2dB seen in this curve is the result of the finite interpolation error of the X-AMP. It occurs with a periodicity of 12dB – twice the separation between the tap points in each amplifier section.

This ripple can be canceled whenever the X-AMP stages are cascaded by introducing a 3dB offset between the two pairs of control voltages. A simple means to achieve this is shown in Figure 3.13: the voltages at C1HI and C2HI are "split" by ±46.875mV, or ±1.5dB. Alternatively, either one of these pins can be individually offset by 3dB, and a 1.5dB gain adjustment made at the input attenuator (R1+R2). The error curve shown in Figure 3.14 demonstrates that over the central portion of the range, the output voltage can be maintained very close to the ideal value. The penalty for this modification is higher errors at both ends of the range.

3

METHOD FOR CANCELING THE GAIN-CONTROL RIPPLE

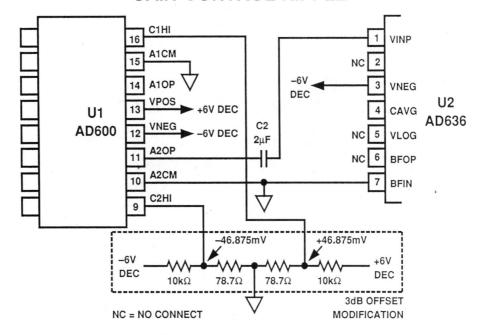

Figure 3.13

LOGARITHMIC ERROR USING THE
PREVIOUS CIRCUIT MODIFICATION

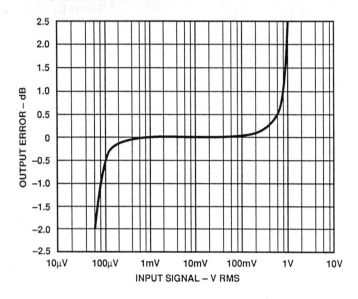

Figure 3.14

A 40MHz, 80dB, LOW-NOISE
AGC AMPLIFIER USING THE AD603

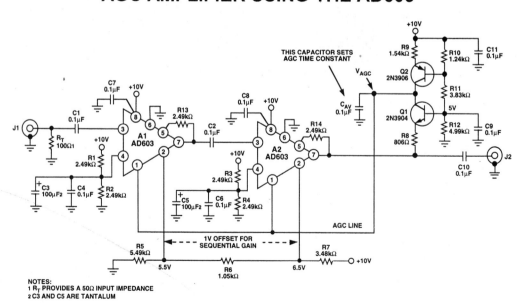

NOTES:
1 R_T PROVIDES A 50Ω INPUT IMPEDANCE
2 C3 AND C5 ARE TANTALUM

Figure 3.15

Figure 3.15 shows the ease with which the AD603 (90MHz X-AMP) can be used as a high speed AGC amplifier. The circuit uses few parts, has a linear-in-dB gain, operates from a single supply, uses two cascaded amplifiers in sequential gain mode for maximum S/N ratio (see the data sheet for the AD600/AD602, or AD603 for a complete description of the methods for cascading X-AMPS), and external resistor programs each amplifier's gain. It also uses a simple temperature-compensated detector.

The circuit operates from a single +10V supply. Resistors R1, R2 and R3, R4 bias the common pins of A1 and A2 at 5V. This pin is a low impedance point and must have a low impedance path to ground, provided by the 100µF tantalum capacitor and the 0.1µF ceramic capacitors.

The cascaded amplifiers operate in sequential gain. The offset voltage between the pins 2 (GNEG) of A1 and A2 is 1.05V (42.14dB x 25mV/dB), provided by a voltage divider consisting of resistors R5, R6, and R7. Using standard values, the offset is not exact but is not critical for this application.

The gain of both A1 and A2 is programmed by resistors R13 and R14, respectively, to be about 42dB; thus the maximum gain of the circuit is twice that, or 84dB. The gain-control range can be shifted up by as much as 20dB by appropriate choices of R13 and R14.

The circuit operates as follows. A1 and A2 are cascaded. Capacitor C1 and the 100Ω of resistance at the input of A1 form a time-constant of 10µs. C2 blocks the small DC offset voltage at the output of A1 (which might otherwise saturate A2 at its maximum gain) and

introduces a high-pass corner at about 16kHz, eliminating low frequency noise.

A half-wave detector is used based on Q1 and R8. The current into capacitor C_{AV} is the difference between the collector current of Q2 (biased to be 300µA at 27°C, 300K) and the collector current of Q1, which increases with the amplitude of the output signal. The automatic gain control voltage, V_{AGC}, is the time-integral of this error current. In order for V_{AGC} (and thus the gain) to remain insensitive to short-term amplitude fluctuations in the output signal, the rectified current in Q1 must, on average, exactly balance the current in Q2. If the output of A2 is too small to do this, V_{AGC} will increase, causing the gain to increase, until Q1 conducts sufficiently.

Consider the case where R8 is zero and the output voltage V_{OUT} is a square wave at, say 455kHz, that is, well above the corner frequency of the control loop.

During the time V_{OUT} is negative with respect to the base voltage of Q1, Q1 conducts; when V_{OUT} is positive, it is cut off. Since the average collector current of Q1 is forced to be 300µA, and the square wave has a duty cycle of 1:1, Q1's collector current when conducting must be 600µA. With R8 omitted, the peak amplitude of V_{OUT} is forced to be just the V_{BE} of Q1 at 600µA, typically about 700mV, or 2V_{BE} peak-to-peak. This voltage, hence the amplitude at which the output stabilizes, has a strong negative temperature coefficient (TC), typically –1.7mV/°C. Although this may not be troublesome in some applications, the correct value of R8 will render the output stable with temperature.

To understand this, first note that the current in Q2 is made to be proportional to absolute temperature (PTAT). For the moment, continue to assume that the signal is a square wave.

When Q1 is conducting, V_{OUT} is now the sum of V_{BE} and a voltage which is PTAT and which can be chosen to have an equal but opposite TC to that of V_{BE}. This is actually nothing more than an application of the "bandgap voltage reference" principle. When R8 is chosen such that the sum of the voltage across it and the V_{BE} of Q1 is close to the bandgap voltage of about 1.2V, V_{OUT} will be stable over a wide range of temperatures, provided, of course, that Q1 and Q2 share the same thermal environment.

Since the average emitter current is 600µA during each half-cycle of the square wave, a resistor of 833Ω would add a PTAT voltage of 500mV at 300K, increasing by 1.66mV/°C. In practice, the optimum value will depend on the type of transistor used, and, to a lesser extent, on the waveform for which the temperature stability is to be optimized; for the inexpensive 2N3904/ 2N3906 pair and sine wave signals, the recommended value is 806Ω.

This resistor also serves to lower the peak current in Q1 when more typical signals (usually sinusoidal) are involved, and the 1.8kHz lowpass filter it forms with C_{AV} helps to minimize distortion due to ripple in V_{AGC}. Note that the output amplitude under sine wave conditions will be higher than for a square wave, since the average value of the current for an ideal rectifier would be 0.637 times as large, causing the output amplitude to be 1.2V/ 0.637=1.88V, or 1.33V rms. In practice, the somewhat nonideal rectifier results in the sine wave output being regulated to about 1.4Vrms, or 3.6V p-p.

The bandwidth of the circuit exceeds 40MHz. At 10.7MHz, the AGC threshold is 100µV (–67dBm) and its maximum gain is 83dB, 20log(1.4V/100µV). The circuit holds its output at 1.4V rms for inputs as low as –67dBm to +15dBm (82dB), where the input signal exceeds the AD603's maximum input rating. For a +10dBm input at 10.7MHz, the second harmonic is 34dB down from the fundamental, and the third harmonic is 35dB down.

LOGARITHMIC AMPLIFIERS

The term "Logarithmic Amplifier" (generally abbreviated to "log amp") is something of a misnomer, and "Logarithmic Converter" would be a better description. The conversion of a signal to its equivalent logarithmic value involves a nonlinear operation, the consequences of which can be confusing if not fully understood. It is important to realize that many of the familiar concepts of linear circuits are irrelevant to log amps. For example, the incremental gain of an ideal log amp approaches infinity as the input approaches zero, and a change of offset at the output of a log amp is equivalent to a change of amplitude at its input - not a change of input offset.

For the purposes of simplicity in our initial discussions, we shall assume that both the input and the output of a log amp are voltages, although there is no particular reason why logarithmic current, transimpedance, or transconductance amplifiers should not also be designed.

If we consider the equation $y = \log(x)$ we find that every time x is multiplied by a constant A, y increases by another constant A1. Thus if $\log(K) = K1$, then $\log(AK) = K1 + A1$, $\log(A^2K) = K1 + 2A1$, and $\log(K/A) = K1 - A1$. This gives a graph as shown in Figure 3.16, where y is zero when x is unity, y approaches minus infinity as x approaches zero, and which has no values for x for which y is negative.

3

GRAPH OF Y = LOG(X)

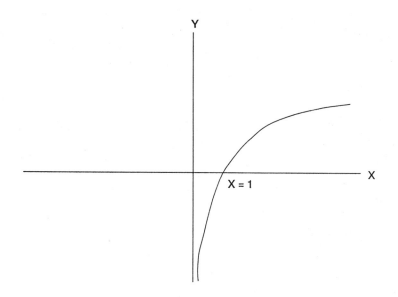

Figure 3.16

On the whole, log amps do not behave in this way. Apart from the difficulties of arranging infinite negative output voltages, such a device would not, in fact, be very useful. A log amp must satisfy a transfer function of the form

$$v_{out} = V_y \log(V_{in}/V_x)$$

over some range of input values which may vary from 100:1 (40dB) to over 1,000,000:1 (120dB).

With inputs very close to zero, log amps cease to behave logarithmically, and most then have a linear V_{in}/V_{out} law. This behavior is often lost in device noise. Noise often limits the dynamic range of a log amp. The constant, V_y, has the dimensions of voltage, because the output is a voltage. The input, V_{in}, is divided by a voltage, V_x, because the argument of a logarithm must be a simple dimensionless ratio.

A graph of the transfer characteristic of a log amp is shown in Figure 3.17. The scale of the horizontal axis (the input) is logarithmic, and the ideal transfer characteristic is a straight line. When $V_{in} = V_x$, the logarithm is zero (log 1 = 0). V_x is therefore known as the *intercept voltage* of the log amp because the graph crosses the horizontal axis at this value of V_{in}.

LOG AMP TRANSFER FUNCTION

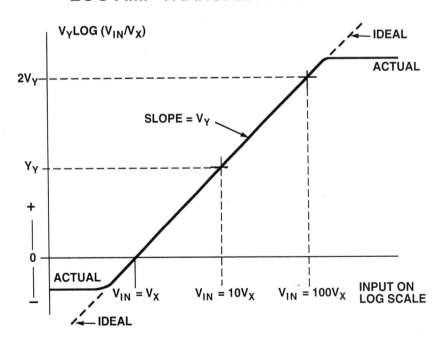

Figure 3.17

The slope of the line is proportional to V_y. When setting scales, logarithms to the base 10 are most often used because this simplifies the relationship to decibel values: when $V_{in} = 10V_x$, the logarithm has the value of 1, so the output voltage is V_y. When $V_{in} = 100V_x$, the output is $2V_y$, and so forth. V_y can therefore be viewed either as the "slope voltage" or as the "volts per decade factor."

The logarithm function is indeterminate for negative values of x. Log amps can respond to negative inputs in three different ways: (1) They can give a fullscale negative output as shown in Figure 3.18. (2) They can give an output which is proportional to the log of the absolute value of the input and disregards its sign as shown in Figure 3.19. This type of log amp can be considered to be a full-wave detector with a logarithmic characteristic, and is often referred to as a *detecting* log amp. (3) They can give an output which is proportional to the log of the absolute value of the input and has the same sign as the input as shown in Figure 3.20. This type of log amp can be considered to be a video amp with a logarithmic characteristic, and may be known as a *logarithmic video* (*log video*) amplifier or, sometimes, a *true log amp* (although this type of log amp is rarely used in video-display-related applications).

3

BASIC LOG AMP
(SATURATES WITH NEGATIVE INPUT)

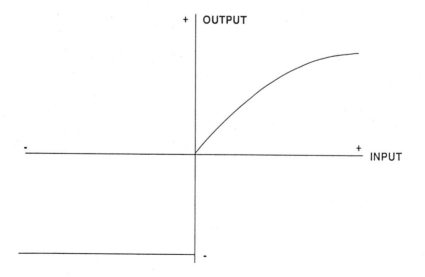

Figure 3.18

DETECTING LOG AMP
(OUTPUT POLARITY INDEPENDENT
OF INPUT POLARITY)

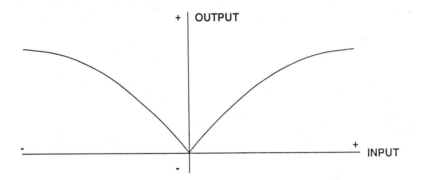

Figure 3.19

LOG VIDEO OR "TRUE LOG AMP"
(SYMMETRICAL RESPONSE
TO POSITIVE OR NEGATIVE SIGNALS)

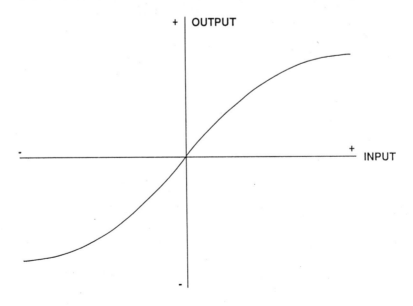

Figure 3.20

There are three basic architectures which may be used to produce log amps: the *basic diode log amp*, the *successive detection log amp*, and the *"true log amp"* which is based on cascaded semi-limiting amplifiers.

The voltage across a silicon diode is proportional to the logarithm of the current through it. If a diode is placed in the feedback path of an inverting op-amp, the output voltage will be proportional to the log of the input current as shown in Figure 3.21. In practice, the dynamic range of this configuration is limited to 40-60dB because of non-ideal diode characteristic, but if the diode is replaced with a diode-connected transistor as shown in Figure 3.22, the dynamic range can be extended to 120dB or more. This type of log amp has three disadvantages: (1) both the slope and intercept are temperature dependent; (2) it will only handle unipolar signals; and (3) its bandwidth is both limited and dependent on signal amplitude.

Where several such log amps are used on a single chip to produce an analog computer which performs both log and antilog operations, the temperature variation in the log operations is unim-

portant, since it is compensated by a similar variation in the antilogging. This makes possible the AD538, a monolithic analog computer which can multiply, divide, and raise to powers. Where actual logging is required, however, the AD538 and similar circuits require temperature compensation (Reference 7). The major disadvantage of this type of log amp for high frequency applications, though, is its limited frequency response - which cannot be overcome. However carefully the amplifier is designed, there will always be a residual feedback capacitance C_c (often known as Miller capacitance), from output to input which limits the high frequency response.

What makes this Miller capacitance particularly troublesome is that the impedance of the emitter-base junction is inversely proportional to the current flowing in it - so that if the log amp has a dynamic range of 1,000,000:1, then its bandwidth will also vary by 1,000,000:1. In practice, the variation is less because other considerations limit the large signal bandwidth, but it is very difficult to make a log amp of this type with a small-signal bandwidth greater than a few hundred kHz.

3

THE DIODE / OP-AMP LOG AMP

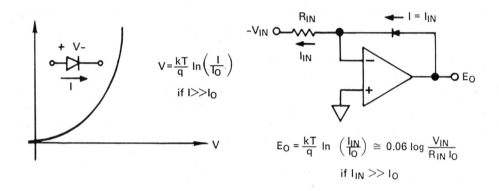

$$V = \frac{kT}{q} \ln \left(\frac{I}{I_O} \right)$$

if $I \gg I_O$

$$E_O = \frac{kT}{q} \ln \left(\frac{I_{IN}}{I_O} \right) \cong 0.06 \log \frac{V_{IN}}{R_{IN} \, I_O}$$

if $I_{IN} \gg I_O$

Figure 3.21

TRANSISTOR / OP-AMP LOG AMP

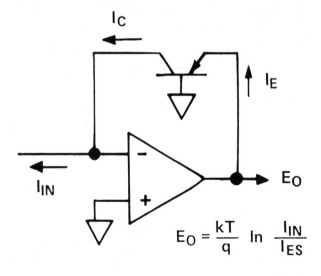

$$E_O = \frac{kT}{q} \ln \frac{I_{IN}}{I_{ES}}$$

Figure 3.22

For high frequency applications, therefore, *detecting* and *true log* architectures are used. Although these differ in detail, the general principle behind their design is common to both: instead of one amplifier having a logarithmic characteristic, these designs use a number of similar cascaded linear stages having well-defined large signal behavior.

Consider N cascaded limiting amplifiers, the output of each driving a summing circuit as well as the next stage (Figure 3.23). If each amplifier has a gain of A dB, the small signal gain of the strip is NA dB. If the input signal is small enough for the last stage not to limit, the output of the summing amplifier will be dominated by the output of the last stage.

As the input signal increases, the last stage will limit. It will now make a

fixed contribution to the output of the summing amplifier, but the incremental gain to the summing amplifier will drop to (N-1)A dB. As the input continues to increase, this stage in turn will limit and make a fixed contribution to the output, and the incremental gain will drop to (N-2)A dB, and so forth - until the first stage limits, and the output ceases to change with increasing signal input.

The response curve is thus a set of straight lines as shown in Figure 3.24. The total of these lines, though, is a very good approximation to a logarithmic curve, and in practical cases, is an even better one, because few limiting amplifiers, especially high frequency ones, limit quite as abruptly as this model assumes.

3

BASIC MULTI-STAGE LOG AMP ARCHITECTURE

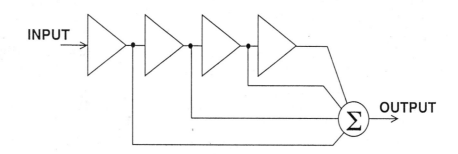

Figure 3.23

BASIC MULTI-STAGE LOG AMP RESPONSE
(UNIPOLAR CASE)

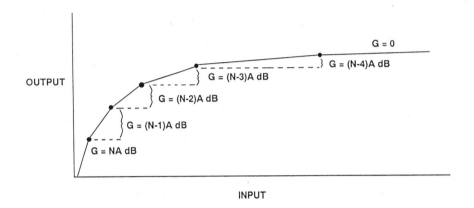

OUTPUT

G = 0

G = (N-4)A dB

G = (N-3)A dB

G = (N-2)A dB

G = (N-1)A dB

G = NA dB

INPUT

Figure 3.24

The choice of gain, A, will also affect the log linearity. If the gain is too high, the log approximation will be poor. If it is too low, too many stages will be required to achieve the desired dynamic range. Generally, gains of 10 to 12dB (3x to 4x) are chosen.

This is, of course, an ideal and very general model - it demonstrates the principle, but its practical implementation at very high frequencies is difficult. Assume that there is a delay in each limiting amplifier of t nanoseconds (this delay may also change when the amplifier limits but let's consider first order effects!). The signal which passes through all N stages will undergo delay of Nt nanoseconds, while the signal which only passes one stage will be delayed only t nanoseconds. This means that a small signal is delayed by Nt nanoseconds, while a large one is

"smeared", and arrives spread over Nt nanoseconds. A nanosecond equals a foot at the speed of light, so such an effect represents a spread in position of Nt feet in the resolution of a radar system-which may be unacceptable in some systems (for most log amp applications this is not a problem).

A solution is to insert delays in the signal paths to the summing amplifier, but this can become complex. Another solution is to alter the architecture slightly so that instead of limiting gain stages, we have stages with small signal gain of A and large signal (incremental) gain of unity (0dB). We can model such stages as two parallel amplifiers, a limiting one with gain, and a unity gain buffer, which together feed a summing amplifier as shown in Figure 3.25.

STRUCTURE AND PERFORMANCE OF "TRUE" LOG AMP ELEMENT AND OF A LOG AMP FORMED BY SEVERAL SUCH ELEMENTS

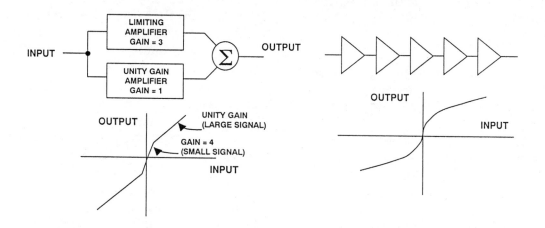

Figure 3.25

SUCCESSIVE DETECTION LOGARITHMIC AMPLIFIER WITH LOG AND LIMITER OUTPUTS

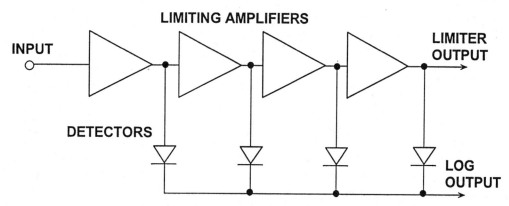

■ DETECTORS MAY BE FULL OR HALF WAVE

■ SHOULD BE CURRENT OUTPUT DEVICES (NOT SIMPLE DIODES) SO THAT OUTPUTS MAY BE SUMMED WITHOUT ADDITIONAL SUMMING COMPONENTS BEING NECESSARY

Figure 3.26

Figure 3.25 shows that such stages, cascaded, form a log amp without the necessity of summing from individual stages. Both the multi-stage architectures described above are *video* log amplifiers, or *true log* amplifiers, but the most common type of high frequency log amplifier is the *successive detection* log amp architecture shown in Figure 3.26.

The *successive detection* log amp consists of cascaded limiting stages as described above, but instead of summing their outputs directly, these outputs are applied to detectors, and the detector outputs are summed as shown in Figure 3.26. If the detectors have current outputs, the summing process may involve no more than connecting all the detector outputs together.

Log amps using this architecture have two outputs: the log output and a limiting output. In many applications, the limiting output is not used, but in some (FM receivers with "S"-meters, for example), both are necessary. The limited output is especially useful in extracting the phase information from the input signal in polar demodulation techniques.

The log output of a successive detection log amplifier generally contains amplitude information, and the phase and frequency information is lost. This is not necessarily the case, however, if a half-wave detector is used, and attention is paid to equalizing the delays from the successive detectors - but the design of such log amps is demanding.

The specifications of log amps will include *noise, dynamic range, frequency response* (some of the amplifiers used as successive detection log amp stages have low frequency as well as high frequency cutoff), the *slope of the transfer characteristic* (which is expressed as V/dB or mA/dB depending on whether we are considering a voltage- or current-output device), the *intercept point* (the input level at which the output voltage or current is zero), and the *log linearity*. (See Figures 3.27 and 3.28)

In the past, it has been necessary to construct high performance, high frequency successive detection log amps (called log strips) using a number of individual monolithic limiting amplifiers such as the Plessey SL-1521-series (see Reference 16). Recent advances in IC processes, however, have allowed the complete log strip function to be integrated into a single chip, thereby eliminating the need for costly hybrid log strips.

The AD641 log amp contains five limiting stages (10dB per stage) and five full-wave detectors in a single IC package, and its logarithmic performance extends from dc to 250MHz. Furthermore, its amplifier and full-wave detector stages are balanced so that, with proper layout, instability from feedback via supply rails is unlikely. A block diagram of the AD641 is shown in Figure 3.29. Unlike many previous integrated circuit log amps, the AD641 is laser trimmed to high absolute accuracy of both slope and intercept, and is fully temperature compensated. Key features of the AD641 are summarized in Figure 3.30. The transfer function for the AD641 as well as the log linearity is shown in Figure 3.31.

KEY PARAMETERS OF LOG AMPS

■ NOISE: The Noise Referred to the Input (RTI) of the Log Amp. It May Be Expressed as a Noise Figure or as a Noise Spectral Density (Voltage, Current, or Both) or as a Noise Voltage, a Noise Current, or Both

■ DYNAMIC RANGE: Range of Signal Over Which the Amplifier Behaves in a Logarithmic Manner (Expressed in dB)

■ FREQUENCY RESPONSE: Range of Frequencies Over Which the Log Amp Functions Correctly

■ SLOPE: Gradient of Transfer Characteristic in V/dB or mA/dB

■ INTERCEPT POINT: Value of Input Signal at Which Output is Zero

■ LOG LINEARITY: Deviation of Transfer Characteristic (Plotted on log/lin Axes) from a Straight Line (Expressed in dB)

Figure 3.27

LOG LINEARITY

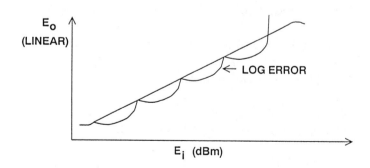

Figure 3.28

BLOCK DIAGRAM OF THE AD641 MONOLITHIC LOG AMP

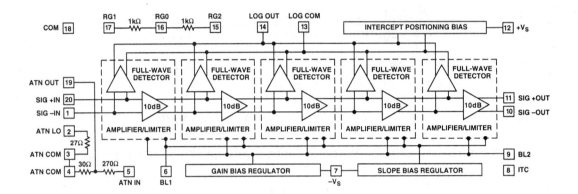

Figure 3.29

AD641 KEY FEATURES

- 44dB Dynamic Range

- Bandwidth dc to 250MHz

- Laser-Trimmed Slope of 1mA/decade - Temperature Stable

- Laser-Trimmed Intercept of 1mV - Temperature Stable

- Less than 2dB Log Non-Linearity

- Limiter Output: ±1.6dB Gain Flatness, ±2° Phase Variation
  for -44dBm to 0dBm inputs @ 10.7MHz

- Balanced Circuitry for Stability

- Minimal External Component Requirement

Figure 3.30

DC LOGARITHMIC TRANSFER FUNCTION
AND ERROR CURVE FOR SINGLE AD641

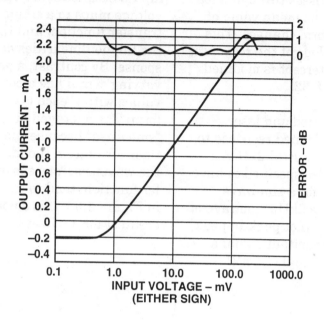

Figure 3.31

THE EFFECT OF WAVEFORM ON INTERCEPT POINT

INPUT WAVEFORM	PEAK OR RMS	INTERCEPT FACTOR	ERROR (RELATIVE TO A DC INPUT)
Square Wave	Either	1	0.00dB
Sine Wave	Peak	2	–6.02dB
Sine Wave	RMS	1.414 (√2)	–3.01dB
Triwave	Peak	2.718 (e)	–8.68dB
Triwave	RMS	1.569 (e/√3)	–3.91dB
Gaussian Noise	RMS	1.887	–5.52dB

Figure 3.32

Because of its high accuracy, the actual waveform driving the AD641 must be considered when calculating responses. When a waveform passes through a log function generator, the mean value of the resultant waveform changes. This does not affect the slope of the response, but the apparent intercept is modified according to Figure 3.32.

The AD641 is calibrated and laser trimmed to give its defined response to a DC level or a symmetrical 2kHz square wave. It is also specified to have an intercept of 2mV for a sinewave input (that is to say a 2kHz sinewave of amplitude 2mV peak [not peak-to-peak] gives the same mean output signal as a DC or square wave signal of 1mV).

The waveform also affects the ripple or nonlinearity of the log response. This ripple is greatest for DC or square wave inputs because every value of the input voltage maps to a single location on the transfer function, and thus traces out the full nonlinearities of the log response. By contrast, a general time-varying signal has a continuum of values within each cycle of its waveform. The averaged output is thereby "smoothed" because the periodic deviations away from the ideal response, as the waveform "sweeps over" the transfer function, tend to cancel. As is clear in Figure 3.33, this smoothing effect is greatest for a triwave.

THE EFFECT OF WAVEFORM ON AD641 LOG LINEARITY

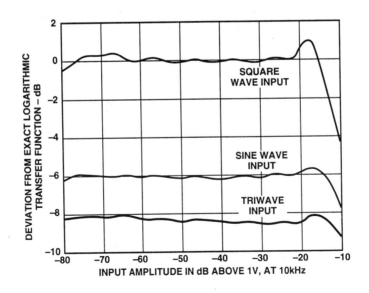

Figure 3.33

3

Each of the five stages in the AD641 has a gain of 10dB and a full-wave detected output. The transfer function for the device was shown in Figure 3.21 along with the error curve. Note the excellent log linearity over an input range of 1 to 100mV (40dB). Although well suited to RF applications, the AD641 is dc-coupled throughout. This allows it to be used in LF and VLF systems, including audio measurements, sonar, and other instrumentation applications requiring operation to low frequencies or even dc.

The limiter output of the AD641 has better than 1.6dB gain flatness (-44dBm to 0dBm @ 10.7MHz) and less than 2° phase variation, allowing it to be used as a polar demodulator

The AD606 is a complete monolithic 50MHz bandwidth log amp using 9 stages of successive detection, and is shown in Figure 3.34. Key specifications are summarized in Figure 3.35. Seven of the amplifier/detector stages handle inputs from –80dBm (32µV rms) up to about –14dBm (45mV rms). The noise floor is about –83dBm (18µV rms). Another two parallel stages receive the input attenuated by 22.3dB, and respond to inputs up to +10dBm (707mV rms). The gain of each stage is 11.15dB and is accurately stabilized over temperature by a precise biasing system.

The AD606 provides both logarithmic and limited outputs. The logarithmic output is from a three-pole post-demodulation lowpass filter and provides an output voltage of +0.1V DC to +4V DC. The logarithmic scaling is such that the output is +0.5V for a sinusoidal input of –75dBm, and +3.5V at an input of +5dBm. Over this range, the log linearity is typically within ±0.4dB.

AD606 50MHz, 80dB LOG AMP BLOCK DIAGRAM

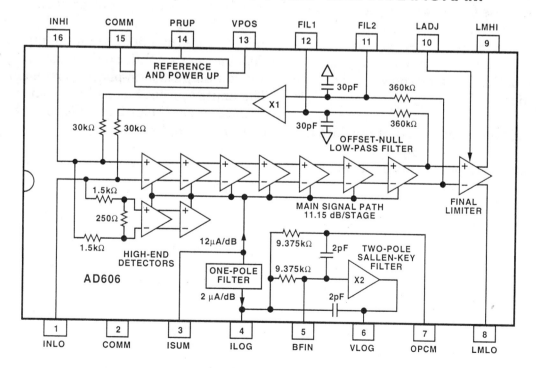

Figure 3.34

AD606 LOG AMP KEY FEATURES

■ Dynamic Range: –75dBm to +5dBm (80dB)

■ Input Noise: < 1.5nV/√Hz

■ Usable from 200Hz to Greater than 50MHz

■ Slope: 37.5mV/dB Voltage Output

■ On-Chip Lowpass Output Filter

■ Limiter Output: ±1.6dB Gain Flatness, ±2° Phase Variation
for -44dBm to 0dBm inputs @ 10.7MHz

■ +5V Single-Supply, 65mW Power Consumption

Figure 3.35

The AD606 can operate above and below these limits, with reduced linearity, to provide as much as 90dB of conversion range. A second lowpass filter automatically nulls the input offset of the first stage down to the submicrovolt level.

The AD606's limiter output provides a hard-limited signal output as a differential current of ±1.2mA from open-collector outputs. In a typical application, both of these outputs are loaded by 200Ω resistors to provide a voltage gain of more than 90dB from the input. This limiting amplifier has exceptionally low amplitude-to-phase conversion. The limiter output has ±1dB output flatness and ±3° phase stability over an 80dB range at 10.7MHz.

RECEIVER OVERVIEW
Walt Kester, Bob Clarke

We will now consider how the previously discussed building blocks can be used in designing a receiver. First, consider the analog superheterodyne receiver invented in 1917 by Major Edwin H. Armstrong (see Figure 3.36). This architecture represented a significant improvement over single-stage direct conversion (homodyne) receivers which had previously been constructed using tuned RF amplifiers, a single detector, and an audio gain stage. A significant advantage of the superheterodyne receiver is that it is much easier and more economical to have the gain and selectivity of a receiver at fixed intermediate frequencies (IF) than to have the gain and frequency-selective circuits "tune" over a band of frequencies.

DUAL CONVERSION SUPERHET RECEIVER
(EXAMPLE FREQUENCIES)

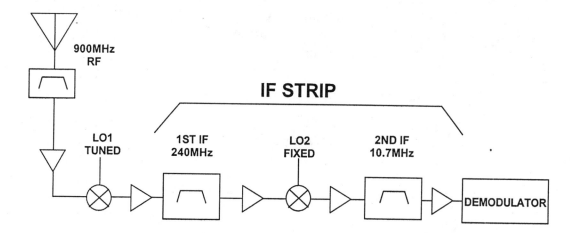

Figure 3.36

The receiver shown is a dual conversion receiver with two intermediate frequency (IF) stages. The frequencies chosen are typical in digital mobile radio (DMR), but the principles apply to other systems as well. The 900MHz RF signal is mixed down to the first IF frequency of 240MHz. Tuning is accomplished by the first local oscillator (LO1). The LO1 frequency is chosen such that the output of the first mixer is at the first IF frequency, 240MHz. Choosing a relatively high first IF frequency eases the requirement on the image frequency rejection filter as will be discussed in the next section on mixers. The first IF is then mixed down to the second IF frequency of 10.7MHz, where it is demodulated (either using analog or digital techniques).

Because of the wide dynamic range of the RF signal, such a receiver requires the use of automatic gain control, voltage controlled amplifiers, and in some cases (depending on the type of demodulation), logarithmic amplifiers.

Receiver design is a complicated art, and there are many tradeoffs that can be made between IF frequencies, single-conversion vs. double-conversion or triple conversion, filter cost and complexity at each stage in the receiver, demodulation schemes, etc. There are many excellent references on the subject, and the purpose of this section is only to acquaint the design engineer with some of the building block ICs which can make receiver design much easier.

Before we look at further details of a receiver, the subject of *mixing* requires further discussion.

MULTIPLIERS, MODULATORS, AND MIXERS
Barrie Gilbert, Bob Clarke

An idealized mixer is shown in Figure 3.37. An RF (or IF) mixer (not to be confused with video and audio mixers) is an active or passive device that converts a signal from one frequency to another. It can either modulate or demodulate a signal. It has three signal connections, which are called *ports* in the language of radio engineers. These three ports are the radio frequency (RF) input, the local oscillator (LO) input, and the intermediate frequency (IF) output.

THE MIXING PROCESS

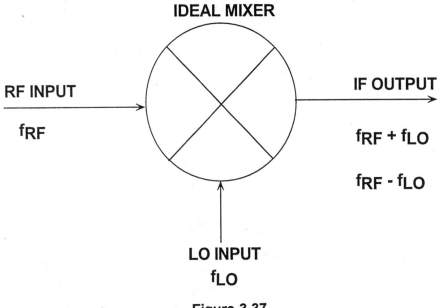

Figure 3.37

A mixer takes an RF input signal at a frequency f_{RF}, mixes it with a LO signal at a frequency f_{LO}, and produces an IF output signal that consists of the sum and difference frequencies, $f_{RF} \pm f_{LO}$. The user provides a bandpass filter that follows the mixer and selects the sum ($f_{RF} + f_{LO}$) or difference ($f_{RF} - f_{LO}$) frequency.

Some points to note about mixers and their terminology:

• When the sum frequency is used as the IF, the mixer called an *upconverter*; when the difference is used, the mixer is called a *downconverter*. The former is often used in a transmit channel, the latter in a receive channel.

• In a receiver, when the LO frequency is below the RF, it is called *low-side injection* and the mixer *a low-side downconverter*; when the LO is above the RF, it is called *high-side injection*, and the mixer *a high-side downconverter*.

• Each of the outputs is only half the amplitude (one-quarter the power) of the individual inputs; thus, there is a loss of 6dB in this ideal linear mixer. (In a practical multiplier, the conversion loss may be greater than 6dB, depending on the scaling parameters of the device. Here, we assume a *mathematical* multiplier, having no dimensional attributes.

A mixer can be implemented in several ways, using active or passive techniques. A brief review of the various classes of nonlinear elements that can be used for frequency translation may be helpful in setting the context. We can identify three subclasses of circuits, sharing certain similarities. All are in the class of signal multipliers, producing at their output a signal which is, in

one way or another, the product of its two inputs. They are *multipliers*, *modulators*, and *mixers*.

An *analog multiplier* generally has two signal input ports, which can be called X and Y, and generates an output W that is the linear product of the voltages applied to these two ports. To retain dimensional consistency, the analog linear multiplication function must invoke the use of a reference voltage, which we can call U, thus $W=XY/U$. In some cases, U is actually a third input that can be used to implement analog division.

There are three functional categories of multipliers: In *single-quadrant* multipliers, X and Y must be unipolar; in *two-quadrant* multipliers, one of the inputs may be bipolar; in *four-quadrant* multipliers, both X and Y may be bipolar. Analog Devices produces a wide range of "linear" multipliers, including the AD534, AD538, AD539, AD633, AD734, AD834 and AD835, providing the highest available accuracy (±0.02% for the AD734) to the highest speed (more than 500MHz for the AD834).

Modulators (sometimes called *balanced-modulators*, *doubly-balanced modulators* or even on occasions *high level mixers*) can be viewed as *sign-changers*. The two inputs, X and Y, generate an output W, which is simply one of these inputs (say, Y) multiplied by just the sign of the other (say, X), that is $W = Y\,\text{sign}(X)$. Therefore, no reference voltage is required. A good modulator exhibits very high linearity in its signal path, with precisely equal gain for positive and negative values of Y, and precisely equal gain for positive and negative values of X. Ideally, the amplitude of the X input needed to fully switch the output sign is very small, that is, the X-input exhibits a comparator-like behavior. In some cases, where this input may be a logic signal, a simpler X-channel can be used. A highly-linear mixer such as the AD831 is well-suited as a modulator.

A *mixer* is a modulator optimized for frequency-translation. Its place in the signal path is usually close to the antenna, where both the wanted and (often large) unwanted signals coexist at its signal input, usually called the *RF port*. Thus, the mixer must exhibit excellent linearity in the sense that its output (at the IF port) is expected to increase by the same number of dB as a test signal applied to the RF port, up to as high as level as possible. This attribute is defined both by the 1dB gain-compression and the 3rd-order intercept (later explained). The conversion process is driven by an input applied to the LO port.

Noise and matching characteristics are crucial to achieving acceptable levels of performance in a receiver's mixer. It is desirable to keep the LO power to a minimum to minimize cross-talk between the three ports, but this often conflicts with other requirements. The gain from the RF port to its IF port at specified RF and LO frequencies is called the *conversion gain* and in classi-

cal diode-bridge mixers is less than -4dB. *Active mixers* provide higher conversion gain, and better port-port isolation, but often at the expense of noise and linearity. It is not usually possibly (nor even desirable) to describe mixer behavior using equations relating the instantaneous values of inputs and outputs; instead, we generally seek to characterize mixers in terms of their non-ideal cross-product terms at the output. In this class, Analog Devices has the AD831, and mixers are found embedded in the AD607, AD608 and other signal-processing ICs.

Thus far, we have seen that multipliers are linear in their response to the instantaneous value of both of their input voltages; modulators are linear in their response to one input, the other merely flipping the sign of this signal at regular intervals, with virtually zero transition time, and beyond that having ideally no other effect on the signal; mixers are a sort of RF half-breed, ideally being very linear on the RF input, and "binary" in their switching function in response to the LO input, but in reality being nonideal in both respects; they are optimized for very low noise and minimal intermodulation distortion.

Mixing Using an Ideal Analog Multiplier

Figure 3.38 shows a greatly simplified RF mixer by assuming the use of an analog multiplier.

Ideally, the multiplier has no noise, no limit to the maximum signal amplitude, and no intermodulation between the various RF signals (that is, no spurious nonlinearities). Figure 3.39 shows the result of *mixing* (= multiplying) an RF input of $\sin\omega_{RF}t$ with (= by) a LO input

of $\sin\omega_{LO}t$, where $\omega_{RF} = 2\pi\times11\text{MHz}$ and $\omega_{LO} = 2\pi\times10\text{MHz}$.

Clearly, to better understand mixer behavior, we will need to consider not only the time-domain waveforms, as shown here, but also the spectrum of the IF output. Figure 3.40 shows the output spectrum corresponding to the above IF waveform.

"MIXING" USING AN ANALOG MULTIPLIER

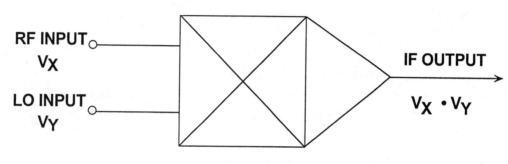

RF INPUT
V_X

LO INPUT
V_Y

IF OUTPUT
$V_X \cdot V_Y$

ANALOG MULTIPLIER, e.g., AD834

3

Figure 3.38

INPUTS AND OUTPUT FOR MULTIPLYING MIXER
FOR $f_{RF} = 11MHz$, $f_{LO} = 10MHz$

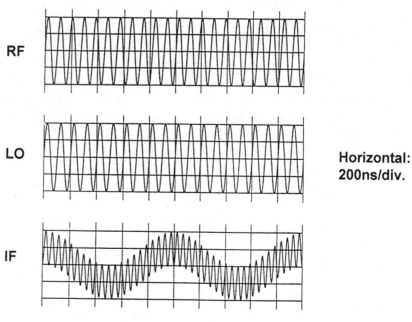

RF

LO

IF

Horizontal:
200ns/div.

Figure 3.39

OUTPUT SPECTRUM FOR MULTIPLYING MIXER
FOR f_{RF} = 11MHz, f_{LO} = 10MHz

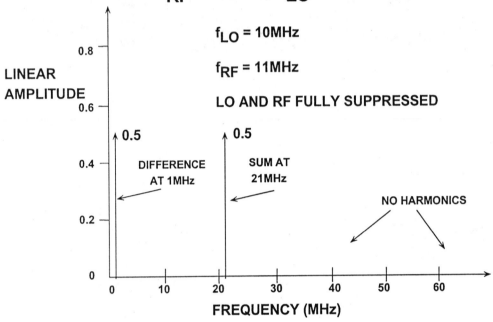

Figure 3.40

There is no mystery so far. The mathematics are simple. Neglecting scaling issues (real signals are voltages; thus a practical multiplier needs an embedded voltage reference, ignored here) the relationship is:

$$\sin\omega_{RF}t \, \sin\omega_{LO}t \; = \; \tfrac{1}{2} \{ \cos(\omega_{RF} + \omega_{LO})t + \cos(\omega_{RF} - \omega_{LO})t \} \qquad \text{Eq. 1}$$

The multiplier has thus transformed the RF input into two, equal-amplitude cosinusoidal components at its output (the IF port), one at the sum frequency, $\omega_{RF} + \omega_{LO}$, and the other at the difference frequency, $\omega_{RF} - \omega_{LO}$.

In practice, an analog multiplier would be a poor choice for a mixer because the two linear inputs bring with them a serious noise penalty.

Image Response

A receiver using even this mathematically perfect mixer suffers a basic problem, that of *image response*. Consider the use of a low-side downconverter. The wanted output is found at the frequency $\omega_{IF} = \omega_{RF} - \omega_{LO}$. So we might suppose

that the only component of the RF spectrum that finds its way through the mixer "sieve" to the narrow IF passband is the wanted component at ω_{RF}. But we could have just as easily written (1) as

$$\sin\omega_{RF}t \, \sin\omega_{LO}t \;=\; \tfrac{1}{2}\{\cos(\omega_{RF} + \omega_{LO})t + \cos(\omega_{LO} - \omega_{RF})t\} \qquad \text{Eq. 1a}$$

because the cosine function is symmetric about t = 0. So there is another spectral component at the RF input that falls in the IF passband, namely the one for which $\omega_{IF} = \omega_{LO} - \omega_{RF}$, in this case, the *image* frequency.

Consider the above example, where f_{LO} = 10MHz and f_{IF} = 1MHz; the wanted response is at the IF frequency, f_{IF} = 1MHz for f_{RF} = 11MHz. However, the mixer produces the same IF in response to the *image frequency*, f_{IMAGE} = 9MHz (see Figure 3.41).

3

IMAGE RESPONSE

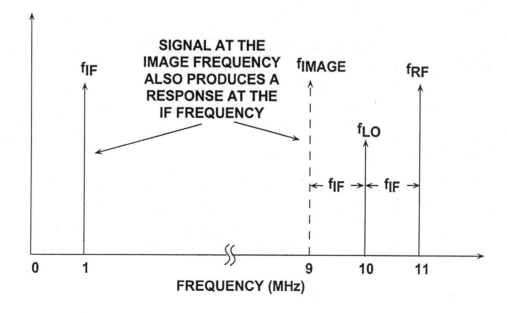

Figure 3.41

The most practical solution to this dilemma is to carefully choose the IF frequency to minimize the likelihood of image sensitivity and also include an image-reject filter at the RF input, just ahead of the mixer. Another approach is to use a special type of mixer circuit that does not respond to the image frequency. This approach requires circuitry which is considerably more complex, and for this reason has generally been unpopular, but it is becoming more practical in a modern IC implementation. It has the further disadvantage of higher power consumption, since two mixer cells operating in quadrature are required.

The Ideal Mixer

Ideally, to meet the low-noise, high-linearity objectives of a mixer we need some circuit that implements a polarity-switching function in response to the LO input. Thus, the mixer can be reduced to Figure 3.42, which shows the RF signal being split into in-phase (0°) and anti-phase (180°) components; a changeover switch, driven by the local oscillator (LO) signal, alternately selects the in-phase and antiphase signals. Thus reduced to essentials, the ideal mixer can be modeled as a sign-switcher.

AN IDEAL SWITCHING MIXER

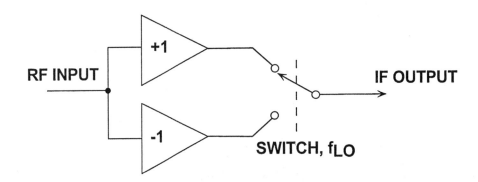

Figure 3.42

In a perfect embodiment, this mixer would have no noise (the switch would have zero resistance), no limit to the maximum signal amplitude, and would develop no intermodulation between the various RF signals. Although simple in concept, the waveform at the intermediate frequency (IF) output can be very complex for even a small number of signals in the input spectrum. Figure 3.43 shows the result of *mixing*

just a single input at 11MHz with an LO of 10MHz.

The *wanted* IF at the difference frequency of 1MHz is still visible in this waveform, and the 21MHz sum is also apparent. But the spectrum of this waveform is clearly more complex than that obtained using the analog multiplier. How are we to analyze this?

INPUTS AND OUTPUT FOR IDEAL SWITCHING MIXER
FOR f_{RF} = 11MHz, f_{LO} = 10MHz

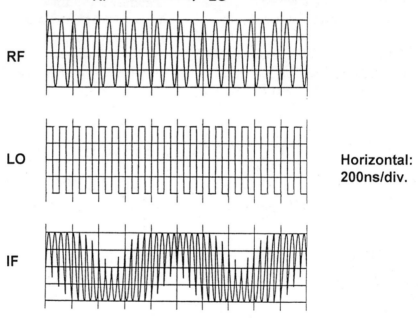

RF

LO

Horizontal:
200ns/div.

IF

Figure 3.43

We still have a product, but now it is that of a sinusoid (the RF input) at ω_{RF} and a variable that can only have the values +1 or -1, that is, a unit square wave at ω_{LO}. The latter can be expressed as a Fourier series

$$S_{LO} = {}^{4}/\pi \{ \sin\omega_{LO}t - {}^{1}/_{3} \sin3\omega_{LO}t + {}^{1}/_{5} \sin5\omega_{LO}t - \ldots \} \qquad \text{Eq. 2}$$

Thus, the output of the switching mixer is its RF input, which we can simplify as $\sin\omega_{RF}t$, multiplied by the above expansion for the square wave, producing

$$S_{IF} = {}^{4}\!/\pi \{ \ \sin\omega_{RF}t \ \sin\omega_{LO}t \ - {}^{1}\!/_3 \ \sin\omega_{RF}t \ \sin3\omega_{LO}t$$
$$+ {}^{1}\!/_5 \ \sin5\omega_{RF}t \ \sin5\omega_{LO}t \ - \ .... \} \qquad \text{Eq. 3}$$

Now expanding each of the products, we obtain

$$S_{IF} = {}^{2}\!/\pi \{ \ \sin(\omega_{RF} + \omega_{LO})t + \sin(\omega_{RF} - \omega_{LO})t$$
$$- {}^{1}\!/_3 \ \sin(\omega_{RF} + 3\omega_{LO})t \ - {}^{1}\!/_3 \ \sin(\omega_{RF} - 3\omega_{LO})t$$
$$+ {}^{1}\!/_5 \ \sin(\omega_{RF} + 5\omega_{LO})t \ + {}^{1}\!/_5 \ \sin(\omega_{RF} - 5 \ \omega_{LO})t \ - ... \} \qquad \text{Eq. 4}$$

or simply

$$S_{IF} = {}^{2}\!/\pi \{ \ \sin(\omega_{RF} + \omega_{LO})t + \sin(\omega_{RF} - \omega_{LO})t \ + \ \text{harmonics} \ \} \qquad \text{Eq. 5}$$

The most important of these harmonic components are sketched in Figure 3.44 for the particular case used to generate the waveform shown in Figure 3.43, that is, $f_{RF} = 11\text{MHz}$ and $f_{LO} = 10\text{MHz}$. Because of the $2/\pi$ term, a mixer has a minimum 3.92 dB insertion loss (and noise figure) in the absence of any gain.

Note that the ideal (switching) mixer has exactly the same problem of image response to $\omega_{LO} - \omega_{RF}$ as the linear multiplying mixer. The image response is somewhat subtle, as it does not immediately show up in the output spectrum: it is a latent response, awaiting the occurrence of the "wrong" frequency in the input spectrum.

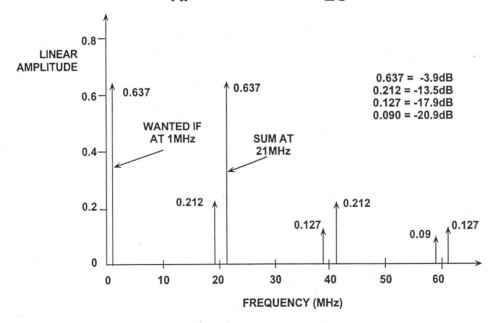

OUTPUT SPECTRUM FOR SWITCHING MIXER
FOR f_{RF} = 11MHz AND f_{LO} = 10MHz

LINEAR AMPLITUDE

0.637 = -3.9dB
0.212 = -13.5dB
0.127 = -17.9dB
0.090 = -20.9dB

0.637

0.637

WANTED IF AT 1MHz

SUM AT 21MHz

0.212

0.127

0.212

0.09

0.127

FREQUENCY (MHz)

Figure 3.44

Diode-Ring Mixer

For many years, the most common mixer topology for high-performance applications has been the diode-ring mixer, one form of which is shown in Figure 3.45. The diodes, which may be silicon junction, silicon Schottky-barrier or gallium-arsenide types, provide the essential switching action. We do not need to analyze this circuit in great detail, but note in passing that the LO drive needs to be quite high — often a substantial fraction of one watt — in order to ensure that the diode conduction is strong enough to achieve low noise and to allow large signals to be converted without excessive spurious nonlinearity.

Because of the highly nonlinear nature of the diodes, the impedances at the three ports are poorly controlled, making matching difficult. Furthermore, there is considerable coupling between the three ports; this, and the high power needed at the LO port, make it very likely that there will be some component of the (highly-distorted) LO signal coupled back toward the antenna. Finally, it will be apparent that a passive mixer such as this cannot provide conversion gain; in the idealized scenario, there will be a conversion loss of $2/\pi$ [as Eq. 4 shows], or 3.92dB. A practical mixer will have higher losses, due to the resistances of the diodes and the losses in the transformers.

3

DIODE-RING MIXER

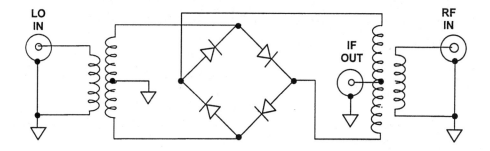

Figure 3.45

Users of this type of mixer are accustomed to judging the signal handling capabilities by a "Level" rating. Thus, a Level-17 mixer needs +17dBm (50mW) of LO drive and can handle an RF input as high as +10dBm (±1V). A typical mixer in this class would be the Mini-Circuits LRMS-1H, covering 2-500MHz, having a nominal insertion loss of 6.25dB (8.5dB max), a worst-case LO-RF isolation of 20dB and a worst-case LO-IF isolation of 22dB (these figures for an LO frequency of 250-500MHz). The price of this component is approximately $10.00 in small quantities. Even the most expensive diode-ring mixers have similar drive power requirements, high losses and high coupling from the LO port.

FET Mixers

A modern alternative to the diode-ring mixer is one in which the diodes are replaced by FETs. The idea here is to reduce the distortion caused by the inherent nonlinearities of junction diodes, whose incremental resistance varies with the instantaneous signal current. To reduce this effect, the diodes are often driven to very high current levels. Indeed, some users of diode-ring mixers push them to extremes, operating at current levels close to those which will cause the diodes to fail by over-dissipation. Thus, in commenting about a certain minor variation to the diode-ring-mixer, we read:

"This helps the mixer to accept higher LO power without burning out the diodes!"

(From Wes Hayward, *Solid State Design for the Radio Amateur*, ARRL, 1986, Chapter 6, p.120)

To avoid "burning out the diodes", some mixers use two or four J-FETs in an analogous way to that shown in Figure 3.45. The idea is that the channel resistance of a large FET driven into its triode region of conduction can be as low as the dynamic resistance of a diode, thus achieving similar conversion gain and noise levels. But this low resistance arises without any current flow in the channel and it is also more linear than that of the diodes when signal current does flow, thus resulting in lower intermodulation, and hence a larger overall dynamic range. MOS-FETs can also be used in a similar way.

This style of FET-based mixers is very attractive for many high-performance applications. However, since the active devices are still used only as switches, they do not provide power gain, and have typical insertion losses of 6 to 8dB. Furthermore, the balance of these mixers is still critically dependent on such things as transistor matching and transformer winding accuracy, large LO drives (volts) are needed, and the overall matching requirements continue to be difficult to achieve over the full frequency range. Finally, of course, they are not directly amenable to monolithic integration.

Another popular circuit, widely used in many inexpensive receivers, is the dual-gate MOS-FET mixer. In this type of mixer, the RF signal is applied to one gate of the FET and the LO signal to the second gate. The multiplication process is not very well-defined, but in general terms relies on the fact that both the first and second gates influence the current in the channel. The structure can be modeled as two FETs, where the drain of the lower FET (having the RF input applied to it) is intimately connected to the source of the upper FET (having the LO input on its gate). The lower FET operates in its triode region, and thus exhibits a g_m that is a function of its drain voltage,

controlled by the LO. Though not readily modeled to great accuracy, this mixer, like many others, can be pragmatically optimized to achieve useful performance, though not without the support of many associated passive components for biasing and matching.

Classic Active Mixer

The diode-ring mixer not only has certain performance limitations, but it is also not amenable to fabrication using integrated circuit technologies, at least in the form shown in Figure 3.45. In the mid 'sixties it was realized that the four diodes could be replaced by four transistors to perform essentially the same switching function. This formed the basis of the now-classical bipolar circuit shown in Figure 3.46,

which is a minimal configuration for the fully-balanced version. Millions of such mixers have been made, including variants in CMOS and GaAs. We will limit our discussion to the BJT form, an example of which is the Motorola MC1496, which, although quite rudimentary in structure, has been a mainstay in semi-discrete receiver designs for about 25 years.

CLASSIC ACTIVE MIXER

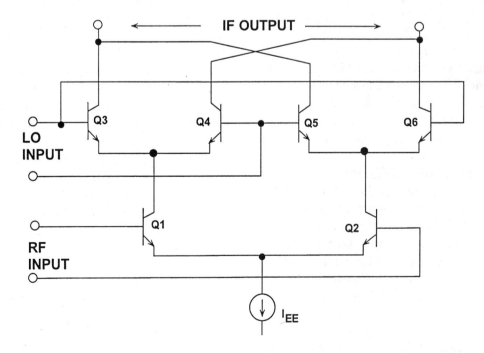

Figure 3.46

The *active mixer* is attractive for the following reasons:

• It can be monolithically integrated with other signal processing circuitry.

• It can provide conversion gain, whereas a diode-ring mixer always has an insertion loss. (Note: Active mixers may have gain. The analog Devices' AD831 active mixer, for example, amplifies the result in Eq. 5 by $\pi/2$ to provide unity gain from RF to IF.)

• It requires much less power to drive the LO port.

• It provides excellent isolation between the signal ports.

• Is far less sensitive to load-matching, requiring neither diplexer nor broadband termination.

Using appropriate design techniques it can provide trade-offs between third-order intercept (3OI or IP3) and the 1dB gain-compression point (P_{1dB}), on the one hand, and total power consumption (P_D) on the other. (That is, including the LO power, which in a passive mixer is "hidden" in the drive circuitry.)

Basic Operation of the Active Mixer

Unlike the diode-ring mixer, which performs the polarity-reversing switching function in the voltage domain, the active mixer performs the switching function in the current domain. Thus the active mixer core (transistors Q3 through Q6 in Figure 3.46) must be driven by current-mode signals. The voltage-to-current converter formed by Q1 and Q2 receives the voltage-mode RF signal at their base terminals and transforms it into a differential pair of currents at the their collectors.

A second point of difference between the active mixer and diode ring mixer, therefore, is that the active mixer responds only to magnitude of the input voltage, not to the input power; that is, the active mixer is not matched to the source. (The concept of matching is that both the current and the voltage at some port are used by the circuitry which forms that port). By altering the bias current, I_{EE}, the transconductance of the input pair Q1-Q2 can be set over

a wide range. Using this capability, an active mixer can provide variable gain.

A third point of difference is that the output (at the collectors of Q3-Q6) is in the form of a current, and can be converted back to a voltage at some other impedance level to that used at the input, hence, can provide further gain. By combining both output currents (typically, using a transformer) this voltage gain can be doubled. Finally, it will be apparent that the isolation between the various ports, in particular, from the LO port to the RF port, is inherently much lower than can be achieved in the diode ring mixer, due to the reversed-biased junctions that exist between the ports.

Briefly stated, though, the operation is as follows. In the absence of any voltage difference between the bases of Q1 and Q2, the collector currents of these two transistors are essentially equal. Thus, a voltage applied to the LO input results in no change of output current. Should a small DC offset voltage be present at the RF input (due typically to mismatch in the emitter areas of Q1 and Q2), this will only result in a small feedthrough of the LO signal to the IF output, which will be blocked by the first IF filter.

Conversely, if an RF signal is applied to the RF port, but no voltage difference is applied to the LO input, the output currents will again be balanced. A small offset voltage (due now to emitter mismatches in Q3-Q6) may cause some RF signal feedthrough to the IF output; as before, this will be rejected by the IF

filters. It is only when a signal is applied to both the RF and LO ports that a signal appears at the output; hence, the term doubly-balanced mixer.

Active mixers can realize their gain in one other way: the matching networks used to transform a 50Ω source to the (usually) high input impedance of the mixer provides an impedance transformation and thus voltage gain due to the impedance step up. Thus, an active mixer that has loss when the input is terminated in a broadband 50Ω termination can have "gain" when an input matching network is used.

The AD831, 500MHz, Low Distortion Active Mixer

The AD831 is a low distortion, wide dynamic range, monolithic mixer for use in such applications as RF to IF down conversion in HF and VHF receivers, the second mixer in digital mobile radio base stations, direct-to-baseband conversion, quadrature modulation and demodulation, and doppler-frequency shift detection in ultrasound imaging applications. The mixer includes a local oscillator driver and a low-noise output amplifier. The AD831 provides a

+24dBm third-order intercept point for −10dBm local oscillator power, thus improving system performance and reducing system cost, compared to passive mixers, by eliminating the need for a high power local oscillator driver and its associated shielding and isolation problems. A simplified block diagram of the AD831 is shown in Figure 3.47, and key specifications in Figure 3.48.

AD831 500MHz LOW DISTORTION ACTIVE MIXER

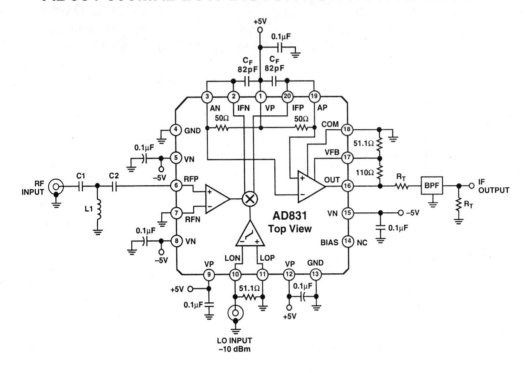

Figure 3.47

AD831 ACTIVE MIXER KEY SPECIFICATIONS

■ Doubly-Balanced Mixer, 10dB Noise Figure

■ Low Distortion (IF = 10.7MHz, RF to 200MHz):

    ◆ +24dBm Third Order Intercept

    ◆ +10dBm 1dB Compression Point

■ Low LO Drive Required: –10dBm

■ Bandwidth:

    ◆ 500MHz RF and LO Input Bandwidths

    ◆ 250MHz Differential Current IF Output

    ◆ DC to > 200MHz Single-Ended Voltage IF Output

Figure 3.48

Noise Figure

Noise Figure (NF) is a figure of merit used to determine how a device degrades the signal-to-noise ratio of its input. Note: in RF systems, the impedance is 50Ω unless otherwise stated. Mathematically, noise figure is defined as:

$$NF = 20 \log_{10} \frac{S_I / N_I}{S_O / N_O},$$

where S_I/N_I is the input signal-to-noise ratio, and S_O/N_O is the output signal-to-noise ratio.

Typical noise figures for passive mixers with post amplifiers are 12 to 15dB.

The NF of the AD831 is 10dB with a matched input, which is adequate for applications in which there is gain in front of the mixer.

Noise Figure is used in a "cascaded noise figure calculation", which gives the overall noise figure of a receiver. Basically, the noise figure of each stage is converted into a noise factor (F = antilog NF/10) and plugged into a spreadsheet containing the Friis Equation:

$$F_{RECEIVER} = F_1 + \frac{F_2 - 1}{G_1} + \frac{F_3 - 1}{G_1 G_2} + \sum_{K=4}^{N} \frac{F_K - 1}{\prod\limits_{J=1}^{K-1} G_J}$$

where F_N and G_N are the noise factor and gain, respectively, of the Nth stage in the receiver.

For a passive diode-ring mixer, the noise figure is the same as the insertion loss. For an active mixer, however, noise is added to the signal by the active devices in the signal path. The difference between the noise figure of a matched active mixer and an unmatched active mixer can be several dB due to the "voltage gain" of the imped-ance-matching network, which acts as a "noiseless" preamplifier (Figure 3.49). In the case of the AD831, the noise figure for the matched circuit is 10 dB (at 70MHz) and the unmatched circuit with its input terminated with a 50Ω resistor is 16dB.

The noise figure is 11.7dB at 220 MHz using the external matching network shown in Figure 3.49. The values shown are for 220 MHz and provide 10 dB of voltage gain.

AD831 ACTIVE MIXER WITH 220MHz
EXTERNAL MATCHING NETWORK

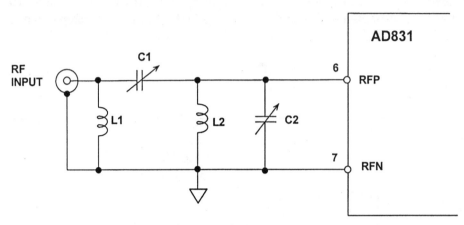

L1: 100nH, COILCRAFT 1008CS-101
L2: 56nH, COILCRAFT 1008CS-560
C1, C2: 2-10pF CERAMIC VARIABLE

Figure 3.49

Intermodulation Distortion

Even before the "mixing" process in the core, the entire signal spectrum co-exists within the RF input stage. This part of the mixer is inevitably nonlinear, to a greater or lesser extent, and, with or without the LO input operative, generates a very large number of intermodulation products.

Thus, the key objectives in the design of a high-performance active mixer are to achieve a very linear RF input section, followed by a near-ideal polarity-switching stage, followed by a very linear IF output amplifier (if used) prior to the first filter.

1dB Compression Point and Third-Order Intercept Point

For a single-sinusoid input to a system, a point will be reached as the input amplitude is increased at which the apparent gain becomes 1dB lower than that observed at lower input amplitudes. This is called the 1dB gain compression level, which we'll abbreviate P_{1dB}, and is usually quoted in dBm, or decibels above 1mW, that is, it is expressed as a power measurement. When using an active mixer with an input matching network, the gain of the input matching network must be taken into account when defining the system in terms of an active mixer's 1dB compression point, since the impedance transformation of the network increases the input voltage to mixer.

Another metric used in characterizing mixers is the third-order intercept, known as P_{3OI} or IP3. If two tones of frequency f_1 and f_2 (representing two adjacent channels in a communications system, for example) are applied to a non-linear system, there will be a large number of intermodulation products generated. The third-order distortion products which fall at $2f_2-f_1$ and $2f_1-f_2$ are particularly troublesome, because they are close to the original frequencies (see Figure 3.50). If the two tones represent true signals, then the third-order IMD products can interfere with signals in the adjacent channels.

Rather than measuring the third-order distortion products for a variety of signal amplitudes, the concept of third-order intercept can be used to extract the IMD information and is often used as a figure of merit for mixers and amplifiers in RF applications.

A plot (Figure 3.51) of the power levels at the output of the system for the fundamental of the output frequency and for its third harmonic, plotted versus the input power, will generally yield a pair of straight lines which eventually intersect (at the 3rd order intercept point, IP3).

3

THIRD-ORDER INTERMODULATION DISTORTION

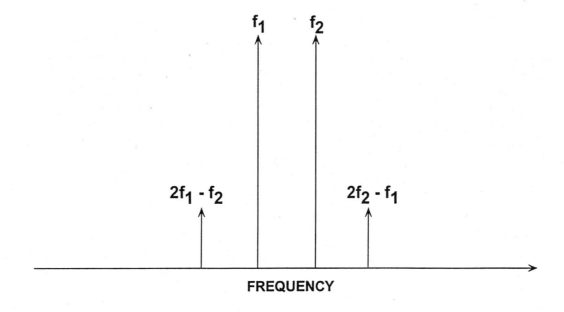

Figure 3.50

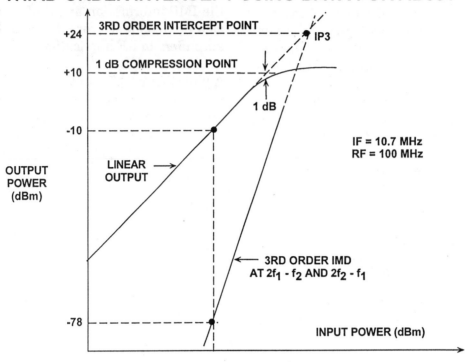

THIRD-ORDER INTERCEPT USING DATA FOR AD831

3RD ORDER INTERCEPT POINT

+24 ⟵ ● IP3

1 dB COMPRESSION POINT

+10

1 dB

-10

OUTPUT
POWER
(dBm)

LINEAR ⟶
OUTPUT

IF = 10.7 MHz
RF = 100 MHz

⟵ 3RD ORDER IMD
AT $2f_1 - f_2$ AND $2f_2 - f_1$

-78

INPUT POWER (dBm)

Figure 3.51

The problem with this metric is that it has meaning only for certain simple cases. In particular, the 3rd harmonic is assumed to increase at three times the rate of the fundamental. The appeal of P_{3OI} lies in the fact that it is easily measured, or at least, it is easy to obtain measurements. (The measurements are not hard to make, but it will be found that the apparent P_{3OI} is signal-dependent). Apply a low level signal, at some known level P_O (in dBm, see Figure 3.51), measure the output power at the fundamental, P_1 (in relative terms, dBc) and at the third harmonic, P_3 (also in dBc) and from simple geometry calculate

$$P_{3OI} = P_O + \frac{1}{2}(P_1 - P_3) \qquad \text{Eq. 6}$$

The non-linearity in some classical circuits, such as the diode-ring mixer, approximates a cubic function, and the above relationship holds, but in practice, the P_{3OI} can be quite misleading, for several reasons. First, other circuits may not, in general, exhibit this type of non-linearity. This type of behavior could easily lead to apparent third-order intercept values which were impressively high (theoretically infinite, if measured using signals of less than the critical amplitude).

A *spur chart* is a compilation of the $nf_1 \pm mf_2$ products that result from the mixing process. The spur chart is useful because it allows an engineer developing a frequency plan for a radio to identify possible problems due to spurious signals created in the mixer. However, the spur chart is also tedious to create; for $n = m = 7$, a chart requires 112 measurements.

The compilation of results is the spur chart (also called a "mixer table").

Mixer Summary

Mixers are a special kind of analog multiplier optimized for use in frequency translation, having one linear input (that associated with the RF signal) and a second (that associated with the LO input) which alternates the phase of the first input by 0/180°. In integrating complete receivers in monolithic form, certain basic circuit forms have proven useful. So far, we have considered a classic form, a six-transistor circuit exemplified by the AD831. Compared to a diode-ring mixer, this circuit has several advantages, including much better isolation between ports, the ability to provide conversion gain (which may also be variable), the need for much lower LO drive levels, and the elimination of special matching networks.

Often cited as a disadvantage of the active mixer is its poorer dynamic

Details of making the spur chart measurements and results are given in the AD831 data sheet (see Reference 17).

range: we have just begun to examine what defines this, beginning with a consideration of the linearity of the RF port, traditionally characterized by the 1dB gain-compression input power, P_{1dB}, and the third-order intercept, P_{3OI}. The second of these measures was shown to be meaningful only if the nonlinearity is essentially cubic in form, which may not always be true. In passing, we pointed out that while inputs and outputs are invariably characterized in terms of a power level of so-many-dBm, active mixers respond to instantaneous signal voltages at their inputs, which are usually not matched to their source, which can be confusing at times.

Now that we have examined each of the fundamental receiver building blocks, we are ready to look at receiver subsystems.

RECEIVER SUBSYSTEMS
Bob Clarke, Walt Kester

In order to design a communications receiver, a clear understanding of the modulation technique is essential. There are many types of modulation, ranging from simple amplitude modulation (AM), phase modulation (PM), and frequency modulation (FM) to multi-level quadrature-amplitude-modulation (QAM) where both amplitude and phase are modulated. Most modern modulation schemes make use of both signal amplitude and phase information. A complex signal can thus be represented in two ways as shown in the diagrams in Figure 3.52. The left-hand diagram represents the signal in rectangular coordinates as an inphase (I) and quadrature (Q) signal of the form:

$$S(t) = I(t) + jQ(t).$$

The right hand diagram represents the same signal expressed in polar coordinates:

$$S(t) = A(t)e^{j\varnothing(t)}.$$

The conversions between the two coordinate systems are:

$$S(t) = A(t)e^{j\varnothing(t)} = I(t) + jQ(t), \text{ where}$$

$$A(t) = \sqrt{I(t)^2 + Q(t)^2}\,,$$

$$\varnothing(t) = \arctan\left[\frac{Q(t)}{I(t)}\right].$$

RECTANGULAR AND POLAR REPRESENTATIONS OF AMPLITUDE AND PHASE MODULATED SIGNAL

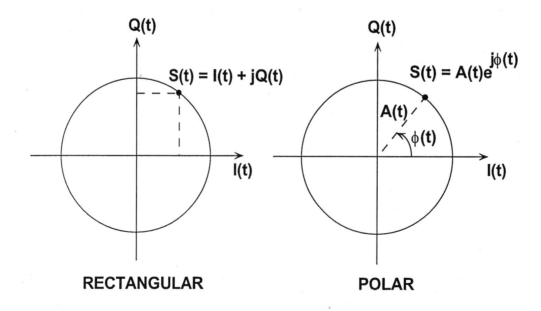

RECTANGULAR

POLAR

Figure 3.52

Note that the signals are identical, only their representation is different.

In the case of the I/Q (rectangular) representation, a linear IF strip is required. Variable gain is required because of the wide dynamic range, and amplitude and phase information must be preserved. This type of IF strip often incorporates an I/Q demodulator whose outputs drive baseband ADCs followed by a DSP. Linear IF amplifiers are used in these systems.

For the case of the polar representation, the signal amplitude is derived from the RSSI (log) output of a log/limiting amplifier and the phase information from the limited output. This type of IF strip operates at a high fixed gain, retains the phase information in the limited output, and often incorporates a phase demodulator.

In order to handle these two fundamental representations of modulation, ADI has developed two IF subsystems, the AD607 and the AD608. These are used in such applications as PHS, PCN, DECT, CT2, and GSM where the modulation mode is some form of phase-shift keying (PSK).

The choice of demodulation technique depends on the receiver architecture.

The standard architecture in GSM and PHS uses a rectangular representation of the signal, that is $S(t) = I(t) + jQ(t)$ and requires a linear IF amplifier stage such as that in the AD607. In this architecture, a baseband converter consisting of two signal inputs; each with individual low-pass filters, digitizes the $I(t)$ and $Q(t)$ outputs of the IF IC's quadrature demodulator. Further demodulation is performed digitally using a DSP. An equalizer in the DSP then determines the correct manual gain control (MGC) voltage (or digital signal) to change the IF gain to center the signal in the dynamic range of the baseband ADCs. The equalizer calculates the RSSI value as part of this process (see Figure 3.53).

A detailed block diagram of the AD607 Mixer/AGC/RSSI 3V receiver IF subsystem is shown in Figure 3.54. The RF input frequency can be as high as 500MHz, and the IF frequency from 400kHz to 12MHz. It consists of a mixer, linear IF amplifiers, I and Q demodulators, a phase-locked quadrature oscillator, AGC detector, and a biasing system with external power-down. Total power on +3V is 25mW.

3

RECEIVER BASED ON AD607 SUBSYSTEM
USING INPHASE/QUADRATURE MODULATION

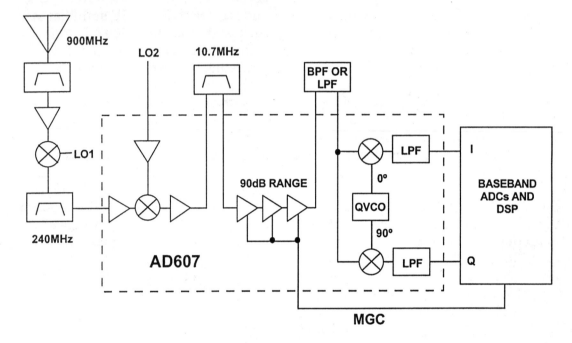

Figure 3.53

AD607 FUNCTIONAL BLOCK DIAGRAM

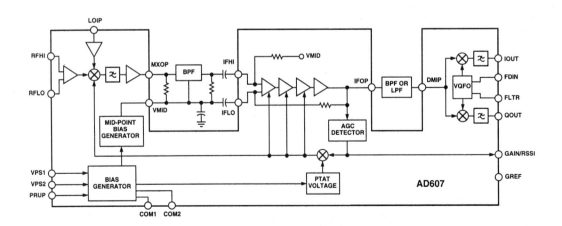

Figure 3.54

The AD607's low noise, high intercept mixer is a doubly-balanced Gilbert cell type. It has a nominal –15dBm input-referred 1dB compression point and a –8dBm input-referred third-order intercept. The mixer section also includes a local oscillator preamplifier, which lowers the required external LO drive to –16dBm.

The variable-gain mixer and the linear four-stage IF amplifier strip together provide a voltage controlled gain range of more than 90dB. The I and Q demodulators, each consisting of a multiplier followed by a 2-pole, 2MHz low-pass filter, are driven by a phase-locked loop providing inphase and quadrature clocks. An internal AGC detector is included, and the temperature stable gain control system provides an accurate RSSI capability.

The I and Q demodulators provide inphase and quadrature baseband outputs to interface with Analog Devices' AD7013 (IS54/IS136, TETRA, MSAT) and AD7015 (GSM) baseband converters.

Key specifications for the AD607 are summarized in Figure 3.55.

AD607 MIXER / AGC / RSSI 3V RECEIVER KEY FEATURES

- ■ Mixer:
  - ◆ –15dBm Input 1dB Compression Point
  - ◆ –8dBm Input Third Order Intercept Point
  - ◆ RF/LO Inputs to 500MHz
  - ◆ 12dB Noise Figure, Matched Input
  - ◆ –16dBm LO Drive

- ■ Linear IF Amplifier:
  - ◆ 45MHz Bandwidth
  - ◆ Linear-in-dB Gain Control Over 90dB Gain Range
  - ◆ –15dBm Input 1dB Compression Point
  - ◆ +18dBm Output Third Order Intercept Point

- ■ In-Phase and Quadrature Demodulators:
  - ◆ 1.5MHz Output Bandwidth
  - ◆ Compatible with Baseband Converters (AD7013, AD7015)

- ■ 25mW Total Power @ Single +3V Supply

Figure 3.55

For cases where the signal is represented in polar form, the AD608 is the proper choice. The AD608 Mixer/Limiter/RSSI 3V Receiver IF Subsystem consists of a mixer followed by a logarithmic amplifier; the logarithmic amplifier has both limited output (phase information) and an RSSI output (amplitude information). This architecture is useful in polar demodulation applications as shown in Figure 3.56.

A block diagram of the AD608 is shown in Figure 3.57, and key specifications in Figure 3.58.

RECEIVER BASED ON AD608 SUBSYSTEM
USING POLAR DEMODULATION

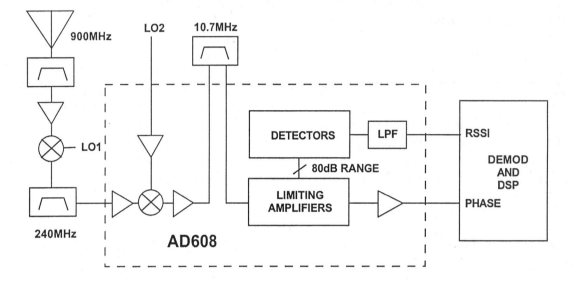

Figure 3.56

AD608 FUNCTIONAL BLOCK DIAGRAM

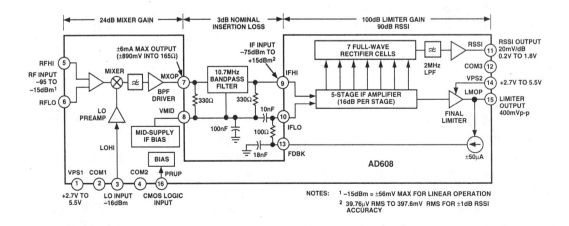

Figure 3.57

AD608 MIXER / LIMITER / RSSI 3V RECEIVER KEY FEATURES

- ■ **Mixer:**
  - ◆ **−15dBm Input 1dB Compression Point**
  - ◆ **−5dBm Input Third Order Intercept Point**
  - ◆ **RF/LO Inputs to 500MHz**
  - ◆ **12dB Noise Figure, Matched Input**
  - ◆ **−16dBm LO Drive**

- ■ **Logarithmic Amplifier / Limiter:**
  - ◆ **100dB Limiter Gain, 90dB RSSI**
  - ◆ **±1dB Log Linearity**
  - ◆ **±3° Phase Variation, −75dBm to +5dBm IF @ 10.7MHz**

- ■ **21mW Total Power @ Single +3V Supply**

3

Figure 3.58

The log amp both measures the level of the signal (like the AD641 and AD606) and limits the signal. The RSSI or Received Signal Strength Indicator output is proportional to the log of the input signal. As a limiting amplifier, the AD608 removes any amplitude changes in the signal and keeps only the phase or frequency changes. These phase or frequency changes are proportional to the modulating signal and contain the intelligence in the signal. The AD608's limiting amplifier is a 5-stage log amp with more than 80dB of dynamic range.

In a typical mobile phone application, the RF signal (typically 900MHz or 1800MHz) is mixed down to the first IF (typically 240MHz), is filtered, and enters the AD608, where it is mixed down to a second IF at 10.7MHz, where it is amplified, limited, and measured. The limited output is demodulated by

an external frequency or phase demodulator. The RSSI output is digitized by an ADC and used for active power control in the phone system.

As a practical note, the cutoff frequency of the log amp's internal low pass filter depends on what range of frequencies the log amp was designed for. In analog cellular systems, where the modulation mode is narrow-band FM, the IF is typically 450kHz. The low pass filters in the IF ICs designed for these standards have a fairly low cutoff frequency, and the filter's voltage output response provides a "slow" RSSI. In GSM (Global System for Mobile Communications) and PHS (Personal Handy System) applications, the IF is typically 10.7MHz or higher, and the filter's voltage output response provides a "fast" RSSI. The cutoff frequency of the low pass filter in the AD608 is 2MHz.

REFERENCES

1.   Barrie Gilbert, **ISSCC Digest of Technical Papers 1968**, pp. 114-115
        February 16, 1968.

2.   Barrie Gilbert, **Journal of Solid State Circuits**, Vol. SC-3, December
        1968, pp. 353-372.

3.   C.L. Ruthroff, *Some Broadband Transformers*, **Proc. I.R.E.**, Vol.47,
        August, 1959, pp.1337-1342.

4.   James M. Bryant, *Mixers for High Performance Radio*, **Wescon 1981:
        Session 24** (Published by Electronic Conventions, Inc., Sepulveda Blvd.,
        El Segundo, CA)

5.   P.E. Chadwick, *High Performance IC Mixers*, **IERE Conference on Radio
        Receivers and Associated Systems**, Leeds, 1981, IERE Conference
        Publication No. 50.

6.   P.E. Chadwick, *Phase Noise, Intermodulation, and Dynamic Range*,
        RF Expo, Anaheim, CA, January, 1986.

7.   Daniel H. Sheingold, Editor, **Nonlinear Circuits Handbook**, Analog
        Devices, Inc., 1974.

8.   Richard Smith Hughes, **Logarithmic Amplifiers**, Artech House, Inc.,
        Dedham, MA., 1986.

9.   William L. Barber and Edmund R. Brown, *A True Logarithmic Amplifier for
        Radar IF Applications*, **IEEE Journal of Solid State Circuits**, Vol. SC-
        15, No. 3, June, 1980, pp. 291-295.

10.   **Broadband Amplifier Applications**, Plessey Co. Publication P.S. 1938,
        September, 1984.

11.   M. S. Gay, **SL521 Application Note**, Plessey Co., 1966.

12.   **Amplifier Applications Guide**, Analog Devices, Inc., 1992. Section 9.

13.   Charles Kitchen and Lew Counts, **RMS-to-DC Conversion Application
        Guide, Second Edition**, Analog Devices, Inc., 1986.

14.   Barrie Gilbert, *A Low Noise Wideband Variable-Gain Amplifier Using
        an Interpolated Ladder Attenuator*, **IEEE ISSCC Technical Digest**, 1991,
        pp. 280, 281, 330.

15.   Barrie Gilbert, *A Monolithic Microsystem for Analog Synthesis of Trigonometric Functions and their Inverses*, **IEEE Journal of Solid State Circuits**, Vol. SC-17, No. 6, December, 1982, pp. 1179-1191.

16.   **Linear Design Seminar**, Analog Devices, 1995, Section 3.

17.   **AD831 Data Sheet**, Rev. B, Analog Devices.

3

SECTION 4

HIGH SPEED SAMPLING AND HIGH SPEED ADCs

- ■ Fundamentals of High Speed Sampling

- ■ Baseband Antialiasing Filters

- ■ Undersampling

- ■ Antialiasing Filters in Undersampling Applications

- ■ Distortion and Noise in an Ideal N-bit ADC

- ■ Distortion and Noise in Practical ADCs

- ■ High Speed ADC Architectures

4

SECTION 4
HIGH SPEED SAMPLING AND
HIGH SPEED ADCs, *Walt Kester*

INTRODUCTION

High speed ADCs are used in a wide variety of real-time DSP signal-processing applications, replacing systems that used analog techniques alone. The major reason for using digital signal processing are (1) the cost of DSP processors has gone down, (2) their speed and computational power has increased, and (3) they are reprogrammable, thereby allowing for system performance upgrades without hardware changes. DSP offers solutions that cannot be achieved in the analog domain, i.e. V.32 and V.34 modems.

However, in order for digital signal processing techniques to be effective in solving an analog signal processing problem, appropriate cost effective high speed ADCs must be available. The ADCs must be tested and specified in such a way that the design engineer can relate the ADC performance to specific system requirements, which can be more demanding than if they were used in purely analog signal processing systems. In most high speed signal processing applications, AC performance and wide dynamic range are much more important than traditional DC performance. This requires that the ADC manufacturer not only design the right ADCs but specify them as completely as possible to cover a wide variety of applications.

Another important aspect of integrating ADCs into a high speed system is a complete understanding of the sampling process and the distortion mecha-

nisms which ultimately limit system performance. High speed sampling ADCs first were used in instrumentation and signal processing applications, where much emphasis was placed on time-domain performance. While this is still important, applications of ADCs in communications also require comprehensive frequency-domain specifications.

Modern IC processes also allow the integration of more analog functionality into the ADC, such as on-board references, sample-and-hold amplifiers, PGAs, etc. This makes them easier to use in a system by minimizing the amount of support circuitry required.

Another driving force in high speed ADC development is the trend toward lower power and lower supply voltages. Most high speed sampling ADCs today operate on either dual or single 5V supplies, and there is increasing interest in single-supply converters which will operate on 3V or less for battery powered applications. Lower supply voltages tend to increase a circuit's sensitivity to power supply noise and ground noise, especially mixed-signal devices such as ADCs and DACs.

The trend toward lower cost and lower power has led to the development of a variety of high speed ADCs fabricated on standard 0.6 micron CMOS processes. Making a precision ADC on a digital process (no thin film resistors are available) is a real challenge to the

IC circuit designer. ADCs which require the maximum in performance still require a high speed complementary bipolar process (such as Analog Devices' XFCB) with thin film resistors.

The purpose of this section is to equip the engineer with the proper tools necessary to understand and select ADCs for high speed systems applications. Making intelligent tradeoffs in the system design requires a thorough understanding of the fundamental capabilities and limitations of state-of-the-art high speed sampling ADCs.

HIGH SPEED SAMPLING ADCs

■ Wide Acceptance in Signal Processing and Communications

■ Emphasis on Dynamic Performance

■ Trend to Low Power, Low Voltage, Single-Supply

■ More On-Chip Functionality: PGAs, SHA, Digital Filters, etc.

■ Process Technology:

◆ Low Cost CMOS: Up to 12-bits @ 10MSPS

◆ High Speed Complementary Bipolar: Up to 12-bits @ 70MSPS

◆ Statistical Matching Techniques Rather than Thin Film Laser Trimming

Figure 4.1

FUNDAMENTALS OF HIGH SPEED SAMPLING

The sampling process can be discussed from either the frequency or time domain or both. Frequency-domain analysis is applicable to communications, so that's what we will consider.

First consider the case of a single frequency sinewave of frequency f_a sampled at a frequency f_s by an ideal impulse sampler (see top diagram in Figure 4.2). Also assume that $f_s > 2f_a$ as shown. The frequency-domain output of the sampler shows *aliases* or *images* of the original signal around every multiple of f_s, i.e. at frequencies equal to
$| \pm Kf_s \pm f_a |$, $K = 1, 2, 3, 4, \ldots$

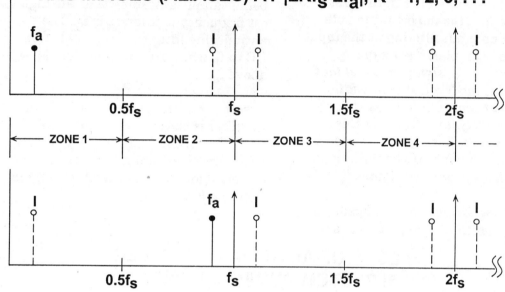

Figure 4.2

4

The *Nyquist* bandwidth is defined to be the frequency spectrum from DC to $f_s/2$. The frequency spectrum is divided into an infinite number of *Nyquist zones*, each having a width equal to $0.5f_s$ as shown. In practice, the ideal sampler is replaced by an ADC followed by an FFT processor. The FFT processor only provides an output from DC to $f_s/2$, i.e., the signals or aliases which appear in the first Nyquist zone.

Now consider the case of a signal which is outside the first Nyquist zone (Figure 4.2, bottom diagram) Notice that even though the signal is outside the first Nyquist zone, its image (or *alias*), f_s-f_a,

falls inside. Returning to Figure 4.2, top diagram, it is clear that if an unwanted signal appears at any of the image frequencies of f_a, it will also occur at f_a, thereby producing a spurious frequency component in the first Nyquist zone. This is similar to the analog mixing process and implies that some filtering ahead of the sampler (or ADC) is required to remove frequency components which are outside the Nyquist bandwidth, but whose aliased components fall inside it. The filter performance will depend on how close the out-of-band signal is to $f_s/2$ and the amount of attenuation required.

BASEBAND ANTIALIASING FILTERS

Baseband sampling implies that the signal to be sampled lies in the first Nyquist zone. It is important to note that with no input filtering at the input of the ideal sampler, *any frequency component (either signal or noise) that falls outside the Nyquist bandwidth in any Nyquist zone will be aliased back into the first Nyquist zone.* For this reason, an antialiasing filter is used in almost all sampling ADC applications to remove these unwanted signals.

Properly specifying the antialiasing filter is important. The first step is to know the characteristics of the signal being sampled. Assume that the highest frequency of interest is f_a. The antialiasing filter passes signals from DC to f_a while attenuating signals above f_a.

Assume that the corner frequency of the filter is chosen to be equal to f_a. The effect of the finite transition from minimum to maximum attenuation on system dynamic range is illustrated in Figure 4.3.

EFFECTS OF ANTIALIASING FILTER ON SYSTEM DYNAMIC RANGE

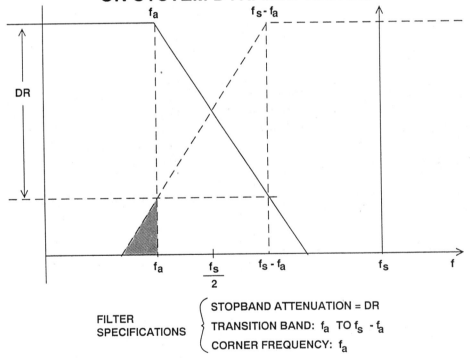

FILTER SPECIFICATIONS

{
STOPBAND ATTENUATION = DR
TRANSITION BAND: f_a TO $f_s - f_a$
CORNER FREQUENCY: f_a
}

Figure 4.3

Assume that the input signal has fullscale components well above the maximum frequency of interest, f_a. The diagram shows how fullscale frequency components above $f_s - f_a$ are aliased back into the bandwidth DC to f_a.

These aliased components are indistinguishable from actual signals and therefore limit the dynamic range to the value on the diagram which is shown as *DR*.

Some texts recommend specifying the antialiasing filter with respect to the Nyquist frequency, $f_s/2$, but this assumes that the signal bandwidth of interest extends from DC to $f_s/2$ which is rarely the case. In the example shown in Figure 4.3, the aliased components between f_a and $f_s/2$ are not of interest and do not limit the dynamic range.

The antialiasing filter transition band is therefore determined by the corner frequency f_a, the stopband frequency $f_s - f_a$, and the stopband attenuation, DR. The required system dynamic range is chosen based on our requirement for signal fidelity.

Filters have to become more complex as the transition band becomes sharper, all other things being equal. For instance, a Butterworth filter gives 6dB attenuation per octave for each filter pole. Achieving 60dB attenuation in a transition region between 1MHz and 2MHz (1 octave) requires a minimum of 10 poles, not a trivial filter, and definitely a design challenge.

Therefore, other filter types are generally more suited to high speed applications where the requirement is for a sharp transition band and in-band flatness coupled with linear phase response. Elliptic filters meet these criteria and are a popular choice.

There are a number of companies which specialize in supplying custom analog filters. TTE is an example of such a company (Reference 1). As an example, the normalized response of the TTE, Inc., LE1182 11-pole elliptic antialiasing filter is shown in Figure 4.4. Notice that this filter is specified to achieve at least 80dB attenuation between f_c and $1.2f_c$. The corresponding passband ripple, return loss, delay, and phase response are also shown in Figure 4.4. This custom filter is available in corner frequencies up to 100MHz and in a choice of PC board, BNC, or SMA with compatible packages.

CHARACTERISTICS OF TTE, INC., LE1182-SERIES 11-POLE ELLIPTICAL FILTER

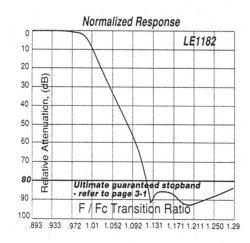

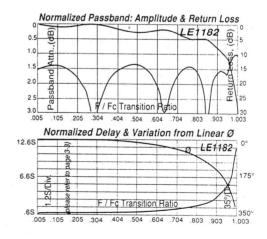

Reprinted with Permission of
TTE, Inc., 2251 Barry Ave., Los Angeles, CA 90064

Figure 4.4

From this discussion, we can see how the sharpness of the antialiasing transition band can be traded off against the ADC sampling frequency. Choosing a higher sampling rate (oversampling) reduces the requirement on transition band sharpness (hence, the filter complexity) at the expense of using a faster ADC and processing data at a faster rate. This is illustrated in Figure 4.5 which shows the effects of increasing the sampling frequency while maintaining the same analog corner frequency, f_a, and the same dynamic range, DR, requirement.

The above design process is started by choosing an initial sampling rate of 2 to 4 times f_a. Determine the filter specifications based on the required dynamic range and see if such a filter is realizable within the constraints of the system cost and performance. If not,

consider a higher sampling rate which may require using a faster ADC.

The antialiasing filter requirements can be relaxed somewhat if it is certain that there will never be a fullscale signal at the stopband frequency $f_s - f_a$. In many applications, it is improbable that fullscale signals will occur at this frequency. If the maximum signal at the frequency $f_s - f_a$ will never exceed XdB below fullscale. Then, the filter stopband attenuation requirement is reduced by that same amount. The new requirement for stopband attenuation at $f_s - f_a$ based on this knowledge of the signal is now only DR – XdB. When making this type of assumption, be careful to treat any noise signals which may occur above the maximum signal frequency f_a as unwanted signals which will also alias back into the signal bandwidth.

INCREASING SAMPLING FREQUENCY RELAXES REQUIREMENT ON ANTIALIASING FILTER

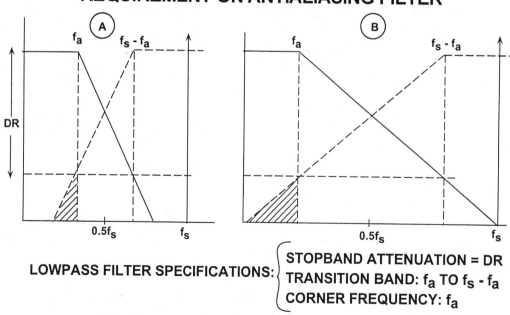

LOWPASS FILTER SPECIFICATIONS:
- STOPBAND ATTENUATION = DR
- TRANSITION BAND: f_a TO $f_s - f_a$
- CORNER FREQUENCY: f_a

Figure 4.5

UNDERSAMPLING (HARMONIC SAMPLING, BANDPASS SAMPLING, IF SAMPLING, DIRECT IF TO DIGITAL CONVERSION)

Thus far we have considered the case of baseband sampling, i.e., all the signals of interest lie within the first Nyquist zone. Figure 4.6A shows such a case, where the band of sampled signals is limited to the first Nyquist zone, and images of the original band of frequencies appear in each of the other Nyquist zones.

Consider the case shown in Figure 4.6B, where the sampled signal band lies entirely within the second Nyquist zone. The process of sampling a signal outside the first Nyquist zone is often referred to as *undersampling*, or *harmonic sampling*. Note that the first Nyquist zone image contains all the information in the original signal, with

the exception of its original location (the order of the frequency components within the spectrum is reversed, but this is easily corrected by re-ordering the output of the FFT).

Figure 4.6C shows the sampled signal restricted to the third Nyquist zone. Note that the first Nyquist zone image has no frequency reversal. In fact, the sampled signal frequencies may lie in *any* unique Nyquist zone, and the first Nyquist zone image is still an accurate representation (with the exception of the frequency reversal which occurs when the signals are located in even Nyquist zones). At this point we can clearly state the Nyquist criteria:

4

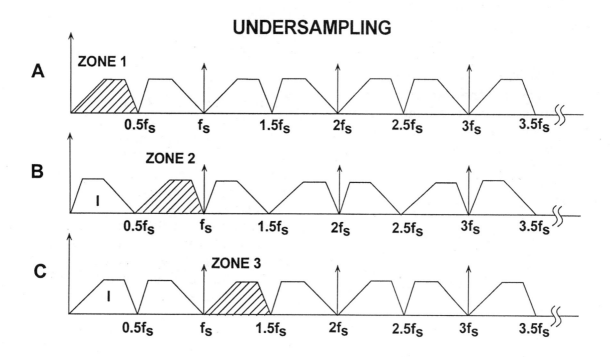

Figure 4.6

*A signal must be sampled at a rate equal to or greater than twice its **band-width** in order to preserve all the signal information.*

Notice that there is no mention of the absolute *location* of the band of sampled signals within the frequency spectrum relative to the sampling frequency. The only constraint is that the band of sampled signals be restricted to a *single* Nyquist zone, i.e., the signals must not overlap any multiple of $f_s/2$ (this, in fact, is the primary function of the antialiasing filter).

Sampling signals above the first Nyquist zone has become popular in communications because the process is equivalent to analog demodulation. It is becoming common practice to sample IF signals directly and then use digital techniques to process the signal, thereby eliminating the need for the IF demodulator. Clearly, however, as the IF frequencies become higher, the dynamic performance requirements on the ADC become more critical. The ADC input bandwidth and distortion performance must be adequate at the IF frequency, rather than only baseband. This presents a problem for most ADCs designed to process signals in the first Nyquist zone, therefore an ADC suitable for undersampling applications must maintain dynamic performance into the higher order Nyquist zones.

ANTIALIASING FILTERS IN UNDERSAMPLING APPLICATIONS

Figure 4.7 shows a signal in the second Nyquist zone centered around a carrier frequency, f_c, whose lower and upper frequencies are f_1 and f_2. The antialiasing filter is a bandpass filter. The desired dynamic range is DR, which defines the filter stopband attenuation. The upper transition band is f_2 to $2f_s-f_2$, and the lower is f_1 to $f_s - f_1$. As in the case of baseband sampling, the antialiasing filter requirements can be relaxed by proportionally increasing the sampling frequency, but f_c must also be increased so that it is always centered in the second Nyquist zone.

Two key equations can be used to select the sampling frequency, f_s, given the carrier frequency, f_c, and the bandwidth of its signal, Δf. The first is the Nyquist criteria:

$$f_s > 2\Delta f \qquad \text{Eq. 1}$$

The second equation ensures that f_c is placed in the center of a Nyquist zone:

$$f_s = \frac{4f_c}{2NZ-1}, \text{ Eq. 2}$$

where NZ = 1, 2, 3, 4, ... and NZ corresponds to the Nyquist zone in which the carrier and its signal fall (see Figure 4.8).

NZ is normally chosen to be as large as possible while still maintaining $f_s > 2\Delta f$. This results in the minimum required sampling rate. If NZ is chosen to be odd, then f_c and it's signal will fall in an odd Nyquist zone, and the image frequencies in the first Nyquist zone will not be reversed. Tradeoffs can be made between the sampling frequency and the complexity of the antialiasing filter by choosing smaller values of NZ (hence a higher sampling frequency).

As an example, consider a 4MHz wide signal centered around a carrier frequency of 71MHz. The minimum required sampling frequency is therefore

ANTIALIASING FILTER FOR UNDERSAMPLING

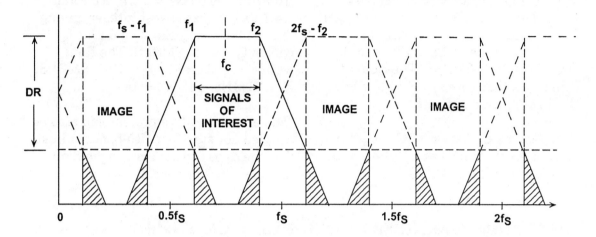

BANDPASS FILTER SPECIFICATIONS:
$$\begin{cases} \text{STOPBAND ATTENUATION} = \text{DR} \\ \text{TRANSITION BAND: } f_2 \text{ TO } 2f_S - f_2 \\ \qquad\qquad\qquad f_1 \text{ TO } f_S - f_1 \\ \text{CORNER FREQUENCIES: } f_1, f_2 \end{cases}$$

Figure 4.7

CENTERING AN UNDERSAMPLED SIGNAL WITHIN A NYQUIST ZONE

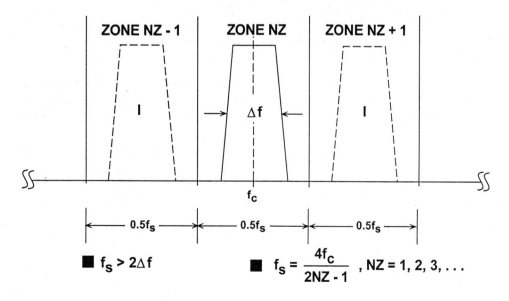

■ $f_S > 2\Delta f$ ■ $f_S = \dfrac{4f_C}{2NZ - 1}$, NZ = 1, 2, 3, . . .

Figure 4.8

8MSPS. Solving Eq. 2 for NZ using $f_c = 71\text{MHz}$ and $f_s = 8\text{MSPS}$ yields NZ = 18.25. However, NZ must be an integer, so we round 18.25 to the next lowest integer, 18. Solving Eq. 2 again for f_s yields $f_s = 8.1143\text{MSPS}$. The final values are therefore $f_s = 8.1143\text{MSPS}$, $f_c = 71\text{MHz}$, and NZ = 18.

Now assume that we desire more margin for the antialiasing filter, and we select f_s to be 10MSPS. Solving Eq.

2 for NZ, using $f_c = 71\text{MHz}$ and $f_s = 10\text{MSPS}$ yields NZ = 14.7. We round 14.7 to the next lowest integer, giving NZ = 14. Solving Eq. 2 again for f_s yields $f_s = 10.519\text{MSPS}$. The final values are therefore $f_s = 10.519\text{MSPS}$, $f_c = 71\text{MHz}$, and NZ = 14.

The above iterative process can also be carried out starting with f_s and adjusting the carrier frequency to yield an integer number for NZ.

DISTORTION AND NOISE IN AN IDEAL N-BIT ADC

Thus far we have looked at the implications of the sampling process without considering the effects of ADC quantization. We will now treat the ADC as an ideal sampler, but include the effects of quantization.

The only errors (DC or AC) associated with an ideal N-bit ADC are those related to the sampling and quantization processes. The maximum error an ideal ADC makes digitizing a DC input signal is ±1/2LSB. Any AC signal applied to an ideal N-bit ADC will produce quantization noise whose rms value (measured over the Nyquist bandwidth, DC to $f_s/2$) is approximately equal to the weight of the least significant bit (LSB), q, divided by $\sqrt{12}$. (See Reference 2). This assumes that the signal is at least a few LSBs in amplitude so that the ADC output always changes state. The quantization error signal from a linear ramp input is approximated as a sawtooth waveform with a peak-to-peak amplitude equal to q, and its rms value is therefore $q/\sqrt{12}$ (see Figure 4.9).

It can be shown that the ratio of the rms value of a full scale sinewave to the rms value of the quantization noise (expressed in dB) is:

$$SNR = 6.02N + 1.76\text{dB},$$

where N is the number of bits in the ideal ADC. *This equation is only valid if the noise is measured over the entire Nyquist bandwidth from DC to $f_s/2$.* If the signal bandwidth, BW, is less than $f_s/2$, then the SNR within the signal bandwidth BW is increased because the amount of quantization noise within the signal bandwidth is smaller. The correct expression for this condition is given by:

$$SNR = 6.02N + 1.76\text{dB} + 10\log\left(\frac{f_s}{2 \cdot BW}\right).$$

The above equation reflects the condition called *oversampling*, where the sampling frequency is higher than twice the signal bandwidth. The correction term is often called *processing gain*. Notice that for a given signal bandwidth, doubling the sampling frequency increases the SNR by 3dB.

Although the rms value of the noise is accurately approximated $q/\sqrt{12}$, its frequency domain content may be highly correlated to the AC input signal. For instance, there is greater correlation for low amplitude periodic

IDEAL N-BIT ADC QUANTIZATION NOISE

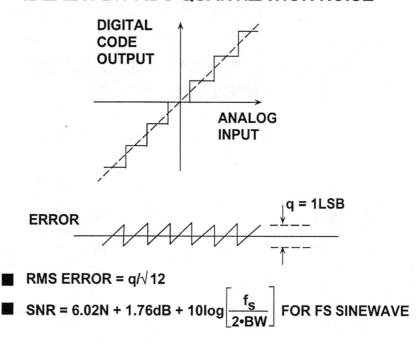

- RMS ERROR = $q/\sqrt{12}$
- SNR = $6.02N + 1.76\text{dB} + 10\log\left[\dfrac{f_s}{2 \cdot BW}\right]$ FOR FS SINEWAVE

Figure 4.9

4

signals than for large amplitude random signals. Quite often, the assumption is made that the theoretical quantization noise appears as white noise, spread uniformly over the Nyquist bandwidth DC to $f_s/2$. Unfortunately, this is not true. In the case of strong correlation, the quantization noise appears concentrated at the various harmonics of the input signal, just where you don't want them.

In most applications, the input to the ADC is a band of frequencies (usually summed with some noise), so the quantization noise tends to be random. In spectral analysis applications (or in performing FFTs on ADCs using spectrally pure sinewaves - see Figure 4.10), however, the correlation between

the quantization noise and the signal depends upon the ratio of the sampling frequency to the input signal. This is demonstrated in Figure 4.11, where an ideal 12-bit ADCs output is analyzed using a 4096-point FFT. In the left-hand FFT plot, the ratio of the sampling frequency to the input frequency was chosen to be exactly 32, and the worst harmonic is about 76dB below the fundamental. The right hand diagram shows the effects of slightly offsetting the ratio, showing a relatively random noise spectrum, where the SFDR is now about 92dBc. In both cases, the rms value of all the noise components is $q/\sqrt{12}$, but in the first case, the noise is concentrated at harmonics of the fundamental.

DYNAMIC PERFORMANCE ANALYSIS
OF AN IDEAL N-BIT ADC

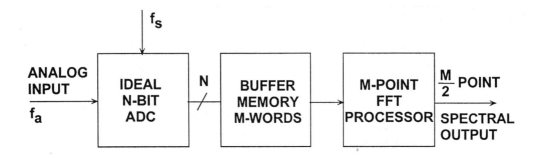

Figure 4.10

EFFECT OF RATIO OF SAMPLING CLOCK TO INPUT
FREQUENCY ON SFDR FOR IDEAL 12-BIT ADC

$f_S / f_a = 32$ M = 4096 $f_S / f_a = 32.25196850394$

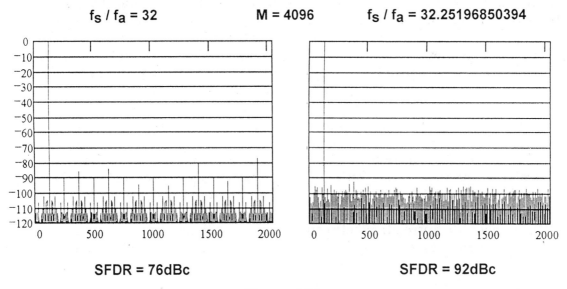

SFDR = 76dBc   SFDR = 92dBc

Figure 4.11

Note that this variation in the apparent harmonic distortion of the ADC is an artifact of the sampling process and the correlation of the quantization error with the input frequency. In a practical ADC application, the quantization error generally appears as random noise because of the random nature of the wideband input signal and the additional fact that there is a usually a small amount of system noise which acts as a *dither* signal to further randomize the quantization error spectrum. (For further discussions on dither, see Section 5 of this book).

It is important to understand the above point, because single-tone sinewave FFT testing of ADCs is a universally accepted method of performance evaluation. In order to accurately measure the harmonic distortion of an ADC, steps must be taken to ensure that the test setup truly measures the ADC distortion, not the artifacts due to quantization noise correlation. This is done by properly choosing the frequency ratio and sometimes by injecting a small amount of noise (dither) with the input signal.

Now, return to Figure 4.11, and note that the average value of the noise floor of the FFT is greater than 100dB below full scale, but the theoretical SNR of a 12-bit ADC is 74dB. The FFT noise floor is *not* the SNR of the ADC, because the FFT acts like an analog spectrum analyzer with a bandwidth of f_s/M, where M is the number of points in the FFT, rather than $f_s/2$. The theoretical FFT noise floor is therefore $10\log_{10}(M/2)$dB below the quantization noise floor due to the so-called *processing gain* of the FFT (see Figure 4.12). In the case of an ideal 12-bit ADC with an SNR of 74dB, a 4096-point FFT would result in a processing gain of $10\log_{10}(4096/2) = 33$dB, thereby resulting in an overall FFT noise floor of 74+33=107dBc. In fact, the FFT noise floor can be reduced even further by going to larger and larger FFTs; just as an analog spectrum analyzer's noise floor can be reduced by narrowing the bandwidth.

4

NOISE FLOOR FOR AN IDEAL 12-BIT ADC USING 4096-POINT FFT

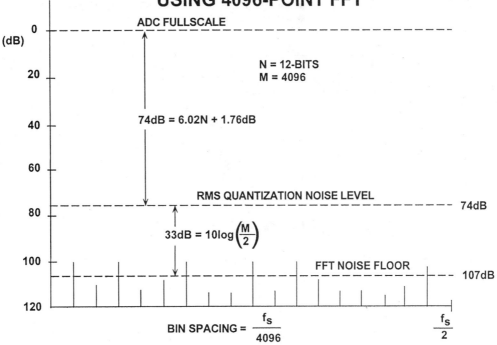

Figure 4.12

DISTORTION AND NOISE IN PRACTICAL ADCs

A practical sampling ADC (one that has an integral sample-and-hold), regardless of architecture, has a number of noise and distortion sources as shown in Figure 4.13. The wideband analog front-end buffer has wideband noise, non-linearity, and also finite bandwidth. The SHA introduces further non-linearity, bandlimiting, and aperture jitter. The actual quantizer portion of the ADC introduces quantization noise, and both integral and differential non-

linearity. In this discussion, assume that sequential outputs of the ADC are loaded into a buffer memory of length M and that the FFT processor provides the spectral output. Also assume that the FFT arithmetic operations themselves introduce no significant errors relative to the ADC. However, when examining the output noise floor, the FFT processing gain (dependent on M) must be considered.

ADC MODEL SHOWING NOISE AND DISTORTION SOURCES

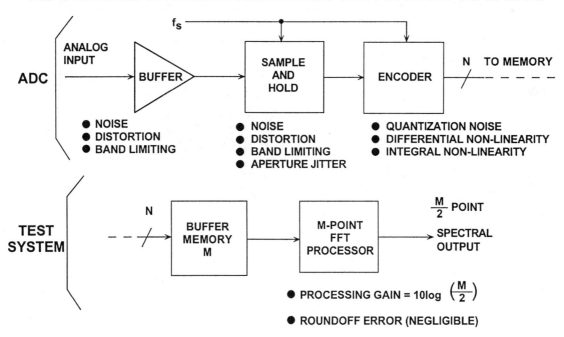

Figure 4.13

Equivalent Input Referred Noise (Thermal Noise)

The wideband ADC internal circuits produce a certain amount of wideband rms noise due to thermal effects. This noise is present even for DC input signals, and accounts for the fact that the output of most wideband ADCs is a distribution of codes, centered around the nominal value of a DC input (see Figure 4.14). To measure its value, the input of the ADC is grounded, and a large number of output samples are collected and plotted as a histogram (sometimes referred to as a *grounded-input* histogram). Since the noise is approximately Gaussian, the standard deviation of the histogram is easily calculated (see Reference 3), corresponding to the effective input rms noise. It is common practice to express this rms noise in terms of LSBs, although it can be expressed as an rms voltage.

HISTOGRAM OF 5000 CONVERSIONS FOR A DC INPUT SHOWS 5 LSB p-p OR 0.8LSB RMS EQUIVALENT INPUT NOISE

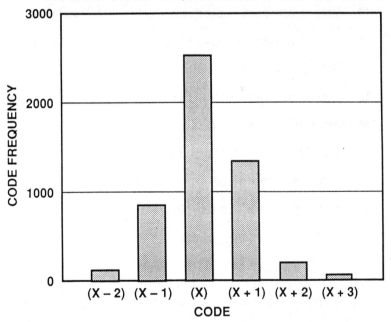

Figure 4.14

Integral and Differential Non-Linearity

The overall integral non-linearity of an ADC is due to the integral non-linearity of the front-end and SHA as well as the overall integral non-linearity in the ADC transfer function. However, *differential non-linearity is due exclusively to the encoding process* and may vary considerably dependent on the ADC encoding architecture. Overall integral non-linearity produces distortion products whose amplitude varies as a function of the input signal amplitude. For instance, second-order intermodulation products increase 2dB for every 1dB increase in signal level, and third-order products increase 3dB for every 1dB increase in signal level.

QUANTIFYING ADC DYNAMIC PERFORMANCE

- Harmonic Distortion
- Worst Harmonic
- Total Harmonic Distortion (THD)
- Total Harmonic Distortion Plus Noise (THD + N)
- Signal-to-Noise-and-Distortion Ratio (SINAD, or S/N +D)
- Effective Number of Bits (ENOB)
- Signal-to-Noise Ratio (SNR)
- Analog Bandwidth (Full-Power, Small-Signal)
- Spurious Free Dynamic Range (SFDR)
- Two-Tone Intermodulation Distortion
- Noise Power Ratio (NPR)

Figure 4.15

The differential non-linearity in the ADC transfer function produces distortion products which not only depend on the amplitude of the signal but the positioning of the differential non-linearity along the ADC transfer function. Figure 4.16 shows two ADC transfer functions containing differential non-linearity. The left-hand diagram shows an error which occurs at midscale. Therefore, for both large and small signals, the signal crosses through this point producing a distortion product which is relatively independent of the signal amplitude. The right-hand diagram shows another ADC transfer function which has differential non-linearity errors at 1/4 and 3/4 full scale. Signals which are above 1/2 scale peak-to-peak will exercise these codes, while those less and 1/2 scale peak-to-peak will not.

The design of most high-speed ADCs is such that differential non-linearity is spread across the entire ADC range. Therefore, for signals which are within a few dB of full scale, the overall inte-

ADC DNL ERRORS

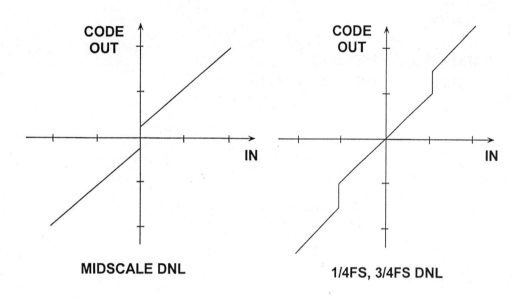

Figure 4.16

gral non-linearity of the transfer function determines the distortion products. For lower level signals, however, the harmonic content becomes dominated by the differential non-linearities and does not generally decrease proportionally with decreases in signal amplitude.

Harmonic Distortion, Worst Harmonic, Total Harmonic Distortion (THD), Total Harmonic Distortion Plus Noise (THD + N)

There are a number of ways to quantify the distortion of an ADC. An FFT analysis can be used to measure the amplitude of the various harmonics of a signal as shown in Figure 4.17. The harmonics of the input signal can be distinguished from other distortion products by their location in the frequency spectrum. The figure shows a 7MHz input signal sampled at 20MSPS and the location of the first 9 harmonics. Aliased harmonics of f_a fall at frequencies equal to $|\pm Kf_s \pm nf_a|$, where n is the order of the harmonic, and K = 0, 1, 2, 3,.... The second and third harmonics are generally the only ones specified on a data sheet because they tend to be the largest, although some data sheets may specify the value of the *worst* harmonic. Harmonic distortion is normally specified in dBc (decibels below carrier), although at audio frequencies it may be specified as a percentage. Harmonic distortion is specified with an input signal near full scale (generally 0.5 to 1dB below full scale to prevent clipping). For signals much lower than full scale, other distortion products (not direct harmonics) may limit performance.

LOCATION OF HARMONIC DISTORTION PRODUCTS: INPUT SIGNAL = 7MHz, SAMPLING RATE = 20MSPS

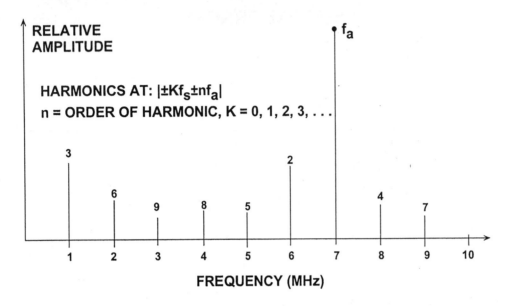

Figure 4.17

Total harmonic distortion (THD) is the ratio of the rms value of the fundamental signal to the mean value of the root-sum-square of its harmonics (generally, only the first 5 are significant). THD of an ADC is also generally specified with the input signal close to full scale.

Total harmonic distortion plus noise (THD+ N) is the ratio of the rms value

of the fundamental signal to the mean value of the root-sum-square of its harmonics plus all noise components (excluding DC). The bandwidth over which the noise is measured must be specified. In the case of an FFT, the bandwidth is DC to $f_s/2$. (If the bandwidth of the measurement is DC to $f_s/2$, THD+N is equal to SINAD - see below).

Signal-to-Noise-and-Distortion Ratio (SINAD), Signal-to-Noise Ratio (SNR), and Effective Number of Bits (ENOB)

SINAD and SNR deserve careful attention, because there is still some variation between ADC manufacturers as to their precise meaning. Signal-to-noise-and Distortion (SINAD, or S/N+D) is the ratio of the rms signal amplitude to the mean value of the root-sum-square (RSS) of all other spectral components, *including harmonics*, but excluding DC. SINAD is a good indication of the over-

all dynamic performance of an ADC as a function of input frequency because it includes all components which make up noise (including thermal noise) and distortion. It is often plotted for various input amplitudes. SINAD is equal to THD+N if the bandwidth for the noise measurement is the same. A typical plot for the AD9220 12-bit, 10MSPS ADC is shown in Figure 4.19.

SINAD, ENOB, AND SNR

■ SINAD (Signal-to-Noise-and-Distortion Ratio):

The ratio of the rms signal amplitude to the mean value of
the root-sum-squares (RSS) of all other spectral components,
including harmonics, but excluding DC

■ ENOB (Effective Number of Bits):

$$ENOB = \frac{SINAD - 1.76dB}{6.02}$$

■ SNR (Signal-to-Noise Ratio, or Signal-to-Noise Ratio
Without Harmonics):

The ratio of the rms signal amplitude to the mean value of
the root-sum-squares (RSS) of all other spectral components,
excluding the first 5 harmonics and DC

Figure 4.18

AD9220 12-BIT, 10MSPS ADC SINAD AND ENOB
VS. INPUT FREQUENCY FOR SAMPLING RATE = 10MSPS:
SINGLE-ENDED DRIVE, V$_{cm}$ = +2.5V, INPUT SPAN = 2V p-p

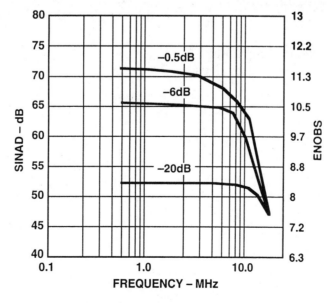

Figure 4.19

The SINAD plot shows where the AC performance of the ADC degrades due to high-frequency distortion and is usually plotted for frequencies well above the Nyquist frequency so that performance in undersampling applications can be evaluated. SINAD is often converted to effective-number-of-bits (ENOB) using the relationship for the theoretical SNR of an ideal N-bit ADC: SNR = 6.02N + 1.76dB. The equation is solved for N, and the value of SINAD is substituted for SNR:

$$ENOB = \frac{SINAD - 1.76dB}{6.02}.$$

Signal-to-noise ratio (SNR, or *SNR-without-harmonics*) is calculated the same as SINAD except that the signal harmonics are excluded from the calculation, leaving only the noise terms. In practice, it is only necessary to exclude the first 5 harmonics since they dominate. The SNR plot will degrade at high frequencies also, but not as rapidly as SINAD because of the exclusion of the harmonic terms.

Many current ADC data sheets somewhat loosely refer to SINAD as SNR, so the engineer must be careful when interpreting these specifications.

Analog Bandwidth

The analog bandwidth of an ADC is that frequency at which the spectral output of the *fundamental* swept frequency (as determined by the FFT analysis) is reduced by 3dB. It may be specified for either a small signal (SSBW- small signal bandwidth), or a full scale signal (FPBW- full power bandwidth), so there can be a wide variation in specifications between manufacturers.

Like an amplifier, the analog bandwidth specification of a converter does not imply that the ADC maintains good distortion performance up to its bandwidth frequency. In fact, the SINAD (or ENOB) of most ADCs will begin to degrade considerably before the input frequency approaches the actual 3dB bandwidth frequency. Figure 4.20 shows ENOB and full scale frequency response of an ADC with a FPBW of 1MHz, however, the ENOB begins to drop rapidly above 100kHz.

ADC GAIN (BANDWIDTH) AND ENOB VERSUS FREQUENCY SHOWS IMPORTANCE OF ENOB SPECIFICATION

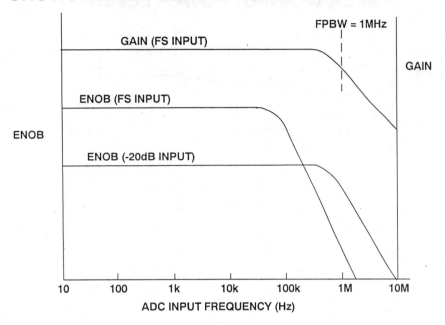

Figure 4.20

Spurious Free Dynamic Range (SFDR)

Probably the most significant specification for an ADC used in a communications application is its spurious free dynamic range (SFDR). The SFDR specification is to ADCs what the third order intercept specification is to mixers and LNAs. SFDR of an ADC is defined as the ratio of the rms signal amplitude to the rms value of the *peak spurious spectral content* (measured over the entire first Nyquist zone, DC to $f_s/2$). SFDR is generally plotted as a function of signal amplitude and may be expressed relative to the signal amplitude (dBc) or the ADC full scale (dBFS).

For a signal near full scale, the peak spectral spur is generally determined by one of the first few harmonics of the fundamental. However, as the signal

falls several dB below full scale, other spurs generally occur which are not direct harmonics of the input signal. This is because of the differential non-linearity of the ADC transfer function as discussed earlier. Therefore, SFDR considers *all* sources of distortion, regardless of their origin.

The AD9042 is a 12-bit, 41MSPS wideband ADC designed for communications applications where high SFDR is important. The SFDR for a 19.5MHz input and a sampling frequency of 41MSPS is shown in Figure 4.21. Note that a minimum of 80dBc SFDR is obtained over the entire first Nyquist zone (DC to 20MHz). The plot also shows SFDR expressed as dBFS.

AD9042 12-BIT, 41MSPS ADC
SFDR VS. INPUT POWER LEVEL

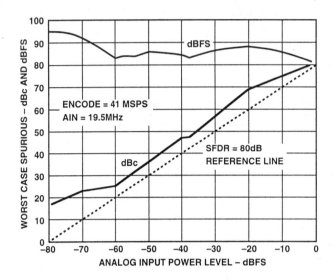

Figure 4.21

SFDR is generally much greater than the ADCs theoretical N-bit SNR (6.02N + 1.76dB). For example, the AD9042 is a 12-bit ADC with an SFDR of 80dBc and a typical SNR of 65dBc (theoretical SNR is 74dB). This is because there is a fundamental distinction between noise and distortion measurements. The process gain of the FFT (33dB for a 4096-point FFT) allows frequency spurs well below the noise floor to be observed. Adding extra resolution to an ADC may serve to increase its SNR but may or may not increase its SFDR.

Two Tone Intermodulation Distortion

Two tone IMD is measured by applying two spectrally pure sinewaves to the ADC at frequencies f1 and f2, usually relatively close together. The amplitude of each tone is set slightly more than 6dB below full scale so that the ADC does not clip when the two tones add in-phase. The location of the second and third-order products are shown in Figure 4.22. Notice that the second-order products fall at frequencies which can be removed by digital filters. However, the third-order products 2f2–f1 and 2f1–f2 are close to the original signals and are more difficult to filter. Unless otherwise specified, two-tone IMD refers to these third-order products. The value of the IMD product is expressed in dBc relative to the value of *either* of the two original tones, and not to their sum.

SECOND AND THIRD-ORDER INTERMODULATION
PRODUCTS FOR f₁ = 5MHz, f₂=6MHz

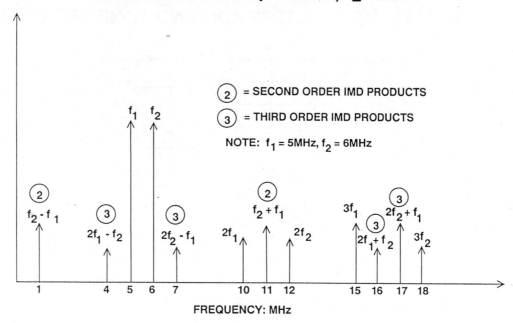

Figure 4.22

Note, however, that if the two tones are close to $f_s/4$, then the aliased third harmonic of the fundamental can make the identification of the actual 2f2–f1 and 2f1–f2 products difficult. Similarly, if the two tones are close to $f_s/3$, the aliased second harmonic may interfere with the measurement.

The concept of *second and third-order intercept points* is not valid for an ADC, because the distortion products do not vary in a predictable manner (as a function of signal amplitude). The ADC does not gradually begin to compress signals approaching full scale (there is

no 1dB compression point), it acts as a *hard limiter* as soon as the signal exceeds the ADC input range, thereby suddenly producing extreme amounts of distortion because of clipping.

On the other hand, for signals much below full scale, the distortion floor remains relatively constant and is independent of signal level. This is illustrated in Figure 4.23 for the AD9042, where two-tone SFDR is plotted as a function of signal level. The plot indicates that the distortion floor ranges from 85 to 90dBFS regardless of the input signal amplitude.

AD9042 12-BIT, 41MSPS ADC TWO-TONE SFDR

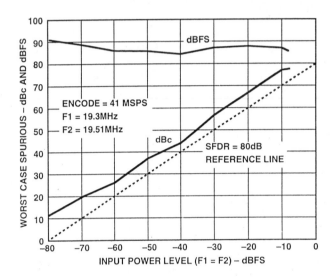

Figure 4.23

Noise Power Ratio (NPR)

Noise power ratio testing has been used extensively to measure the transmission characteristics of Frequency Division Multiplexed (FDM) communications links (see Reference 4). In a typical FDM system, 4kHz wide voice channels are "stacked" in frequency bins for transmission over coaxial, microwave, or satellite equipment. At the receiving end, the FDM data is demultiplexed and returned to 4kHz individual baseband channels. In an FDM system having more than approximately 100 channels, the FDM signal can be approximated by Gaussian noise with the appropriate bandwidth. An individual 4kHz channel can be measured for "quietness" using a narrow-band notch (bandstop) filter and a specially tuned receiver which measures the noise power inside the 4kHz notch (see Figure 4.24).

Noise Power Ratio (NPR) measurements are straightforward. With the notch filter out, the rms noise power of the signal inside the notch is measured by the narrowband receiver. The notch filter is then switched in, and the residual noise inside the slot is measured. The ratio of these two readings expressed in dB is the NPR. Several slot frequencies across the noise bandwidth (low, midband, and high) are tested to characterize the system adequately. NPR measurements on ADCs are made in a similar manner except the analog receiver is replaced by a buffer memory and an FFT processor.

NPR is usually plotted on an NPR curve. The NPR is plotted as a function of rms noise level referred to the peak range of the system. For very low noise loading level, the undesired noise (in non-digital systems) is primarily thermal noise and is independent of the input noise level. Over this region of the curve, a 1dB increase in noise loading level causes a 1dB increase in NPR. As the noise loading level is increased, the amplifiers in the system begin to overload, creating intermodulation products which cause the noise floor of the system to increase. As the input noise increases further, the effects of "overload" noise predominate, and the NPR is reduced dramatically. FDM systems are usually operated at a noise loading level a few dB below the point of maximum NPR.

In a digital system containing an ADC, the noise within the slot is primarily quantization noise when low levels of noise input are applied. The NPR curve is linear in this region. As the noise level increases, there is a one-for-one correspondence between the noise level and the NPR. At some level, however, "clipping" noise caused by the hard-limiting action of the ADC begins to dominate. A theoretical curve for 10, 11, and 12-bit ADCs is shown in Figure 4.25 (see Reference 5). Peak NPR and corresponding loading levels are shown in Figure 4.26.

NOISE POWER RATIO (NPR) MEASUREMENTS

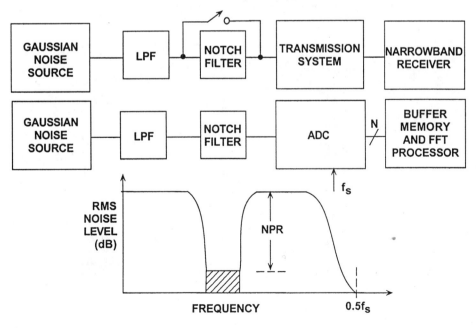

Figure 4.24

THEORETICAL NPR FOR 10, 11, 12-BIT ADCs

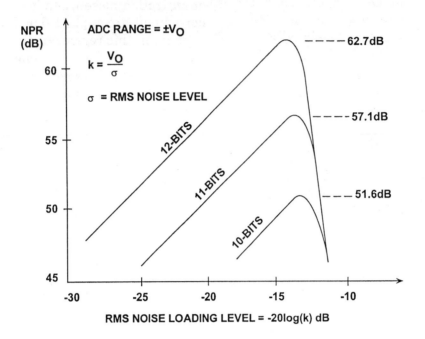

Figure 4.25

THEORETICAL NPR SUMMARY

BITS	k OPTIMUM	k(dB)	MAX NPR (dB)
8	3.92	11.87	40.60
9	4.22	12.50	46.05
10	4.50	13.06	51.56
11	4.76	13.55	57.12
12	5.01	14.00	62.71
13	5.26	14.41	68.35
14	5.49	14.79	74.01
15	5.72	15.15	79.70
16	5.94	15.47	85.40

ADC Range = $\pm V_O$

$k = V_O / \sigma$

σ = RMS Noise Level

Figure 4.26

In multi-channel high frequency communication systems, NPR can also be used to simulate the distortion caused by a large number of individual channels, similar to an FDM system. A notch filter is placed between the noise source and the ADC, and an FFT output is used in place of the analog receiver. The width of the notch filter is set for several MHz as shown in Figure

4.27 for the AD9042. NPR is the "depth" of the notch. An ideal ADC will only generate quantization noise inside the notch, however a practical one has additional noise components due to intermodulation distortion caused by ADC non-linearity. Notice that the NPR is about 60dB compared to 62.7dB theoretical.

AD9042 12-BIT, 41MSPS ADC NPR MEASURES 60dB (62.7dB THEORETICAL)

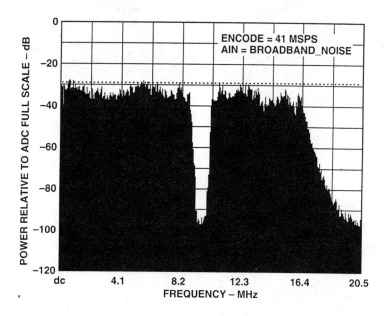

Figure 4.27

Aperture Jitter and Aperture Delay

Another reason that the SNR of an ADC decreases with input frequency may be deduced from Figure 4.28, which shows the effects of phase jitter (or aperture time jitter) on the sampling clock of an ADC (or internal in the sample-and-hold). The phase jitter causes a voltage error which is a func-

tion of slew rate and results in an overall degradation in SNR as shown in Figure 4.29. This is quite serious, especially at higher input/output frequencies. Therefore, extreme care must be taken to minimize phase noise in the sampling/reconstruction clock of any sampled data system. This care must extend to all aspects of the clock signal: the oscillator itself (for example, a 555 timer is absolutely inadequate, but even a quartz crystal oscillator can give problems if it uses an active device which shares a chip with noisy logic); the transmission path (these clocks are very vulnerable to interference of all sorts), and phase noise introduced in the ADC or DAC. A very common source of phase noise in converter circuitry is aperture jitter in the integral sample-and-hold (SHA) circuitry.

A decade or so ago, sampling ADCs were built up from a separate SHA and ADC. Interface design was difficult, and a key parameter was aperture jitter in the SHA. Today, most sampled data systems use *sampling* ADCs which contain an integral SHA. The aperture jitter of the SHA may not be specified

EFFECTS OF APERTURE AND SAMPLING CLOCK JITTER

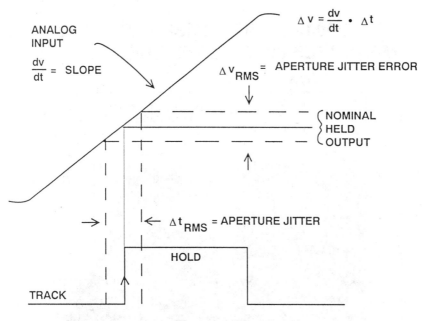

Figure 4.28

as such, but this is not a cause of concern if the SNR or ENOB is clearly specified, since a guarantee of a specific SNR is an implicit guarantee of an adequate aperture jitter specification. However, the use of an additional high-performance SHA will sometimes improve the high-frequency ENOB of a even the best sampling ADC by presenting "DC" to the ADC, and may be more cost-effective than replacing the ADC with a more expensive one.

It should be noted that there is also a fixed component which makes up the

ADC aperture time. This component, usually called *effective aperture delay time,* does not produce an error. It simply results in a time offset between the time the ADC is asked to sample and when the actual sample takes place (see Figure 4.30), and may be positive or negative. The variation or tolerance placed on this parameter from part to part is important in simultaneous sampling applications or other applications such as I and Q demodulation where two ADCs are required to track each other.

SNR DUE TO APERTURE AND SAMPLING CLOCK JITTER

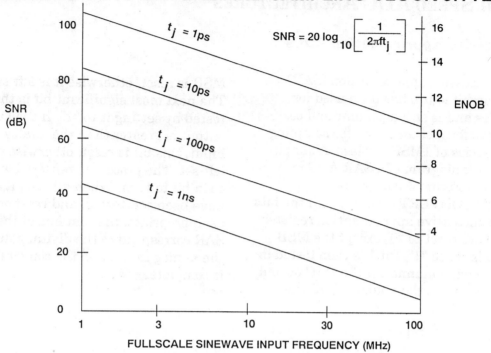

$$SNR = 20 \log_{10}\left[\frac{1}{2\pi f t_j}\right]$$

Figure 4.29

EFFECTIVE APERTURE DELAY TIME

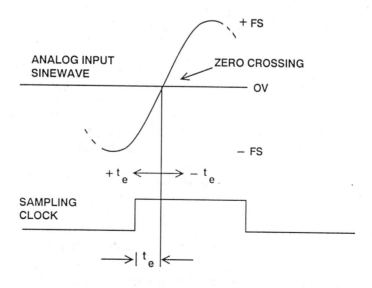

Figure 4.30

HIGH SPEED ADC ARCHITECTURES

Successive Approximation ADCs

The successive approximation (SAR) ADC architecture has been used for decades and is still a popular and cost effective form of converter for sampling frequencies of 1MSPS or less. A simplified block diagram of a SAR ADC is shown in Figure 4.31. On the START CONVERT command, all the bits of the successive approximation register (SAR) are reset to "0" except the MSB which is set to "1". Bit 1 is then tested in the following manner: If the DAC output is greater than the analog input, the

MSB is reset, otherwise it is left set. The next most significant bit is then tested by setting it to "1". If the DAC output is greater than the analog input, this bit is reset, otherwise it is left set. The process is repeated with each bit in turn. When all the bits have been set, tested, and reset or not as appropriate, the contents of the SAR correspond to the digital value of the analog input, and the conversion is complete.

SUCCESSIVE APPROXIMATION ADC

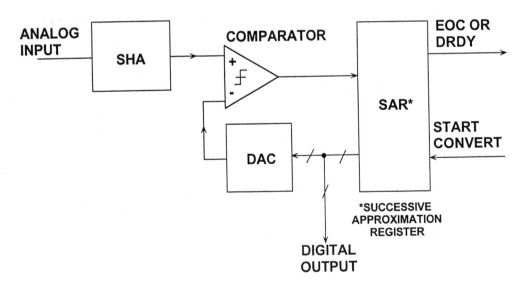

Figure 4.31

An N-bit conversion takes N steps. It would seem on superficial examination that a 16-bit converter would have a conversion time that is twice as long as an 8-bit one, but this is not the case. In an 8-bit converter, the DAC must settle

to 8-bit accuracy before the bit decision is made, whereas in a 16-bit converter, it must settle to 16-bit accuracy, which takes a lot longer. In practice, 8-bit successive approximation ADCs can convert in a few hundred nanoseconds, while 16-bit ones will generally take several microseconds.

The classic SAR ADC is only a quantizer: no sampling takes place, and for an accurate conversion, the input must remain constant for the entire conversion period. Most modern SAR ADCs are sampling types and have an internal sample-and-hold so that they can process AC signals. They are specified for both AC and DC applications. A SHA is required in a SAR ADC because the signal must remain constant during the entire N-bit conversion cycle.

The accuracy of a SAR ADC depends primarily on the accuracy (differential and integral linearity, gain, and offset) of the internal DAC. Until recently, this accuracy was achieved using laser trimmed thin film resistors. Modern SAR ADCs utilize CMOS switched capacitor charge redistribution DACs. This type of DAC depends on the accurate ratio matching and stability of on-chip capacitors rather than thin film resistors. For resolutions greater than 12-bits, on-chip autocalibration techniques using an additional *calibration DAC* and the accompanying logic can accomplish the same thing as thin film laser trimmed resistors, at much less cost. Therefore, the entire ADC can be made on a standard sub-micron CMOS process.

The successive approximation ADC has a very simple structure, is low power, and has reasonably fast conversion times (<1MSPS). It is probably the most widely used ADC architecture, and will continue to be used for medium speed and medium resolution applications.

Current 12-bit SAR ADCs achieve sampling rates up to about 1MSPS, and 16-bit ones up to about 300kSPS. Examples of typical state-of-the-art SAR ADCs are the AD7892 (12-bits at 600kSPS), the AD976/977 (16-bits at 100kSPS), and the AD7882 (16-bits at 300kSPS).

4

Flash Converters

Flash ADCs (sometimes called *parallel* ADCs) are the fastest type of ADC and use large numbers of comparators. An N-bit flash ADC consists of 2^N resistors and 2^N-1 comparators arranged as in Figure 4.32. Each comparator has a reference voltage which is 1 LSB higher than that of the one below it in the chain. For a given input voltage, all the comparators below a certain point will have their input voltage larger than their reference voltage and a "1" logic output, and all the comparators above that point will have a reference voltage larger than the input voltage and a "0" logic output. The 2^N-1 comparator outputs therefore behave in a way analogous to a mercury thermometer, and the output code at this point is sometimes called a *thermometer* code. Since 2^N-1 data outputs are not really practical, they are processed by a decoder to an N-bit binary output.

FLASH OR PARALLEL ADC

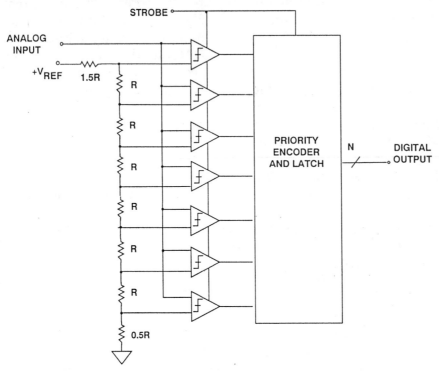

Figure 4.32

The input signal is applied to all the comparators at once, so the thermometer output is delayed by only one comparator delay from the input, and the encoder N-bit output by only a few gate delays on top of that, so the process is very fast. However, the architecture uses large numbers of resistors and comparators and it limited to low resolutions, and if it is to be fast, each comparator must run at relatively high power levels. Hence, the problems of flash ADCs include limited resolution, high power dissipation because of the large number of high speed comparators (especially at sampling rates greater than 50MSPS), and relatively large (and therefore expensive) chip sizes. In addition, the resistance of the reference resistor chain must be kept low to supply adequate bias current to the fast comparators, so the voltage reference has to source quite large currents (>10 mA).

In practice, flash converters are available up to 10-bits, but more commonly they have 8-bits of resolution. Their maximum sampling rate can be as high as 500 MSPS, and input full-power bandwidths in excess of 300 MHz.

But as mentioned earlier, full-power bandwidths are not necessarily full-resolution bandwidths. Ideally, the comparators in a flash converter are well matched both for DC and AC characteristics. Because the strobe is applied to all the comparators simultaneously, the flash converter is inherently a sampling converter. In practice, there are delay variations between the comparators and other AC mismatches which cause a degradation in ENOB at high input frequencies. This is because the inputs are slewing at a rate comparable to the comparator conversion time.

The input to a flash ADC is applied in parallel to a large number of comparators. Each has a voltage-variable junction capacitance, and this signal-dependent capacitance results in all flash ADCs having reduced ENOB and higher distortion at high input frequencies. A model is shown in Figure 4.33, where the input capacitance is modeled as a fixed 10pF capacitor in parallel with a variable capacitor

(modeled as a diode with a zero-bias junction capacitance of 6pF). As the input changes from −FS to +FS, the total input capacitance changes from about 12.5 to 16pF. The wideband external drive amplifier is isolated from the flash converter by a 50Ω series resistor. The distortion of this circuit degrades from about 70dBc at 1MHz to 35dBc at 100MHz.

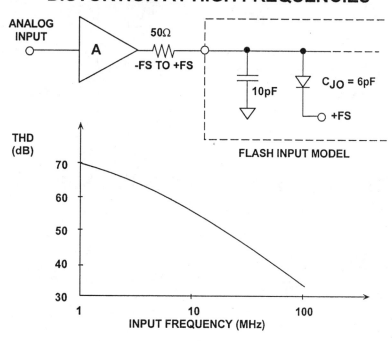

Figure 4.33

High data rate digital communications applications such as set-top boxes for direct broadcast satellites (DBS) require dual 6 or 8-bit high speed ADCs to perform quadrature demodulation. A dual flash converter ensures good matching between the two ADCs. The AD9066 (dual 6-bit, 60MSPS) flash converter is representative of this type

of converter. The AD9066 is fabricated on a BiCMOS process, operates on a single +5V supply, and dissipates 400mW. The effective bit performance of the device is shown in Figure 4.34. Note that the device maintains greater than 5 ENOBs up to 60MSPS analog input.

AD9066 DUAL 6-BIT, 60MSPS ADC ENOB
VS. ANALOG INPUT FREQUENCY

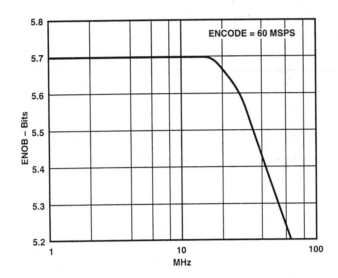

Figure 4.34

"INTERPOLATING" FLASH REDUCES THE NUMBER
OF PREAMPLIFIERS BY FACTOR OF TWO

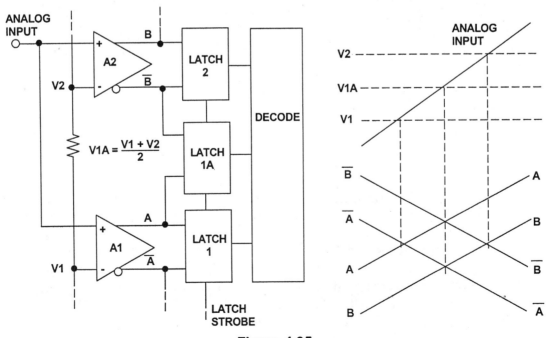

Figure 4.35

Part of the reason for the excellent performance of the AD9066 is the use of an interpolation scheme that reduces the number of differential amplifiers required by a factor of two (see Reference 6). The architecture enables 64 possible quantization levels to be determined with only 32 preamplifiers which drive 63 latches. This keeps the input capacitance to a minimum (10pF) and reduces total power dissipation of the device. The basic interpolation circuit is shown in Figure 4.35.

The preamplifiers are low-gain g_m stages whose bandwidth is proportional to the tail currents of the differential pairs. Consider the case for a positive-going ramp input which is initially below the reference to AMP A1, V1. As the input signal approaches V1, the differential output of A1 approaches zero (i.e., $A = \overline{A}$), and the decision point is reached. The output of A1 drives the differential input of LATCH 1. As the input signals continues to go positive, A continues to go positive, and $\overline{B}$ begins to go negative. The interpolated decision point is determined when $A = \overline{B}$. As the input continues positive, the third decision point is reached when $B = \overline{B}$. This novel architecture reduces the ADC input capacitance and thereby minimizes its change with signal level and the associated distortion. The input capacitance of the AD9066 is only about 10pF. Key specifications for the device are summarized in Figure 4.36.

4

AD9066 DUAL 6-BIT, 60MSPS FLASH ADC
KEY SPECIFICATIONS

■ Input Range: 500mV p-p

■ Input Impedance: 50kΩ || 10pF

■ ENOB: 5.7bits @ 15.5MHz Input

■ On-Chip Reference

■ Power Supply: Single +5V

■ Power Dissipation: 400mW

■ Package: 28-pin SOIC

■ Ideal for Quadrature Demodulation

Figure 4.36

Subranging (Pipelined) ADCs

Although it is not practical to make flash ADCs with high resolution, flash ADCs are often used as subsystems in "subranging" ADCs (sometimes known as "half-flash ADCs"), which are capable of much higher resolutions (up to 16-bits).

A block diagram of an 8-bit subranging ADC based upon two 4-bit flash converters is shown in Figure 4.37. Although 8-bit flash converters are readily available at high sampling rates, this example will be used to illustrate the theory. The conversion process is done in two steps. The first

four significant bits (MSBs) are digitized by the first flash (to better than 8-bits accuracy), and the 4-bit binary output is applied to a 4-bit DAC (again, better than 8-bit accurate). The DAC output is subtracted from the held analog input, and the resulting residue signal is amplified and applied to the second 4-bit flash. The outputs of the two 4-bit flash converters are then combined into a single 8-bit binary output word. If the residue signal range does not exactly fill the range of the second flash converter, non-linearities and perhaps missing codes will result.

8-BIT SUBRANGING ADC

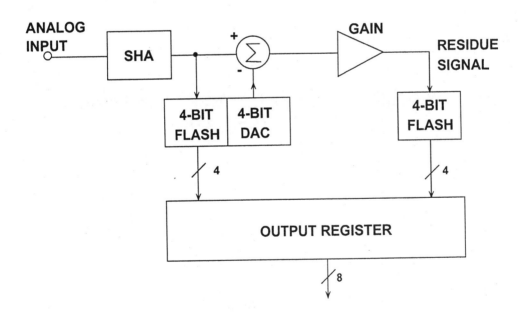

Figure 4.37

Modern subranging ADCs use a technique called *digital correction* to eliminate problems associated with the architecture of Figure 4.37. A simplified block diagram of a 12-bit digitally corrected subranging (DCS) ADC is shown in Figure 4.38. The architecture

is similar to that used in the AD9042 12-bit, 41MSPS ADC. Note that a 6-bit and an 7-bit ADC have been used to achieve an overall 12-bit output. These are not flash ADCs, but utilize a *magnitude-amplifier (MagAmp™)* architecture which will be described shortly.

AD9042 12-BIT, 41MSPS PIPELINED SUBRANGING ADC WITH DIGITAL ERROR CORRECTION

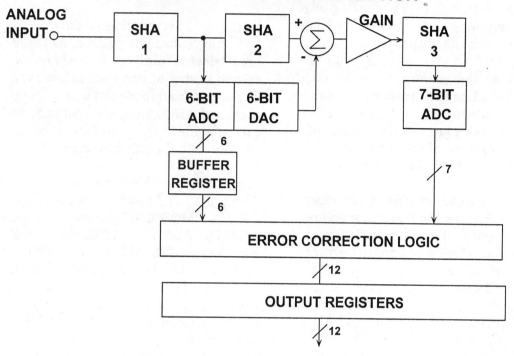

Figure 4.38

If there were no errors in the first-stage conversion, the 6-bit "residue" signal applied to the 7-bit ADC by the summing amplifier would never exceed one-half of the range of the 7-bit ADC. The extra range in the second ADC is used in conjunction with the error correction logic (usually just a full adder) to correct the output data for most of the errors inherent in the traditional uncorrected subranging converter architecture. It is important to note that the 6-bit DAC must be better than 12-bit accurate, because the digital error correction does not correct for DAC errors. In practice, "thermometer" or "fully-decoded" DACs using one current switch per level (63 switches in the case of a 6-bit DAC) are often used instead of a "binary" DAC to ensure excellent differential and integral linearity and minimum switching transients.

The second SHA delays the held output of the first SHA while the first-stage conversion occurs, thereby maximizing throughput. The third SHA serves to *deglitch* the residue output signal, thereby allowing a full conversion cycle for the 7-bit ADC to make its decision (the 6 and 7-bit ADCs in the AD9042 are bit-serial *MagAmp* ADCs which require more settling time than a flash converter).

This multi-stage conversion technique is sometimes referred to as "pipelining." Additional shift registers in series with the digital outputs of the first-stage ADC ensure that its output is ultimately time-aligned with the last 7 bits from the second ADC when their outputs are combined in the error correction logic. A pipelined ADC therefore has a specified number of clock cycles of *latency*, or *pipeline delay* associated with the output data. The leading edge of the sampling clock (for sample N) is used to clock the output register, but the data which appears as a result of that clock edge corresponds to sample N − L, where L is the number of clock cycles of latency. In the case of the AD9042, there are two clock cycles of latency. Key specifications for the AD9042 are shown in Figure 4.39.

The error correction scheme described above is designed to correct for errors made in the first conversion. Internal ADC gain, offset, and linearity errors are corrected as long as the residue signal fall within the range of the second-stage ADC. These errors will not affect the linearity of the overall ADC transfer characteristic. Errors made in the final conversion, however, do translate directly as errors in the overall transfer function. Also, linearity errors or gain errors either in the DAC or the residue amplifier will not be corrected and will show up as nonlinearities or

non-monotonic behavior in the overall ADC transfer function.

So far, we have considered only two-stage subranging ADCs, as these are easiest to analyze. There is no reason to stop at two stages, however. Three-pass and four-pass subranging pipelined ADCs are quite common, and can be made in many different ways, usually with digital error correction.

A simplified block diagram of the AD9220 12-bit, 10MSPS single-supply, 250mW CMOS ADC is shown in Figure 4.40. The AD9221 (1.25MSPS, 60mW) and the AD9223 (3MSPS, 100mW) ADCs use the identical architecture but operate at lower power and lower sampling rates. This is a four-stage pipelined architecture with an additional bit in the second, third, and fourth stage for error correction. Because of the pipelined architecture, these ADCs have a 3 clock-cycle latency (see Figure 4.41). Key specifications for the AD9220/9221/9223 are given in Figure 4.42.

AD9042 12-BIT, 41MSPS ADC KEY SPECIFICATIONS

- Input Range: 1V peak-to-peak, V_{cm} = +2.4V

- Input Impedance: 250Ω to V_{cm}

- Effective Input Noise: 0.33LSBs rms

- SFDR at 20MHz Input: 80dB minimum

- SINAD (S/N+D) at 20MHz Input = 67dB

- Digital Outputs: TTL Compatible

- Power Supply: Single +5V

- Power Dissipation: 595mW

- Fabricated on High Speed Dielectrically Isolated Complementary Bipolar Process

Figure 4.39

AD9220/9221/9223 12-BIT PIPELINED CMOS ADC

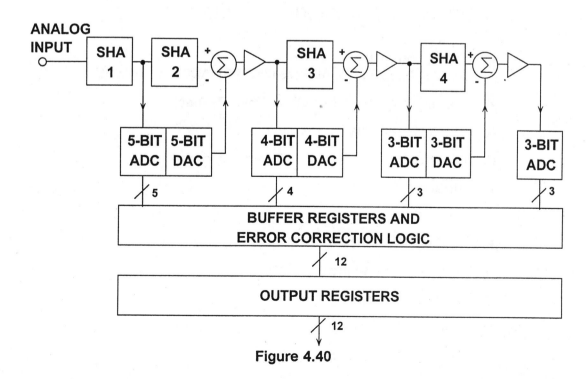

Figure 4.40

LATENCY (PIPELINE DELAY)
OF AD9220/9221/9223 ADC

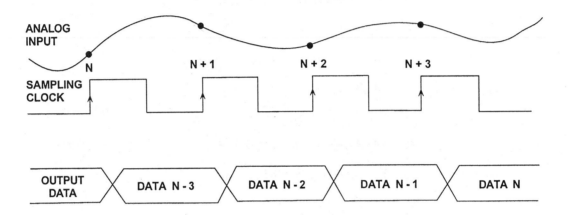

Figure 4.41

AD9220, AD9221, AD9223
CMOS 12-BIT ADCs KEY SPECIFICATIONS

- ■ Family Members:
  AD9221 (1.25MSPS), AD9223 (3MSPS), AD9220 (10MSPS)

- ■ Power Dissipation: 60, 100, 250mW, Respectively

- ■ FPBW: 25, 40, 60MHz, Respectively

- ■ Effective Input Noise: 0.1LSB rms (Span = 5V)

- ■ SINAD: 71dB

- ■ SFDR: 88dBc

- ■ On-Chip Reference

- ■ Differential Non-Linearity: 0.3LSB

- ■ Single +5V Supply

- ■ 28-Pin SOIC Package

Figure 4.42

Bit-Per-Stage (Serial, or Ripple) ADCs

Various architectures exist for performing A/D conversion using one stage per bit. In fact, a multistage subranging ADC with one bit per stage and no error correction is one form. Figure 4.43 shows the overall concept. The SHA holds the input signal constant during the conversion cycle. There are N stages, each of which have a bit output and a residue output. The residue output of one stage is the input to the next. The last bit is detected with a single comparator as shown.

BIT-PER-STAGE, SERIAL, OR RIPPLE ADC

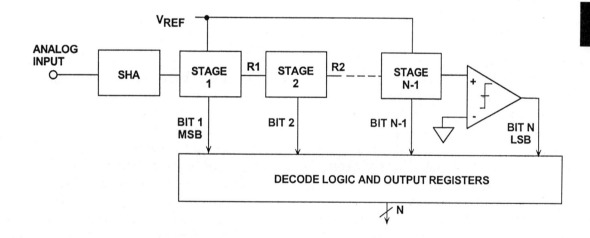

Figure 4.43

The basic stage for performing a single binary bit conversion is shown in Figure 4.44. It consists of a gain-of-two amplifier, a comparator, and a 1-bit DAC. The comparator detects the zero-crossing of the input and is the binary bit output for that stage. The comparator also switches a 1-bit DAC whose output is summed with the output of the gain-of-two amplifier. The resulting residue output is then applied to the next stage.

SINGLE-STAGE OF BINARY ADC

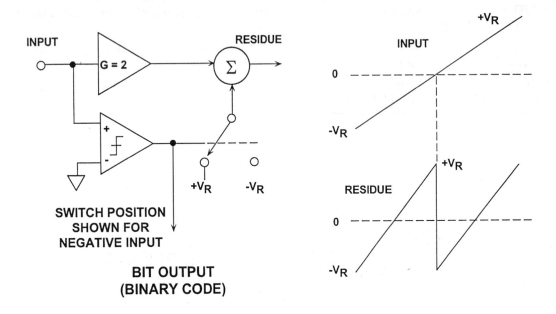

Figure 4.44

A simplified 3-bit serial-binary ADC is shown in Figure 4.45, and the residue outputs are shown in Figure 4.46. Each residue output signal has discontinuities which correspond to the point where the comparator changes state and causes the DAC to switch. The fundamental problem with this architecture is the discontinuity in the residue output waveforms. Adequate settling time must be allowed for these transients to propagate through all the stages and settle at the final comparator input. The prospects of making this architecture operate at high speed are therefore dismal.

A much better bit-per-stage architecture was developed by F.D. Waldhauer (Reference 7) based on absolute value amplifiers (magnitude amplifiers, or simply *MagAmps*™). This scheme has often been referred to as *serial-Gray* (since the output coding is in Gray code), or *folding* converter (References 8, 9, 10). The basic stage is shown functionally in Figure 4.47. The comparator detects the polarity of the input signal and provides the Gray bit output for the stage. It also determines whether the overall stage gain is +2 or –2. The reference voltage V_R is summed with the switch output to generate the residue signal which is applied to the next stage. The transfer function for the folding stage is also shown in Figure 4.47.

3-BIT SERIAL ADC WITH BINARY OUTPUT

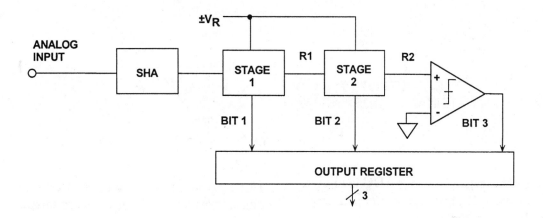

Figure 4.45

INPUT AND RESIDUE WAVEFORMS OF
3-BIT BINARY RIPPLE ADC

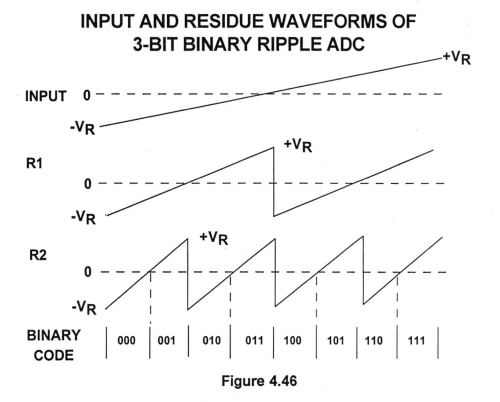

Figure 4.46

MagAmp STAGE FUNCTIONAL EQUIVALENT CIRCUIT

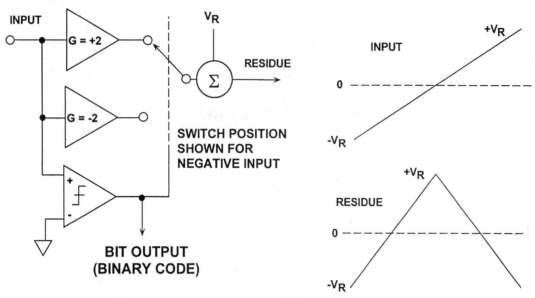

Figure 4.47

A 3-bit MagAmp folding ADC is shown in Figure 4.48, and the corresponding residue waveforms in Figure 4.49.

Notice that there is no abrupt transition in any of the folding stage output waveforms.

3-BIT MagAmp™ (FOLDING) ADC BLOCK DIAGRAM

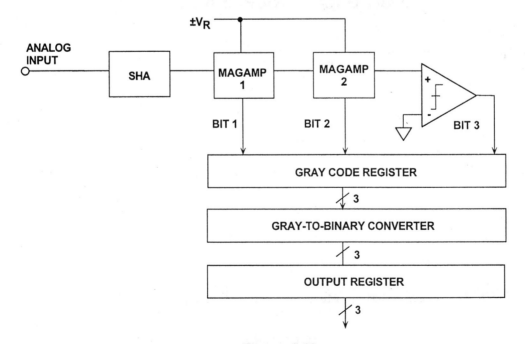

Figure 4.48

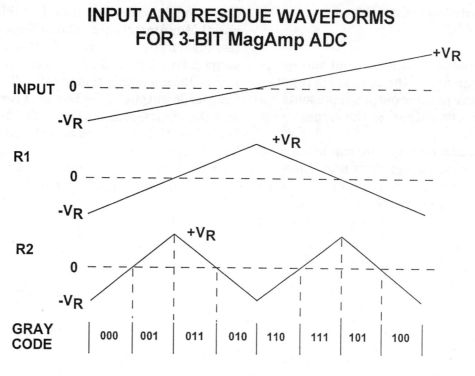

INPUT AND RESIDUE WAVEFORMS
FOR 3-BIT MagAmp ADC

Figure 4.49

The key to operating this architecture at high speeds is the folding stage. Early designs (see References 7, 8, 9) used discrete op amps with diodes inside the feedback loop to generate the folding transfer function. Modern IC circuit designs implement the transfer function using current-steering open-loop gain techniques which can be made to operate much faster. Fully differential stages (including the SHA) also provide speed, lower distortion, and yield 8-bit accurate folding stages with no requirement for thin film resistor laser trimming.

An example of a fully differential gain-of-two MagAmp folding stage is shown in Figure 4.50 (see References 11, 12, 13). The differential input signal is applied to the degenerated-emitter differential pair Q1,Q2 and the comparator. The differential input voltage is converted into a differential current which flows in the collectors of Q1, Q2. If +IN is greater than −IN, cascode-connected transistors Q3, Q6 are on, and Q4, Q6 are off. The differential signal currents therefore flow through the collectors of Q3, Q6 into level-shifting transistors Q7, Q8 and into the output load resistors, developing the differential output voltage between +OUT and −OUT. The overall differential voltage gain of the circuit is two.

If +IN is less than −IN (negative differential input voltage), the comparator changes stage and turns Q4, Q5 on and Q3, Q6 off. The differential signal currents flow from Q5 to Q7 and from Q4 to Q8, thereby maintaining the same relative polarity at the differential output as for a positive differential input voltage. The required offset voltage is developed by adding a current I_{OFF} to the emitter current of Q7 and subtracting it from the emitter current of Q8.

The differential residue output voltage of the stage drives the next stage input, and the comparator output represents the Gray code output for the stage.

The MagAmp architecture can be extended to sampling rates previously dominated by flash converters. The AD9059 8-bit, 60MSPS dual ADC is shown in Figure 4.51. The first five bits (Gray code) are derived from five differential MagAmp stages. The differential residue output of the fifth MagAmp stage drives a 3-bit flash converter, rather than a single comparator. The Gray-code output of the five MagAmps and the binary-code output of the 3-bit flash are latched, all converted into binary, and latched again in the output data register. Key specifications for the AD9059 are shown in Figure 4.52.

CIRCUIT DETAILS OF MagAmp STAGE

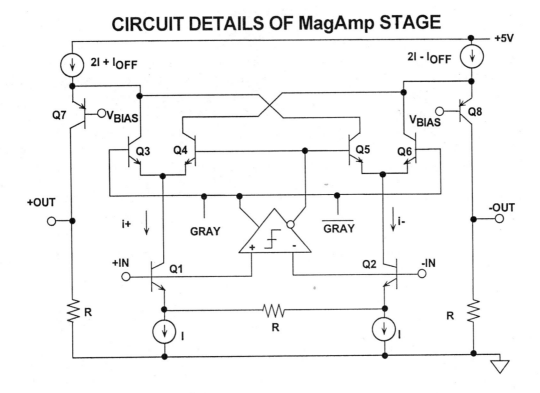

Figure 4.50

AD9059 DUAL 8-BIT, 60MSPS ADC FUNCTIONAL DIAGRAM

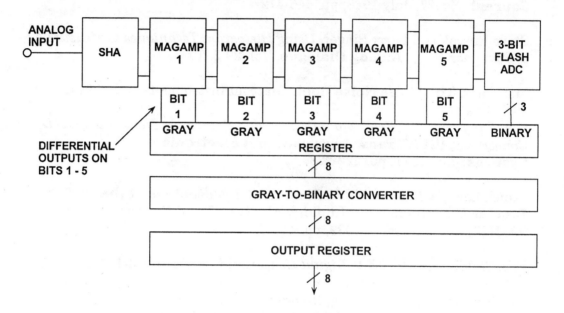

Figure 4.51

AD9059 DUAL 8-BIT, 60MSPS ADC KEY SPECIFICATIONS

- Input Range: 1V p-p, Vcm = +2.5V

- Input Impedance: 200kΩ || 5pF

- ENOB: 7.3 @ 10.3MHz Input

- On-Chip Reference

- Power Supply: Single +5V Supply (+5 or +3V Digital)

- Power Dissipation: 375mW (Power Down: 10mW)

- Package: 28-lead SSOP

- Ideal for Quadrature Demodulation in DBS Set-Top Boxes

Figure 4.52

REFERENCES

1. **Active and Passive Electrical Wave Filter Catalog**, Vol. 34, TTE, Incorporated, 2251 Barry Avenue, Los Angeles, CA 90064.

2. W. R. Bennett, "Spectra of Quantized Signals", **Bell System Technical Journal**, No. 27, July 1948, pp. 446-472.

3. Steve Ruscak and Larry Singer, *Using Histogram Techniques to Measure A/D Converter Noise*, **Analog Dialogue**, Vol. 29-2, 1995.

4. M.J. Tant, **The White Noise Book**, Marconi Instruments, July 1974.

5. G.A. Gray and G.W. Zeoli, *Quantization and Saturation Noise due to A/D Conversion*, **IEEE Trans. Aerospace and Electronic Systems**, Jan. 1971, pp. 222-223.

6. Chuck Lane, *A 10-bit 60MSPS Flash ADC*, **Proceedings of the 1989 Bipolar Circuits and Technology Meeting**, IEEE Catalog No. 89CH2771-4, September 1989, pp. 44-47.

7. F.D. Waldhauer, *Analog to Digital Converter*, **U.S. Patent 3-187-325**, 1965.

8. J.O. Edson and H.H. Henning, *Broadband Codecs for an Experimental 224Mb/s PCM Terminal*, **Bell System Technical Journal**, 44, November 1965, pp. 1887-1940.

9. **J.S. Mayo**, *Experimental 224Mb/s PCM Terminals*, **Bell System Technical Journal**, 44, November 1965, pp. 1813-1941.

10. Hermann Schmid, **Electronic Analog/Digital Conversions**, Van Nostrand Reinhold Company, New York, 1970.

11. Carl Moreland, *An 8-bit 150MSPS Serial ADC*, **1995 ISSCC Digest of Technical Papers**, Vol. 38, p. 272.

12. Roy Gosser and Frank Murden, *A 12-bit 50MSPS Two-Stage A/D Converter*, **1995 ISSCC Digest of Technical Papers**, p. 278.

13. Carl Moreland, **An Analog-to-Digital Converter Using Serial-Ripple Architecture**, Masters' Thesis, Florida State University College of Engineering, Department of Electrical Engineering, 1995.

14. **Practical Analog Design Techniques**, Analog Devices, 1995, Chapter 4, 5, and 8.

15. **Linear Design Seminar**, Analog Devices, 1995, Chapter 4, 5.

16. **System Applications Guide**, Analog Devices, 1993, Chapter 12, 13,15,16.

17.   **Amplifier Applications Guide**, Analog Devices, 1992, Chapter 7.

18.   Walt Kester, *Drive Circuitry is Critical to High-Speed Sampling ADCs*, **Electronic Design Special Analog Issue**, Nov. 7, 1994, pp. 43-50.

19.   Walt Kester, *Basic Characteristics Distinguish Sampling A/D Converters*, **EDN**, Sept. 3, 1992, pp. 135-144.

20.   Walt Kester, *Peripheral Circuits Can Make or Break Sampling ADC Systems*, **EDN**, Oct. 1, 1992, pp. 97-105.

21.   Walt Kester, *Layout, Grounding, and Filtering Complete Sampling ADC System*, **EDN**, Oct. 15, 1992, pp. 127-134.

22.   Robert A. Witte, *Distortion Measurements Using a Spectrum Analyzer*, **RF Design**, September, 1992, pp. 75-84.

23.   Walt Kester, *Confused About Amplifier Distortion Specs?*, **Analog Dialogue**, 27-1, 1993, pp. 27-29.

24.   **System Applications Guide**, Analog Devices, 1993, Chapter 16.

25.   Frederick J. Harris, *On the Use of Windows for Harmonic Analysis with the Discrete Fourier Transform*, **IEEE Proceedings**, Vol. 66, No. 1, Jan. 1978, pp. 51-83.

26.   Joey Doernberg, Hae-Seung Lee, David A. Hodges, *Full Speed Testing of A/D Converters*, **IEEE Journal of Solid State Circuits**, Vol. SC-19, No. 6, Dec. 1984, pp. 820-827.

27.   Brendan Coleman, Pat Meehan, John Reidy and Pat Weeks, *Coherent Sampling Helps When Specifying DSP A/D Converters*, **EDN**, October 15, 1987, pp. 145-152.

28.   Robert W. Ramierez, **The FFT: Fundamentals and Concepts**, Prentice-Hall, 1985.

29.   R. B. Blackman and J. W. Tukey, **The Measurement of Power Spectra**, Dover Publications, New York, 1958.

30.   James J. Colotti, *Digital Dynamic Analysis of A/D Conversion Systems Through Evaluation Software Based on FFT/DFT Analysis*, **RF Expo East 1987 Proceedings**, Cardiff Publishing Co., pp. 245-272.

31.   **HP Journal**, Nov. 1982, Vol. 33, No. 11.

32.   **HP Product Note** 5180A-2.

33.   **HP Journal**, April 1988, Vol. 39, No. 2.

4

34.   **HP Journal**, June 1988, Vol. 39, No. 3.

35.   Dan Sheingold, Editor, **Analog-to-Digital Conversion Handbook, Third Edition**, Prentice-Hall, 1986.

36.   Lawrence Rabiner and Bernard Gold, **Theory and Application of Digital Signal Processing**, Prentice-Hall, 1975.

37.   Matthew Mahoney, **DSP-Based Testing of Analog and Mixed-Signal Circuits**, IEEE Computer Society Press, Washington, D.C., 1987.

38.   **IEEE Trial-Use Standard for Digitizing Waveform Recorders**, No. 1057-1988.

39.   Richard J. Higgins, **Digital Signal Processing in VSLI**, Prentice-Hall, 1990.

40.   M. S. Ghausi and K. R. Laker, **Modern Filter Design: Active RC and Switched Capacitors**, Prentice Hall, 1981.

41.   Mathcad™ 4.0 software package available from MathSoft, Inc., 201 Broadway, Cambridge MA, 02139.

42.   Howard E. Hilton, *A 10MHz Analog-to-Digital Converter with 110dB Linearity*, **H.P. Journal**, October 1993, pp. 105-112.

SECTION 5

HIGH SPEED ADC APPLICATIONS

■ Driving ADC Inputs for Low Distortion and Wide
Dynamic Range

■ Applications of High Speed ADCs in CCD Imaging

■ High Speed ADC Applications in Digital Receivers

5

SECTION 5
HIGH SPEED ADC APPLICATIONS
Walt Kester, Brad Brannon, Paul Hendricks

DRIVING ADC INPUTS FOR LOW DISTORTION AND WIDE DYNAMIC RANGE

In order to achieve wide dynamic range in high speed ADC applications, careful attention must be given to the analog interface. Many ADCs are designed so that analog signals can be interfaced directly to their inputs without the necessity of a drive amplifier. This is especially true in ADCs such as the AD9220/21/23 family and the AD9042, where even a low distortion drive amplifier may result in some degradation in AC performance. If a buffer amplifier is required, it must be carefully selected so that its distortion and noise performance is better than that of the ADC.

Single-supply ADCs generally yield optimum AC performance when the common-mode input voltage is centered between the supply rails (although the optimum common-mode voltage may be skewed slightly in either direction about this point depending upon the particular design). This also eases the drive requirement on the input buffer amplifier (if required) since even "rail-to-rail" output op amps give best distortion performance if their output is centered about mid-supply, and the peak signals are kept at least 1V from either rail.

Typical high speed single-supply ADC peak-to-peak input voltage ranges may vary from about 0.5V to 5V, but in most cases, 1V to 2V peak-to-peak represents the optimum tradeoff between noise and distortion performance.

In single-supply applications requiring DC coupling, careful attention must be given to the input and output common-mode range of the driving amplifier. Level shifting is often required in order to center a ground-referenced signal within the allowable common-mode input range of the ADC.

Small RF transformers are quite useful in AC coupled applications, especially if the ADC has differential inputs. Significant improvement in even-order distortion products and common-mode noise rejection may be realized, depending upon the characteristics of the ADC.

An understanding of the input structure of the ADC is therefore necessary in order to properly design the analog interface circuitry. ADCs designed on CMOS processes typically connect the sample-and-hold switches directly to the analog input, thereby generating transient current pulses. These transients may significantly degrade performance if the settling time of the op amp is not sufficiently fast. On the other hand, ADCs designed on bipolar processes may present a relatively benign load to the drive amplifier with minimal transient currents.

5

The data sheet for the ADC is the prime source an engineer should use in designing the interface circuits. It should contain recommended interface circuits and spell out relevant tradeoffs. However, no data sheet can substitute for a fundamental understanding of what's inside the ADC.

HIGH SPEED ADC INPUT CONSIDERATIONS

- Selection of Drive Amplifier (Only if Needed!)

- Single Supply Implications

- Input Range (Span): Typically 1V to 2V peak-to-peak for best distortion / noise tradeoff

- Input Common-Mode Range: V_S / 2 (Nominally) for Single Supply ADCs

- Differential vs. Single-Ended

- AC Coupling Using Transformers

- Input Transient Currents

Figure 5.1

Switched-Capacitor Input ADCs

The AD9220/21/23-series of ADCs are excellent examples of the progress that has been made in utilizing low-cost CMOS processes to achieve a high level of performance. A functional block diagram is shown in Figure 5.2. This family of ADCs offers sampling rates of 1.25MSPS (AD9221), 3MSPS (AD9223), and 10MSPS (AD9220) at power dissipations of 60, 100, and 250mW respectively. Key specifications for the family of ADCs are given in Figure 5.3. The devices contain an on-chip reference voltage which allows the full scale span to be set at 2V or 5V peak-to-peak (full scale spans between 2V and 5V can be set by adding two external gain setting resistors).

AD922X-SERIES ADC FUNCTIONAL DIAGRAM

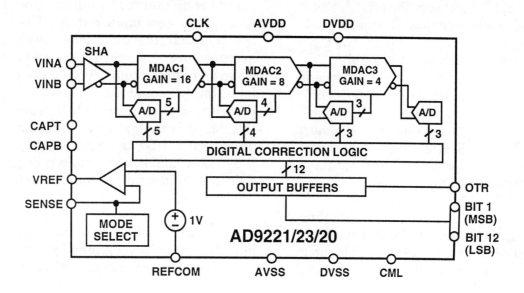

Figure 5.2

AD9220, AD9221, AD9223
CMOS 12-BIT ADCs KEY SPECIFICATIONS

- ■ Family Members:
  AD9221 (1.25MSPS), AD9223 (3MSPS), AD9220 (10MSPS)

- ■ Power Dissipation: 60, 100, 250mW, Respectively

- ■ FPBW: 25, 40, 60MHz, Respectively

- ■ Effective Input Noise: 0.1LSB rms (Span = 5V)

- ■ SINAD: 71dB

- ■ SFDR: 88dBc

- ■ On-Chip Reference

- ■ Differential Non-Linearity: 0.3LSB

- ■ Single +5V Supply

- ■ 28-Pin SOIC Package

Figure 5.3

5

The input circuit of the AD9220/21/23-series of CMOS ADCs contains the differential sample-and-hold as shown in Figure 5.4. The switches are shown in the track mode. They open and close at the sampling frequency. The 16pF capacitors represent the effective capacitance of switches S1 and S2 plus the stray input capacitance. The C_S capacitors (4pF) are the sampling capacitors, and the C_H capacitors are the hold capacitors. Although the input circuit is completely differential, the ADC can be driven either single-ended or differential. Optimum SFDR, however, is obtained using a differential transformer drive.

In the track mode, the differential input voltage is applied to the C_S capacitors. When the circuit enters the hold mode, the voltage across the sampling capacitors is transferred to the C_H hold capacitors and buffered by the amplifier A. (The switches are controlled by the appropriate phases of the sampling clock). When the SHA returns to the track mode, the input source must charge or discharge the voltage stored on C_S to the new input voltage. This action of charging and discharging C_S, averaged over a period of time and for a given sampling frequency f_S, makes the input impedance appear to have a benign resistive component. However, if this action is analyzed within a sampling period $(1/f_S)$, the input impedance is dynamic, and hence certain precautions on the input drive source should be observed.

The resistive component to the input impedance can be computed by calculating the average charge that is drawn

SIMPLIFIED INPUT CIRCUIT OF AD922X ADC FAMILY

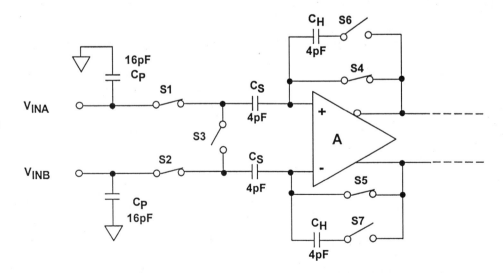

SWITCHES SHOWN IN TRACK MODE

Figure 5.4

AD922X ADC INPUT VOLTAGE RANGE OPTIONS

SINGLE-ENDED INPUT

Input Signal Range (Volts)	Peak-to-Peak Signal (Volts)	Common-Mode Voltage (Volts)
0 to +2	2	+1
0 to +5	5	+2.5
+1.5 to +3.5	2	+2.5

DIFFERENTIAL INPUT

Input Signal Range (Volts)	Peak-to-Peak Signal Differential (Volts)	Common-Mode Voltage (Volts)
+2 to +3	2	+2.5
+1.25 to +3.75	5	+2.5

Figure 5.5

AD9220 THD VS. INPUT FREQUENCY: SINGLE-ENDED DRIVE
2V p-p INPUT, V_{cm} = +1V AND V_{cm} = +2.5V, f_S = 10MSPS

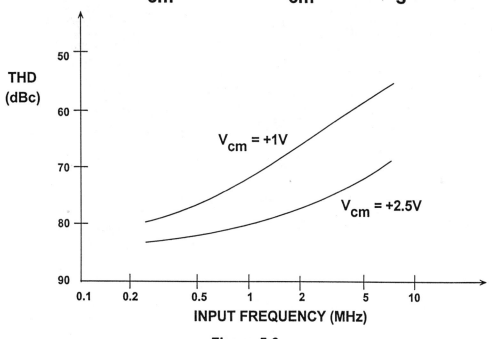

Figure 5.6

by C_H from the input drive source. It can be shown that if C_S is allowed to fully charge to the input voltage before switches S1 and S2 are opened that the average current into the input is the same as if there were a resistor equal to $1/(C_S f_S)$ connected between the inputs. Since C_S is only a few picofarads, this resistive component is typically greater than several kΩ for an $f_S = 10$MSPS.

If one considers the SHA's input impedance over a sampling period, it appears as a dynamic load to the input drive source. When the SHA returns to the track mode, the input source should ideally provide the charging current through the R_{on} of switches S1 and S2 in an exponential manner. The requirement of exponential charging means that the source impedance should be both low and resistive up to and beyond the sampling frequency.

The output impedance of an op amp can be modeled as a series inductor and resistor. When a capacitive load is switched onto the output of the op amp, the output will momentarily change due to its effective high frequency output impedance. As the output recovers, ringing may occur. To remedy this situation, a series resistor can be inserted between the op amp and the SHA input. The optimum value of this resistor is dependent on several factors including the sampling frequency and the op amp selected, but in most applications, a 30 to 50Ω resistor is optimum.

The input voltage span of the AD922X-family is set by pin-strap options using the internal voltage reference (see Figure 5.5). The common-mode voltage can be set by either pin strap or applying the common-mode voltage to the

SINGLE-ENDED AC-COUPLED
DRIVE CIRCUIT FOR AD922X ADC

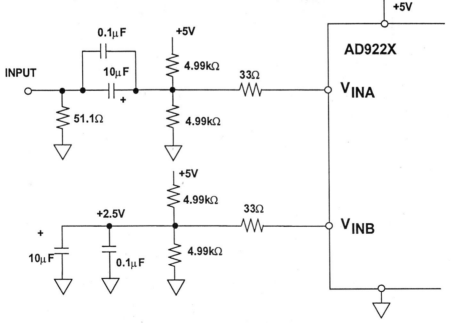

Figure 5.7

BUFFERED AC-COUPLED INPUT DRIVE
CIRCUIT FOR AD922X ADC

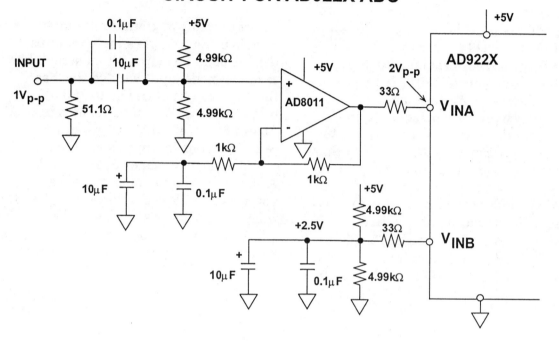

Figure 5.8

VINB pin. Tradeoffs can be made between noise and distortion performance. Maximum input range allowable is 5V peak-to-peak, in which case, the common-mode input voltage must be one-half the supply voltage, or +2.5V. The minimum input range is 2V peak-to-peak, in which case the common-mode input voltage can be set from +1V to +4V. For best DC linearity and maximum signal-to-noise ratio, the ADC should be operated with an input signal of 5V peak-to-peak. However, for best high frequency noise and distortion performance, 2V peak-to-peak with a common-mode voltage of +2.5V is preferred. This is because the CMOS FET on-resistance is a minimum at this voltage, and the non-linearity caused by the signal-dependence of R_{on} (R_{on} modulation effect) is also minimal.

Figure 5.6 shows the THD performance of the AD9220 for a 2V peak-to-peak input signal span and common-mode input voltage of 2.5V and 1V. The data was taken with a single-ended drive. Note that the performance is significantly better for $V_{cm} = +2.5V$.

A simple single-ended circuit for AC coupling into the inputs of the AD9220-family is shown in Figure 5.7. Note that the common-mode input voltage is set for +2.5V by the 4.99kΩ resistors. The input impedance is also balanced for optimum distortion performance.

If the input to the ADC is coming from a long coaxial cable run, it may be desirable to buffer the transient currents at the ADC inputs from the cable to prevent problems resulting from reflections, especially if the cable is not source-terminated. The circuit shown in Figure 5.8 uses the low distortion AD8011 op amp as a buffer which can optionally provide signal gain. In all cases, the feedback resistor should be fixed at 1kΩ for best op amp perfor- mance, since the AD8011 is a current- feedback type. In this type of arrangement, care must be taken to observe the allowable input and output range of the op amp. The AD8011 input common-mode range (operating on a single +5V supply) is from +1.5 to +3.5V, and its output +1V to +4V. The ADC should be operated with a 2V peak-to-peak input range. The 33Ω series resistor is required to isolate the output of the AD8011 from the effective

input capacitance of the ADC. The value was empirically determined to yield the best high-frequency SINAD.

Direct coupling of ground-referenced signals using a single supply requires the use of an op amp with an acceptable common-mode input voltage, such as the AD8041 (input can go to 200mV below ground). The circuit shown in Figure 5.9 level shifts the ground- referenced bipolar input signal to a common-mode voltage of +2.5V at the ADC input. The common-mode bias voltage of +2.5V is developed directly from an AD780 reference, and the AD8041 common-mode voltage of +1.25V is derived with a simple divider.

DIRECT-COUPLED LEVEL SHIFTER FOR DRIVING AD922X ADC INPUT

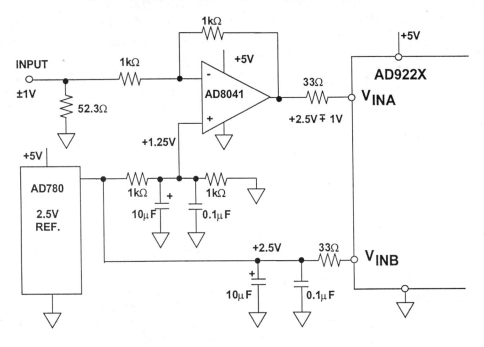

Figure 5.9

Transformer coupling provides the best CMR and the lowest distortion. Figure 5.10 shows the suggested circuit. The transformer is a Mini-Circuits RF transformer, model #T4-6T which has an impedance ratio of four (turns ratio of 2). The schematic assumes that the signal source has a 50Ω source impedance. The 1:4 impedance ratio requires the 200Ω secondary termination for optimum power transfer and VSWR. The Mini-Circuits T4-6T has a 1dB bandwidth from 100kHz to 100MHz. The center tap of the transformer provides a convenient means of level shifting the input signal to the optimum common-mode voltage. The AD922X CML pin is used to provide the +2.5 common-mode voltage.

Transformers with other turns ratios may also be selected to optimize the performance for a given application. For example, a given input signal source or amplifier may realize an improvement in distortion performance at reduced output power levels and signal swings. Hence, selecting a transformer with a higher impedance ratio (i.e. Mini-Circuits #T16-6T with a 1:16 impedance ratio, turns ratio 1:4) effectively "steps up" the signal level thus reducing the driving requirements of the signal source.

Note the 33Ω series resistors inserted between the transformer secondary and the ADC input. These values were specifically selected to optimize both the SFDR and the SNR performance of the ADC. They also provide isolation from transients at the ADC inputs. Transients currents are approximately equal on the VINA and VINB inputs, so they

TRANSFORMER COUPLING INTO AD922X ADC

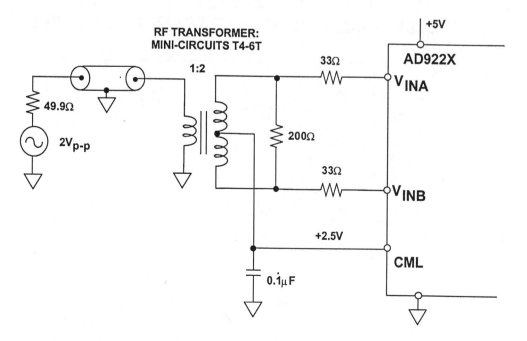

Figure 5.10

are isolated from the primary winding of the transformer by the transformer's common-mode rejection.

Transformer coupling using a common-mode voltage of +2.5V provides the maximum SFDR when driving the AD922X-series. By driving the ADC differentially, even-order harmonics are reduced compared with the single-ended circuit. Figure 5.11 shows a plot of SFDR and SNR for the transformer-coupled differential drive circuit using 2V p-p and 5V p-p inputs and a common-mode voltage of +2.5V. Note that the SFDR is greater than 80dBc for input signals up to full scale with a 5MHz input signal.

Figure 5.11 also shows differences between the SFDR and SNR performance for 2V p-p and 5V p-p inputs. Note that the SNR with a 5V p-p input is approximately 2dB to 3dB better than that for a 2V p-p input because of the additional dynamic range provided by the larger input range. Also, the SFDR performance using a 5V p-p input is 3 to 5dB better for signals between about –6dBFS and –36dBFS. This improvement in SNR and SFDR for the 5V p-p input range may be advantageous in systems which require more than 6dB headroom to minimize clipping of the ADC.

AD9220 SFDR AND SNR FOR 5Vp-p AND 2Vp-p INPUT:
Vcm = +2.5V, 5MHz INPUT, fs = 10MSPS
TRANSFORMER-COUPLED DIFFERENTIAL DRIVE

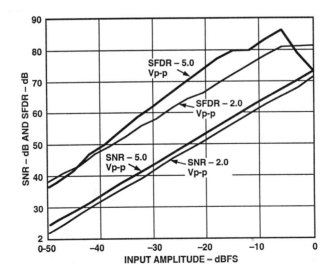

Figure 5.11

Driving Bipolar Input ADCs

Bipolar technology is typically used for extremely high performance ADCs with wide dynamic range and high sampling rates such as the AD9042. The AD9042 is a state-of-the-art 12-bit, 41MSPS two stage subranging ADC consisting of a 6-bit coarse ADC and a 7-bit residue ADC with one bit of overlap to correct for any DNL, INL, gain or offset errors of the coarse ADC, and offset errors in the residue path. A block diagram is shown in Figure 5.12 and key specifications in Figure 5.13. A proprietary gray-code architecture is used to implement the two internal ADCs. The gain alignments of the coarse and residue, likewise the subtraction DAC, rely on the statistical matching of the devices on the process. As a result, 12-bit integral and differential linearity is obtained without laser trim. The internal DAC consists of 126 interdigitated current sources. Also on the DAC reference, there are an additional 20 interdigitated current sources to set the coarse gain, residue gain, and full scale gain. The interdigitization removes the requirement for laser trim. The AD9042 is fabricated on a high speed dielectrically isolated complementary bipolar process. The total power dissipation is only 575mW when operating on a single +5V supply.

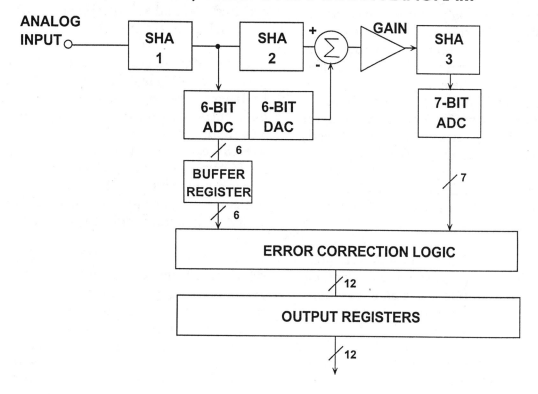

AD9042 12-BIT, 41MSPS ADC BLOCK DIAGRAM

Figure 5.12

AD9042 12-BIT, 41MSPS ADC KEY SPECIFICATIONS

- Input Range: 1V peak-to-peak, V_{cm} = +2.4V

- Input Impedance: 250Ω to V_{cm}

- Effective Input Noise: 0.33LSBs rms

- SFDR at 20MHz Input: 80dB

- SINAD at 20MHz Input = 66dB

- Digital Outputs: TTL Compatible

- Power Supply: Single +5V

- Power Dissipation: 575mW

- Fabricated on High Speed Dielectrically Isolated
  Complementary Bipolar Process

Figure 5.13

The outstanding performance of the AD9042 is partly due to the use of differential techniques throughout the device. The low distortion input amplifier converts the single-ended input signal into a differential one. If maximum SFDR performance is desired, the signal source should be coupled directly into the input of the AD9042 without using a buffer amplifier. Figure 5.14 shows a method using capacitive coupling. Transformer coupling can also be used if desired.

The AD9050 is a 10-bit, 40MSPS single supply ADC designed for wide dynamic range applications such as ultrasound, instrumentation, digital communications, and professional video. Like the AD9042, it is fabricated on a high speed complementary bipolar process. A block diagram of the AD9050 (Figure 5.15) illustrates the two-step subranging

architecture, and key specifications are summarized in Figure 5.16.

The analog input circuit of the AD9050 (see Figure 5.17) is differential, but can be driven either single-endedly or differentially with equal performance. The input signal range of the AD9050 is ±0.5V centered around a common-mode voltage of +3.3V, which makes single supply op amp selection more difficult since the amplifier has to drive +3.8V peak signals with low distortion.

The input circuit of the AD9050 is a relatively benign and constant 5kΩ in parallel with approximately 5pF. Because of its well-behaved input, the AD9050 can be driven directly from 50, 75, or 100Ω sources without the need for a low-distortion buffer amplifier. In ultrasound applications, it is normal to AC couple the signal (generally be-

INPUT STRUCTURE OF AD9042 ADC IS DESIGNED TO BE DRIVEN DIRECTLY FROM 50Ω SOURCE FOR BEST SFDR

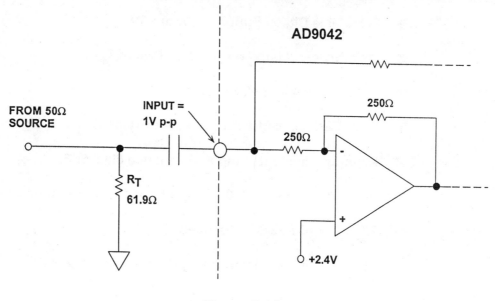

Figure 5.14

AD9050 10-BIT, 40MSPS SINGLE SUPPLY ADC

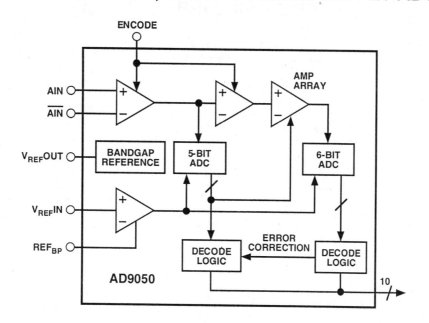

Figure 5.15

AD9050 10-BIT, 40MSPS ADC KEY SPECIFICATIONS

- ■ 10-Bits, 40MSPS, Single +5V Supply

- ■ Selectable Digital Supply: +5V, or +3V

- ■ Low Power: 300mW on BiCMOS Process

- ■ On-Chip SHA and +2.5V reference

- ■ 56dB S/(N+D), 9 Effective Bits, with 10.3MHz Input Signal

- ■ No input transients, Input Impedance 5kΩ, 5pF

- ■ Input Range +3.3V ±0.5V Single-Ended or Differential

- ■ 28-pin SOIC / SSOP Packages

- ■ Ideal for Digital Beamforming Ultrasound Systems

Figure 5.16

AD9050 SIMPLIFIED INPUT CIRCUIT

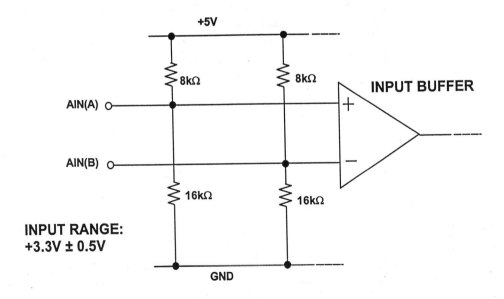

Figure 5.17

tween 1MHz and 15MHz) into the AD9050 differential inputs using a wideband transformer as shown in Figure 5.18. The Mini-Circuits T1-1T transformer has a 1dB bandwidth from 200kHz to 80MHz. Signal-to-noise plus

distortion (SINAD) values of 57dB (9.2 ENOB) are typical for a 10MHz input signal. If the input signal comes directly from a 50, 75, or 100Ω single-ended source, capacitive coupling as shown in Figure 5.18 can be used.

AC COUPLING INTO THE INPUT OF THE AD9050 ADC

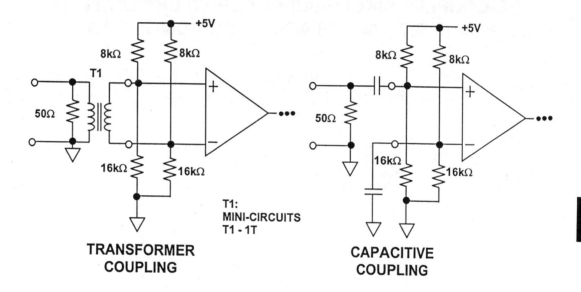

Figure 5.18

If DC coupling is required, the AD8041 (zero-volt in, rail-to-rail output) op amp can be used as a low distortion driver. The circuit shown in Figure 5.19 level shifts a ground-referenced video signal to fit the +3.3V ±0.5V input range of the AD9050. The source is a ground-referenced 0 to +2V signal which is series-terminated in 75Ω. The termina-

tion resistor, R_T, is chosen such that the parallel combination of R_T and R1 is 75Ω. The AD8041 op amp is configured for a signal gain of –1. Assuming that the video source is at zero volts, the corresponding ADC input voltage should be +3.8V. The common-mode voltage, V_{cm}, is determined from the following equation:

$$V_{cm} = 3.8\left(\frac{R_S \| R_T + R1}{R_S \| R_T + R1 + R2}\right) = 3.8\left(\frac{38.8 + 1000}{38.8 + 1000 + 1000}\right) = 1.94V$$

The common-mode voltage, V_{cm}, is derived from the common-mode voltage at the inverting input of the AD9050. The +3.3V is buffered by the AD820 single-supply FET-input op amp. A divider network generates the required +1.94V for the AD8041, and a potentiometer provides offset adjustment capability.

The AD8041 voltage feedback op amp was chosen because of its low power

(26mW), wide bandwidth (160MHz), and low distortion (–69dBc at 10MHz). It is fully specified for both ±5V,+5V, and +3V operation. When operating on a single +5V supply, the input common-mode range is –0.2V to +4V, and the output swing is +0.1V to +4.9V. Distortion performance of the entire circuit including the ADC is better than –60dBc for an input frequency of 10MHz and a sampling rate of 40MSPS.

DC-COUPLED SINGLE-SUPPLY DRIVE CIRCUIT FOR AD9050 10-BIT, 40MSPS ADC USING AD8041 OP AMP

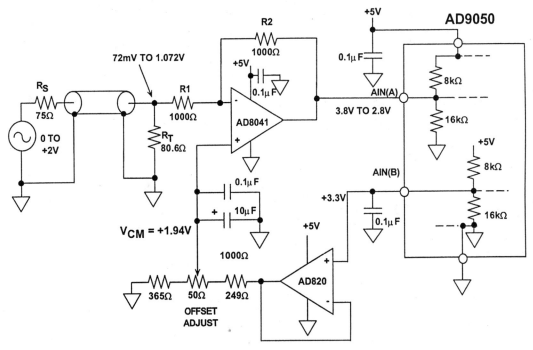

Figure 5.19

APPLICATIONS OF HIGH SPEED ADCs IN CCD IMAGING

Charge coupled devices (CCDs) contains a large number of small photocells called photosites or pixels which are arranged either in a single row (linear arrays) or in a matrix (area arrays). CCD area arrays are commonly used in video applications, while linear arrays are used in facsimile machines, graphics scanners, and pattern recognition equipment.

The linear CCD array consists of a row of image sensor elements (photosites, or pixels) which are illuminated by light from the object or document. During one exposure period each photosite acquires an amount of charge which is proportional to its illumination. These photosite charge packets are subsequently switched simultaneously via transfer gates to an analog shift register. The charge packets on this shift register are clocked serially to a charge detector (storage capacitor) and buffer amplifier (source follower) which convert them into a string of photo-dependent output voltage levels (see Figure 5.20). While the charge packets from one exposure are being clocked out to the charge detector, another exposure is underway. The analog shift register typically operates at frequencies between 1 and 10MHz.

LINEAR CCD ARRAY

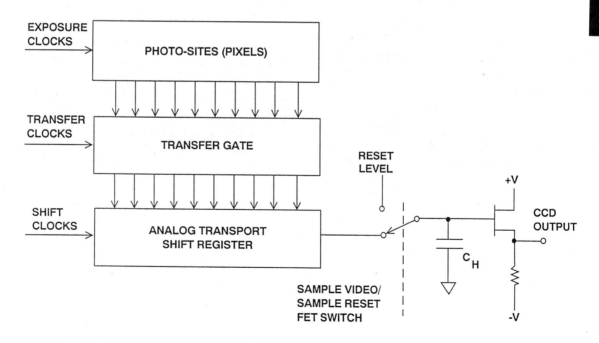

Figure 5.20

The charge detector readout cycle begins with a reset pulse which causes a FET switch to set the output storage capacitor to a known voltage. Switching the FET causes capacitive feedthrough which results in a reset glitch at the output as shown in Figure 5.21. The switch is then opened, isolating the capacitor, and the charge from the last pixel is dumped onto the capacitor causing a voltage change. The difference between the reset voltage and the final voltage (video level) shown in Figure 5.21 represents the amount of charge in the pixel. CCD charges may be as low as 10 electrons, and a typical CCD output sensitivity is 0.6µV/electron. Most CCDs have a saturation output voltage of about 1V (see Reference 1).

Since CCDs are generally fabricated on MOS processes, they have limited capability to perform on-chip signal conditioning. Therefore, the CCD output is generally processed by external conditioning circuits.

CCD output voltages are small and quite often buried in noise. The largest source of noise is the thermal noise in the resistance of the FET reset switch. This noise may have a typical value of 100 to 300 electrons rms (approximately 60 to 180mV rms). This noise occurs as a *sample-to-sample* variation in the CCD output level and is common to both the reset level and the video level for a given pixel period. A technique called *correlated double sampling* (CDS) is often used to reduce the effect of this noise. Figure 5.22 shows two circuit implementations of the CDS scheme. In the top circuit, the CCD output drives both SHAs. At the end of the reset interval, SHA1 holds the reset voltage level. At the end of the video interval, SHA2 holds the video level. The SHA outputs are applied to a difference amplifier which subtracts one from the other. In this scheme, there is only a short interval during which both SHA outputs are stable, and their difference represents ΔV, so the difference amplifier must settle quickly to the desired resolution.

Another arrangement is shown in the bottom half of Figure 5.22, which uses three SHAs and allows either for faster operation or more time for the difference amplifier to settle. In this circuit, SHA1 holds the reset level so that it occurs simultaneously with the video level at the input to SHA2 and SHA3. When the video clock is applied simultaneously to SHA2 and SHA3, the input to SHA2 is the reset level, and the input to SHA3 the video level. This arrangement allows the entire pixel period (less the acquisition time of SHA2 and SHA3) for the difference amplifier to settle.

CCD OUTPUT WAVEFORM

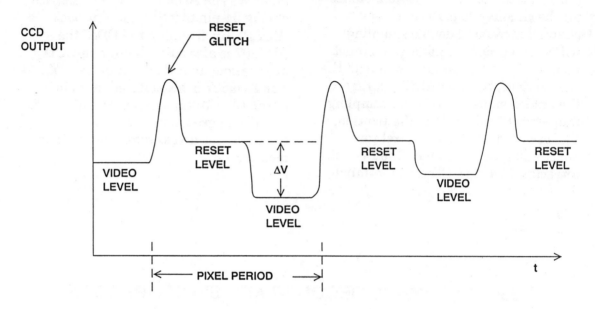

Figure 5.21

CORRELATED DOUBLE SAMPLING (CDS) MINIMIZES SWITCHING NOISE AT OUTPUT

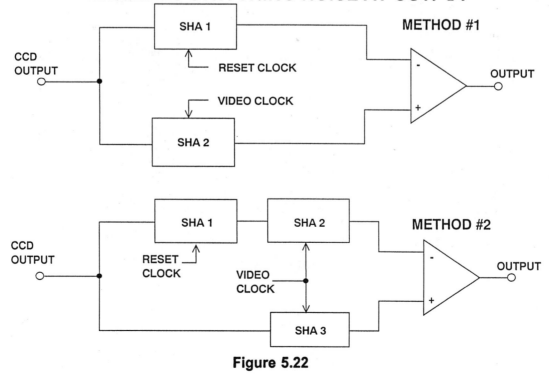

Figure 5.22

The AD9807 is a complete CCD imaging decoder and signal processor on a single chip (see Figure 5.23). The input of the AD9807 allows direct AC coupling of the CCD outputs and includes all the circuitry to perform three-channel correlated double sampling (CDS) and programmable gain adjustment (1X to 4X in 16 increments) of the CCD output. A 12-bit ADC quantizes the analog signal (maximum sampling frequency 6MSPS). After digitization, the on-board DSP allows pixel rate offset and gain correction. The DSP also corrects odd/even CCD register imbal-

ance errors. A parallel control bus provides a simple interface to 8-bit microcontrollers. The device operates on a single +5V supply and dissipates 500mW. The AD9807 comes in a space saving 64-pin plastic quad flat pack (PQFP). By disabling the CDS, the AD9807 is also suitable for non-CCD applications that do not require CDS. The AD9807 is also offered in a pin-compatible 10-bit version, the AD9805, to allow upgradeability and simplify design issues across different scanner models.

AD9807 CCD IMAGE DECODER AND SIGNAL PROCESSOR

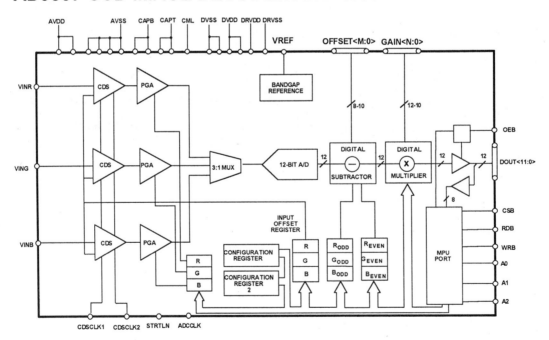

Figure 5.23

HIGH SPEED ADC APPLICATIONS IN DIGITAL RECEIVERS

Introduction

Consider the analog superheterodyne receiver invented in 1917 by Major Edwin H. Armstrong (see Figure 5.24). This architecture represented a significant improvement over single-stage direct conversion (homodyne) receivers which had previously been constructed using tuned RF amplifiers, a single detector, and an audio gain stage. A significant advantage of the superhetrodyne receiver is that it is much easier and more economical to have the gain and selectivity of a receiver at fixed intermediate frequencies (IF) than to have the gain and frequency-selective circuits "tune" over a band of frequencies.

The frequencies shown in Figure 5.24 correspond to the AMPS (Advanced Mobile Phone Service) analog cellular phone system currently used in the U.S. The receiver is designed for AMPS signals at 900MHz RF. The signal bandwidth for the "A" or "B" carriers serving a particular geographical area is 12.5MHz (416 channels, each 30kHz wide). The receiver shown uses triple conversion, with a first IF frequency of 70MHz and a second IF of 10.7MHz, and a third of 455kHz. The image frequency at the receiver input is separated from the RF carrier frequency by an amount equal to twice the first IF frequency (illustrating the point

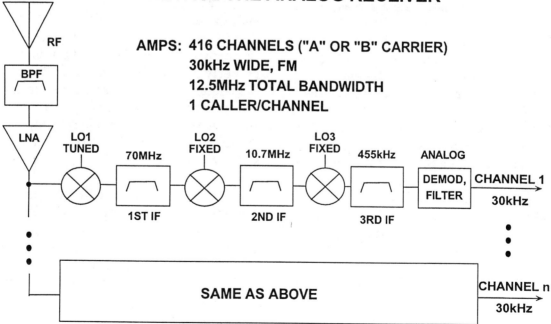

U.S. ADVANCED MOBILE PHONE SERVICE (AMPS) SUPERHETRODYNE ANALOG RECEIVER

Figure 5.24

that using relatively high first IF frequencies makes the design of the image rejection filter easier).

The output of the third IF stage is demodulated using analog techniques (discriminators, envelope detectors, synchronous detectors, etc.). In the case of AMPS the modulation is FM. An important point to notice about the above scheme is that there is *one receiver required per channel*, and only the antenna, prefilter, and LNA can be shared.

It should be noted that in to make the receiver diagrams more manageable, the interstage amplifiers are not shown.

They are, however, an important part of the receiver, and the reader should be aware that they must be present.

Receiver design is a complicated art, and there are many tradeoffs that can be made between IF frequencies, single-conversion vs. double-conversion or triple conversion, filter cost and complexity at each stage in the receiver, demodulation schemes, etc. There are many excellent references on the subject, and the purpose of this section is only to acquaint the design engineer with some of the emerging architectures, especially in the application of digital techniques in the design of advanced communications receivers.

A Receiver Using Digital Processing at Baseband

With the availability of high performance high speed ADCs and DSPs (such as ADSP-2181 and the ADSP-21062), it is now becoming common practice to use digital techniques in at least part of the receive and transmit path, and various chipsets are available from Analog Devices to perform these functions for GSM and other cellular standards. This is illustrated in Figure 5.25 where the output of the last IF stage is converted into a baseband in-phase (I) and quadrature (Q) signal using a quadrature demodulator. The I and Q signals are then digitized by two ADCs. The DSPs then perform the additional signal processing. The signal can then be converted into analog format using a DAC, or it can be processed, mixed with other signals, upconverted, and retransmitted.

At this point, we should make it clear that *a digital receiver is not the same thing as digital modulation*. In fact, a digital receiver will do an excellent job of receiving an analog signal such as AM or FM. Digital receivers can be

used to receive any type of modulation standard including analog (AM, FM) or digital (QPSK, QAM, FSK, GMSK, etc.). Furthermore, since the core of a digital radio is its digital signal processor (DSP), the same receiver can be used for both analog and digitally modulated signals (simultaneously if necessary), assuming that the RF and IF hardware in front of the DSP is properly designed. Since it is software that determines the characteristics of the radio, changing the software changes the radio. For this reason, digital receivers are often referred to as *software radios*.

The fact that a radio is software programmable offers many benefits. A radio manufacturer can design a generic radio in hardware. As interface standards change (as from FM to CDMA or TDMA), the manufacturer is able to make timely design changes to the radio by reprogramming the DSP. From a user or service-providers point of view, the software radio can be upgraded by loading the new software

DIGITAL RECEIVER USING
BASEBAND SAMPLING AND DIGITAL PROCESSING

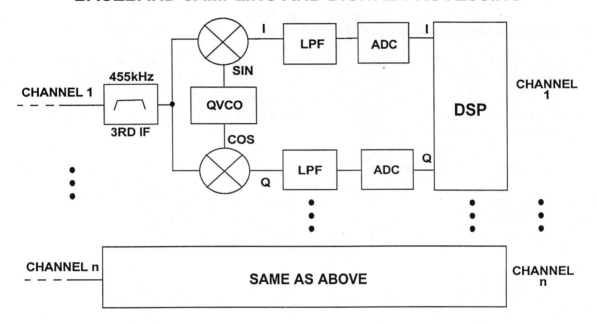

Figure 5.25

at a small cost, while retaining all of the initial hardware investment. Additionally, the receiver can be tailored for custom applications at very low cost, since only software costs are involved.

A digital receiver performs the same function as an analog one with one difference; some of the analog functions have been replaced with their digital equivalent. The main difference between Figure 5.24 and Figure 5.25 is that the FM discriminator in the analog radio has been replaced with two ADCs and a DSP. While this is a very simple example, it shows the fundamental beginnings of a digital, or *software* radio.

An added benefit of using digital techniques is that some of the filtering in the radio is now performed digitally. This eliminates the requirement of tight tolerances and matching for

frequency-sensitive components such as inductors and capacitors. In addition, since filtering is performed within the DSP, the filter characteristics can be implemented in software instead of costly and sensitive SAW, ceramic, or crystal filters. In fact, many filters can be synthesized digitally that could never be implemented in a strictly analog receiver.

This simple example is only the beginning. With current technology, much more of the receiver can be implemented in digital form. There are numerous advantages to moving the digital portion of the radio closer to the antenna. In fact, placing the ADC at the output of the RF section and performing direct RF sampling might seem attractive, but does have some serious drawbacks, particularly in terms of selectivity and out-of-band (image) rejection. However, the concept makes clear one key advantage of software radios: they are programmable and require little or no component selection or adjustments to attain the required receiver performance.

Narrowband IF-Sampling Digital Receivers

A reasonable compromise in many digital receivers is to convert the signal to digital form at the output of the first or the second IF stage. This allows for out-of-band signals to be filtered before reaching the ADC. It also allows for some automatic gain control (AGC) in the analog stage ahead of the ADC to reduce the possibility of in-band signals overdriving the ADC and allows for maximum signal gain prior to the A/D conversion. This relieves some of the dynamic range requirements on the ADC. Additionally, IF sampling and digital receiver technology reduce costs by elimination of further IF stages (mixers, filters, and amplifiers) and adds flexibility by the replacement of fixed analog filter components with programmable digital ones.

In analyzing an analog receiver design, much of the signal gain is after the first IF stage. This prevents front-end overdrive due to out-of-band signals or strong in-band signals. However, in an IF sampling digital receiver, all of the gain is in the front end, and great care must be taken to prevent in-band and out-of-band signals from saturating the ADC, which results in excessive distortion. Therefore, a method of attenuation must be provided when large in-band signals occur. While additional signal gain can be obtained digitally after the ADC, there are certain restrictions. Gain provided in the analog domain improves the SNR of the signal and only reduces the performance to the degree that the noise figure (NF) degrades noise performance.

NARROWBAND IF SAMPLING GSM DIGITAL RECEIVER

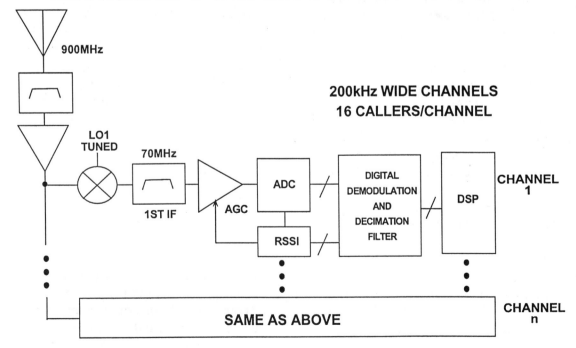

Figure 5.26

Figure 5.26 shows a detailed IF sampling digital receiver for the GSM system . The receiver has RF gain, automatic gain control (AGC), a high performance ADC, digital demodulator/filter, and a DSP.

The heart of the system is the AD6600 dual channel, gain ranging 11-bit, 20MSPS ADC with RSSI (Received Signal Strength Indicator) and the AD6620 dual channel decimating receiver. A detailed block diagram of the AD6600 is shown in Figure 5.27 and key specifications in Figure 5.28.

The AD6600 is a mixed signal chip that directly samples narrow band signals at IF frequencies up to 250MHz. The device includes an 11-bit, 20MSPS ADC, input attenuators, automatic gain ranging circuitry, a 450MHz bandwidth track-and-hold, digital RSSI outputs, references, and control circuitry. The device accepts two inputs (for use with diversity antennas) which are multiplexed to the single ADC.

The AD6600 provides greater than 92dB dynamic range from the ADC and the auto gain-ranging/RSSI circuits. The gain range is 36dB in 6dB increments (controlled by a 3-bit word from the RSSI circuit). This sets the smallest input range at 31mV peak-to-peak, and the largest at 2V peak-to-peak. SFDR is 70dBc @ 100MHz and 53dBc @ 250MHz. Channel isolation is 70dB @ 100MHz and 60dB @ 250MHz. The SNR performance of the AD6600 is shown in Figure 5.29. The dynamic range of the AD6600 is greater than the minimum GSM specification of 91dB.

5

AD6600 DUAL CHANNEL GAIN RANGING ADC WITH RECEIVED SIGNAL STRENGTH INDICATOR (RSSI)

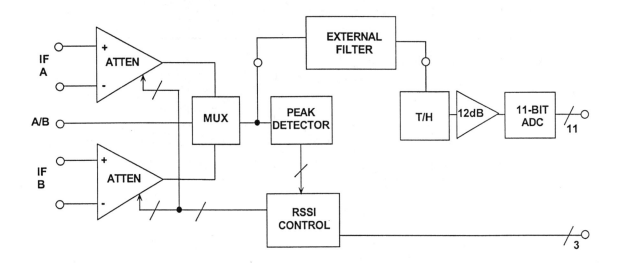

Figure 5.27

AD6600 KEY SPECIFICATIONS

- ■ Dual Input, 11-bit, 20MSPS ADC Plus 3-bits RSSI

- ■ Dynamic Range > 100dB
  - ◆ 11-bit ADC → 62dB
  - ◆ 3-bits RSSI → 30dB (5 levels, 6dB / level)
  - ◆ Process Gain → 12dB (6.5MSPS Sampling, 30kHz channel)

- ■ On-Chip Reference and Timing

- ■ Single +5V Supply, 400mW

- ■ 44-pin TQFP Package

- ■ Optimum Design for Narrowband Digital Receivers with IF Frequencies to 250MHz

Figure 5.28

AD6600 INPUT VS. SNR

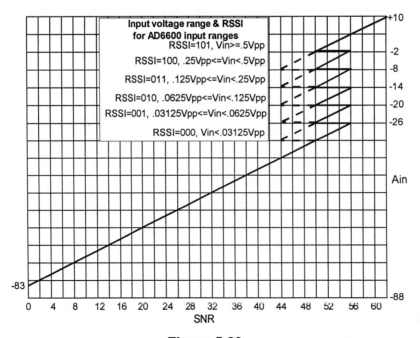

Figure 5.29

The analog input to the AD6600 consists of two parallel attenuator stages followed by an output selection multiplexer. The attenuation levels can be set either by the on-chip automatic RSSI circuit (synchronous peak detector) or can be set digitally with external logic. The ADC T/H input can also be accessed directly by by-passing the front-end attenuators.

An external analog filter is required between the attenuator output and the track-and-hold input of the ADC section. This filter may be either a lowpass or a bandpass depending on the system architecture. Since the input bandwidth of the ADC is 450MHz, the filter minimizes the wideband noise entering the track-and-hold. The bandwidth of the filter should be set to allow sufficient settling time (1/2 the sampling period) during the RSSI peak detection period.

The ADC is based on the high dynamic range AD9042 architecture covered previously. The ADC input is designed to take advantage of the excellent small-signal linearity of the track-and-hold. Therefore, the full scale input to the ADC section is only 50mV peak-to-peak. The track-and-hold is followed by a gain block with a 6dB gain-select to increase the signal level for digitization by the 11-bit ADC. This amplifier only requires enough bandwidth to accurately settle to the next value during the sampling period (77ns for f_s = 13MSPS). Because of its reduced bandwidth, any high frequency track-and-hold feed through is also minimized.

The RSSI peak detector function consists of a bank of 5 high speed comparators with separate reference inputs. Each reference input is 6dB lower than the previous one. Each comparator has 6dB of built-in hysteresis to eliminate level uncertainty at the threshold points. Once one of the comparators is tripped, it stays in that state until it is reset by the negative-going edge of the sampling clock. The 5 comparator outputs are decoded into a 3-bit word that is used to select the proper input attenuation.

The RSSI follows the IF signal one clock cycle before the conversion is made. During this time period, the RSSI looks for the signal peaks. Prior to digitization, the RSSI word selects the correct attenuator factor to prevent the ADC from over-ranging on the following conversion cycle. The peak signal is set 6dB below the full scale range of the 11-bit ADC. The RSSI word can be read via the RSSI pins. The 11-bit ADC output functions as the mantissa, while the RSSI word is the exponent, and the combination forms a floating point number.

The AD6600 is ideal for use in a GSM narrowband basestation. Figure 5.30 shows a block diagram of the fundamental receiver. Two separate antennas and RF sections are used (this is often called *diversity*) to reduce the signal strength variations due to multipath effects. The IF output (approximately 70MHz) of each channel is digitized by the AD6600 at a sampling rate of 6.5MSPS (one-half the master GSM clock frequency of 13MHz). The two antennas need only be separated by a few feet to provide the required signal strength diversity (the wavelength of a 900MHz signal is about 1 foot). The DSP portion of the receiver selects the channel which has the largest signal amplitude.

5

The bandwidth of a single GSM channel is 200kHz, and each channel can handle up to 8 simultaneous callers for full-rate systems and 16 simultaneous callers for the newer one-half-rate systems. A typical basestation may be required to handle 50 to 60 simultaneous callers, thereby requiring 4 separate signal processing channels (assuming a one-half-rate system).

The IF frequency is chosen to be 69.875MHz, thus centering the 200kHz signal in the 22nd Nyquist zone (see Figure 5.31). The dual channel digital decimating receiver (AD6620) reverses the frequency sense of the signal and shifts it down to baseband.

We now have a 200kHz baseband signal (generated by undersampling) which is being *oversampled* by a factor of approximately 16 .

The signal is then passed through a digital filter (part of the AD6620) which removes all frequency components above 200kHz, including the quantization noise which falls in the region between 200kHz and 3.25MHz (the Nyquist frequency) as shown in Figure 5.32. The resultant increase in SNR is 12dB (processing gain). There is now no information contained in the signal above 200kHz, and the output data rate can be reduced (decimated) from 6.5MSPS to 406.25kSPS, a data rate which the DSP can handle. The data corresponding to the 200kHz channel is transmitted to the DSP over a simple 3-wire serial interface. The DSP performs such functions as channel equalization, decoding, and spectral shaping.

NARROWBAND GSM BASESTATION WITH DIVERSITY

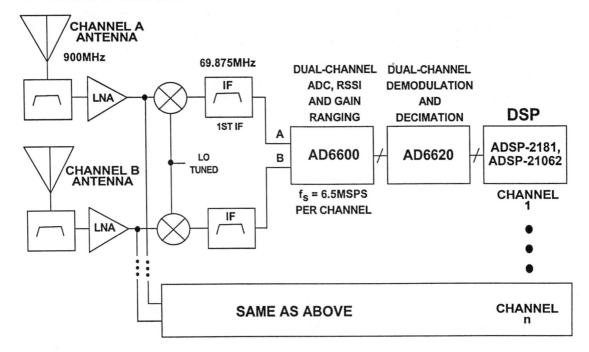

Figure 5.30

NARROWBAND GSM RECEIVER BANDPASS SAMPLING
OF A 200kHz CHANNEL AT 6.5MSPS

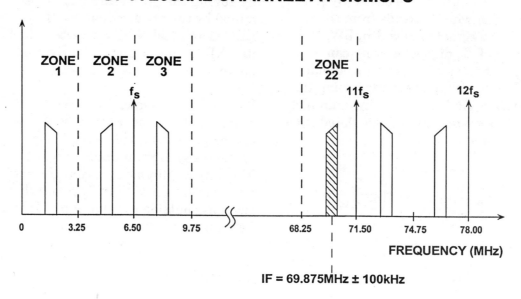

Figure 5.31

DIGITAL FILTERING AND DECIMATION
OF THE 200kHz CHANNEL

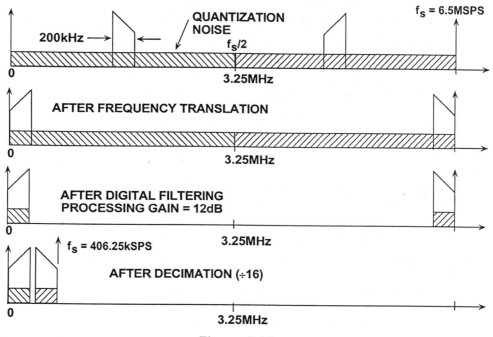

Figure 5.32

The concept of *processing gain* is common to all communications systems, analog or digital. In a sampling system, the quantization noise produced by the ADC is spread over the entire Nyquist bandwidth which extends from DC to $f_s/2$. If the signal bandwidth, BW, is less than $f_s/2$, digital filtering can remove the noise components outside this bandwidth, thereby increasing the effective SNR. The processing gain in a sampling system can be calculated from the formula:

$$\text{Processing Gain} = 10\log\left(\frac{f_s}{2\cdot\text{BW}}\right).$$

The SINAD (noise and distortion measured over $f_s/2$ bandwidth) of the ADC at the bandwidth of the signal should be used to compute the actual SINAD by adding the processing gain determined by the above equation. If the ADC is an ideal N-bit converter, then its SNR (measured over the Nyquist bandwidth) is 6.02N + 1.76dB.

Notice that as shown in the previous narrowband receiver example, there can be processing gain even if the original signal is an undersampled one. The only requirement is that the signal bandwidth be less than $f_s/2$, and that the noise outside the signal bandwidth be removed with a digital filter.

PROCESSING GAIN

- Measure ADC SINAD (6.02N + 1.76dB Theoretical)

- Sampling Frequency = f_s

- Signal Bandwidth = BW

- Processing Gain $= 10\log\left(\dfrac{f_s}{2\cdot\text{BW}}\right)$

- SINAD in Signal Bandwidth = SINAD + $10\log\left(\dfrac{f_s}{2\cdot\text{BW}}\right)$

- SINAD (Theoretical) = 6.02N + 1.76dB + $10\log\left(\dfrac{f_s}{2\cdot\text{BW}}\right)$

- Processing Gain Increases 3dB each time f_s is doubled

Figure 5.33

Wideband IF-Sampling Digital Receivers

Thus far, we have avoided a detailed discussion of *narrowband* versus *wideband* digital receivers. A digital receiver can be either, but more detailed definitions are important at this point. By *narrowband*, we mean that sufficient pre-filtering has been done such that all undesired signals have been eliminated and that only the signal of interest is presented to the ADC input. This is the case for the GSM basestation example previously discussed.

Wideband simply means that a number of channels are presented to input of

the ADC and further filtering, tuning, and processing is performed digitally. Usually, a wideband receiver is designed to receive an entire band; cellular or other similar wireless services such as PCS (Personal Communications Systems). In fact, one wideband digital receiver can be used to receive *all* channels within the band simultaneously, allowing almost all of the analog hardware (including the ADC) to be shared among all channels as shown in Figure 5.34 which compares the narrowband and the wideband approaches.

NARROWBAND VERSUS WIDEBAND DIGITAL RECEIVER

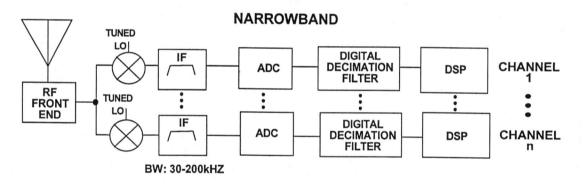

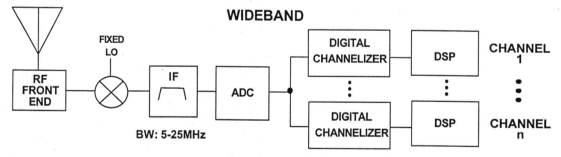

Figure 5.34

Note that in the narrowband digital radio, there is one front-end LO and mixer required per channel to provide individual channel tuning. In the

wideband digital radio, however, the first LO frequency is fixed, and the "tuning" is done in the *digital channelizer* circuits following the ADC.

A typical wideband digital receiver may process a 5 to 25MHz band of signals simultaneously. This approach is frequently called *block conversion*. In the wideband digital receiver, the variable local oscillator in the narrowband receiver has been replaced with a fixed oscillator, so tuning must be accomplished digitally. Tuning is performed using a digital down converter (DDC) and filter chip frequently called a *channelizer*. The term channelizer is used because the purpose of these chips is to select one channel out of the many within the broadband spectrum actually present in the ADC output. A typical channelizer is shown in Figure 5.35.

DIGITAL CHANNELIZER IN WIDEBAND RECEIVER

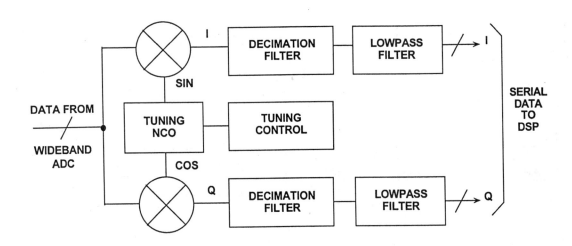

Figure 5.35

It consists of an NCO (Numerically Controlled Oscillator) with tuning capability, dual mixer, and matched digital filters. These are the same functions that would be required in an analog receiver, but implemented in digital form. The digital output from the channelizer is the demodulated signal in I and Q format, and all other signals have been filtered and removed. Since the channelizer output consists of one selected RF channel, one channelizer is required for each channel. The channelizer also serves to decimate the output data rate such that it can be processed by a DSP such as the ADSP-2181 or the ADSP-21062. The DSP extracts the signal information from the I and Q data and performs further processing. Another effect of the filtering provided by the channelizer is to increase the SNR by adding processing gain.

In the case of an AMPS signal, there are 416 channels, each 30kHz wide, for a total bandwidth of 12.5MHz (each of the two carriers in a given region are allocated 12.5MHz of the total 25MHz cellular band). Each channel carries one call, so there is a clear advantage in using the wideband approach versus the narrowband one in an AMPS basestation which must handle between 50 and 60 simultaneous calls. On the other hand, a 200kHz GSM channel can carry 16 calls simultaneously (for half-rate systems), so only three or four channels are required in the typical GSM basestation, and the narrowband approach is more cost-effective. Using today's technology (1996), the break-even cost point between narrowband and wideband ranges from two and eight channels.

In an ADC used for narrowband applications, the key specifications are SINAD, SFDR, and SNR. The narrowband ADC can take advantage of automatic gain ranging (as in the AD6600) to account for signal amplitude variations between individual channels and thereby achieve extra dynamic range.

On the other hand, an ADC used in a wideband receiver must digitize all channels simultaneously, thereby eliminating the possibility of per-channel analog gain ranging. For example, the GSM (European Digital Cellular) system specification requires the receiver to process signals between –13dBm and –104dBm (with a noise floor of –114dBm) in the presence of many other signals. This is a dynamic range of 91dB! This implies that the SFDR of the ADC and the analog front end must be approximately 95 to 100dBFS, allowing for additional headroom. In addition, the GSM system has 124 channels, each having a bandwidth of 200kHz for a total signal bandwidth of 25MHz. The minimum required sampling rate for an ADC suitable for wideband GSM is therefore greater than 50MSPS.

SFDR is a very important specification when a mobile phone is near the basestation because it is an indication of how strong signals interfere with signals in other channels. Strong signals usually produce the largest spurs due to front-end distortion, and these spurs can mask weaker signals from mobile phones near the cell fringes. The SFDR for weak signals provides an indication of the overall noise floor, or SINAD which can ultimately be related to the receiver bit error rate (BER).

When digitizing a wideband signal, full scale single-tone evaluations are no longer sufficient. Two-tone and multiple-tone intermodulation testing in conjunction with SFDR amplitude sweeps are better indicators of performance.

The AMPS cellular system basestation is ideally suited to the wideband digital receiver design, and a simplified diagram of one is shown in Figure 5.37. The AD9042 sampling frequency of 30.72MSPS is chosen to be a power-of-two multiple of the channel bandwidth (30kHz x 1024). Another popular AMPS wideband receiver sampling frequency is 40.96MSPS. The choice of IF frequency is flexible, and a second IF stage may be required if lower IF frequencies are chosen.

5

GSM VERSUS AMPS COMPARISONS

	GSM	AMPS
Digital Receiver	Narrowband	Wideband
# of Channels	124	416
Channel BW	200kHz	30kHz
Total BW	25MHz	12.5MHz
Callers/Channel	16 (one-half rate)	1
ADC Requirements	11-bits with RSSI	12-bits
	6.5 MSPS	30.72 MSPS
	92dB Dynamic Range	80dB SFDR
Process Gain	12dB	27dB

Figure 5.36

AMPS WIDEBAND DIGITAL RECEIVER

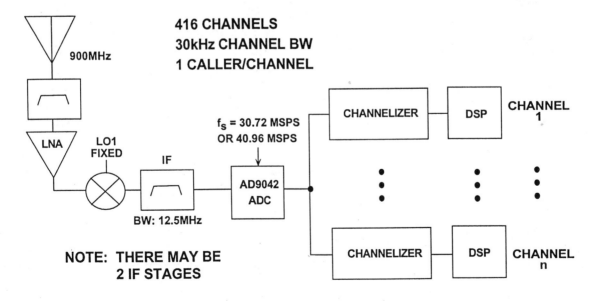

416 CHANNELS
30kHz CHANNEL BW
1 CALLER/CHANNEL

Figure 5.37

With a sampling frequency of 30.72MSPS, the 12.5MHz bandwidth signal can be positioned in the first Nyquist zone (DC to 15.36MHz) with an IF frequency of 7.68MHz, or in the second Nyquist zone (15.36MHz to 30.72MHz) with an IF frequency of 23.04MHz.

With a sampling frequency of 40.96MSPS, the 12.5 MHz bandwidth signal can be positioned in the first Nyquist zone (DC to 20.48MHz) with an IF frequency of 10.24MHz, or in the second Nyquist zone (20.48MHz to 40.96MHz) with an IF frequency of 30.72MHz.

The digital channelizers provide the receiver tuning and demodulate the signal into the I and Q components. The output data rate to the DSPs after decimation is 60kSPS. The processing gain incurred is calculated as follows:

Processing Gain =

$$10\log\left(\frac{30.72}{2 \times 0.03}\right) = 27.1\text{dB}.$$

AMPS WIDEBAND RECEIVER PROCESS GAIN

- f_s = 30.72MSPS   (1024 · 30kHz)

- Channel BW = 30kHz

- Process Gain = $10\log\left(\frac{f_s}{2 \cdot BW}\right)$ = 27.1dB

Figure 5.38

In addition to SFDR, two-tone and multi-tone intermodulation distortion is important in an ADC for wideband receiver applications. Figure 5.39 shows two strong signals in two adjacent channels at frequencies f1 and f2. If the ADC has third-order intermodulation distortion, these products will fall at $2f_2-f_1$ and $2f_1-f_2$ and are indistinguishable from signals which might be present in these channels. This is one reason the GSM system is difficult to implement using the wideband approach, since the dynamic range requirement is greater than 91dB.

TWO-TONE INTERMODULATION DISTORTION
IN MULTICHANNEL SYSTEM
(GSM REQUIREMENTS SHOWN)

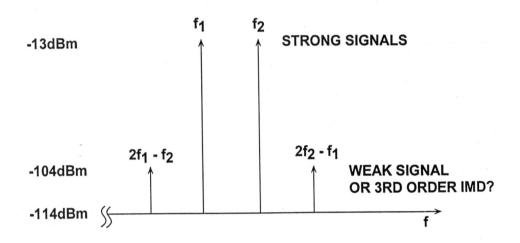

Figure 5.39

The two-tone SFDR of the AD9042 is greater than 80dB with input tones at 15.3MHz and 19.5MHz as shown in Figure 5.40. Note than the amplitude of each tone must be 6dB below full scale in order to prevent the ADC from being overdriven. The two-tone SFDR as a function of input signal amplitude is shown in Figure 5.41 for tone frequencies of 19.3MHz and 19.51MHz. The upper curve is in dBFS, and the lower in dBc. Note that the SFDR is greater than 80dBFS for all input amplitudes. Figure 5.42 shows a multitone FFT output for the AD9042, and the ADC still maintains 85dBFS of SFDR.

AD9042 TWO-TONE FFT OUTPUT
F1 = 15.3MHz, F2 = 19.5MHz, f$_S$ = 41MSPS

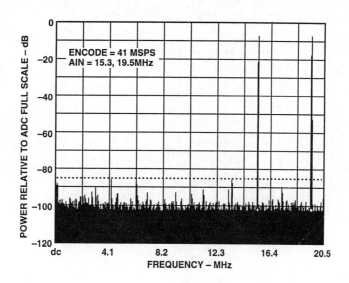

Figure 5.40

AD9042 TWO-TONE SFDR
F1 = 19.3MHz, F2 = 19.51MHz, f$_S$ = 41MSPS

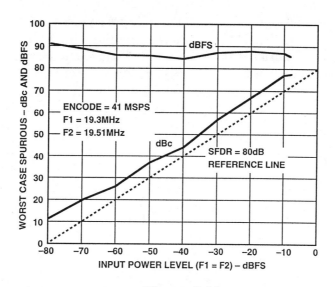

Figure 5.41

AD9042 MULTITONE PERFORMANCE (4 TONES)
f_S = 41MSPS

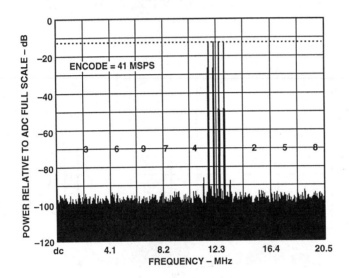

Figure 5.42

Direct IF-to-Digital Considerations

The dynamic performance of the AD9042 extends well beyond 20MHz analog input signals (see Figure 5.43). Therefore it can be used to perform direct IF-to-digital conversions using a wide range of IF frequencies. These IF signals can be undersampled as previously described, and the minimum sampling frequency required is determined by the bandwidth of the IF signal. Figure 5.44 shows a 21.4MHz signal sampled at 10MSPS using the AD9042. Note that under these conditions, the SFDR performance is greater than 80dBFS.

AD9042 SFDR VERSUS INPUT FREQUENCY

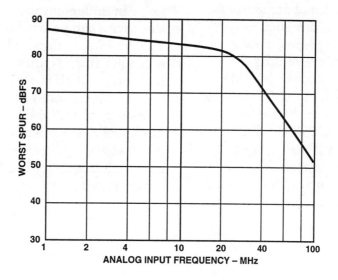

Figure 5.43

AD9042 FFT OUTPUT FOR IF SAMPLED INPUT:
f_S = 10MSPS, ANALOG INPUT = 21.4MHz

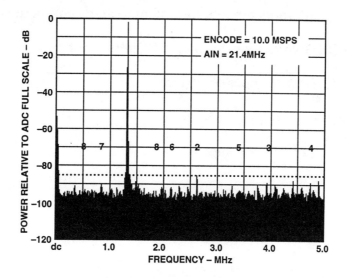

Figure 5.44

The AD6640 represents the next generation in IF sampling ADCs. Key specifications for the AD6640 are summarized in Figure 5.45. The architecture is similar to that of the AD9042, but the device is fabricated on a faster XFCB process. The input structure is fully differential and designed for transformer coupling for minimum distortion. Maximum sampling frequency is 65MSPS, and the SINAD performance is 67dB at 60MHz analog input. SFDR is greater than 80dBFS for frequencies up to 25MHz. This device allows direct IF sampling in wideband communications systems having bandwidths up to 25MHz (such as the AMPS system, where each carrier is allocated 12.5MHz of spectrum). For systems with smaller bandwidths, the higher sampling frequency provided by the AD6640 will allow analog antialiasing filter requirements to be relaxed and provide processing gain. In undersampling applications, the device can be used to digitize 70MHz IF signals which lie in the second or third Nyquist zone. For instance, a 30MHz wideband signal bandwidth centered around a carrier frequency of 48.75MHz can be digitized at 65MSPS as shown in Figure 5.46. In narrowband applications, the high sampling frequency can be used to achieve additional processing gain.

AD6640 12-BIT, 65MSPS ADC KEY SPECIFICATIONS

- ■ 12-bit, 65MSPS IF-SAMPLING ADC

- ■ Based on AD9042 architecture, but 1.5X faster CB process

- ■ Fully differential inputs for optimum distortion performance

- ■ SFDR Greater than 80dB up to 25MHz Input

- ■ 68dB SINAD for 60MHz IF input

- ■ Single +5V Supply, 695mW

- ■ 44-Lead TQFP Package

Figure 5.45

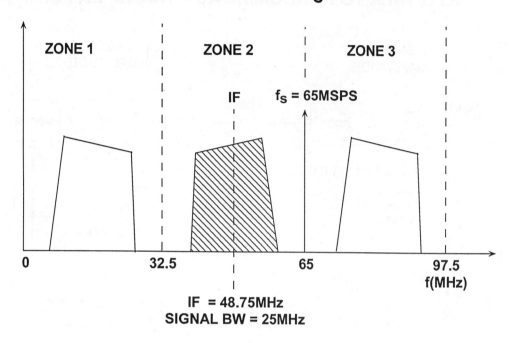

SAMPLING A 25MHz BW SIGNAL USING AD6640: IF FREQUENCY = 48.75MHz, f_S = 65MSPS

Figure 5.46

Achieving Wide Dynamic Range in High Speed ADCs Using Dither

There are two fundamental limitations to maximizing SFDR in a high speed ADC. The first is the distortion produced by the front-end amplifier and the sample-and-hold circuit. The second is that produced by non-linearity in the actual transfer function of the encoder portion of the ADC. The key to wide SFDR is to minimize the non-linearity of each.

There is nothing that can be done externally to the ADC to significantly reduce the inherent distortion caused by the ADC front end. However, the non-linearity in the ADC encoder transfer function can be reduced by the proper use of dither (external noise which is summed with the analog input signal to the ADC).

Dithering improves ADC SFDR under certain conditions. For example, even in a perfect ADC, there is some correlation between the quantization noise and the input signal. This can reduce the SFDR of the ADC, especially if the input signal is an exact sub-multiple of the sampling frequency. Summing broadband noise (about 1/2 LSB rms in amplitude) with the input signal tends to randomize the quantization noise and minimize this effect (see Figure 5.47). In most systems, however, there is enough noise riding on top of the signal so that adding additional dither noise is not required. Increasing the wideband rms noise level beyond an LSB will proportionally reduce the ADC SNR.

5

USING DITHER TO RANDOMIZE ADC TRANSFER FUNCTION

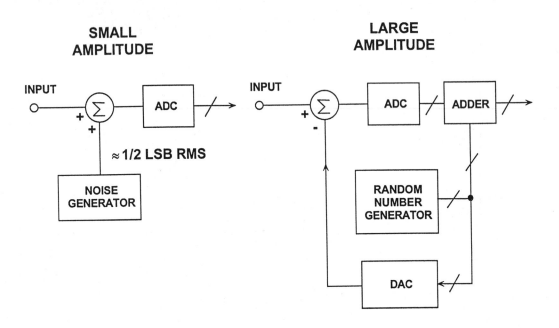

Figure 5.47

Other schemes have been developed which use larger amounts of dither noise to randomize the transfer function of the ADC. Figure 5.47 also shows a dither noise source comprised of a pseudo-random number generator which drives a DAC. This signal is subtracted from the ADC input signal and then digitally added to the ADC output, thereby causing no significant degradation in SNR. An inherent disadvantage of this technique is that the allowable input signal swing is reduced as the amplitude of the dither signal is increased. This reduction in signal amplitude is required to prevent overdriving the ADC. It should be noted that this scheme does not significantly improve distortion created by the front-end of the ADC, only that produced by

the non-linearity of the ADC encoder transfer function.

Another method which is easier to implement, especially in wideband receivers, is to inject a narrowband dither signal *outside the signal band of interest* as shown in Figure 5.48. Usually, there are no signal components located in the frequency range near DC, so this low-frequency region is often used for such a dither signal. Another possible location for the dither signal is slightly below $f_s/2$. Because the dither signal occupies only a small bandwidth relative to the signal bandwidth, there is no significant degradation in SNR, as would occur if the dither was broad-band.

INJECTING OUT-OF-BAND DITHER TO IMPROVE ADC SFDR

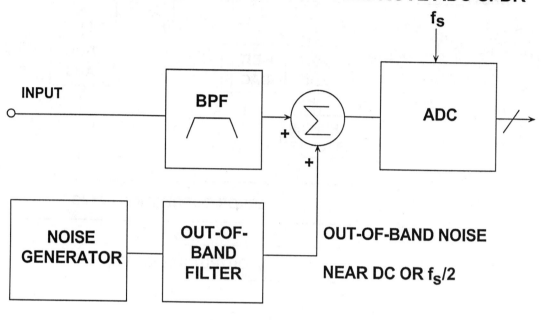

Figure 5.48

A subranging ADC such as the AD9042 (see Figure 5.49) has small differential non-linearity errors that occur at specific regions across the ADC range. For instance, the AD9042 uses a 6-bit ADC followed by a 7-bit one. There are 64 decision points associated with the main-range 6-bit ADC, and they occur every 15.625mV for a 1V full scale input range. Figure 5.50 shows a greatly exaggerated representation of these non-linearities.

The distortion components produced by the front end of the AD9042 up to about 20MHz analog input are negligible compared to those produced by the encoder. That is, *the static non-linearity of the AD9042 transfer function* is the chief limitation to SFDR.

The goal is to select the proper amount of out-of-band dither so that the effect of these small DNL errors are *randomized* across the ADC input range, thereby reducing the average DNL error. The first plot shown in Figure 5.51 shows the undithered DNL over a small portion of the input signal range. The horizontal axis has been expanded to show two of the subranging points which are spaced 15.625mV (64 LSBs) apart. The second plot shows the DNL after adding 5.3mV rms (22 LSBs rms) of dither. This amount of dither corresponds to −32.5dBm (1V p-p full scale corresponds to +4dBm). It was determined that further increases in dither amplitude provided no improvement in the AD9042 SFDR and would only serve to cause a loss in headroom and a decrease in SNR.

AD9042 12-BIT, 41MSPS PIPELINED SUBRANGING ADC WITH DIGITAL ERROR CORRECTION

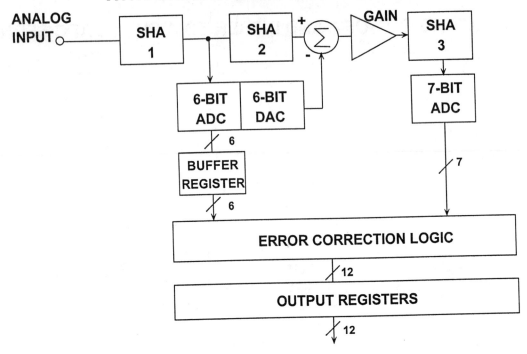

Figure 5.49

AD9042 SUBRANGING POINT DNL ERRORS (EXAGGERATED)

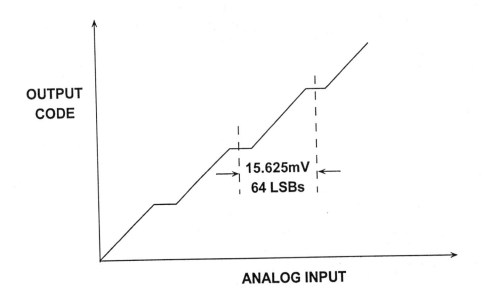

Figure 5.50

AD9042 UNDITHERED AND DITHERED DNL

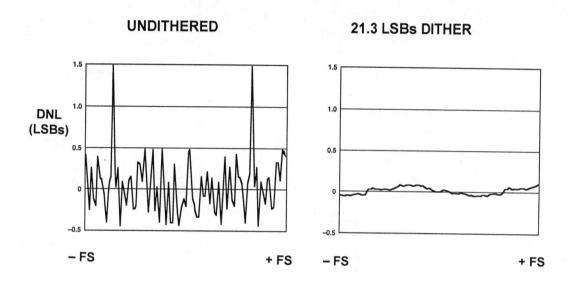

Figure 5.51

The dither signal was generated using a voltage feedback op amp (AD8048, 3.8nV/√Hz input voltage noise, 200MHz gain-bandwidth product) as the noise source (see Figure 5.52). The op amp is configured for a gain of +26, and the output noise spectral density is about 100nV/√Hz over an 8MHz bandwidth. The output of the noise generator is then amplified by the AD600 dual wideband VCA which provides a gain (in dB) which is proportional to the control voltage. The control voltage can be fixed, or programmed using a DAC as shown. The gain of the AD600 can be set from 0dB to 80dB by varying the control voltage from 0 to +1V. The bandwidth of the noise is limited to about 300kHz with a lowpass filter. The filter can be either passive or active, but requires at least 4 poles in order to attenuate the out-of-band noise. The output of the lowpass filter is buffered with the AD797 low-noise op amp which also provides a gain of +2. The filtered noise is summed directly into the input circuit of the AD9042 through a capacitor and a 1kΩ series resistor. The net input impedance of the AD9042 is 50Ω (61.9Ω in parallel with the 250Ω AD9042 internal impedance).

5

DITHER NOISE GENERATOR

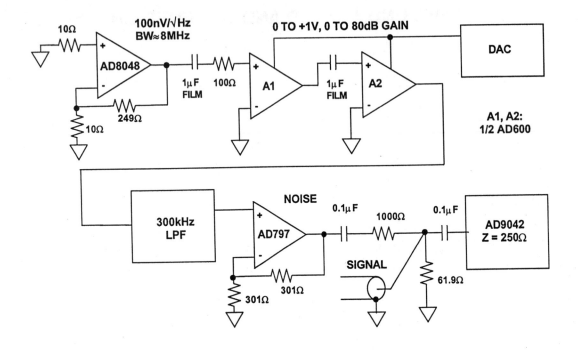

Figure 5.52

The dramatic improvement in SFDR obtained with out-of-band dither is shown in Figure 5.53 using a 4k FFT, where the AD9042 is sampling a 19.5MHz signal (–29dBFS) at 41MSPS. Note that the SFDR without dither is approximately 80dBFS compared to 94dBFS with dither, representing a 14dB improvement! This improvement is also shown in the SFDR amplitude sweeps shown in Figure 5.54. Note the similar improvement.

AD9042 UNDITHERED AND DITHERED 4k FFT OUTPUT

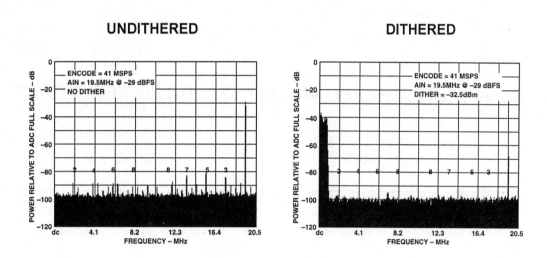

Figure 5.53

AD9042 UNDITHERED AND DITHERED SFDR

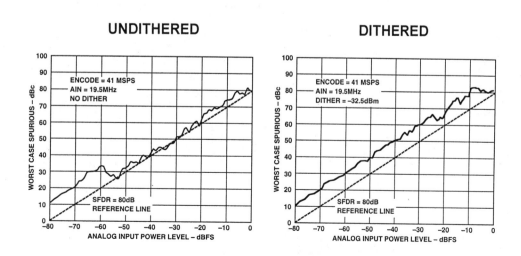

Figure 5.54

At lower frequencies, the FFT size must be increased from 4k to 128k (reducing the FFT noise floor by 15dB) in order to measure the dithered SFDR. Figure

5.55 shows the effects of dither using a 128k FFT and a 2.5MHz input signal. The SFDR with dither is greater than 100dBFS.

AD9042 UNDITHERED AND DITHERED 128k FFT OUTPUTS

UNDITHERED   DITHERED

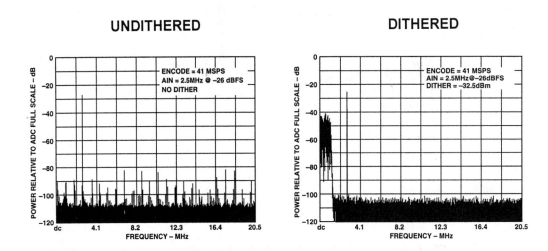

Figure 5.55

High Speed ADC Applications in Digital Communications Systems and Direct Broadcast Satellite (DBS) Set-Top Boxes

In a digital communications system, digital data (which can be digitized analog signals) is formatted and transmitted serially over an appropriate medium. The GSM cellular telephone system is an example. The ubiquitous modem (modulator/demodulator), which PCs and FAX machines use to transmit and receive data over the standard dial-up telephone connection, uses sophisticated modulation techniques to place huge amounts of data in the 4kHz bandwidth telephone channel.

Most digital transmission schemes use some form of in-phase and quadrature (I and Q) modulation to maximize the amount of data transmitted over a given channel bandwidth. Two examples are shown in Figure 5.56 and Figure 5.57. The first is called Quadrature Phase Shift Keying (QPSK) and is

used in Direct Broadcast Satellite systems. The diagram (*constellation*) shows the four possible data points, each representing 2-bits of binary information. Each point in the constellation is called a *symbol* and has a specific I and Q value. In the case of QPSK, there are two bits of information per symbol. The symbol rate is often referred to as the *baud* rate. For example, in QPSK, if the symbol (or baud) rate is 30Mbaud (1baud = 1symbol/sec), the bit rate is 60Mbits/sec. It is common practice to sample these types of signals at twice the symbol (or baud) rate. The I and Q ADC and DSP must identify the signal as representing one of two possible levels, and ADCs of 4, 5, or 6-bits are commonly used in this application for additional noise margin and to achieve the overall system bit-error-rate (BER) requirement.

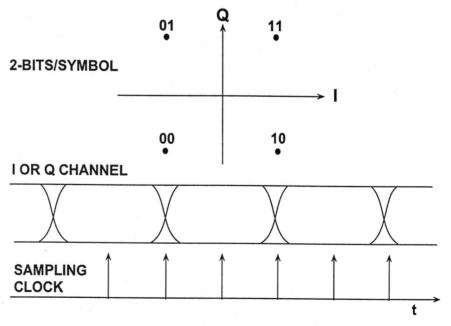

Figure 5.56

In the QPSK system, the magnitude of each symbol is equal, and only the phase is modulated. More complex modulation schemes such as QAM (Quadrature Amplitude Modulation), use more symbols on the constellation and thereby transmit more bits of information per symbol (at the expense of more sensitivity to noise and more complex digital signal processing). Figure 5.57 shows a 16-QAM constella-

tion which contains 4-bits of information per symbol. Note that the I and Q channel receiver DSP must now identify the signal as representing one of the four possible levels. Although the 16-QAM signal carries more bits per symbol, it is more sensitive to noise, and the ADC requires more resolution (typically 8-bits) than for QPSK modulation (typically 4, 5, or 6 bits).

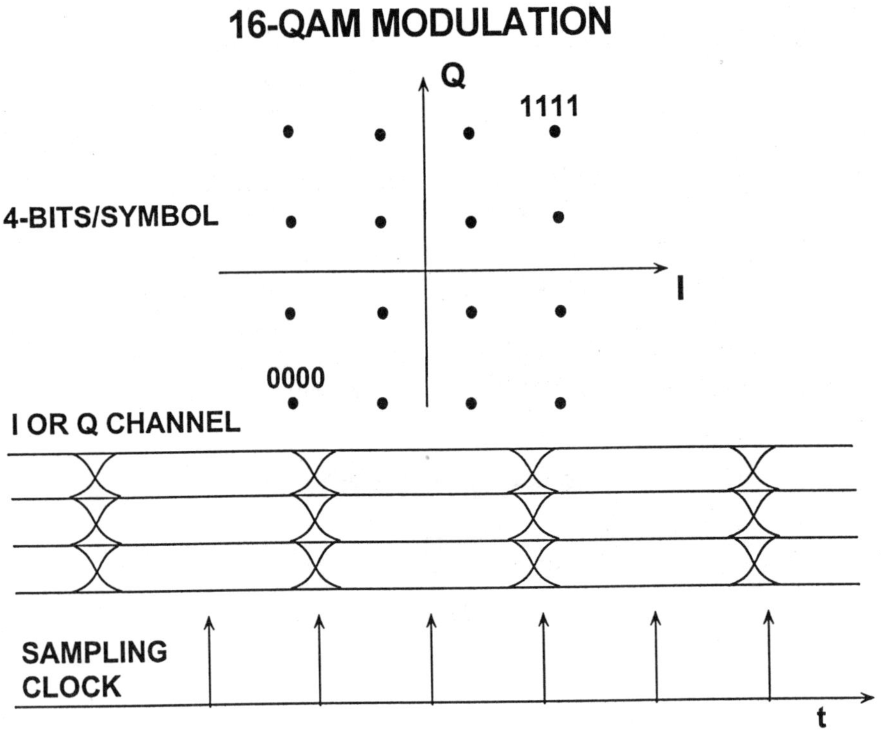

16-QAM MODULATION

Figure 5.57

In the digital receiver, the I and Q components are separated by a quadrature demodulator and digitized by two ADCs operating in parallel. The ADC sampling rate is generally twice the symbol rate. In the case of Direct Broadcast Satellite (DBS), the symbol rate is 30Mbaud (1baud = 1symbol/sec), the bit rate 60Mbits/sec, and the ADC sampling rate is 60MSPS. The actual

signals at the ADC input are called "eye patterns" because the intersymbol interference due to noise and limited bandwidth *smears* the level transitions so that the regions where the data is valid are located in the center of the *eye* opening. Figure 5.58 shows a typical I/Q demodulator followed by a dual ADC such as the AD9066 (6-bits, 60MSPS).

IF SAMPLING USING AD9066 6-BIT, 60MSPS ADC

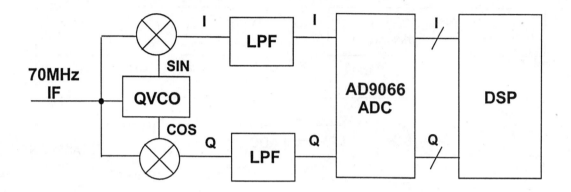

FOR DBS, SYMBOL (BAUD) RATE = 30MBAUD, QPSK
SAMPLING RATE = 60MSPS

Figure 5.58

A recent popular consumer application of digital communications is in Direct Broadcast Satellite (DBS) systems. A simplified block diagram of a DBS system is shown in Figure 5.59. The objective is to transmit up to 150 channels of video programming to home receivers which use a small (18 inch) dish and an inexpensive (less than $500) receiver (set-top box). The subscription costs of the services is compatible with cable TV, but picture quality (because of digital transmission inherent noise immunity) is generally superior over all 150 channels.

MPEG encoding and decoding reduces the data rates to fit the channel bandwidth. The MPEG (Motion Picture Experts Group) standard supports various data rates and minimizes the bandwidth used. For example, a typical 24-frame-per-second NTSC-quality movie needs about 3Mbits/sec after encoding. A more complex and fast-moving show, such as a soccer game, requires 5 to 6 Mbits/sec. In a DBS system, the MPEG encoding rate is kept at a minimum value compatible with the anticipated video signal characteristics. Multiple MPEG data streams are multiplexed and sent through a single satellite transponder. In addition, statistical multiplexing dynamically varies the data rate given to each source as the program content changes.

5

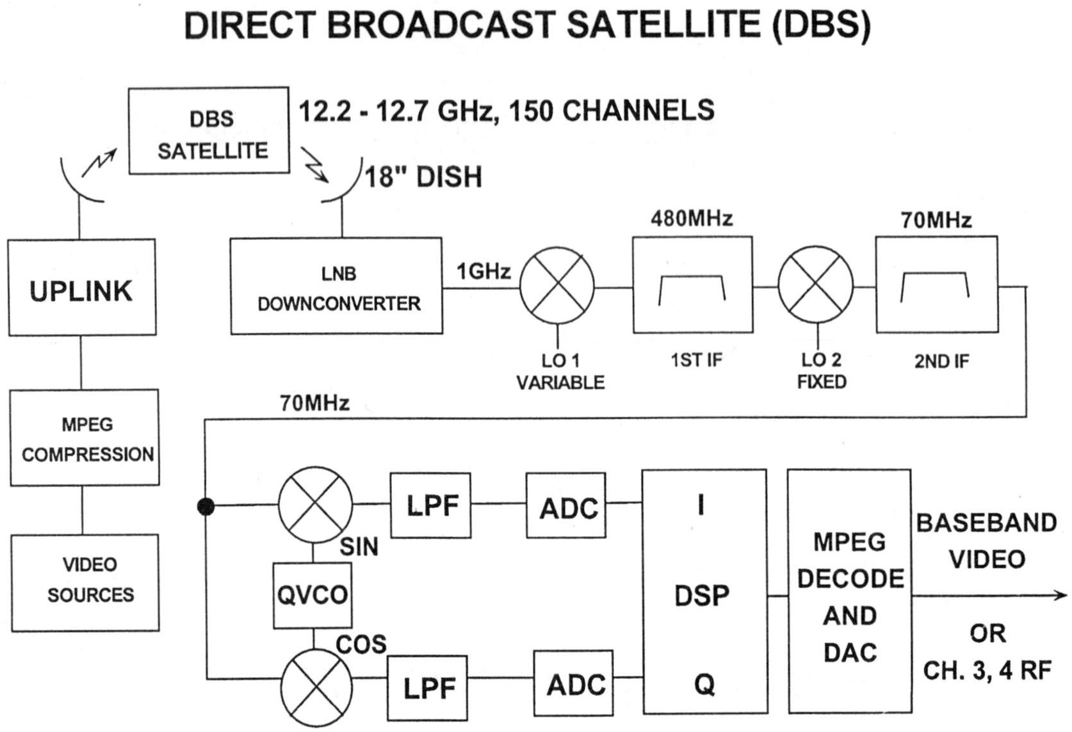

DIRECT BROADCAST SATELLITE (DBS)

Figure 5.59

The satellite downlink frequency is Ku-band (12.2 to 12.7GHz), and the transponder output power is about 120W (10 to 20 times that of a typical communications satellite which is designed for much larger receiver antennas). The LNB (Low Noise Block Converter) converts the 12.2 to 12.7GHz untuned band down to 950MHz to 1450MHz, where the signal is easier to tune, filter, and bring into the home over standard coaxial cable. The lower frequency signal (1GHz) incurs less loss over standard coaxial cable from the outside antenna to the inside of the house (generally 50 feet or more) than the Ku-band signal (12GHz).

The set-top box mixes the RF (1GHz) signal down to the first fixed IF frequency of 480MHz. The LO which drives the mixer is used for channel tuning. A second fixed-frequency IF

stage brings the tuned signal down to 70MHz where it is synchronously demodulated into baseband I and Q components. The modulation scheme is QPSK, the symbol rate is 30Mbaud, and the ADC sampling rate 60MSPS.

Figure 5.60 shows a two-chip solution to the front-end of the set-top box using the AD6461 (quadrature demodulator and baseband filter) and the AD6462 (dual 5-bit ADC and digital receiver). The input to the AD6461 is the 480MHz DBS IF signal. The chip-set is designed to support symbol rates up to 42.5Mbaud. The AD6461 utilizes Analog Devices' XFCB process and is packaged in 28-pin SOIC dissipating about 500mW. The AD6462 utilizes a 0.6 micron CMOS process and is packaged in an 80-pin PQFP dissipating approximately 1.2W (operating dynamically).

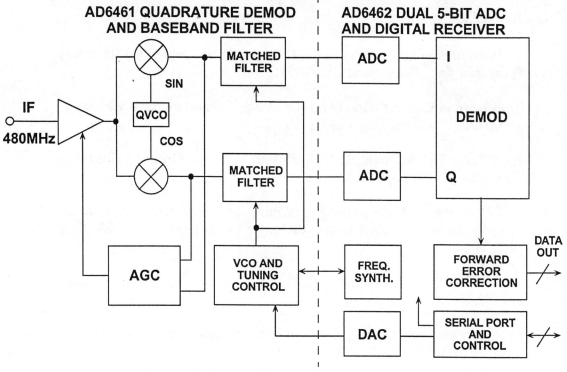

Figure 5.60

REFERENCES

1. *An Introduction to the Imaging CCD Array*, Technical Note 82W-4022, Tektronix, Inc., Beaverton, OR., 1987.

2. Brad Brannon, *Using Wide Dynamic Range Converters for Wide Band Radios*, **RF Design**, May 1995, pp.50-65.

3. Joe Mitola, *The Software Radio Architecture*, **IEEE Communications Magazine**, Vol. 33, No.5, May 1995, pp. 26-38.

4. Jeffery Wepman, *Analog-to-Digital Converters and Their Applications in Radio Receivers*, **IEEE Communications Magazine**, Vol. 33, No.5, May 1995, pp. 39-45.

5. Rupert Baines, *The DSP Bottleneck*, **IEEE CommunicationsMagazine**, Vol. 33, No.5, May 1995, pp. 46-54.

6. Brad Brannon, *Overcoming Converter Nonlinearities with Dither*, **Application Note AN-410**, Analog Devices, 1995.

7. Chris Keate and Mark O'Brien, *DBS Receiver Chip Simplifies Set-Top Box Design*, **RF Design**, November 1995, pp. 36-42.

8. Bill Schweber, *Direct Satellite Broadcast*, **EDN**, December 21, 1995, pp. 53-58.

SECTION 6

HIGH SPEED DACs AND DDS SYSTEMS

- Introduction to DDS

- Aliasing in DDS Systems

- 125MSPS DDS System (AD9850)

- DDS Systems as ADC Clock Drivers

- Amplitude Modulation in a DDS System

- The AD9831/AD9832 Complete DDS System

- Spurious Free Dynamic Range Considerations in DDS Systems

- High Speed Low Distortion DAC Architectures

- Improving SFDR Using Sample-and-Hold Deglitchers

- High Speed Interpolating DACs

- QPSK Signal Generation Using DDS (AD9853)

6

SECTION 6
HIGH SPEED DACs AND DDS SYSTEMS
Walt Kester

INTRODUCTION

A frequency synthesizer generates multiple frequencies from one or more frequency references. These devices have been used for decades, especially in communications systems. Many are based upon switching and mixing frequency outputs from a bank of crystal oscillators. Others have been based upon well understood techniques utilizing phase-locked loops (PLLs). This mature technology is illustrated in Figure 6.1. A fixed-frequency reference drives one input of the phase comparator. The other phase comparator input

is driven from a divide-by-N counter which is in turn driven by a voltage-controlled-oscillator (VCO). Negative feedback forces the output of the internal loop filter to a value which makes the VCO output frequency N-times the reference frequency. The time constant of the loop is controlled by the loop filter. There are many tradeoffs in designing a PLL, such a phase noise, tuning speed, frequency resolution, etc., and there are many good references on the subject (see References 1, 2, and 3).

FREQUENCY SYNTHESIS USING
OSCILLATORS AND PHASE-LOCKED LOOPS

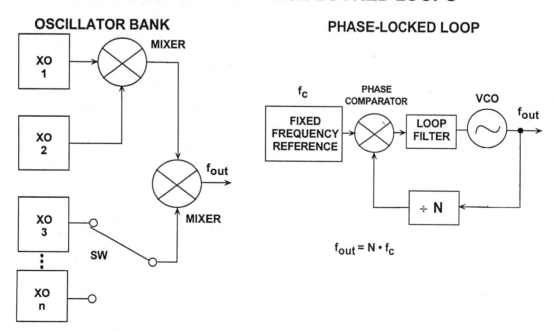

$$f_{out} = N \cdot f_c$$

Figure 6.1

With the widespread use of digital techniques in instrumentation and communications systems, a digitally-controlled method of generating multiple frequencies from a reference frequency source has evolved called Direct Digital Synthesis (DDS). The basic architecture is shown in Figure 6.2. In this simplified model, a stable clock drives a programmable-read-only-memory (PROM) which stores one or more integral number of cycles of a sinewave (or other arbitrary waveform, for that matter). As the address counter steps through each memory location, the corresponding digital amplitude of the signal at each location drives a DAC which in turn generates the analog output signal. The spectral purity of the final analog output signal is determined primarily by the DAC. The phase noise is basically that of the reference clock.

The DDS system differs from the PLL in several ways. Because a DDS system is a sampled data system, all the issues involved in sampling must be considered: quantization noise, aliasing, filtering, etc. For instance, the higher order harmonics of the DAC output frequencies fold back into the Nyquist bandwidth, making them unfilterable, whereas, the higher order harmonics of the output of PLL-based synthesizers can be filtered. There are other considerations which will be discussed shortly.

FUNDAMENTAL DIRECT DIGITAL SYNTHESIS SYSTEM

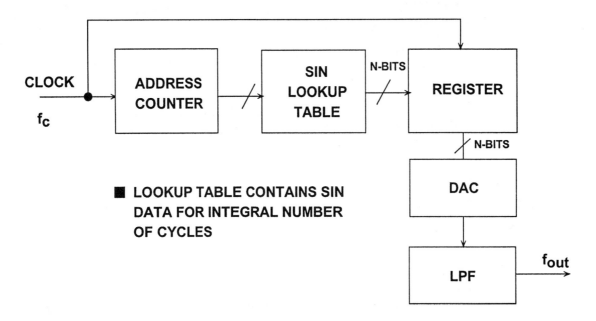

■ LOOKUP TABLE CONTAINS SIN
DATA FOR INTEGRAL NUMBER
OF CYCLES

Figure 6.2

A FLEXIBLE DDS SYSTEM

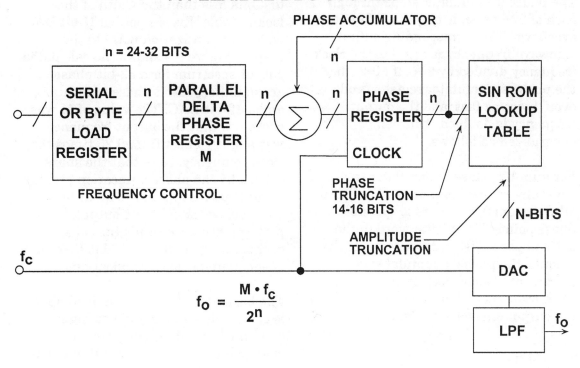

Figure 6.3

A fundamental problem with this simple DDS system is that the final output frequency can be changed only by changing the reference clock frequency or by reprogramming the PROM, making it rather inflexible. A practical DDS system implements this basic function in a much more flexible and efficient manner using digital hardware called a Numerically Controlled Oscillator (NCO). A block diagram of such a system is shown in Figure 6.3.

The heart of the system is the *phase accumulator* whose contents is updated once each clock cycle. Each time the phase accumulator is updated, the digital number, M, stored in the *delta phase register* is added to the number in the phase accumulator register. Assume that the number in the delta phase register is 00...01 and that the

initial contents of the phase accumulator is 00...00. The phase accumulator is updated by 00...01 on each clock cycle. If the accumulator is 32-bits wide, 2^{32} clock cycles (over 4 billion) are required before the phase accumulator returns to 00...00, and the cycle repeats.

The truncated output of the phase accumulator serves as the address to a sine (or cosine) lookup table. Each address in the lookup table corresponds to a phase point on the sinewave from 0° to 360°. The lookup table contains the corresponding digital amplitude information for one complete cycle of a sinewave. (Actually, only data for 90° is required because the quadrature data is contained in the two MSBs). The lookup table therefore maps the phase information from the phase accumulator into a digital amplitude word, which in turn drives the DAC.

6

Consider the case for n=32, and M=1. The phase accumulator steps through each of 2^{32} possible outputs before it overflows. The corresponding output sinewave frequency is equal to the clock frequency divided by 2^{32}. If M=2, then the phase accumulator register "rolls over" twice as fast, and the output frequency is doubled. This can be generalized as follows.

For an n-bit phase accumulator (n generally ranges from 24 to 32 in most DDS systems), there are 2^n possible phase points. The digital word in the delta phase register, M, represents the amount the phase accumulator is incremented each clock cycle. If f_c is the clock frequency, then the frequency of the output sinewave is equal to:

$$f_o = \frac{M \cdot f_c}{2^n}.$$

This equation is known as the DDS "tuning equation." Note that the frequency resolution of the system is equal to $f_c/2^n$. For n=32, the resolution is greater than one part in four billion! In a practical DDS system, all the bits out of the phase accumulator are not passed on to the lookup table, but are truncated, leaving only the first 13 to 15 MSBs. This reduces the size of the lookup table and does not affect the frequency resolution. The phase truncation only adds a small but acceptable amount of phase noise to the final output.

The resolution of the DAC is typically 2 to 4 bits less than the width of the lookup table. Even a perfect N-bit DAC will add quantization noise to the output. Figure 6.4 shows the calculated output spectrum for a 32-bit phase accumulator, 15-bit phase truncation, and a 12-bit DAC. The value of M was chosen so that the output frequency was slightly offset from 0.25 times the clock frequency. Note that the spurs caused by the phase truncation and the finite DAC resolution are all at least 90dB below the fullscale output. This performance far exceeds that of any commercially available 12-bit DAC and is adequate for most applications.

The basic DDS system described above is extremely flexible and has high resolution. The frequency can be changed instantaneously with no phase discontinuity by simply changing the contents of the M-register. However, practical DDS systems first require the execution of a serial, or byte-loading sequence to get the new frequency word into an internal buffer register which precedes the parallel-output M-register. This is done to minimize package pin count. After the new word is loaded into the buffer register, the parallel-output delta phase register is clocked, thereby changing all the bits simultaneously. The number of clock cycles required to load the delta-phase buffer register determines the maximum rate at which the output frequency can be changed.

CALCULATED OUTPUT SPECTRUM SHOWS 90dB SFDR FOR 15-BIT PHASE TRUNCATION AND 12-BIT OUTPUT DATA TRUNCATION

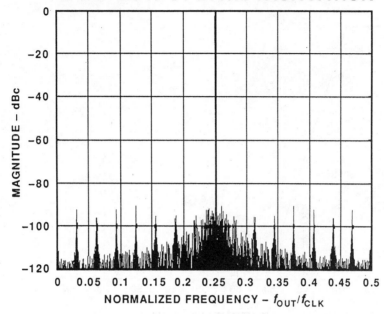

Figure 6.4

ALIASING IN DDS SYSTEMS

There is one important limitation to the range of output frequencies that can be generated from the simple DDS system. The Nyquist Criteria states that the clock frequency (sample rate) must be at least twice the output frequency. Practical limitations restrict the actual highest output frequency to about 1/3 the clock frequency. Figure 6.5 shows the output of a DAC in a DDS system where the output frequency is 30MHz and the clock frequency is 100MHz. An antialiasing filter must follow the reconstruction DAC to remove the lower image frequency (100–30=70MHz) as shown in the figure.

Note that the amplitude response of the DAC output (before filtering) follows a sin(x)/x response with zeros at the clock frequency and multiples thereof. The

exact equation for the normalized output amplitude, $A(f_0)$, is given by:

$$A(f_0) = \frac{\sin\left(\frac{\pi f_0}{f_c}\right)}{\frac{\pi f_0}{f_c}},$$

where f_0 is the output frequency and f_c is the clock frequency.

This rolloff is because the DAC output is not a series of zero-width impulses (as in a perfect re-sampler), but a series of rectangular pulses whose width is equal to the reciprocal of the update rate. The amplitude of the sin(x)/x response is down 3.92dB at the Nyquist frequency (1/2 the DAC update rate). In

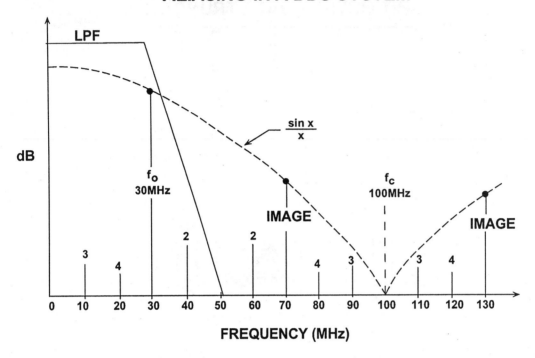

Figure 6.5

practice, the transfer function of the antialiasing filter is designed to compensate for the $\sin(x)/x$ rolloff so that the overall frequency response is relatively flat up to the maximum output DAC frequency (generally 1/3 the update rate).

Another important consideration is that, unlike a PLL-based system, the higher order harmonics of the fundamental output frequency in a DDS system will fold back into the baseband because of aliasing. These harmonics cannot be removed by the antialiasing filter. For instance, if the clock frequency is 100MHz, and the output frequency is 30MHz, the second harmonic of the 30MHz output signal appears at 60MHz (out of band), but also at 100–60=40MHz (the aliased component. Similarly, the third harmonic (90MHz) appears inband at 100–90=10MHz, and the fourth at 120–100MHz=20MHz. Higher order harmonics also fall within the Nyquist bandwidth (DC to $f_c/2$). The location of the first four harmonics is shown in the diagram.

125MSPS DDS System (AD9850)

The AD9850 125MSPS DDS system (Figure 6.6) uses a 32-bit phase accumulator which is truncated to 14-bits (MSBs) before being passed to the lookup table. The final digital output is 10-bits to the internal DAC. The AD9850 allows the output phase to be modulated using an additional register and an adder placed between the output of the phase accumulator register and the input to the lookup table. The AD9850 uses a 5-bit word to control the phase which allows shifting the phase

in increments of 180°, 90°, 45°, 22.5°, 11.25°, and any combination thereof. The device also contains an internal high speed comparator which can be configured to accept the (externally) filtered output of the DAC to generate a low-jitter output pulse suitable for driving the sampling clock input of an ADC. The full scale output current can be adjusted from 10 to 20mA using a single external resistor, and the output voltage compliance is +1V. Key specifications are summarized in Figure 6.7.

AD9850 CMOS 125MSPS DDS/DAC SYNTHESIZER

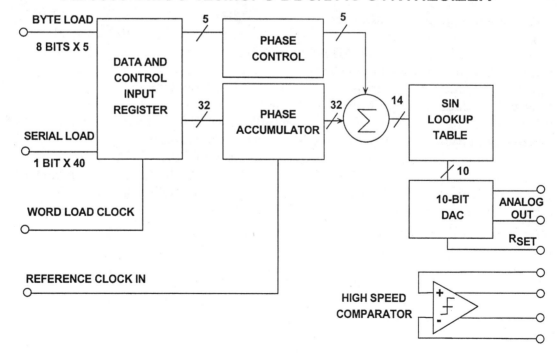

Figure 6.6

AD9850 DDS/DAC SYNTHESIZER KEY SPECIFICATIONS

- ■ 125MSPS Clock Rate

- ■ On-Chip 10-bit DAC and High Speed Comparator

- ■ DAC SFDR > 50dBc @ 40MHz Output

- ■ 32-bit Frequency Tuning

- ■ 5-bit Phase Modulation

- ■ Simplified Control Interface: Byte-Parallel or Serial Load

- ■ +5V or +3.3V Supplies

- ■ 380mW Dissipation @ 125MSPS on +5V Supply
  (30mW Power-Down Mode)

- ■ 28-Pin Shrink Small Outline Package (SSOP)

Figure 6.7

The frequency tuning (delta-phase register input word) and phase modulation words are loaded into the AD9850 via a parallel or serial loading format. The parallel load format consists of five consecutive loads of an 8-bit control word (byte). The first 8-bit byte controls phase modulation (5-bits), power-down enable (1-bit), and loading format (2-bits). Bytes 2-5 comprise the 32-bit frequency tuning word. The maximum control register update frequency is 23MHz. Serial loading of the AD9850 is accomplished via a 40-bit serial data stream on a single pin. Maximum update rate of the control register in the serial-load mode is 3MHz.

The AD9850 consumes only 380mW of power on a single +5V supply at a maximum 125MSPS clock rate. The device is available in a 28-pin surface mount SSOP (Shrink Small Outline Package).

DDS SYSTEMS AS ADC CLOCK DRIVERS

DDS systems such as the AD9850 provide an excellent method of generating the sampling clock to the ADC, especially when the ADC sampling frequency must be under software control and locked to the system clock (see Figure 6.8). The *true* DAC output current I_{out}, drives a 200Ω, 42MHz lowpass filter which is source and load terminated, thereby making the equivalent load 100Ω. The filter removes spurious frequency components above 42MHz. The filtered output drives one input of the AD9850 internal comparator. The *complementary* DAC output current drives a 100Ω load. The output of the 100kΩ resistor divider placed between the two outputs is

decoupled and generates the reference voltage for the internal comparator.

The comparator output has a 2ns rise and fall time and generates a TTL/CMOS-compatible square wave. The jitter of the comparator output edges is less than 20ps rms. True and complementary outputs are available if required.

In the circuit shown (Figure 6.8), the total output rms jitter for a 40MSPS ADC clock is 50ps rms, and the resulting degradation in SNR must be considered in wide dynamic range applications.

USING DDS SYSTEMS AS ADC CLOCK DRIVERS

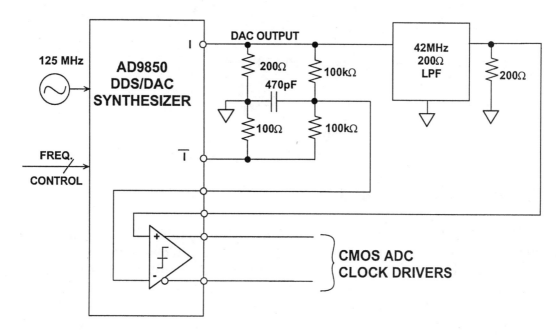

Figure 6.8

6

AMPLITUDE MODULATION IN A DDS SYSTEM

Amplitude modulation in a DDS system can be accomplished by placing a digital multiplier between the lookup table and the DAC input as shown in Figure 6.9. Another method to modulate the DAC output amplitude is to vary the reference voltage to the DAC. In the case of the AD9850, the bandwidth of the internal reference control amplifier is approximately 1MHz. This method is useful for relatively small output amplitude changes as long as the output signal does not exceed the +1V compliance specification.

AMPLITUDE MODULATION IN A DDS SYSTEM

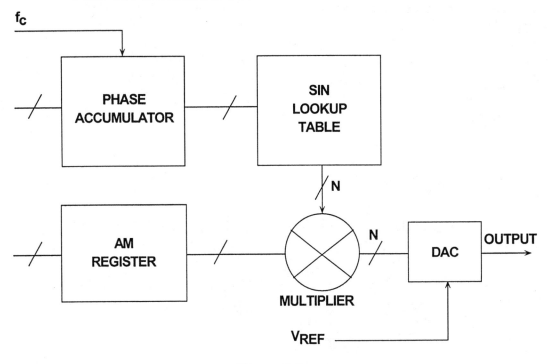

Figure 6.9

THE AD9830/9831 COMPLETE DDS SYSTEMS

The AD9830/9831 CMOS DDS systems (see Figure 6.10) contain two frequency registers and four phase registers thereby allowing both frequency and phase modulation. The registers are loaded through a parallel microprocessor port. The DDS chips contain a 32-bit phase accumulator register, 12-bit sin ROM lookup table, and a 10-bit DAC. The AD9830 operates at 50MSPS and dissipates 250mW on the +5V supply. The AD9831 operates at 25MSPS and dissipates 150mW on a +5V supply and 35mW on +3V. Key specifications for the devices are summarized in Figure 6.11.

AD9830/9831, 50/25MSPS COMPLETE DDS SYSTEMS

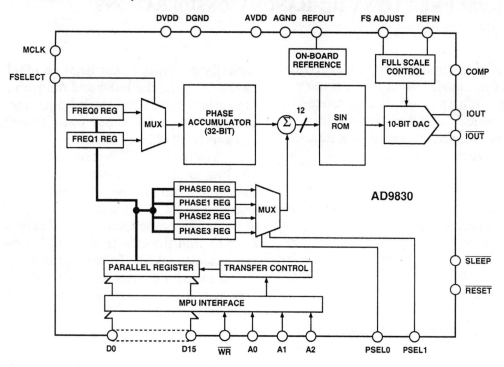

Figure 6.10

AD9830/9831 DDS SYSTEMS KEY SPECIFICATIONS

■ 50MSPS (AD9830), 25MSPS (AD9831) Update Rate

■ Single +5V (AD9830), +5V/+3V (AD9831) Supply

■ 32-bit Phase Accumulator, 12-bit Address Sine ROM

■ On Chip 10-bit DAC (70dB SFDR)

■ Two On-Chip Frequency Modulation Registers

■ Four On-Chip Phase Modulation Registers

■ On-Chip Reference

■ Power Dissipation: 250mW (AD9830),
  150mW (AD9831 @ +5V), 35mW (AD9831 @ +3V)

■ 48-pin TQFP

Figure 6.11

SPURIOUS FREE DYNAMIC RANGE CONSIDERATIONS IN DDS SYSTEMS

In many DDS applications, the spectral purity of the DAC output is of primary concern. Unfortunately, the measurement, prediction, and analysis of this performance is complicated by a number of interacting factors.

Even an ideal N-bit DAC will produce harmonics in a DDS system. The amplitude of these harmonics is highly dependent upon the ratio of the output frequency to the clock frequency. This is because the spectral content of the DAC quantization noise varies as this ratio varies, even though its theoretical rms value remains equal to $q/\sqrt{12}$ (where q is the weight of the LSB). The assumption that the quantization noise appears as white noise and is spread uniformly over the Nyquist bandwidth is simply not true in a DDS system (it is more apt to be a true assumption in an ADC-based system, because the ADC adds a certain amount of noise to the signal which tends to "dither" or randomize the quantization error. However, a certain amount of correlation still exists). For instance, if the DAC output frequency is set to an exact submultiple of the clock frequency, then the quantization noise will be concentrated at multiples of the output frequency, i.e., it is highly signal dependent. If the output frequency is slightly offset, however, the quantization noise will become more random, thereby giving an improvement in the effective SFDR.

This is illustrated in Figure 6.12, where a 4096 point FFT is calculated based on digitally generated data from an ideal 12-bit DAC. In the left-hand diagram, the ratio between the clock frequency and the output frequency was chosen to be exactly 32 (128 cycles of the sinewave in the FFT record length), yielding an SFDR of about 78dBc. In the right-hand diagram, the ratio was changed to 32.25196850394 (127 cycles of the sinewave within the FFT record length), and the effective SFDR is now increased to 92dBc. In this ideal case, we observed a change in SFDR of 14dB just by slightly changing the frequency ratio.

Best SFDR can therefore be obtained by the careful selection of the clock and output frequencies. However, in some applications, this may not be possible. In ADC-based systems, adding a small amount of random noise to the input tends to randomize the quantization errors and reduce this effect. The same thing can be done in a DDS system as shown in Figure 6.13 (Reference 5). The pseudo-random digital noise generator output is added to the DDS sine amplitude word before being loaded into the DAC. The amplitude of the digital noise is set to about 1/2 LSB. This accomplishes the randomization process at the expense of a slight increase in the overall output noise floor. In most DDS applications, however, there is enough flexibility in selecting the various frequency ratios so that dithering is not required.

EFFECT OF RATIO OF CLOCK TO OUTPUT FREQUENCY ON THEORETICAL 12-BIT DAC SFDR USING 4096-POINT FFT

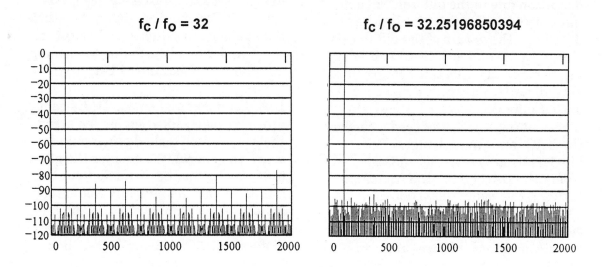

Figure 6.12

INJECTION OF DIGITAL DITHER IN A DDS SYSTEM TO RANDOMIZE QUANTIZATION NOISE AND INCREASE SFDR

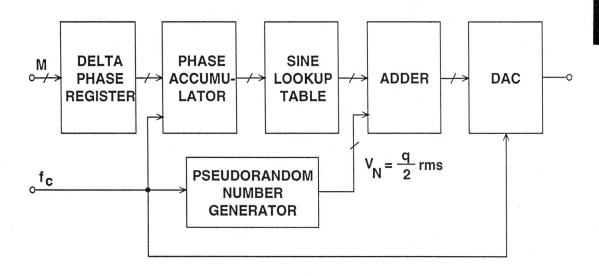

Figure 6.13

A non-ideal DAC will introduce several other mechanisms of distortion. First, the overall integral non-linearity of the DAC transfer function will introduce harmonic distortion. This distortion behaves much like that produced by the non-linearity of an amplifier. The distortion due to the differential non-linearity of the DAC is highly dependent upon the nature of the differential non-linearity and is difficult to predict mathematically. The third source of DAC distortion are code-dependent output glitches. In a DAC there is a transient (or glitch) produced whenever the DAC input code changes. This glitch is usually worst at midscale, where the DAC makes the transition between the codes 1000...000 and 0111...111, and all the DAC bits must switch. These glitches occur because of the unequal turn-on/turn-off times of the DAC current switches. They also occur at 1/4 scale, 1/8 scale, etc., with decreasing amplitude. Because the glitches are code-dependent (hence signal-dependent) they produce harmonics of the fundamental output DAC frequency. For instance, each time the sinewave crosses through mid-scale, a glitch occurs, thereby producing a second harmonic - since the sinewave passes through midscale twice each cycle. The harmonics produced by these code-dependent glitches fold back into the Nyquist bandwidth due to aliasing and thereby affect the SFDR.

Low distortion high-speed DACs generally have a specification for the area of the worst glitch (called *glitch impulse area*). In general, the smaller the glitch area, the better the distortion-but it is difficult to mathematically relate the distortion performance to the glitch area. The glitch impulse area for low distortion DACs is usually less than 30pV-sec. A typical midscale glitch impulse is shown for the AD9721 DAC in Figure 6.15.

CONTRIBUTORS TO DDS DAC DISTORTION

- Resolution

- Integral Non-Linearity

- Differential Non-Linearity

- Code-Dependent Glitches

- Ratio of Clock Frequency to Output Frequency (Even in an Ideal DAC)

- Mathematical Analysis is Difficult !

Figure 6.14

AD9720/AD9721 DAC MIDSCALE GLITCH SHOWS 1.34pV-s
NET IMPULSE AREA AND SETTLING TIME OF 4.5ns

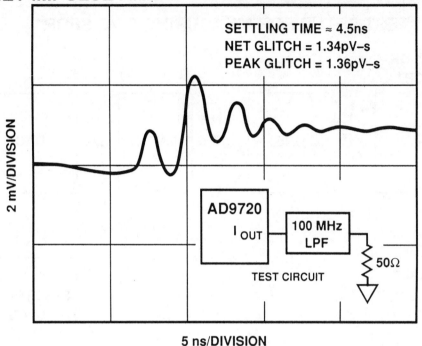

Figure 6.15

The best way to measure DAC performance is with a spectrum analyzer, with a DDS system used to drive the DAC (Figure 6.16). Because there are nearly an infinite combination of possible clock and output frequencies, SFDR is generally specified for only a few selected combinations. One method is to plot the SFDR as a function of clock frequency for the output frequency slightly offset from 1/3 or 1/4 the clock frequency. The small frequency offset randomizes the quantization noise and also allows the distortion products to be easily observed.

Note that for the output slightly offset from $f_c/3$, the even harmonics will be aliased very close to the output signal as shown in Figure 6.17. Similarly, for the output slightly offset from $f_c/4$, the odd harmonics will fall close to the output frequency (Figure 6.18).The SFDR at $f_c/3$ is usually considered a worse case condition and is often plotted as a function of clock frequency as shown in Figure 6.19 for the AD9721 10-bit, 100MSPS TTL-compatible DAC.

6

TEST SETUP FOR MEASURING DAC SFDR

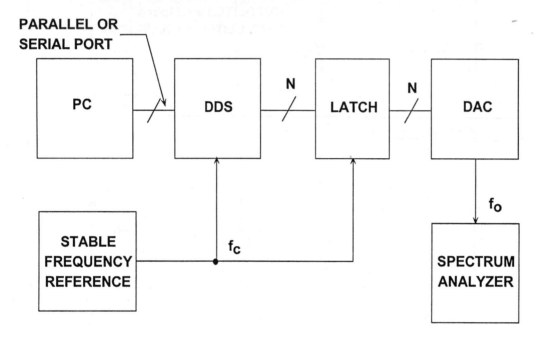

Figure 6.16

LOCATION OF EVEN HARMONICS FOR
$$f_O = f_C / 3 - \Delta f$$

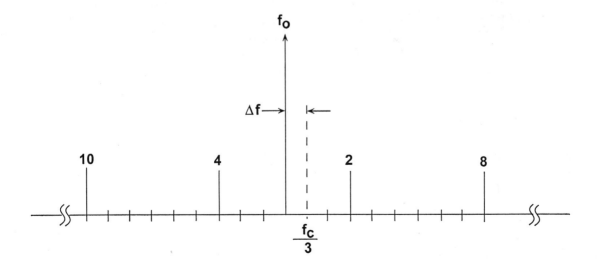

Figure 6.17

LOCATION OF ODD HARMONICS FOR
$f_O = f_C / 4 - \Delta f$

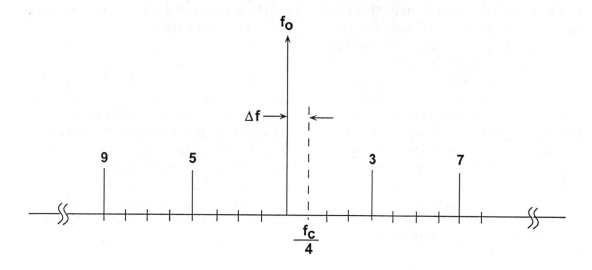

Figure 6.18

SFDR OF AD9721 10-BIT DAC FOR
$f_O \sim f_C / 3$ (BANDWIDTH: DC TO $f_C / 2$)

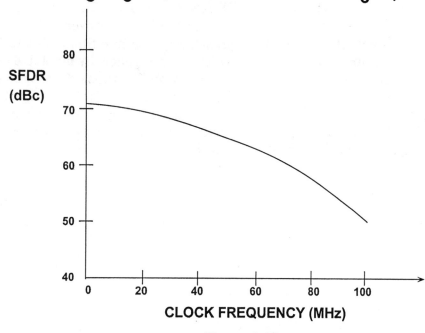

Figure 6.19

HIGH SPEED LOW DISTORTION DAC ARCHITECTURES

Because of the emphasis in communications systems for DDS DACs with high SFDR, much effort has been placed on determining optimum DAC architectures. Practically all low distortion high speed DACs make use of some form of non-saturating current-mode switching. A straight binary DAC with one current switch per bit produces code-dependent glitches as discussed above and is certainly not the most optimum architecture (Figure 6.20). A DAC with one current source per code level can be shown not to have code-dependent glitches, but it is not practical to implement for high resolutions. However, this performance can be approached by decoding the first few MSBs into a "thermometer" code and have one current switch per level. For example, a 5-bit thermometer DAC would have an architecture similar to that shown in Figure 6.21.

The input binary word is latched and then decoded into 31 outputs which drive a second latch. The output of the second latch drives 31 equally weighted current switches whose outputs are summed together. This scheme effectively removes nearly all the code-dependence of the output glitch. The residual glitch that does occur at the output is equal regardless of the output code change and can be filtered. The distortion mechanisms associated with the full-decoded architecture are primarily asymmetrical output slewing, finite switch turn-on and turn-off times, and integral nonlinearity.

The obvious disadvantage of this type of thermometer DAC is the large number of latches and switches required to make a 12, 10, or even 8-bit DAC. However, if this technique is used on the 5 MSBs of an 8, 10, or 12-bit DAC, a significant reduction in the code-dependent glitch is possible. This process is called *segmentation* and is quite common in low distortion DACs.

Figure 6.22 shows a scheme whereby the first 5 bits of a 10-bit DAC are decoded as described above and drive 31 equally weighted switches. The last 5 bits are derived from binarily weighted current sources. Equally weighted current sources driving an R/2R resistor ladder could be used to derive the LSBs, however, this approach requires thin film resistors which are not generally available on a low-cost CMOS process. Also, the use of R/2R networks lowers the DAC output impedance, thereby requiring more drive current to develop the same voltage across a fixed load resistance.

5-BIT BINARY DAC ARCHITECTURES

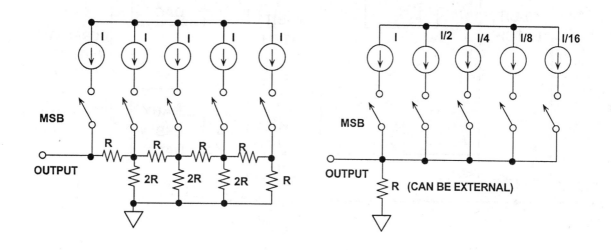

Figure 6.20

5-BIT "THERMOMETER" OR "FULLY-DECODED" DAC

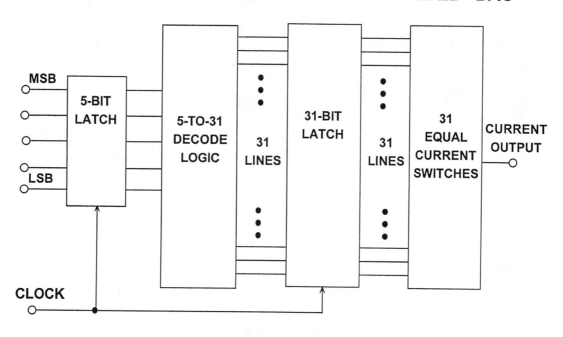

Figure 6.21

10-BIT SEGMENTED DAC

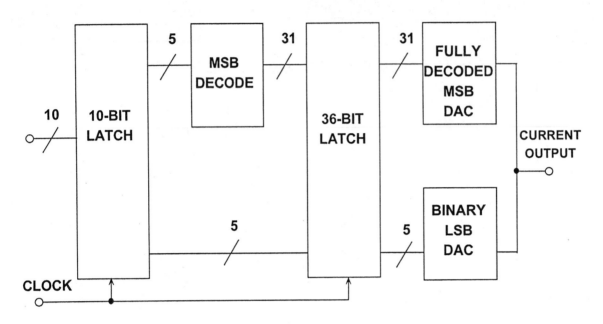

Figure 6.22

AD9850 10-BIT CMOS CURRENT SWITCH DAC CORE

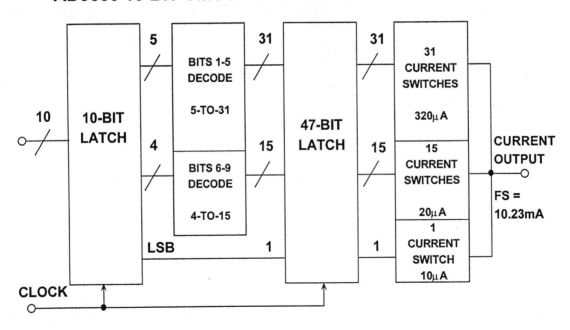

Figure 6.23

The AD9850 internal 10-bit DAC uses two major stages of segmentation as shown in Figure 6.23. The first 5 bits (MSBs) are fully decoded and drive 31 equally weighted current switches (320µA each). The next 4 bits are decoded into 15 lines which drive 15 current switches, each supplying 20µA (1/16 the current supplied by each MSB switch). The LSB is latched and drives a single current switch which supplies 10µA (1/32 the current supplied by each MSB switch). A total of 47 current switches and latches are required to implement this architecture.

The basic current switching cell is made up of a differential PMOS transistor pair as shown in Figure 6.24. The differential pairs are driven with low-level logic to minimize switching tran-sients and time skew. The DAC outputs are symmetrical differential currents which help to minimize even-order distortion products (especially which driving a differential output such as a transformer or an op amp differential I/V converter).

The overall architecture of the AD9850 is an excellent tradeoff between power/performance and allows the entire DDS function to be implemented on a stan-dard CMOS process with no thin film resistors. Single-supply operation on +3.3V or +5V makes the device ex-tremely attractive for portable and low power applications. The SFDR perfor-mance is typically 60, 55, and 45dBc for output frequencies of 1, 20, and 40MHz, respectively (clock frequency = 125MSPS).

PMOS TRANSISTOR CURRENT SWITCHES

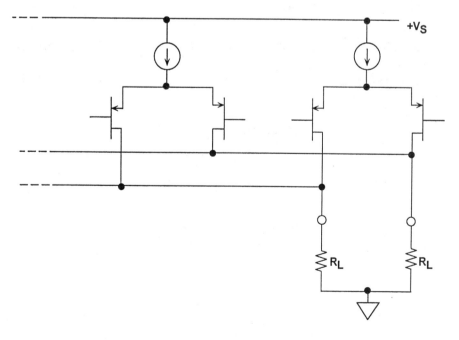

Figure 6.24

The AD9760 (10-bit), AD9762 (12-bit) and AD9764 (14-bit) 100MSPS DACs utilize the same basic switching core as the AD9850. This family of DACs is pin-compatible, and offers exceptional AC and DC performance. They operate on single +5V or +3V supplies and contain on-chip latches, reference, and are ideal for the transmit channel in wireless basestations, ADSL/HFC modems, and DDS applications. Key specifications for the family are summarized in Figure 6.25.

AD9760/9762/9764 FAMILY OF 100MSPS DACs

■ Pin-Compatible 10-bit (AD9760), 12-bit (AD9762), and 14-bit (AD9764)

■ SFDR for 15MHz Output: -60dBc

■ Low Glitch Impulse: 5pVsec

■ On-Chip Reference

■ Single +5V or +3V Supplies

■ Power Dissipation: 175mW @ 5V

■ Power-Down Mode: 30mW

Figure 6.25

IMPROVING SFDR USING SAMPLE-AND-HOLD DEGLITCHERS

High-speed sample-and-hold amplifiers (such as the AD9100 and AD9101) can be used to deglitch DAC outputs as shown in Figure 6.26. Just prior to latching new data into the DAC, the SHA is put into the *hold* mode so that the DAC switching glitches are isolated from the output. The switching transients produced by the SHA are code-independent and occur at the clock frequency and hence are easily filtered.

However, great care must be taken so that the relative timing between the SHA clock and the DAC update clock is optimum. In addition, the distortion performance of the SHA must be at least 6 to 10dB better than the DAC, or no improvement in SFDR will be realized. Achieving good results using an external SHA deglitcher becomes increasingly more difficult as clock frequencies approach 100MSPS.

SAMPLE-AND-HOLD (SHA) USED AS DAC DEGLITCHER

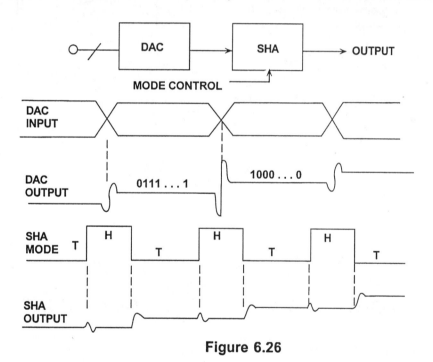

Figure 6.26

The AD6742 is a 12-bit, 65MSPS low distortion DAC with on-chip SHA deglitcher designed for communications applications. This DAC is fabricated on the XFCB process and provides 75dB SFDR for a 20MHz output. A functional diagram is shown in Figure 6.27, and key specifications in Figure 6.28.

AD6742 12-BIT, 65MSPS DEGLITCHED DAC

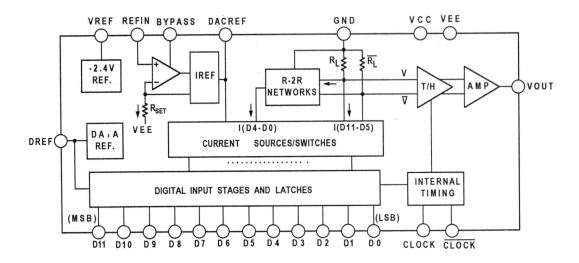

Figure 6.27

AD6742 12-BIT, 65MSPS DAC KEY SPECIFICATIONS

- ■ 12-bit, 65MSPS Communications DAC

- ■ High SFDR: 75dB (min) @ 65MSPS and 20MHz Output

- ■ Fabricated on XFCB process

- ■ On-Chip Reference

- ■ Dual 5V Supplies, 800mW power dissipation

Figure 6.28

HIGH SPEED INTERPOLATING DACs

Consider a DDS system which operates at a clock frequency of 100MSPS and outputs a 30MHz sinewave (see Figure 6.29). The first aliased (or image) frequency occurs at 100–30 = 70MHz. Assume we wish the antialiasing filter to attenuate this image frequency component by 60dB. The filter must go from a passband of 30MHz to 60dB stopband attenuation over the transi-

tion band lying between 30 and 70MHz (approximately one octave). A Butterworth filter design gives 6dB attenuation per octave for each pole. Therefore, a minimum of 10 poles is required to provide the desired attenuation. Filters become even more complex as the transition band becomes narrower.

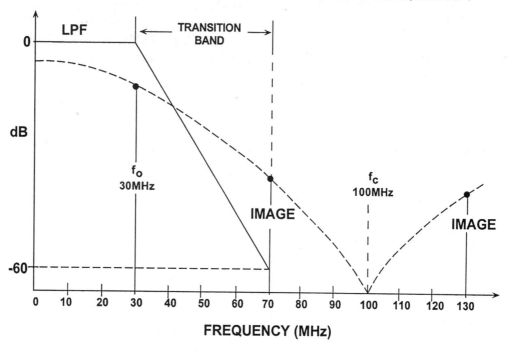

LPF REQUIRED TO REJECT IMAGE FREQUENCY

Figure 6.29

In ADC-based systems, oversampling can ease the requirements on the antialiasing filter, and a sigma-delta ADC has this inherent advantage. In a DAC-based system (such as DDS), the concept of interpolation can be used in a similar manner. This concept is common in digital audio CD players, where the basic update rate of the data from

the CD is about 44kSPS. "Zeros" are inserted into the parallel data, thereby increasing the effective update rate to 4-times, 8-times, or 16-times the fundamental throughput rate. The 4x, 8x, or 16x data stream is passed through a digital interpolation filter which generates the extra data points. The high oversampling rate moves the image frequencies higher, thereby allowing a less complex filter with a wider transition band.

The same concept can be applied to a high speed DDS DAC. Assume a traditional DAC is driven at an input word rate of 30MSPS (see Figure 6.30). The maximum realizable DAC output frequency is about 10MHz. The image frequency component at 30–10 = 20MHz must be attenuated by the analog antialiasing filter, and the transition band of the filter is 10 to 20MHz.

Assume that we increase the update rate to 60MSPS by inserting a "zero" between each original data sample. The parallel data stream is now 60MSPS and is passed through the digital interpolation filter which computes the

additional data points. The response of the digital filter relative to the 2-times oversampling frequency is shown in Figure 6.30. The analog antialiasing filter transition zone is now 10 to 50MHz (the first image occurs at $2f_c-f_0=60-10=50$MHz).

The AD977x is a 4-times oversampling interpolating 10-bit DAC, and a simplified block diagram is shown in Figure 6.31. The device is designed to handle 10-bit input word rates up to about 30MSPS. The internal digital filter consists of a 15-tap filter operating at $2f_c$ followed by a 7-tap filter operating at $4f_c$. The output word rate is 120MSPS, putting the image frequency at $4f_c-f_0=120-10=110$MHz. SFDR of the DAC for a 10MHz output is approximately 60dBc.

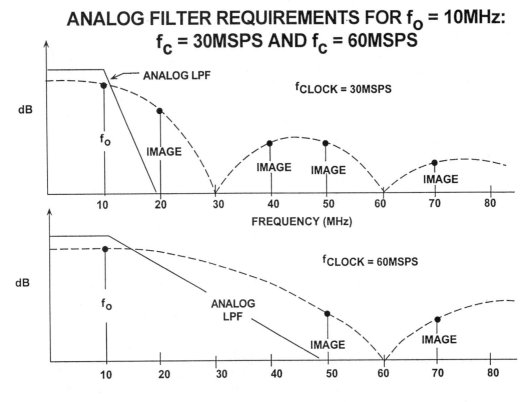

ANALOG FILTER REQUIREMENTS FOR f_O = 10MHz: f_C = 30MSPS AND f_C = 60MSPS

Figure 6.30

INCREASING THE DAC THROUGHPUT RATE BY "K" USING A PLL AND A DIGITAL INTERPOLATION FILTER (INTERPOLATING DAC)

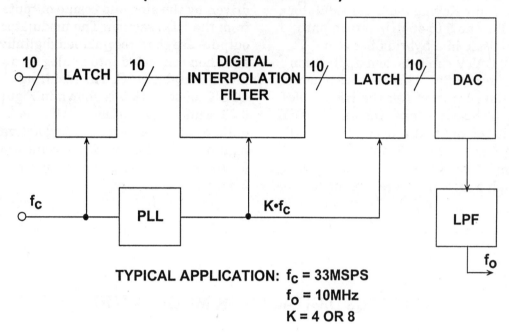

TYPICAL APPLICATION: f_C = 33MSPS

f_O = 10MHz

K = 4 OR 8

Figure 6.31

6

QPSK SIGNAL GENERATION USING DDS (AD9853)

The AD9853 is a digital Quadrature Phase Shift Keying (QPSK) modulator useful in the 5 to 40MHz return path transmitter in a hybrid fiber coax (HFC) CATV cable modem application (see Figure 6.32). This allows asynchronous data transfer over the HFC cable plant. The device takes the serial QPSK data input, splits it into an in-phase (I) and quadrature (Q) signal. The I and Q channel data is then filtered and passed through a digital quadrature modula-

tor. The quadrature modulators are driven by the sine and cosine outputs from the DDS section. The modulator outputs are then recombined digitally and then converted into analog by an internal 10-bit DAC. The resulting QPSK constellation is shown in Figure 6.33. This scheme of modulation is quite common, and results in relatively high noise immunity. Key specifications for the AD9853 are given in Figure 6.34.

AD9853 DIGITAL QPSK MODULATOR

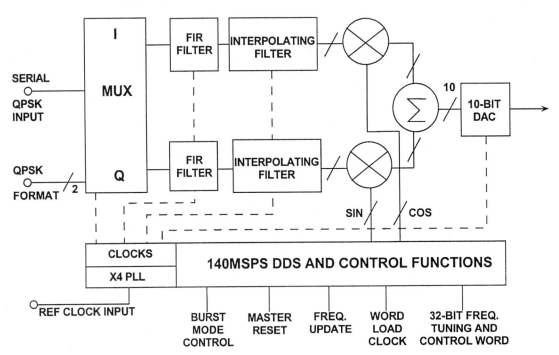

Figure 6.32

QPSK CONSTELLATION

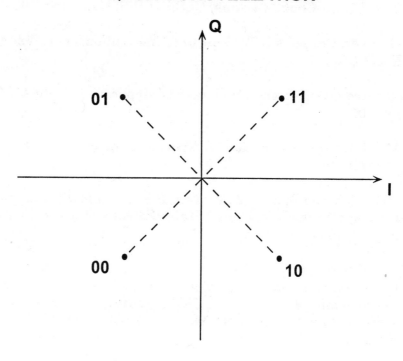

Figure 6.33

AD9853 DIGITAL QPSK MODULATOR KEY SPECIFICATIONS

- Performs Transmit Function for QPSK 5-40MHz Hybrid Fiber Coax (HFC) Return Path

- Includes Raised Cosine Pulse-Shaping Filter (Alpha = 0.5) and Interpolation Filters

- 140MSPS Clock Frequency

- 46dBc SFDR @ 40MHz Output

- +5V or +3.3V Operation

- 300mW Dissipation @ 125MSPS Clock Frequency (30mW Power-Down Mode)

- 28-Pin SSOP Surface-Mount Package

Figure 6.34

6

REFERENCES

1. R.E. Best, **Phase-Locked Loops,** McGraw-Hill, New York, 1984.

2. F.M. Gardner, **Phaselock Techniques,** 2nd Edition, John Wiley, New York, 1979.

3. *Phase-Locked Loop Design Fundamentals*, Applications Note AN-535, Motorola, Inc.

4. **The ARRL Handbook for Radio Amateurs,** American Radio Relay League, Newington, CT, 1992.

5. Richard J. Kerr and Lindsay A. Weaver, *Pseudorandom Dither for Frequency Synthesis Noise*, United States Patent Number 4,901,265, February 13, 1990.

6. Henry T. Nicholas, III and Henry Samueli, *An Analysis of the Output Spectrum of Direct Digital Frequency Synthesizers in the Presence of Phase-Accumulator Truncation*, **IEEE 41st Annual Frequency Control Symposium Digest of Papers**, 1987, pp. 495-502, IEEE Publication No. CH2427-3/87/0000-495.

7. Henry T. Nicholas, III and Henry Samueli, *The Optimization of Direct Digital Frequency Synthesizer Performance in the Presence of Finite Word Length Effects*, **IEEE 42nd Annual Frequency Control Symposium Digest of Papers**, 1988, pp. 357-363, IEEE Publication No. CH2588-2/88/0000-357.

SECTION 7

HIGH SPEED HARDWARE DESIGN TECHNIQUES

- Analog Circuit Simulation

- Prototyping Analog Circuits

- Evaluation Boards

- Grounding in High Speed Systems

- Power Supply Noise Reduction and Filtering

- Power Supply Regulation/Conditioning

- Thermal Management

- EMI/RFI Considerations

- Shielding Concepts

7

SECTION 7

HIGH SPEED HARDWARE DESIGN TECHNIQUES
Walt Kester, James Bryant, Walt Jung, Adolfo Garcia, John McDonald, Joe Buxton

ANALOG CIRCUIT SIMULATION
Walt Kester, Joe Buxton

In recent years there has been much pressure placed on system designers to verify their designs with computer simulations before committing to actual printed circuit board layouts and hardware. Simulating complex digital designs is extremely beneficial, and very often, the prototype phase can be eliminated entirely. However, bypassing the prototype phase in high-speed/high-performance analog or mixed-signal circuit designs can be risky for a number of reasons.

For the purposes of this discussion, an *analog* circuit is any circuit which uses ICs such as op amps, instrumentation amps, programmable gain amps (PGAs), voltage controlled amps (VCAs), log amps, mixers, analog multipliers, etc. A *mixed-signal* circuit is an A/D converter (ADC), D/A converter (DAC), or combinations of these in conjunction with some amount of digital signal processing which may or may not be on the same IC as the converters.

Consider a typical IC operational amplifier. It may contain some 20-40 transistors, almost as many resistors, and a few capacitors. A complete SPICE (Simulation Program with Integrated

Circuit Emphasis, see Reference 1) model will contain all these components, and probably a few of the more important parasitic capacitances and spurious diodes formed by the various junctions in the op-amp chip. For high-speed ICs, the package and wirebond parasitics may also be included. This is the type of model that the IC designer uses to optimize the device during the design phase and is typically run on a CAD workstation. Because it is a detailed model, it will be referred to as a *micromodel*. In simulations, such a model will behave very much like the actual op-amp, but not exactly.

The IC designer uses transistor and other device models based on the actual process upon which the component is fabricated. Semiconductor manufacturers invest considerable time and money developing and refining these device models so that the IC designers can have a high degree of confidence that the first silicon will work and that mask changes (costing additional time and money) required for the final manufactured product are minimized.

However, these *device* models are not published, neither are the IC *micromodels*, as they contain propri-

7

etary information which would be of use to other semiconductor companies who might wish to copy or improve on the design. It would also take far too long for a simulation of a system containing several ICs (each represented by its own micromodel) to reach a useful result. SPICE micromodels of analog ICs often fail to converge (especially under transient conditions), and multiple IC circuits make this a greater possibility.

For these reasons, the SPICE models of analog circuits published by manufacturers or software companies are *macromodels* (as opposed to *micromodels*), which simulate the major features of the component, but lack fine detail. Most manufacturers of linear ICs (including Analog Devices) provide these macromodels for components such as operational amplifiers, analog multipliers, references, etc. (Reference 2 and 3). These models represent *approximations* to the actual circuit, and parasitic

effects such as package capacitance and inductance and PC board layout are rarely included. The models are designed to work with various versions of SPICE simulation programs such as PSpice® (Reference 4) and run on workstations or personal computers. The models are simple enough so that circuits using multiple ICs can be simulated in a reasonable amount of computation time and with good certainty of convergence. Consequently, SPICE modeling does not always reproduce the exact performance of a circuit and should always be verified experimentally using a carefully built prototype.

Finally, there are mixed-signal ICs such as A/D and D/A converters which have *no* SPICE models, or if they exist, the models do not simulate dynamic performance (Signal-to-noise, effective bits, etc.), and prototypes of circuits using them should always be built.

SPICE SIMULATIONS: MACROMODEL OR MICROMODEL?

	METHODOLOGY	ADVANTAGES	DISADVANTAGES
MACROMODEL	Ideal Elements Model the Device Behavior	Fast Simulation Time, Easy to Modify	May Not Model All Characteristics
MICROMODEL	Fully Characterized Transistor Level	Most Complete Model	Slow Simulation, Difficulty in Convergence Not Available to Customers

Figure 7.1

The ADSpice Model

The ADSpice model was developed to advance the state-of-the-art in op amp macromodelling and provide a tool for designers to simulate accurately their circuits. Previously, the dominant model architecture was the Boyle model (Reference 3). However, this model was developed over 20 years ago and does not accurately model many of today's higher speed amplifiers. The primary reason for this is that the Boyle model has only two frequency shaping poles and no zeroes. In contrast, the ADSpice model has an open architecture that allows for unlimited poles and zeroes, leading to much more accurate AC and transient responses.

The ADSpice model is comprised of three main portions: the input and gain stage, the pole/zero stages, and the output stage. The input stage shown in Figure 7.2 uses the only two transistors in the entire model. These are needed to model properly an op amp's differential input stage characteristics. Although the example here uses NPN transistors, the input stage can easily be modified to include PNP, JFET, or CMOS devices. The rest of the input stage uses simple SPICE elements such as resistors, capacitors, and controlled sources.

ADSpice INPUT AND GAIN STAGE MODEL

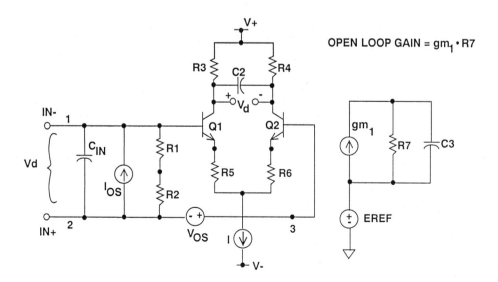

Figure 7.2

An example of a controlled source is gm_1 in the gain stage, which is a voltage controlled current source. It senses the differential collector voltage from the input stage and converts that to a current. When the current flows through R7, a single-ended voltage is produced. By making the product of gm_1 and R7 equal to the open loop gain, the entire open-loop gain is produced in the gain stage, which means that all other stages are set to unity gain. This leads to significant flexibility in adding and deleting stages.

Following the gain stage are an unlimited number of pole / zero stages and their combinations. The typical topology of these stages is shown in Figure 7.3, which is similar to the gain stage. The main difference is that now the product of gm_2 times R8 is equal to unity. The pole or zero frequency is set by the parallel combination of the resistor and capacitor, R8-C4 for the pole and Rg-C5 for the zero. Because these stages are unity gain, any number of them can be added or deleted without affecting the low frequency response of the model. Instead, the high frequency gain and phase response can be tailored to match accurately the actual amplifier's response. The benefits are especially apparent in closed loop pulse response and stability analysis.

POLE AND ZERO STAGE

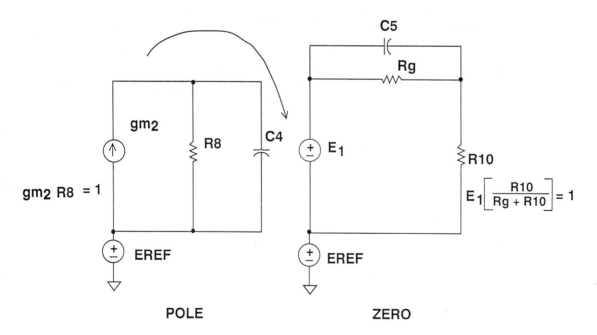

Figure 7.3

The output stage in Figure 7.4 not only models the open loop output impedance at DC but with the inclusion of an inductor also models the rise in impedance at high frequencies. Additionally, the output current is correctly reflected in the supply currents. This is a signifi-

cant improvement over the Boyle model because now the power consumption of the circuit under load can be analyzed accurately. Furthermore, circuits that use the supply currents for feedback can also be simulated.

OUTPUT STAGE

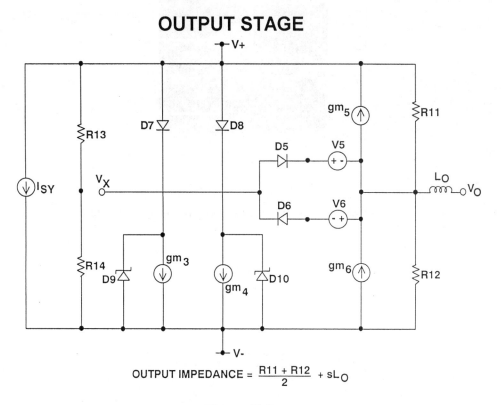

$$\text{OUTPUT IMPEDANCE} = \frac{R11 + R12}{2} + sL_O$$

Figure 7.4

As an illustration of using the ADSpice model to predict circuit performance, the AD847 op amp (50MHz unity gain-bandwidth product) output was loaded in a 65pF capacitor and the response measured (both in ADSpice and in the circuit). The results shown in Figure 7.5

illustrate good correlation between the simulated and the actual response. As an additional example, extra parasitic capacitances were added as shown in Figure 7.6, and the simulated and actual responses compared. Again, note the excellent general agreement.

7

AD847 PULSE RESPONSE

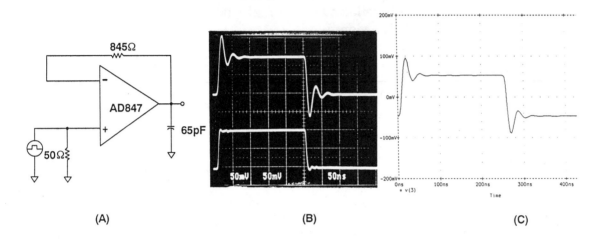

(A) (B) (C)

Properly laid out PC board and simulation agree closely

Figure 7.5

PC BOARD PARASITICS WILL ALTER THE RESULTS

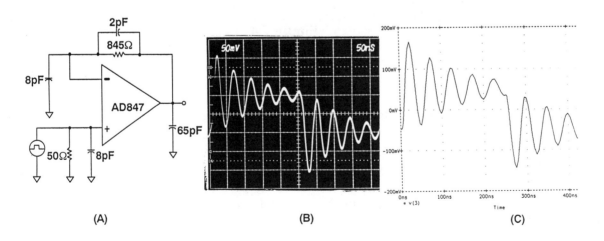

(A) (B) (C)

- Parasitic capacitances worsen the circuit's response
- Properly modelling the parasitics in SPICE yields good results

Figure 7.6

Other Features of ADSpice Models

In addition to offering models of op amps (both voltage and current feedback), which allow simulation of AC and DC performance, Analog Devices has included noise in many of its amplifier models. The capability to model a circuit's noise performance in SPICE can be appreciated by anyone who has tried to analyze noise by hand. A complete analysis is a very involved and tedious task which requires calculating all the individual noise contributors and reflecting them to the input or output. The procedure is further complicated by the fact that noise gain is generally a function of frequency and can significantly affect results if not carefully considered.

To greatly simplify this task, the ADSpice model was enhanced to include noise generators which accurately predict the broadband and 1/f noise of the actual amplifier. Noise is currently modeled in a number of ADI op amps, variable gain amplifiers, and voltage references. For further discussion on the noise model details, see Reference 2.

In addition to amplifiers, ADSpice models exist for instrumentation amplifiers, analog multipliers, voltage references, analog switches, multiplexers, matched transistors, and buffers. A complete set of ADSpice models is available from Analog Devices upon request.

ADSpice will give good approximations to actual performance, if used correctly. However, the user must include the external components and parasitics which may affect the device performance in the circuit. This becomes a difficult task at frequencies much above 100MHz, and caution must be used in interpreting the simulation results. There is no substitute for prototyping at these frequencies.

While pulse and frequency response can be successfully simulated using the ADSpice models, distortion performance cannot be predicted since non-linear effects are not included in the models. As mentioned previously, models for ADCs and DACs are not available due to the difficulty in modeling their AC performance.

7

SUMMARY: ADSpice FEATURES

- ■ **Transistor-Level Input Stage Model**

- ■ **Unlimited Poles and Zeros**

- ■ **Noise is Included in Some Models**

- ■ **Distortion is not Modeled**

- ■ **Over 500 Models Exist for:**
  - ◆ **Amplifiers**
  - ◆ **Instrumentation Amplifiers**
  - ◆ **Analog Multipliers**
  - ◆ **Voltage References**
  - ◆ **VCAs**
  - ◆ **Multiplexers and Switches**

- ■ **But There is no Substitute for a Good Prototype!!**

Figure 7.7

PROTOTYPING TECHNIQUES
James Bryant, Walt Kester

The basic principle of a breadboard or prototype is that it is a *temporary* structure, designed to test the performance of a circuit or system, and must therefore be easy to modify.

There are many commercial prototyping systems, but almost all of them are designed to facilitate the prototyping of *digital* systems, where noise immunities are hundreds of millivolts or more. Non copper-clad Matrix board, Vectorboard, wire-wrap, and plug-in breadboard systems are, without exception, unsuitable for high performance or high frequency analog prototyping because their resistance, inductance, and capacitance are too high. Even the use of standard IC

sockets is inadvisable in many prototyping applications.

An important consideration in selecting a prototyping method is the requirement for a large-area ground plane. This is required for high frequency circuits as well as low speed precision circuits, especially when prototyping circuits involving ADCs or DACs. The differentiation between *high-speed* and *high-precision* mixed-signal circuits is difficult to make. For example, 16+ bit ADCs (and DACs) may operate on high speed clocks (>10MHz) with rise and fall times of less than a few nanoseconds, while the effective throughput rate of the converters may be less than 100kSPS. Successful prototyping of these circuits requires that equal attention be given to good high-speed and high-precision circuit techniques.

The simplest technique for analog prototyping uses a solid copper-clad board as a ground plane (Reference 5 and 6). The ground pins of the ICs are soldered directly to the plane, and the other components are wired together above it. This allows HF decoupling paths to be very short indeed. All lead lengths should be as short as possible, and signal routing should separate high-level and low-level signals. Connection wires should be located close to the surface of the board to minimize the possibility of stray inductive coupling. In most cases, 18-gauge or larger insulated wire should be used. Parallel runs should not be "bundled" because of possible coupling. Ideally the layout (at least the relative placement of the components on the board) should be similar to the layout to be used on the final PCB. This approach is often referred to as *deadbug prototyping* because the ICs are often mounted upside down with their leads up in the air (with the exception of the ground

pins, which are bent over and soldered directly to the ground plane). The upside-down ICs look like deceased insects, hence the name.

Figure 7.8 shows a hand-wired breadboard using two high speed op amps which gives excellent performance in spite of its lack of esthetic appeal. The IC op amps are mounted upside down on the copper board with the leads bent over. The signals are connected with short point-to-point wiring. The characteristic impedance of a wire over a ground plane is about 120Ω, although this may vary as much as ±40% depending on the distance from the plane. The decoupling capacitors are connected directly from the op amp power pins to the copper-clad ground plane. When working at frequencies of several hundred MHz, it is a good idea to use only one side of the board for ground. Many people drill holes in the board and connect both sides together with short pieces of wire soldered to both sides of the board. If care is not taken, however, this may result in unexpected ground loops between the two sides of the board, especially at RF frequencies.

7

"DEADBUG" PROTOTYPE

Figure 7.8

Pieces of copper-clad board may be soldered at right angles to the main ground plane to provide screening, or circuitry may be constructed on both sides of the board (with connections through holes) with the board itself providing screening. In this case, the board will need standoffs at the corners to protect the components on the underside from being crushed.

When the components of a breadboard of this type are wired point-to-point in the air (a type of construction strongly advocated by Robert A. Pease of National Semiconductor (Reference 6) and sometimes known as "bird's nest" construction) there is always the risk of the circuitry being crushed and resulting short-circuits. Also, if the circuitry rises high above the ground plane, the screening effect of the ground plane is diminished, and interaction between different parts of the circuit is more likely. Nevertheless, the technique is very practical and widely used because the circuit may easily be modified (assuming the person doing the modifications is adept at using a soldering iron, solder-wick, and a solder-sucker).

Another prototype breadboard is shown in Figure 7.9. The single-sided copper-clad board has pre-drilled holes on 0.1" centers (Reference 7). Power busses are at the top and bottom of the board. The decoupling capacitors are used on the power pins of each IC. Because of the loss of copper area due to the pre-drilled holes, this technique does not provide as low a ground impedance as a completely covered copper-clad board.

"DEADBUG" PROTOTYPE USING PRE-DRILLED SINGLE-SIDED COPPER-CLAD BOARD

Figure 7.9

In a variation of this technique, the ICs and other components are mounted on the non-copper-clad side of the board. The holes are used as vias, and the point-to-point wiring is done on the copper-clad side of the board. The copper surrounding each hole used for a via must be drilled out to prevent shorting. This approach requires that all IC pins be on 0.1" centers. Low profile sockets can be used for low frequency circuits, and the socket pins allow easy point-to-point wiring.

There is a commercial breadboarding system which has most of the advantages of the above techniques (robust ground, screening, ease of circuit alteration, low capacitance and low inductance) and several additional advantages: it is rigid, components are close to the ground plane, and where necessary, node capacitances and line impedances can be calculated easily. This system is made by Wainwright Instruments and is available in Europe as "Mini-Mount" and in the USA (where the trademark "Mini-Mount" is the property of another company) as "Solder-Mount" (Reference 8).

Solder-Mount consists of small pieces of PCB with etched patterns on one side and contact adhesive on the other. These pieces are stuck to the ground plane, and components are soldered to them. They are available in a wide variety of patterns, including ready-made pads for IC packages of all sizes from 8-pin SOICs to 64-pin DILs,

7

strips with solder pads at intervals (which intervals range from 0.040" to 0.25", the range includes strips with 0.1" pad spacing which may be used to mount DIL devices), strips with conductors of the correct width to form microstrip transmission lines (50Ω, 60Ω, 75Ω or 100Ω) when mounted on the ground plane, and a variety of pads for mounting various other components.

Self-adhesive tinned copper strips and rectangles (LO-PADS) are also available as tie-points for connections. They have a relatively high capacitance to ground and therefore serve as low-inductance decoupling capacitors. They come in sheet form and may be cut with a knife or scissors. A few of the many types of Solder-Mount building-block components are shown in Figure 7.10.

SAMPLES OF "SOLDER-MOUNT" COMPONENTS

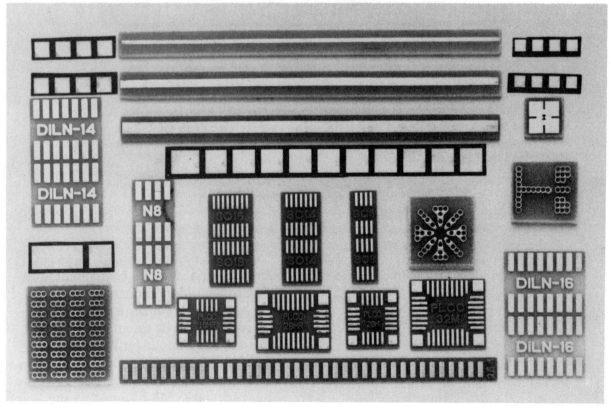

Figure 7.10

The main advantage of Solder-Mount construction over "bird's nest" or "deadbug" is that the resulting circuit is far more rigid, and, if desired, may be made far smaller (the latest Solder-Mounts are for surface-mount devices and allow the construction of breadboards scarcely larger than the final PC board, although it is generally more convenient if the prototype is somewhat larger). Solder-Mount is sufficiently durable that it may be used for small quantity production as well as prototyping.

Figure 7.11 shows an example of a 2.5GHz phase-locked-loop prototype built with Solder-Mount. This is a high speed circuit, but the technique is equally suitable for the construction of high resolution low frequency analog circuitry. A particularly convenient feature of Solder-Mount at VHF is the ease with which it is possible to make a transmission line.

"SOLDER-MOUNT" PROTOTYPE

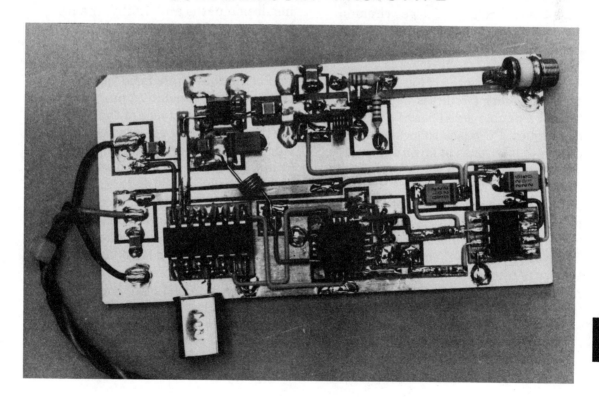

Figure 7.11

7

If a conductor runs over a ground plane, it forms a microstrip transmission line. The Solder-Mount components include strips which form microstrip lines when mounted on a ground plane (they are available with impedances of 50Ω, 60Ω, 75Ω, and 100Ω). These strips may be used as transmission lines, for impedance matching, or simply as power buses. (Glass fiber/epoxy PCB is somewhat lossy at VHF and UHF, but the losses will probably be tolerable if microstrip runs are short.)

Both the "deadbug" and the "Solder-Mount" prototyping techniques become somewhat tedious for complex analog or mixed-signal circuits. Larger circuits are often better prototyped using more formal layout techniques.

An approach to prototyping more complex analog circuits is to actually lay out a double-sided board using CAD techniques. PC-based software layout packages offer ease of layout as well as schematic capture to verify connections (Reference 9). Although most layout software has some amount of auto-routing capability, this feature is best left to digital designs. After the components are placed in their desired positions, the interconnections should be routed manually following good analog layout guidelines. After the layout is complete, the software verifies the connections per the schematic diagram net list.

Many design engineers find that they can use CAD techniques to lay out simple boards themselves, or work closely with a layout person who has experience in analog circuit boards. The result is a pattern-generation tape (or Gerber file) which would normally be sent to a PCB manufacturing facility where the final board is made. Rather than use a PC board manufacturer, however, automatic drilling and milling machines are available which accept the PG tape directly (Reference 10). These systems produce single and double-sided circuit boards directly by drilling all holes and using a milling technique to remove copper and create insulation paths and finally, the finished board. The result is a board very similar to the final manufactured double-sided PC board, the chief exception being that there is no "plated-through" hole capability, and any "vias" between the two layers of the board must be wired and soldered on both sides. Minimum trace widths of 25 mils (1 mil = 0.001") and 12 mil spacing between traces are standard, although smaller trace widths can be achieved with care. The minimum spacing between lines is dictated by the size of the milling bit, typically 10 to 12 mils. An example of such a prototype board is shown in Figure 7.12 (top view) and Figure 7.13 (bottom view).

"MILLED" PROTOTYPE - TOP VIEW

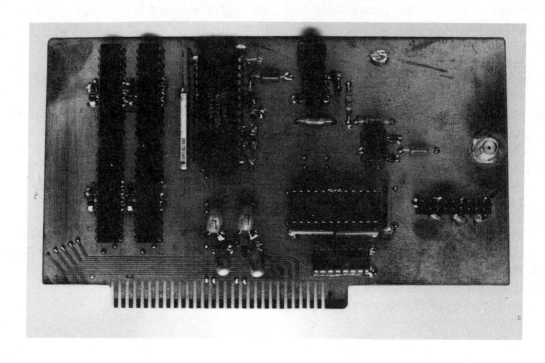

Figure 7.12

"MILLED" PROTOTYPE - BOTTOM VIEW

Figure 7.13

7

IC sockets can degrade the performance of high speed or high precision analog ICs. Although they make prototyping easier, even *low-profile* sockets often introduce enough parasitic capacitance and inductance to degrade the performance of the circuit. If sockets must be used in high speed circuits, an IC socket made of individual *pin sockets* (sometimes called *cage jacks*) mounted in the ground plane board may be acceptable (clear the copper, on both sides of the board, for about 0.5mm around each ungrounded pin socket and solder the grounded ones to ground on both sides of the board). Both capped and uncapped versions of these pin sockets are available (AMP part numbers 5-330808-3, and 5-330808-6, respec-

tively). The pin sockets protrude through the board far enough to allow point-to-point wiring interconnections between them (see Figure 7.14).

The spring-loaded gold-plated contacts within the pin socket makes good electrical and mechanical connection to the IC pins. Multiple insertions, however, may degrade the performance of the pin socket. The uncapped versions allow the IC pins to extend out the bottom of the socket. After the prototype is functional and no further changes are to be made, the IC pins can be soldered directly to the bottom of the socket, thereby making a permanent and rugged connection.

PIN SOCKETS (CAGE JACKS) HAVE MINIMUM PARASITIC RESISTANCE, INDUCTANCE, AND CAPACITANCE

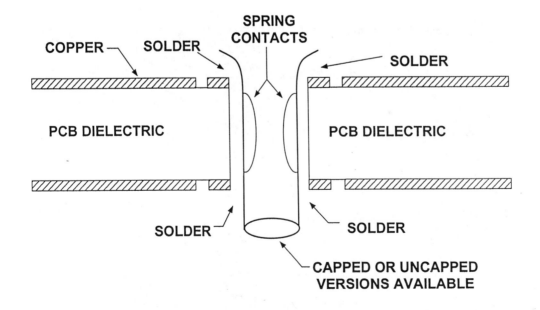

Figure 7.14

The prototyping techniques discussed so far have been limited to single or double-sided PC boards. Multilayer PC boards do not easily lend themselves to standard prototyping techniques. If multilayer board prototyping is required, one side of a double-sided board can be used for ground and the other side for power and signals. Point-to-point wiring can be used for additional runs which would normally be placed on the additional layers provided by a multi-layer board. However, it is difficult to control the impedance of the point-to-point wiring runs, and the high frequency performance of a circuit prototyped in this manner may differ significantly from the final multilayer board.

Other difficulties in prototyping may occur with op amps or other linear devices having bandwidths greater than a few hundred megahertz. Small variations in parasitic capacitance (<1pF) between the prototype and the final board may cause subtle differences in bandwidth and settling time. Oftentimes prototyping is done with DIP packages, when the final production package is an SOIC. This can account for differences between prototype and final PC board performance.

EVALUATION BOARDS
Walt Kester

Most manufacturers of analog ICs provide evaluation boards (usually at a nominal cost) which allow customers to evaluate products without constructing their own prototypes. Regardless of the product, the manufacturer has taken proper precautions regarding grounding, layout, and decoupling to ensure optimum device performance. The artwork or CAD file is usually made available free of charge, should the customer wish to copy the layout directly or make modifications to suit the application.

Figure 7.15 shows the schematic for the AD8001 (SOIC package) 800MHz op amp evaluation board. Figures 7.16 and 7.17, respectively, show the top and bottom side of the PCB. The amplifier is connected in the non-inverting mode. The top side (Figure 7.16) shows the top side of the SOIC package along with input and output SMA connectors. Notice that the ground plane is cut away around the SOIC in order to minimize parasitic capacitance. The bottom side of the board (Figure 7.17) shows the surface mount resistors and capacitors which comprise the op amp gain-setting and power supply decoupling circuits, respectively.

7

AD8001AR (SOIC) 800MHz OP AMP: NON-INVERTING MODE EVALUATION BOARD SCHEMATIC

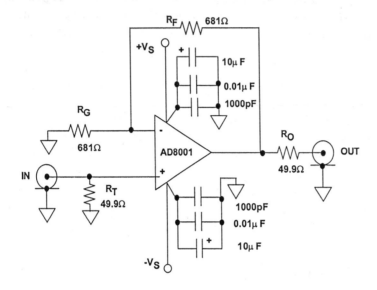

Figure 7.15

AD8001AR (SOIC) EVALUATION BOARD - TOP VIEW

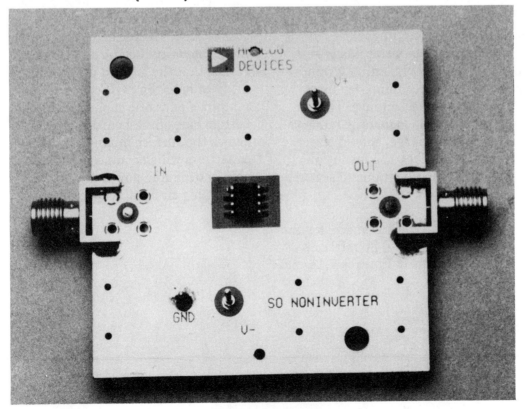

Figure 7.16

AD8001AR (SOIC) EVALUATION BOARD - BOTTOM VIEW

Figure 7.17

In high speed/high precision ICs, special attention must be given to power supply decoupling. For example, fast slewing signals into relatively low impedance loads produce high speed transient currents at the power supply pins of an op amp. The transient currents, in turn, produce corresponding voltages across any parasitic impedance which may exist in the power supply traces. These voltages, in turn, may couple to the amplifier output because of the op amp's finite power supply rejection at high frequencies.

A three-capacitor decoupling scheme was chosen for the AD8001 evaluation board to ensure a low impedance path to ground at all transient frequencies. The highest frequency transients are

shunted to ground by the 1000pF and the 0.01µF ceramic capacitors. These are located as close to the power supply pins as possible to minimize any series inductance and resistance. Because the devices are surface mount, there is minimum stray inductance and resistance in the path to the ground plane. The lower frequency transient currents are shunted to ground by the 10µF tantalum capacitors.

The input and output signal traces are of the AD8001 evaluation board are 50Ω microstrip transmission lines. Notice that there is considerable continuous ground plane area on both sides of the PCB. Plated-through holes connect the top and bottom side ground planes at several points in order to

7

maintain low impedance ground continuity at high frequencies.

Evaluation boards can range from relatively simple ones (op amps, for example) to rather complex ones for mixed-signal ICs such as A/D converters. ADC evaluation boards often have on-board memory and DSPs for analyzing the ADC performance. Software is often provided with these more complex evaluation boards so that they can interface with a personal computer to perform complex signal analysis such as histogram and FFT testing.

Complete evaluations of ADCs requires the use of FFTs to fully characterize the devices AC performance. A typical test

setup is shown in Figure 7.18. The manufacturer's evaluation board is used as a means for interfacing to the ADC. The evaluation board is designed to allow easy access to the ADC inputs and outputs while also providing a good layout (including all necessary references, buffer amplifiers, and decoupling). The evaluation board allows the ADC output data to be captured on a parallel output connector. Most ADC evaluation boards contain an on-board DAC which can be used to check the functionality of the ADC, but is somewhat limited in performing meaningful AC testing. A block diagram of the AD9042 (12-bits, 41MSPS) evaluation board is shown in Figure 7.19, and a photo in Figure 7.20.

TEST SETUP REQUIRED TO EVALUATE HIGH SPEED ADCs

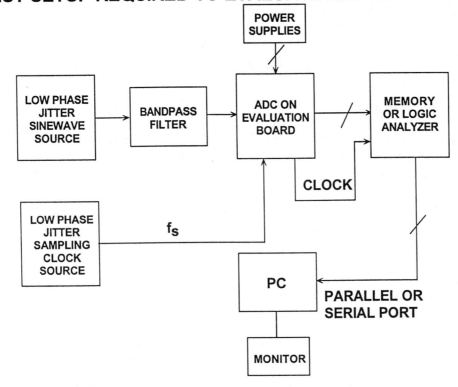

Figure 7.18

AD9042 12-BIT, 41MSPS ADC EVALUATION BOARD FUNCTIONAL DIAGRAM

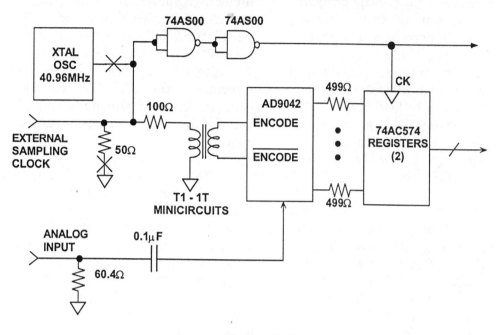

Figure 7.19

AD9042 EVALUATION BOARD - TOP VIEW

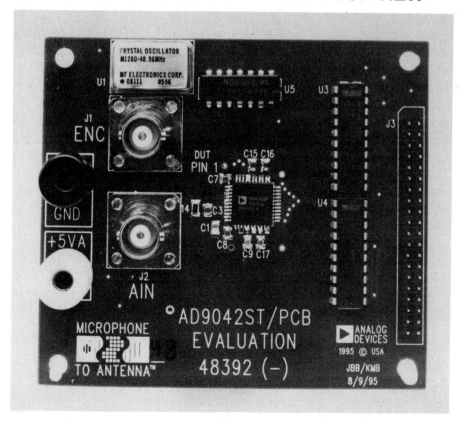

Figure 7.20

The most complex part of the problem is usually designing the buffer memory module. A high speed logic analyzer is one method of capturing the ADC output data, and interfaces easily to the ADC evaluation board. Data from the logic analyzer can be loaded into a PC through either parallel or serial ports. Once the ADC data is inside the PC, software packages such as Mathcad can be used to perform the actual FFT.

Another alternative is to use a commercially-available data acquisition module that plugs directly into a card slot of the PC. These modules come complete with FFT and other ADC test software, but are not easily portable from one PC to another and are generally difficult to interface with laptop computers.

Although fast and relatively low power memories (FIFOs) are available commercially, designing a buffer memory, the interfaces to the ADC and the PC, and the necessary software can be a time-consuming project. Analog Devices has designed a simple 16-bit by 16k deep 100MHz memory board (3 x 4 inches) and the necessary software to allow high speed ADC evaluation boards to interface directly with the parallel printer port of most PCs. The core of the memory design is the IDT72265 16k by 18-bit wide FIFO or alternately, the IDT72255 is an 8k pin compatible device which may be substituted if the deeper memory is not required.

This FIFO chip features fully independent I/O ports that allow data to be loaded at up to 100MSPS and downloaded at the rate of a parallel printer port. Since the ports are independent, both can operate simultaneously, i.e., data may be read out while new data is being written. The chip takes care of all addressing, overhead and much of the hand-shaking for these operations. Included is circuitry that prevents unread data from being overwritten, eliminating the need for extensive write control circuitry.

A photograph of the *Fifo Memory* board is shown in Figure 7.21, and Figure 7.22 shows it connected to the AD9042 evaluation board.

BUFFER MEMORY FIFO BOARD - TOP VIEW

Figure 7.21

MEMORY BOARD / AD9042 EVALUATION BOARD

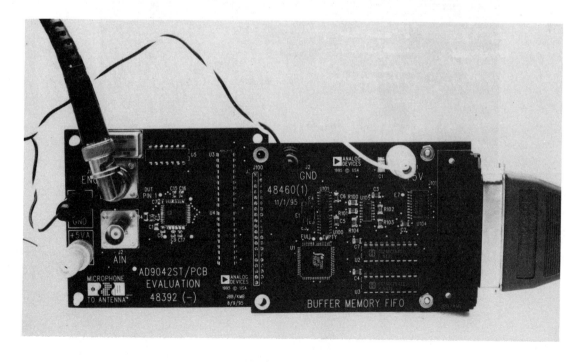

Figure 7.22

Using this hardware and Windows-based software to capture the ADC data, many testing possibilities exist. Figure 7.23 shown a time-domain plot of data captured using the fifo memory. Once the data is captured, FFT analysis (Figure 7.24) or DNL histograms (Figure 7.25) are easily generated.

In summary, good analog designers utilize as many tools as possible to ensure that the final system design performs correctly. The first step is the intelligent use of IC macromodels, where available, to simulate the circuit. The second step is the construction of a prototype board to further verify the

design and the simulation. The final PCB layout should be then be based on the prototype layout as much as possible.

Finally, evaluation boards can be extremely useful in evaluating new analog ICs, and allow designers to verify the IC performance with a minimum amount of effort. The layout of the components on the evaluation board can serve as a guide to both the prototype and the final PC board layout. Gerber files are generally available for all evaluation board layouts and may be obtained at no charge.

DATA CAPTURE PC OUTPUT DISPLAY

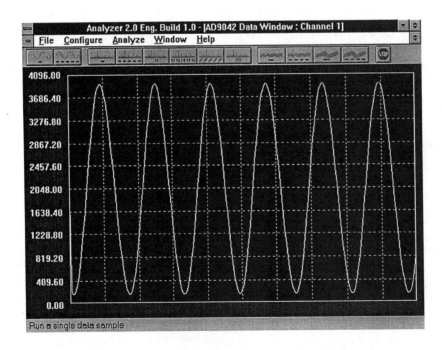

Figure 7.23

FFT OUTPUT

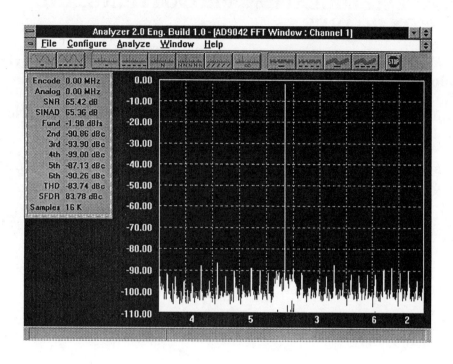

Figure 7.24

DNL HISTOGRAM

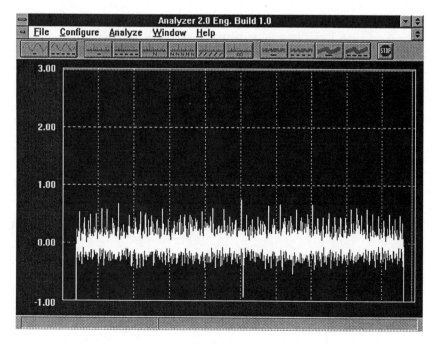

Figure 7.25

REFERENCES: SIMULATION, PROTOTYPING, AND EVALUATION BOARDS

1.   Paolo Antognetti and Guiseppe Massobrio, Ed, **Semiconductor Device Modeling with SPICE**, McGraw Hill, 1988.

2.   **Amplifier Applications Guide**, Section 13, Analog Devices, Inc., Norwood, MA, 1992.

3.   Boyle, et al, *Macromodelling of Integrated Circuit Operational Amplifiers*, **IEEE Journal of Solid State Circuits**,Vol. SC-9, no.6, December 1974.

4.   PSpice® Simulation software. MicroSim Corporation, 20 Fairbanks, Irvine, CA 92718, 714-770-3022

5.   Jim Williams, **High Speed Amplifier Techniques**, Linear Technology Application Note 47, August, 1991.

6.   Robert A. Pease, **Troubleshooting Analog Circuits**, Butterworth-Heinemann, 1991.

7.   Vector Electronic Company, 12460 Gladstone Ave., Sylmar, CA 91342, Tel. 818-365-9661, Fax. 818-365-5718.

8.   Wainwright Instruments Inc., 69 Madison Ave., Telford, PA, 18969-1829, Tel. 215-723-4333, Fax. 215-723-4620.

      Wainwright Instruments GmbH, Widdersberger Strasse 14, DW-8138 Andechs-Frieding, Germany. Tel: +49-8152-3162, Fax: +49-8152-40525.

9.   Schematic Capture and Layout Software:
          PADS Software, INC, 165 Forest St., Marlboro, MA, 01752 and
          ACCEL Technologies, Inc., 6825 Flanders Dr., San Diego, CA, 92121

10.   Prototype Board Cutters:

          LPKF CAD/CAM Systems, Inc., 1800 NW 169th Place,
          Beaverton, OR, 97006 and
          T-Tech, Inc., 5591-B New Peachtree Road, Atlanta, GA, 34341

11.   Howard W. Johnson and Martin Graham, **High-Speed Digital Design**, PTR Prentice Hall, 1993.

12.   **Practical Analog Design Techniques**, Analog Devices, 1995.

GROUNDING IN HIGH SPEED SYSTEMS
Walt Kester, James Bryant

The importance of maintaining a low impedance large area ground plane is critical to practically all analog circuits today, especially at high speeds. The ground plane not only acts as a low impedance return path for high frequency currents but also minimizes EMI/RFI emissions. Because of the shielding action of the ground plane, the circuits susceptibility to external EMI/RFI is also reduced.

All IC ground pins should be soldered directly to the ground plane to minimize series inductance. Power supply pins should be decoupled to the ground plane using low inductance ceramic surface mount capacitors. If through-hole mounted ceramic capacitors must be used, their leads should be less than 1mm. Ferrite beads may be also required.

The ground plane allows the impedance of PCB traces to be controlled, and high frequency signals can be terminated in the characteristic impedance of the trace to minimize reflections when necessary.

Each PCB in the system should have at least one complete layer dedicated to the ground plane. Ideally, a double-sided board should have one side dedicated to ground and the other side for interconnections. In practice, this is not possible, since some of the ground plane will certainly have to be removed to allow for signal and power crossovers and vias. Nevertheless, as much area as possible should be preserved, and at least 75% should remain. After completing an initial layout, the ground layer should be checked carefully to make sure there are no isolated ground "islands." IC ground pins located in a ground "island" have no current return path to the ground plane.

The best way of minimizing ground impedance in a multicard system is to use another PCB as a backplane for interconnections between cards, thus providing a continuous ground plane to the mother card. The PCB connector should have at least 30-40% of its pins devoted to ground, and these pins should be connected to the ground plane on the backplane mother card. To complete the overall system grounding scheme there are two possibilities: (1) The backplane ground plane can be connected to chassis ground at numerous points, thereby diffusing the various ground current return paths. (2) The ground plane can be connected to a single system "star ground" point (generally at the power supply).

The first approach is often used at very high frequencies and where the return currents are relatively constant. The low ground impedance is maintained all the way through the PC boards, the backplane, and ultimately the chassis. It is critical that good electrical contact be made where the grounds are connected to the sheet metal chassis. This requires self-tapping sheet metal screws or "biting" washers. Special care must be taken where anodized aluminum is used for the chassis material, since its surface acts as an insulator.

In other systems, especially high speed ones with large amounts of digital circuitry, it is highly desirable to physically separate sensitive analog components from noisy digital components. It is usually desirable to use separate

7

ground planes for the analog and the digital circuitry. On PCBs which have both analog and digital circuits, there are two separate ground planes. These planes should not overlap in order to minimize capacitive coupling between the two. The separate analog and digital ground planes are continued on the backplane using either motherboard ground planes or "ground screens" which are made up of a series of wired interconnections between the connector ground pins. The arrangement shown in Figure 7.26 illustrates

that the two planes are kept separate all the way back to a common system "star" ground, generally located at the power supplies. The connections between the ground planes, the power supplies, and the "star" should be made up of multiple bus bars or wide copper brads for minimum resistance and inductance. The back-to-back Schottky diodes on each PCB are inserted to prevent accidental DC voltage from developing between the two ground systems when cards are plugged and unplugged.

SEPARATING ANALOG AND DIGITAL GROUNDS

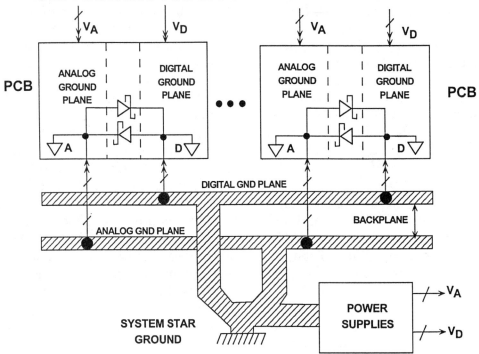

Figure 7.26

Sensitive analog components such as amplifiers and voltage references are referenced and decoupled to the analog ground plane. *The ADCs and DACs (and even some mixed-signal ICs) should be treated as analog components and also grounded and decoupled to the analog ground plane.* At first glance,

this may seem somewhat contradictory, since a converter has an analog and digital interface and usually pins designated as analog ground (AGND) and digital ground (DGND). The diagram shown in Figure 7.27 will help to explain this seeming dilemma.

PROPER GROUNDING OF ADCs, DACs, AND OTHER MIXED-SIGNAL ICs

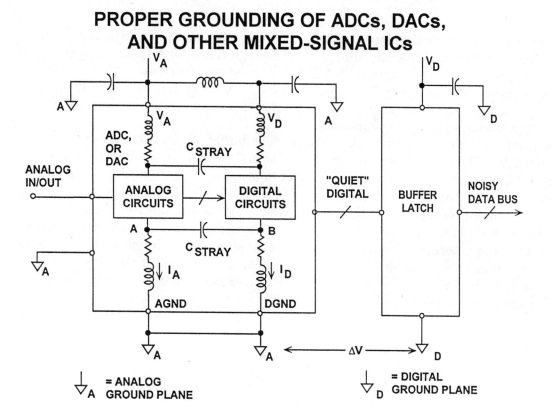

Figure 7.27

Inside an IC that has both analog and digital circuits, such as an ADC or a DAC, the grounds are usually kept separate to avoid coupling digital signals into the analog circuits. Figure 7.27 shows a simple model of a converter. There is nothing the IC designer can do about the wirebond inductance and resistance associated with connecting the pads on the chip to the package pins except to realize it's there. The rapidly changing digital currents produce a voltage at point B which will inevitably couple into point A of the analog circuits through the stray capacitance, C_{STRAY}. In addition, there is approximately 0.2pF unavoidable stray capacitance between every pin of the IC package! It's the IC designer's job to make the chip work in spite of this. However, in order to prevent further coupling, the AGND and DGND pins should be joined together exter-

nally to the *analog* ground plane with minimum lead lengths. Any extra impedance in the DGND connection will cause more digital noise to be developed at point B; it will, in turn, couple more digital noise into the analog circuit through the stray capacitance.

The name "DGND" on an IC tells us that this pin connects to the digital ground of the IC. This does not imply that this pin must be connected to the digital ground of the system.

It is true that this arrangement will inject a small amount of digital noise on the analog ground plane. These currents should be quite small, and can be minimized by ensuring that the converter input/or output does not drive a large fanout (they normally can't by design). Minimizing the fanout on the converter's digital port will also keep the converter logic transitions relatively free from ringing, and thereby minimize any potential coupling into the analog port of the converter. The logic supply pin (V_D) can be further isolated from the analog supply by the insertion of a small lossy ferrite bead as shown in Figure 7.27. The internal digital currents of the converter will return to ground through the V_D pin decoupling capacitor (mounted as close to the converter as possible) and will not appear in the external ground circuit. It is always a good idea (as shown in Figure 7.27) to place a buffer latch adjacent to the converter to isolate the converter's digital lines from any noise which may be on the data bus. Even though a few high speed converters have three-state outputs/inputs, this isolation latch represents good design practice.

The buffer latch and other digital circuits should be grounded and decoupled to the digital ground plane of the PC board. Notice that any noise between the analog and digital ground plane reduces the noise margin at the converter digital interface. Since digital noise immunity is of the orders of hundreds or thousands of millivolts, this is unlikely to matter.

POWER SUPPLY, GROUNDING, AND DECOUPLING POINTS

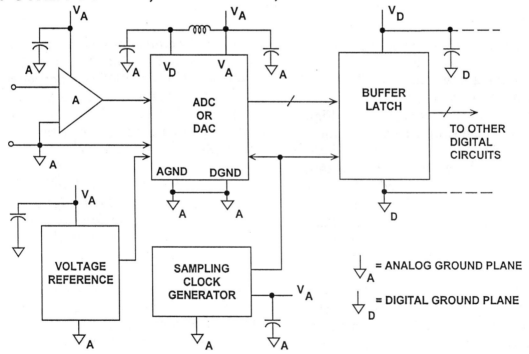

Figure 7.28

Separate power supplies for analog and digital circuits are also highly desirable. The analog supply should be used to power the converter. If the converter has a pin designated as a digital supply pin (V_D), it should either be powered from a separate analog supply, or filtered as shown in the diagram. All converter power pins should be decoupled to the analog ground plane, and all logic circuit power pins should be decoupled to the digital ground plane. If the digital power supply is relatively quiet, it may be possible to use it to supply analog circuits as well, but be very cautious.

The sampling clock generation circuitry should also be grounded and heavily-decoupled to the analog ground plane. As previously discussed, phase noise on the sampling clock produces degradation in system SNR.

A low phase-noise crystal oscillator should be used to generate the ADC sampling clock, because sampling clock jitter modulates the input signal and raises the noise and distortion floor. The sampling clock generator should be isolated from noisy digital circuits and grounded and decoupled to the analog ground plane, as is true for the op amp and the ADC.

Ideally, the sampling clock generator should be referenced to the analog ground plane in a split-ground system. However, this is not always possible because of system constraints. In many cases, the sampling clock must be derived from a higher frequency multi-purpose system clock which is generated on the digital ground plane. If it is passed between its origin on the digital ground plane to the ADC on the analog ground plane, the ground noise between the two planes adds directly to the clock and will produce excess jitter. The jitter can cause degradation in the signal-to-noise ratio and also produce unwanted harmonics. This can be remedied somewhat by transmitting the sampling clock signal as a differential one using either a small RF transformer or a high speed differential driver and receiver as shown in Figure 7.29. The driver and receiver should be ECL to minimize phase jitter. In either case, the original master system clock should be generated from a low phase noise crystal oscillator.

It is evident that noise can be minimized by paying attention to the system layout and preventing different signals from interfering with each other. High level analog signals should be separated from low level analog signals, and both should be kept away from digital signals. We have seen elsewhere that in waveform sampling and reconstruction systems the sampling clock (which is a digital signal) is as vulnerable to noise as any analog signal, but is as liable to cause noise as any digital signal, and so must be kept isolated from both analog and digital systems.

If a ground plane is used, as it should in be most cases, it can act as a shield where sensitive signals cross. Figure 7.30 shows a good layout for a data acquisition board where all sensitive areas are isolated from each other and signal paths are kept as short as possible. While real life is rarely as tidy as this, the principle remains a valid one.

7

SAMPLING CLOCK DISTRIBUTION FROM DIGITAL TO ANALOG GROUND PLANES

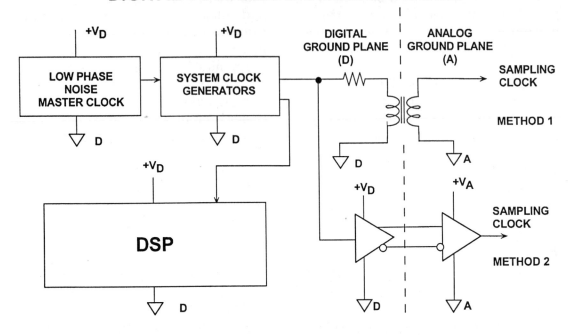

Figure 7.29

A PC BOARD LAYOUT SHOWING GOOD SIGNAL ROUTING

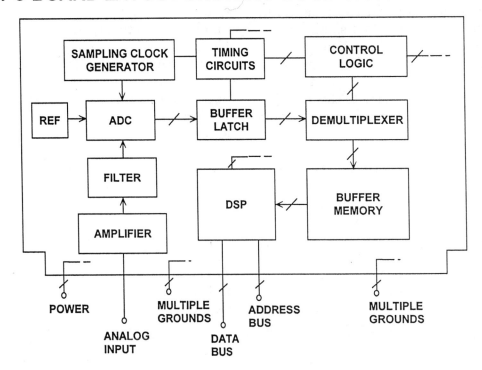

Figure 7.30

There are a number of important points to be considered when making signal and power connections. First of all a connector is one of the few places in the system where all signal conductors must run parallel - it is therefore a good idea to separate them with ground pins (creating a faraday shield) to reduce coupling between them.

Multiple ground pins are important for another reason: they keep down the ground impedance at the junction between the board and the backplane. The contact resistance of a single pin of a PCB connector is quite low (of the order of 10 mOhms) when the board is new - as the board gets older the contact resistance is likely to rise, and the board's performance may be compromised. It is therefore well worthwhile to afford extra PCB connector pins so that there are many ground connections (perhaps 30-40% of all the pins on the PCB connector should be ground pins). For similar reasons there should be several pins for each power connection, although there is no need to have as many as there are ground pins.

7

POWER SUPPLY NOISE REDUCTION AND FILTERING
Walt Jung and John McDonald

Precision analog circuitry has traditionally been powered from well regulated, low noise linear power supplies. During the last decade however, switching power supplies have become much more common in electronic systems. As a consequence, they also are being used for analog supplies. Good reasons for the general popularity include their high efficiency, low temperature rise, small size, and light weight.

In spite of these benefits, switchers *do* have drawbacks, most notably high output noise. This noise generally extends over a broad band of frequencies, resulting in both conducted and radiated noise, as well as unwanted electric and magnetic fields. Voltage output noise of switching supplies are short-duration voltage transients, or spikes. Although the fundamental switching frequency can range from 20kHz to 1MHz, the spikes can contain frequency components extending to 100MHz or more. While specifying switching supplies in terms of RMS noise is common vendor practice, as a user you should also specify the *peak* (or p-p) amplitudes of the switching spikes, with the output loading of your system.

The following section discusses filter techniques for rendering a noisy switcher output *analog ready*, that is sufficiently quiet to power precision analog circuitry with relatively small loss of DC terminal voltage. The filter solutions presented are generally applicable to all power supply types incorporating switching element(s) in their energy path. This includes various DC-DC converters as well as popular 5V (PC type) supplies.

An understanding of the EMI process is necessary to understand the effects of supply noise on analog circuits and systems. Every interference problem has a *source*, a *path*, and a *receptor* [Reference 1]. In general, there are three methods for dealing with interference. First, source emissions can be minimized by proper layout, pulse-edge rise time control/reduction, filtering, and proper grounding. Second, radiation and conduction paths should be reduced through shielding and physical separation. Third, receptor immunity to interference can be improved, via supply and signal line filtering, impedance level control, impedance balancing, and utilizing differential techniques to reject undesired common-mode signals. This section focuses on reducing switching power supply noise with external post filters.

Tools useful for combating high frequency switcher noise are shown by Figure 7.31. They differ in electrical characteristics as well as practicality towards noise reduction, and are listed roughly in an order of priorities. Of these tools, L and C are the most powerful filter elements, and are the most cost-effective, as well as small sized.

Capacitors are probably the single most important filter component for switchers. There are many different types of capacitors, and an understanding of their individual characteristics is absolutely mandatory to the design of effective practical supply filters. There are generally three classes of capacitors useful in 10kHz-100MHz filters, broadly distinguished as the generic dielectric types; *electrolytic*, *film*, and *ceramic*. These can in turn can be further sub-divided. A thumbnail sketch of capacitor characteristics is shown in the chart of Figure 7.32.

NOISE REDUCTION TOOLS

- Capacitors

- Inductors

- Ferrites

- Resistors

- Linear Post Regulation

- PHYSICAL SEPARATION FROM SENSITIVE ANALOG CIRCUITS !!

Figure 7.31

CAPACITOR SELECTION

	Aluminum Electrolytic (General Purpose)	Aluminum Electrolytic (Switching Type)	Tantalum Electrolytic	Polyester (Stacked Film)	Ceramic (Multilayer)
Size	100 µF (1)	120 µF (1)	100 µF (1)	1 µF	0.1 µF
Rated Voltage	25 V	25 V	20 V	400 V	50 V
ESR	0.6 Ω @ 100 kHz	0.18 Ω @ 100 kHz	0.12 Ω @ 100 kHz	0.11 Ω @ 1 MHz	0.12 Ω @ 1 MHz
Operating Frequency (2)	≅ 100 kHz	≅ 500 kHz	≅ 1 MHz	≅ 10 MHz	≅ 1 GHz

(1) Types shown in Figure 9.26 data
(2) Upper frequency limit is strongly size and package dependent

Figure 7.32

With any dielectric, a major potential filter loss element is ESR (equivalent series resistance), the net parasitic resistance of the capacitor. ESR provides an ultimate limit to filter performance, and requires more than casual consideration, because it can vary both with frequency and temperature in some types. Another capacitor loss element is ESL (equivalent series inductance). ESL determines the frequency where the net impedance characteristic switches from capacitive to inductive. This varies from as low as 10kHz in some electrolytics to as high as 100MHz or more in chip ceramic types. Both ESR and ESL are minimized when a leadless package is used. All capacitor types mentioned are available in surface mount packages, preferable for high speed uses.

The *electrolytic* family provides an excellent, cost-effective low-frequency filter component, because of the wide range of values, a high capacitance-to-volume ratio, and a broad range of working voltages. It includes *general purpose aluminum electrolytic* types, available in working voltages from below 10V up to about 500V, and in size from 1 to several thousand μF (with proportional case sizes). All electrolytic capacitors are polarized, and thus cannot withstand more than a volt or so of reverse bias without damage. They also have relatively high leakage currents (up to tens of μA, and strongly dependent upon design specifics).

A subset of the general electrolytic family includes *tantalum* types, generally limited to voltages of 100V or less, with capacitance of 500μF or less[Reference 3]. In a given size, tantalums exhibit a higher capacitance-to-volume ratios than do general pur-

pose electrolytics, and have both a higher frequency range and lower ESR. They are generally more expensive than standard electrolytics, and must be carefully applied with respect to surge and ripple currents.

A subset of aluminum electrolytic capacitors is the *switching* type, designed for handling high pulse currents at frequencies up to several hundred kHz with low losses [Reference 4]. This capacitor type competes directly with tantalums in high frequency filtering applications, with the advantage of a broader range of values.

A more specialized high performance aluminum electrolytic capacitor type uses an organic semiconductor electrolyte [Reference 5]. The *OS-CON* capacitors feature appreciably lower ESR and higher frequency range than do other electrolytic types, with an additional feature of low low-temperature ESR degradation.

Film capacitors are available in very broad value ranges and an array of dielectrics, including polyester, polycarbonate, polypropylene, and polystyrene. Because of the low dielectric constant of these films, their volumetric efficiency is quite low, and a 10μF/50V polyester capacitor (for example) is actually a handful. Metalized (as opposed to foil) electrodes does help to reduce size, but even the highest dielectric constant units among film types (polyester, polycarbonate) are still larger than any electrolytic, even using the thinnest films with the lowest voltage ratings (50V). Where film types excel is in their low dielectric losses, a factor which may not necessarily be a practical advantage for filtering switchers. For example, ESR in film capacitors can be as low as 10mΩ or less, and the behavior of films generally is very high in terms of Q. In fact, this can cause problems of spurious resonance in filters, requiring damping components.

Typically using a wound layer-type construction, film capacitors can be inductive, which can limit their effectiveness for high frequency filtering. Obviously, only non-inductively made film caps are useful for switching regulator filters. One specific style which is non-inductive is the *stacked-film* type, where the capacitor plates are cut as small overlapping linear sheet sections from a much larger wound drum of dielectric/plate material. This technique offers the low inductance attractiveness of a plate sheet style capacitor with conventional leads [see References 4, 5, 6]. Obviously, minimal lead length should be used for best high frequency effectiveness. Very high current polycarbonate film types are also available, specifically designed for switching power supplies, with a variety of low inductance terminations to minimize ESL [Reference 7].

Dependent upon their electrical and physical size, film capacitors can be useful at frequencies to well above 10MHz. At the highest frequencies, only stacked film types should be considered. Some manufacturers are now supplying film types in leadless surface mount packages, which eliminates the lead length inductance.

Ceramic is often the capacitor material of choice above a few MHz, due to its compact size, low loss, and availability up to several μF in the high-K dielectric formulations (X7R and Z5U), at voltage ratings up to 200V [see ceramic families of Reference 3]. NP0 (also called COG) types use a lower dielectric constant formulation, and have nominally zero TC, plus a low voltage coefficient (unlike the less stable high-K types). NP0 types are limited to values of 0.1μF or less, with 0.01μF representing a more practical upper limit.

Multilayer ceramic "chip caps" are very popular for bypassing/ filtering at 10MHz or more, simply because their very low inductance design allows near optimum RF bypassing. For smaller values, ceramic chip caps have an operating frequency range to 1GHz. For high frequency applications, a useful selection can be ensured by selecting a value which has a self-resonant frequency *above* the highest frequency of interest.

All capacitors have some finite ESR. In some cases, the ESR may actually be helpful in reducing resonance peaks in filters, by supplying "free" damping. For example, in most electrolytic types, a nominally flat broad series resonance region can be noted in an impedance vs. frequency plot. This occurs where |Z| falls to a minimum level, nominally equal to the capacitor's ESR at that frequency. This low Q resonance can generally be noted to cover a relatively wide frequency range of several octaves. Contrasted to the very high Q sharp resonances of film and ceramic caps, the low Q behavior of electrolytics can be useful in controlling resonant peaks.

In most electrolytic capacitors, ESR degrades noticeably at low temperature, by as much as a factor of 4-6 times at –55°C vs. the room temperature value. For circuits where ESR is critical to performance, this can lead to problems. Some specific electrolytic types do address this problem, for example within the HFQ switching types, the –10°C ESR at 100kHz is no

7

more than 2× that at room temperature. The OSCON electrolytics have a ESR vs. temperature characteristic which is relatively flat.

Figure 7.33 illustrates the high frequency impedance characteristics of a number of electrolytic capacitor types, using nominal 100µF/20V samples. In these plots, the impedance, |Z|, vs. frequency over the 20Hz-200kHz range is displayed using a high resolution 4-terminal setup [Reference 8]. Shown in this display are performance samples

for a 100µF/25V general purpose aluminum unit (top curve @ right), a 120µF/25V HFQ unit (next curve down @ right), a 100µF/20V tantalum bead type (next curve down @ right), and a 100µF/20V OS-CON unit (lowest curve @ right). While the HFQ and tantalum samples are close in 100kHz impedance, the general purpose unit is about 4 times worse. The OS-CON unit is nearly an order of magnitude lower in 100kHz impedance than the tantalum and switching electrolytic types.

IMPEDANCE Z (Ω) VS. FREQUENCY (Hz) FOR 100µF ELECTROLYTIC CAPACITORS (AC CURRENT = 50mA RMS)

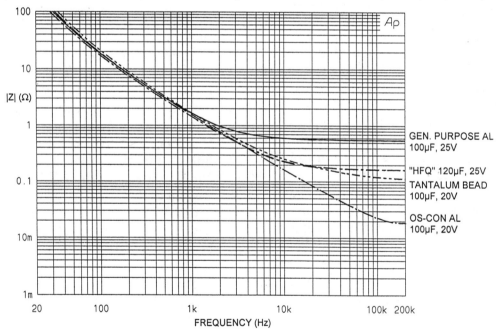

Figure 7.33

As noted, all real capacitors have parasitic elements which limit their performance. The equivalent electrical network representing a real capacitor models both ESR and ESL as well as the basic capacitance, plus some shunt resistance. In such a practical capacitor, at low frequencies the net impedance is almost purely capacitive (noted in Figure 7.33 by the 100Hz impedance). At intermediate frequencies, the net impedance is determined by ESR, for example about 0.12Ω to 0.4Ω at 125kHz, for several types. Above about 1MHz these capacitor types become inductive, with impedance dominated by the effect of ESL (not shown). All electrolytics will display impedance curves similar in general shape. The minimum impedance will vary with the ESR, and the inductive region will vary with ESL (which in turn is strongly effected by package style).

Regarding inductors, *Ferrites* (non-conductive ceramics manufactured from the oxides of nickel, zinc, manganese, or other compounds) are extremely useful in power supply filters [Reference 9]. At low frequencies (<100kHz), ferrites are inductive; thus they are useful in low-pass LC filters. Above 100kHz, ferrites become resistive, an important characteristic in high-frequency filter designs. Ferrite impedance is a function of material, operating frequency range, DC bias current, number of turns, size, shape, and temperature. Figure 7.34 summarize a number ferrite characteristics.

CHARACTERISTICS OF FERRITES

- Good for frequencies above 25kHz

- Many sizes and shapes available including leaded "resistor style"

- Ferrite impedance at high frequencies is primarily resistive -- Ideal for HF filtering

- Low DC loss: Resistance of wire passing through ferrite is very low

- High saturation current

- Low cost

Figure 7.34

Several ferrite manufacturers offer a wide selection of ferrite materials from which to choose, as well as a variety of packaging styles for the finished network (see References 10 and 11). A simple form is the *bead* of ferrite material, a cylinder of the ferrite which is simply slipped over the power supply lead to the decoupled stage. Alternately, the *leaded ferrite bead* is the same bead, pre-mounted on a length of wire and used as a component (see Reference 11). More complex beads offer multiple holes through the cylinder for increased decoupling, plus other variations. Surface mount beads are also available.

PSpice ferrite models for Fair-Rite materials are available, and allow ferrite impedance to be estimated [see Reference 12]. These models have been designed to match measured impedances rather than theoretical impedances.

A ferrite's impedance is dependent upon a number of inter-dependent variables, and is difficult to quantify analytically, thus selecting the proper ferrite is not straightforward. However, knowing the following system characteristics will make selection easier. First, determine the frequency range of the noise to be filtered. Second, the expected temperature range of the filter should be known, as ferrite impedance varies with temperature. Third, the DC current flowing through the ferrite must be known, to ensure that the ferrite does not saturate. Although models and other analytical tools may prove useful, the general guidelines given above, coupled with some experimentation with the actual filter connected to the supply output under system load conditions, should lead to a proper ferrite selection.

CHOOSING THE RIGHT FERRITE DEPENDS ON

- ■ Source of Interference

- ■ Interference Frequency Range

- ■ Impedance Required at Interference Frequency

- ■ Environmental Conditions:

    Temperature, AC and DC Field Strength,
    Size / Space Available

- ■ Don't fail to Test the Design -------

    EXPERIMENT! EXPERIMENT!

Figure 7.35

Using proper component selection, low and high frequency band filters can be designed to smooth a noisy switcher's DC output so as to produce an *analog ready* 5V supply. It is most practical to do this over two (and sometimes more) stages, each stage optimized for a range of frequencies. A basic stage can be used to carry all of the DC load current, and filter noise by 60dB or more up to a 1-10MHz range. This larger filter is used as a *card entry filter* providing broadband filtering for all power entering a PC card. Smaller, more simple local filter stages are also used to provide higher frequency decoupling right at the power pins of individual stages.

Figure 7.36 illustrates a card entry filter suitable for use with switching supplies. With a low rolloff point of 1.5kHz and mV level DC errors, it is effective for a wide variety of filter applications just as shown. This filter is a single stage LC low-pass filter covering the 1kHz to 1MHz range, using carefully chosen parts. Because of component losses, it begins to lose effectiveness above a few MHz, but is still able to achieve an attenuation approaching 60dB at 1MHz.

"CARD-ENTRY" SWITCHING SUPPLY FILTER

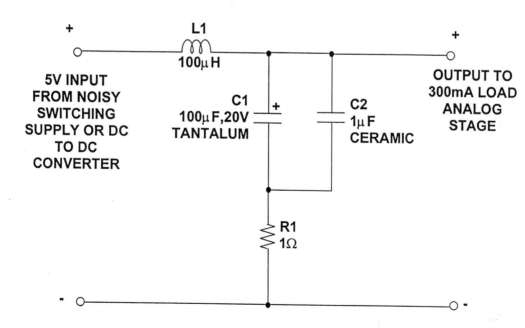

Figure 7.36

The key to low DC losses is the use of input choke, L1, a ferrite-core unit selected for a low DC resistance (DCR) of <0.25Ω at the 100μH inductance (either an axial lead type 5250 or a radial style 6000-101K choke should give comparable results) [Reference 13]. These chokes have low inductance shift with a 300mA load current, and the low DCR allows the 300mA to be passed with no more than 75mV of DC error. Alternately, resistive filtering might be used in place of L1, but a basic tradeoff

here is that load current capacity will be compromised for comparable DC errors. C1, a 100μF/20V tantalum type, provides the bulk of the capacitive filtering, shunted by a 1μF multilayer ceramic.

Figure 7.37 shows the frequency response of this filter in terms of SPICE simulation and lab measurements, with good agreement between the simulation and the measurements below 1MHz.

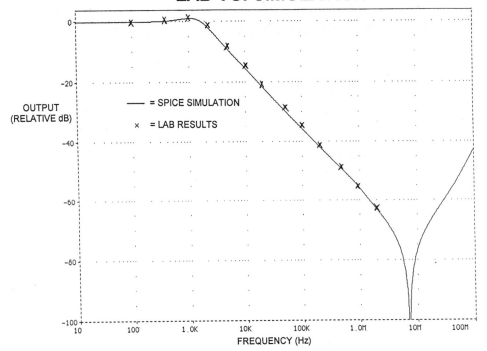

Figure 7.37

This type of filter does have some potential pitfalls, and one of them is the control of resonances. If the LCR circuit formed does not have sufficiently high resistance at the resonant frequency, amplitude peaking will result. This peaking can be minimized with resistance at two locations: in series with L1, or in series with C1+C2. Obviously, limited resistance is usable in series with L1, as this increases the DC errors.

In the filter, R1 is a damping resistor, used to control resonant peaks, and it should not be eliminated. A 1Ω value provides a slightly underdamped response, with peaking on the order of 1dB. Alternately, 1.5Ω can be used for less peaking, with a tradeoff of less

attenuation below 1MHz. Note that for wide temperature range applications, all temperature sensitive filter components will need consideration.

A local high frequency filter useful with the card entry filter is shown in Figure 7.38. This simple filter can be considered an option, one which is exercised dependent upon the high frequency characteristics of the associated IC and the relative attenuation desired. It uses Z1, a leaded ferrite bead such as the Panasonic EXCELSA39, providing a resistance of more than 80Ω at 10MHz, increasing to over 100Ω at 100MHz. The ferrite bead is best used with a local high frequency decoupling cap right at the IC power pins, such as a 0.1μF ceramic unit shown.

HIGH FREQUENCY LOCALIZED DECOUPLING

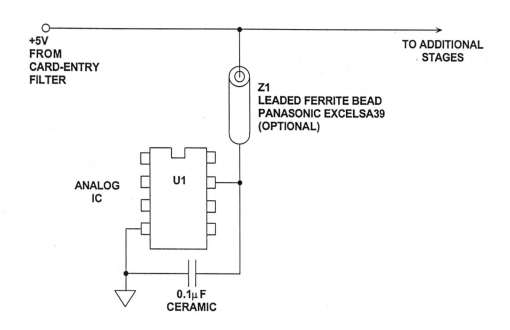

Figure 7.38

Both the card entry filter and the local high frequency decoupling filters are designed to filter differential-mode noise only, and use common, off the shelf components [Reference 14].

The following list summarizes the switching power supply filter layout/ construction guidelines which will help ensure that the filter does the best possible job:

(1) *Pick the highest electrical value and voltage rating for filter capacitors which is consistent with budget and space limits. This minimizes ESR, and maximizes filter performance. Pick chokes for low ΔL at the rated DC current, as well as low DCR.*

(2) *Use short and wide PCB tracks to decrease voltage drops and minimize inductance. Make track widths at least 200 mils for every inch of track length for lowest DCR, and use 1 oz or 2 oz copper PCB traces to further reduce IR drops and inductance.*

(3) *Use short leads or better yet,* leadless *components, to minimize lead inductance. This minimizes the tendency to add excessive ESL and/or ESR. Surface mount packages are preferred.*

(4) *Use a large-area ground plane for minimum impedance.*

(5) *Know what your components do over frequency, current and temperature variations! Make use of vendor component models for the simulation of prototype designs, and make sure that lab measurements correspond reasonably with the simulation. While simulation is not absolutely necessary, it does instill* confidence in a design when correlation is achieved*(see Reference 15).*

The discussion above assumes that the incoming AC power is relatively clean, an assumption not always valid. The AC power line can also be an EMI entry/exit path! To remove this noise path and reduce emissions caused by the switching power supply or other circuits, a *power line filter* is required.

It is important to remember that AC line power can potentially be lethal! Do not experiment without proper equipment and training! All components used in power line filters should be UL approved, and the best way to provide this is to specify a packaged UL approved filter. It should be installed in such a manner that it is the first thing the AC line sees upon entering the equipment (see Figure 7.39). Standard three wire IEC style line cords are designed to mate with three terminal male connectors integral to many line filters. This is the best way to achieve this function, as it automatically grounds the third wire to the shell of the filter and equipment chassis via a low inductance path.

Commercial power line filters can be quite effective in reducing AC power-line noise. This noise generally has both common-mode and differential-mode components. Common-mode noise is noise that is found on any two of the three power connections (black, white, or green) with the same amplitude and polarity. In contrast, differential-mode noise is noise found only between two lines. By design, most commercially available filters address both noise modes (see Reference 16).

POWER LINE FILTERING IS ALSO IMPORTANT

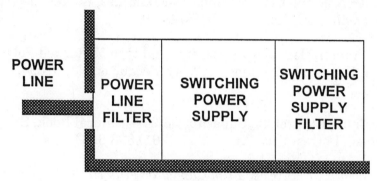

Power Line Filter Blocks EMI from
Entering or Exiting Box Via Power Lines

Figure 7.39

REFERENCES: NOISE REDUCTION AND FILTERING

1. **EMC Design Workshop Notes**, Kimmel-Gerke Associates, Ltd., St. Paul, MN. 55108, (612) 330-3728.

2. Walt Jung, Dick Marsh, *Picking Capacitors, Parts 1 & 2*, **Audio,** February, March, 1980.

3. Tantalum Electrolytic and Ceramic Capacitor Families, Kemet Electronics, Box 5928, Greenville, SC, 29606, (803) 963-6300.

4. Type HFQ Aluminum Electrolytic Capacitor and type V Stacked Polyester Film Capacitor, Panasonic, 2 Panasonic Way, Secaucus, NJ, 07094, (201) 348-7000.

5. OS-CON Aluminum Electrolytic Capacitor 93/94 Technical Book, Sanyo, 3333 Sanyo Road, Forrest City, AK, 72335, (501) 633-6634.

6. Ian Clelland, *Metalized Polyester Film Capacitor Fills High Frequency Switcher Needs*, **PCIM**, June 1992.

7. Type 5MC Metallized Polycarbonate Capacitor, Electronic Concepts, Inc., Box 1278, Eatontown, NJ, 07724, (908) 542-7880.

8. Walt Jung, *Regulators for High-Performance Audio, Parts 1 and 2*, **The Audio Amateur,** issues 1 and 2, 1995.

9. Henry Ott, **Noise Reduction Techniques in Electronic Systems, 2d Ed.,** 1988, Wiley.

10. Fair-Rite Linear Ferrites Catalog, Fair-Rite Products, Box J, Wallkill, NY, 12886, (914) 895-2055.

11. Type EXCEL leaded ferrite bead EMI filter, and type EXC L leadless ferrite bead, Panasonic, 2 Panasonic Way, Secaucus, NJ, 07094, (201) 348-7000.

12. Steve Hageman, *Use Ferrite Bead Models to Analyze EMI Suppression*, **The Design Center Source,** MicroSim Newsletter, January, 1995.

13. Type 5250 and 6000-101K chokes, J. W. Miller, 306 E. Alondra Blvd., Gardena, CA, 90247, (310) 515-1720.

14. DIGI-KEY, PO Box 677, Thief River Falls, MN, 56701-0677, (800) 344-4539.

15. Tantalum Electrolytic Capacitor SPICE Models, Kemet Electronics, Box 5928, Greenville, SC, 29606, (803) 963-6300.

16. Eichhoff Electronics, Inc., 205 Hallene Road, Warwick, RI., 02886, (401) 738-1440.

POWER SUPPLY REGULATION/CONDITIONING
Walt Jung

Many analog circuits require stable regulated voltages relatively close in potential to an unregulated source. An example would be a linear post regulator for a switching power supply, where voltage loss (dropout) is critical. This *low dropout* type of regulator is readily implemented with a rail-rail output op amp. The wide output swing and low saturation voltage enables outputs to come within a fraction of a volt of the

source for medium current (<30mA) loads, such as reference applications. For higher output currents, the rail-rail voltage swing feature allows direct drive to low saturation voltage pass devices, such as power PNPs or P-channel MOSFETs. Op amps working from 3V up with the rail-rail features are most suitable here, providing power economy and maximum flexibility.

LOW DROPOUT REFERENCES

Basic references

Among the many problems in making stable DC voltage references work from 5V and lower supplies are quiescent power consumption, overall efficiency, the ability to operate down to 3V, low input/output (dropout) capability, and minimum noise output. Because low voltage supplies can't support zeners of $\cong 6V$, low voltage references must necessarily be bandgap based— a basic $\cong 1.2V$ potential. With low voltage systems, power conservation can be a critical issue with references, as can output DC precision.

For many applications, simple one-package fixed (or variable) voltage references with minimal external circuitry and high accuracy are attractive. Two unique features of the three terminal REF19X bandgap reference family are low power, and shutdown capability. The series allows fixed outputs from 2.048-5V to be controlled between ON and OFF, via a TTL/CMOS power control input. It provides precision reference quality for those popular voltages shown in Figure 7.40.

The REF19X family can be used as a simple three terminal fixed reference as per the table by tying pins 2 and 3 together, or as an ON/OFF controlled device, by programming pin 3 as noted. In addition to the shutdown capacity, the distinguishing functional features are a low dropout of 0.5V at 10mA, and a low current drain for both quiescent and shutdown states, 45 and 15µA (max.), respectively. For example, working from inputs in the range of 6.3 to 15V, a REF195 used as shown drives 5V loads at up to 30mA, with grade dependent tolerances of ±2 to ±5mV, and max TCs of 5 to 25ppm/°C. Other devices in the series provide comparable accuracy specifications, and all have low dropout features.

To maximize DC accuracy in this circuit, the output of U1 should be connected directly to the load with short heavy traces, to minimize IR drops. The common terminal (pin 4) is less critical due to lower current in this leg.

7

30 mA REFERENCE FAMILY WITH OPTIONAL SHUTDOWN

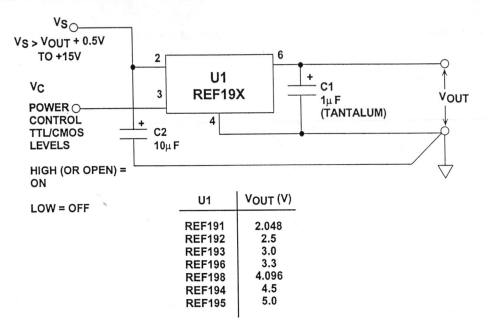

U1	V_{OUT} (V)
REF191	2.048
REF192	2.5
REF193	3.0
REF196	3.3
REF198	4.096
REF194	4.5
REF195	5.0

Figure 7.40

RAIL-TO-RAIL OUTPUT OP AMPS ALLOW GREATEST FLEXIBILITY IN LOW DROPOUT FREQUENCIES

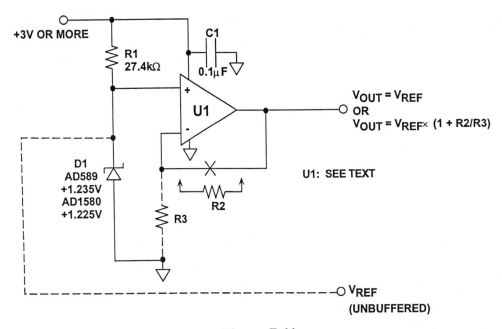

Figure 7.41

Scaled References

Another approach, one with the advantage of voltage flexibility, is to buffer/scale a low voltage reference diode. With this approach, one difficulty is getting an amplifier to work well at 3V. A workhorse solution is the low power reference and scaling buffer shown in Figure 7.41. Here a low current 1.2V, two-terminal reference diode is used for D1, either the 1.235V AD589 or the 1.225V AD1580. Resistor R1 sets the diode current, chosen for 50µA at a minimum supply of 2.7V. Obviously, loading on the unbuffered diode must be minimized at the V_{REF} node.

Amplifier U1 both buffers and optionally scales up the nominal 1.2V refer-

ence, allowing much higher source/sink currents. A higher op amp quiescent current is expended in doing this, but this is a basic tradeoff of the approach. Quiescent current is amplifier dependent, ranging from 45µA/channel with the OP196/296/496 series to 1000-2000µA/channel with the OP284 and OP279. The former series is most useful for very light loads (<2mA), while the latter series provide device dependent outputs up to 50mA. Various devices can be used in the circuit as shown, and their key specs are summarized in Figure 7.42.

OP AMPS USEFUL IN LOW VOLTAGE RAIL-RAIL REFERENCES AND REGULATORS

Device*	Iq/channel mA	Vsat(+), V(min @ mA)	Vsat(-), V (max @ mA)	Isc, mA (min)
OP193/293/493	0.017	4.20 @ 1	0.280 @ 1 (typ)	± 8
OP196/296/496	0.045	4.30 @ 1	0.430 @ 1	± 4
OP295/495	0.150 (max)	4.50 @ 1	0.110 @ 1	± 11
OP191/291/491	0.300	4.80 @ 2.5	0.075 @ 2.5	± 8.75
AD820/822/824	0.620	4.89 @ 2	0.055 @ 2	± 15
OP184/284/484	1.250 (max)	4.85 @ 2.5	0.125 @ 2.5	± 7.5
OP279	2.000	4.80 @ 10	0.075 @ 10	± 45

*Typical device specifications @ Vs = +5V, T_A = 25°C, unless otherwise noted.

Figure 7.42

In Figure 7.41, without gain scaling resistors R2-R3, V_{OUT} is simply equal to V_{REF}. With the scaling resistors, V_{OUT} can be set anywhere between V_{REF} and the positive rail, due to the op amp's rail-rail output swing. Also, this buffered reference is inherently low dropout, allowing a +4.5V reference output on a +5V supply, for example. The general expression for V_{OUT} is shown in the figure, where V_{REF} is the reference voltage.

Amplifier standby current can be further reduced below 20µA, if an amplifier from the OP193/293/493 series is used. This will be at the expense of current drive and positive rail saturation, but does provide the lowest possible quiescent current if necessary. All devices in Figure 7.42 operate from voltages down to 3V (except the OP279, which operates at 5V).

Low Dropout Regulators

By adding a boost transistor to the basic rail-rail output low dropout reference of Figure 7.41, output currents of 100mA or more are possible, still retaining features of low standby

current and low dropout voltage. Figure 7.43 shows a low dropout regulator with 800µA standby current, suitable for a variety of outputs at current levels of 100mA.

100mA LOW NOISE, LOW DROPOUT REGULATOR

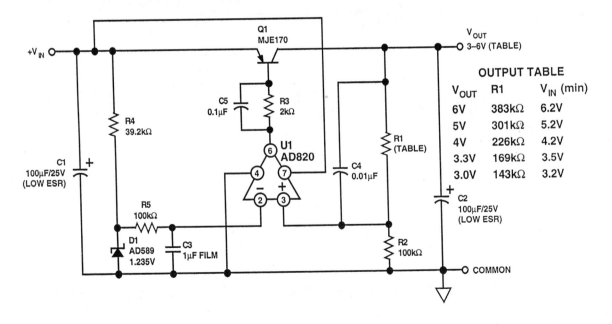

Figure 7.43

The 100mA output is achieved with a controlled gain bipolar power transistor for pass device Q1, an MJE170. Maximum output current control is provided by limiting base drive to Q1 via series resistor R3. This limits the base current to about 2mA, so the max H_{FE} of Q1 then allows no more than 500mA. This limits Q1's short circuit power dissipation to safe levels.

Overall, the circuit operates as a follower with gain, as was true in the case of Figure 7.41, so V_{OUT} has a similar output expression. The circuit is adapted for different voltages simply by programming R1 via the table. Dropout with a 100mA load is about 200mV, thus a 5V output is maintained for inputs above 5.2V (see table), and V_{OUT} levels down to 3V are possible. Step load response of this circuit is quite good, and transient error is only a

few mVp-p for a 30-100mA load change. This is achieved with low ESR switching type capacitors at C1-C2, but the circuit also works with conventional electrolytics (with higher transient errors).

If desired, lowest output noise with the AD820 is reached by including the optional reference noise filter, R5-C3. Lower current op amps can also be used for lower standby current, but with larger transient errors due to reduced bandwidth.

While the 30mA rated output current of the REF19X series is higher than most reference ICs, it can be boosted to much higher levels if desired, with the addition of a PNP transistor, as shown in Figure 7.44. This circuit uses full time current limiting for protection of pass transistor shorts.

150mA BOOSTED OUTPUT REGULATOR/REFERENCE WITH CURRENT LIMITING

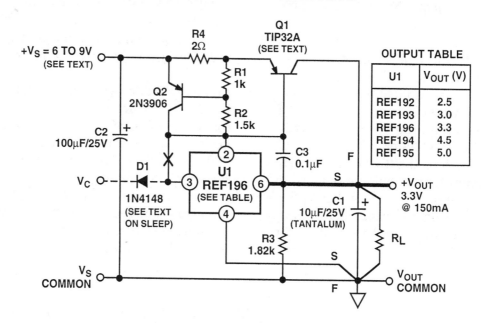

U1	V_{OUT} (V)
REF192	2.5
REF193	3.0
REF196	3.3
REF194	4.5
REF195	5.0

Figure 7.44

In this circuit the supply current of reference U1 flows in R1-R2, developing a base drive for pass device Q1, whose collector provides the bulk of the output current. With a typical gain of 100 in Q1 for 100-200mA loads, U1 is never required to furnish more than a few mA, and this factor minimizes temperature related drift. Short circuit protection is provided by Q2, which clamps drive to Q1 at about 300mA of load current. With separation of control/power functions, DC stability is optimum, allowing best advantage of premium grade REF19X devices for U1. Of course, load management should still be exercised. A short, heavy, low resistance conductor should be used from U1-6 to the V_{OUT} sense point "S", where the collector of Q1 connects to the load.

Because of the current limiting, dropout voltage is raised about 1.1V over that of the REF19X devices. However, overall dropout typically is still low enough to allow operation of a 5 to 3.3V regulator/reference using the 3.3V REF-196 for U1, with a Vs of 4.5V and a load current of 150mA.

The heat sink requirements of Q1 depend upon the maximum power. With Vs = 5V and a 300mA current limit, the worst case dissipation of Q1 is 1.5W, less than the TO-220 package 2W limit. If TO-39 or TO-5 packaged devices such as the 2N4033 are used, the current limit should be reduced to keep maximum dissipation below the package rating, by raising R4. A tantalum output capacitor is used at C1 for its low ESR, and the higher value is

required for stability. Capacitor C2 provides input bypassing, and can be an ordinary electrolytic.

Shutdown control of the booster stage is shown as an option, and when used, some cautions are in order. To enable shutdown control, the connection to U1-2 and U1-3 is broken at "X", and diode D1 allows a CMOS control source to drive U1-3 for ON/OFF control. Startup from shutdown is not as clean under heavy load as it is with the basic REF19X series stand-alone, and can require several milliseconds under load. Nevertheless, it is still effective, and can fully control 150mA loads. When shutdown control is used, heavy capacitive loads should be minimized.

Dedicated low dropout linear IC regulators offer all the virtues of the discrete approaches, but in a easier-to-use compact format. The ADP3367 is such a device, providing either a fixed output of 5V ±2%, or adjustable outputs over a range of 1.3 to 16.5V, with current outputs up to 300mA. Using a CMOS architecture with a PNP pass transistor, it has a quiescent current of 25µA (max., unloaded), and a dropout voltage of 175mV (max.) with a 100mA output.

Figure 7.45 shows the basic hookup for the ADP3367, which uses the "thermal coastline" 8 pin SOIC package, which is designed for power dissipation up to 960mW. For fixed 5V outputs, R1 and R2 aren't used, and the SET pin is grounded as shown. With the SHDN pin also grounded, this simple hookup provides a constant 5V at V_{OUT}, with the low dropout features mentioned.

30mA LOW DROPOUT FIXED/VARIABLE REGULATOR WITH OPTIONAL SHUTDOWN

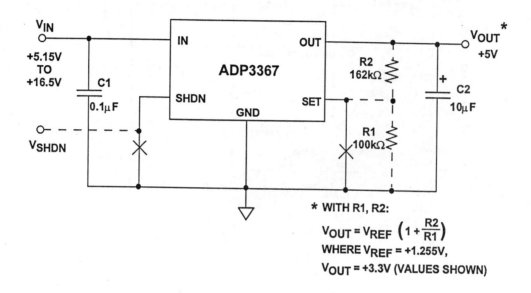

Figure 7.45

The ADP3367's useful output current capacity will be dependent upon the V_{IN}-V_{OUT} differential, such that the resulting power it dissipates is contained to 960 mW or less. For example, at low input-output differences of 2.5V, up to 300mA is available. For higher input-output differences, the allowable current is reduced according to the curves shown in Figure 7.46. The upper shaded curve corresponds to the output current which is consistent with the ADP3367's package limitations. Note that the allowable output current is appreciably higher than that of a standard SO package, shown in the lower shaded curve.

The ADP3367 can be placed in a shutdown mode, which reduces the output voltage to zero and drops the standby current to less than 1μA. When imple-

mented, shutdown is accomplished by applying a control voltage of more than 1.5V to V_{SHDN}. Otherwise, this pin should be tied to ground as shown. The SET pin has a dual function, and can be used either to select an internal divider (which provides the fixed 5V output), or it can be used with an external divider, R1-R2. When the SET pin is grounded, the internal divider is active, and the 5 V output results. When the SET pin is used with the external divider, V_{OUT} is programmed as:

$$V_{OUT} = V_{REF} * \left(1 + \frac{R2}{R1}\right)$$

where V_{REF} is 1.255V, the internal reference voltage of the ADP3367. The divider's absolute resistance values are not critical, since the input current at

ADP3367 LOAD CURRENT VS. INPUT - OUTPUT VOLTAGE

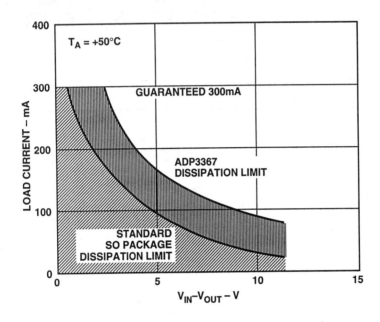

Figure 7.46

the SET pin is low, typically 10pA. This allows resistances of 100k - 1meg, consistent with the overall low standby power objectives. The example 1% values shown provide a 3.3V output. They can be further increased, if it is desired to lower standby current consumption below the $\cong 12\mu A$ resulting with the values shown.

C2, the output capacitor, is a 10µF type, and is required for regulator stability. Larger sizes are permissible, and will help improve transient re-

sponse. An input bypass is also recommended, C1.

To achieve the full power capability inherent to the design, the ADP3367 should be mounted on a PCB in such as way that internally-generated heat can flow outward easily from the die to the PCB. Large area PCB copper traces should be used beneath and around the IC, and mounting should be such that the part is exposed to unrestricted air flow [see Reference 5].

REFERENCES: POWER SUPPLY REGULATION/CONDITIONING

1.   Walt Jung, *Build an Ultra-Low-Noise Voltage Reference*, **Electronic Design Analog Applications Issue**, June 24, 1993.

2.   Walt Jung, *Getting the Most from IC Voltage References*, **Analog Dialogue 28-1**, 1994.

3.   Walt Jung, *The Ins and Outs of 'Green' Regulators/References*, **Electronic Design Analog Applications Issue**, June 27, 1994.

4.   Walt Jung, *Very-Low-Noise 5-V Regulator*, **Electronic Design**, July 25, 1994.

5.   *"Power Dissipation"* Discussions, **ADP3367 Data Sheet**, Analog Devices.

7

THERMAL MANAGEMENT
Walt Jung

For reliability reasons, modern semiconductor based systems are increasingly called upon to observe some form of *thermal management*. All semiconductors have some specified safe upper limit to junction temperature (T_J), usually on the order of 150°C (but sometimes 175°). Like maximum power supply potentials, maximum junction temperature is a worst case limitation which shouldn't be exceeded. In conservative designs, it won't be approached by less than an ample safety margin. This is a critical point, since the lifetime of all semiconductors is inversely related to their operating junction temperature. The cooler semiconductors can be kept during operation, the more closely they will approach maximum useful life.

Thermal basics

The general symbol θ is used for *thermal resistance*, that is:

θ = thermal resistance, in units of °C/watt (or, °C/W).

$θ_{JA}$ and $θ_{JC}$ are two more specific terms used in dealing with semiconductor thermal issues, which are further explained below.

In general, a device with a thermal resistance θ equal to 100°C/W will exhibit a temperature differential of 100°C for a power dissipation of 1W, as measured between two reference points. Note that this is a linear relation, so a 500mW dissipation in the same part will produce a 50°C differential, and so forth. For any power P (in watts), calculate the effective temperature differential (ΔT) in °C as:

$$ΔT = P \times θ$$

where θ is the total applicable thermal resistance. Figure 7.47 summarizes these thermal relationships.

A real example illustrating this relationship is shown by Figure 7.48. These curves indicate the maximum power dissipation vs. temperature characteristic for a device using 8 pin DIP and SOIC packaging. For a T_J(max) of 150°C, the upper curve shows the allowable power in a DIP package. This corresponds to a θ which can be calculated by dividing the ΔT by P at any point. For example, 1W of power is allowed at a T_A of 60°C, so the ΔT is 150°C − 60°C = 90°C. Dividing by 1W gives this DIP package's θ of 90°C/W. Similarly, the SOIC package yields 160°C/W. These figures are in fact the $θ_{JA}$ for the AD823 op amp, but they also happen to be quite similar to other 8 pin devices. Given such data as these curves, the $θ_{JA}$ for a given device can be readily determined, as above.

As the relationship signifies, to maintain a low T_J, either θ or the power dissipated (or both) must be kept low. A low ΔT is the key to extending semiconductor lifetimes, as it

THERMAL BASICS

- θ = Thermal Resistance (°C/W)

- $\Delta T = P \times \theta$

- θ_{JA} = Junction - to - Ambient Thermal Resistance

- θ_{JC} = Junction - to - Case Thermal Resistance

- θ_{CA} = Case - to - Ambient Thermal Resistance

- $\theta_{JA} = \theta_{JC} + \theta_{CA}$

- $T_J = T_A + (P \times \theta_{JA})$, P = Total Device Power Dissipation

- $T_{J(Max)}$ = 150°C   (Sometimes 175°C)

Figure 7.47

MAXIMUM POWER DISSIPATION VS. TEMPERATURE FOR 8-PIN MINI-DIP AND 8-PIN SOIC PACKAGES

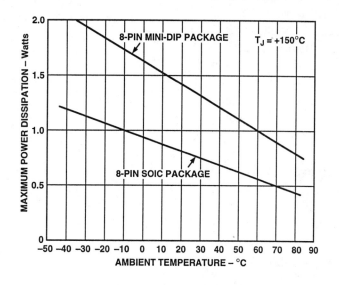

Figure 7.48

leads to low maximum junction temperatures.

In semiconductors, one temperature reference point is always the device junction, taken to mean the hottest spot inside the chip operating within a given package. The other relevant reference point will be either the case of the device, or the *ambient temperature*, T_A, that of the surrounding air. This then leads in turn to the above mentioned individual thermal resistances, θ_{JA} and θ_{JC}.

Taking the more simple case first, θ_{JA} is the thermal resistance of a given device measured between its *junction* and the *ambient* air. This thermal resistance is most often used with small, relatively low power ICs which do not dissipate serious amounts of power, that is 1W or less. θ_{JA} figures typical of op amps and other small devices are on the order of 90-100°C/W for a plastic 8 pin DIP package. It must be understood that thermal resistances are highly package dependent, as different materials have differing degrees of thermal conductivity. As a general rule of thumb, thermal resistance for the conductors within packaging materials is closely analogous to electrical resistances, that is copper is the best, followed by aluminum, steel, and so on. Thus copper lead frame packages offer the highest performance (lowest θ).

A summary of the thermal resistances of various IC packages is shown in Figures 7.49 and 7.50. In general, most of these packages do not lend themselves to easy heat sink attachment (with notable exceptions, such as the older round metal can types). Devices which *are* amenable to heat

sink attachment will often be noted by a θ_{JC} dramatically lower than the θ_{JA}. See for example the 15 pin SIP package (used by the AD815).

θ_{JC} is the thermal resistance of a given device as measured between its *junction* and the device *case*. This form is most often used with larger power semiconductors which do dissipate significant amounts of power, that is typically more than 1W. The reason for this is that a *heat sink* generally must be used with such devices, to maintain a sufficiently low internal junction temperature. A heat sink is simply an additional low thermal resistance device attached externally to a semiconductor part to aid in heat removal. It will have some additional thermal resistance of its own, also rated in °C/W.

Rather than just a single number, θ in this case will be composed of more than one component, i.e., θ_1, θ_2, etc. Like series resistors, thermal impedances add, making a net calculation relatively simple. For example, to compute a net θ_{JA} given a relevant θ_{JC}, the thermal resistance of the heat sink, θ_{CA}, or *case* to *ambient* is added to the θ_{JC} as:

$$\theta_{JA} = \theta_{JC} + \theta_{CA}$$

and the result is the θ_{JA} for that specific circumstance.

A second form of the general overall relationship between T_J, T_A, P and θ is:

$$T_J = T_A + (P \times \theta)$$

To take a real world example, the AD815AVR power-tab packaged op

STANDARD PACKAGE THERMAL RESISTANCES - 1

Package	ADI designation	θJA (°C/W)	θJC (°C/W)	Comment
8 pin plastic DIP	N-8	90		AD823
8 pin ceramic DIP	D-8	110	22	AD712
8 pin SOIC	R-8	160	60	
8 pin SOIC	R-8	90	60	ADP3367 Thermal Coastline
8 pin metal can	H-08A (TO-99)	150	45	OP07
10 pin metal can	H-10A (TO-100)	150	25	AD582
12 pin metal can	H-12A (TO-8)	100	30	AD841
14 pin plastic DIP	N-14	150		AD713
14 pin ceramic DIP	D-14	110	30	AD585
14 pin SOIC	R-14	120		AD813
15 pin SIP	Y-15	41	2	AD815 Through-Hole
16 pin plastic DIP	N-16	120	40	
16 pin ceramic DIP	D-16	95	22	AD524
16 pin SOIC	R-16	85		AD811

Figure 7.49

STANDARD PACKAGE THERMAL RESISTANCES - 2

Package	ADI designation	θJA (°C/W)	θJC (°C/W)	Comment
18 pin ceramic DIP	D-18	120	35	AD7575
20 pin plastic DIP	N-20	102	31	
20 pin ceramic DIP	D-20	70	10	
20 pin SOIC	R-20	74	24	
24 pin plastic DIP	N-24	105	35	
24 pin ceramic DIP	D-24	120	35	AD7547
28 pin plastic DIP	N-28	74	24	
28 pin ceramic DIP	D-28	51	8	
28 pin SOIC	R-28	71	23	

Figure 7.50

7

amp has a θ_{JA} of 41°C/W with no additional heat sinking (the device simply operating in still air). Using it just as this would allow a power of:

$$P = (T_J - T_A)/\theta_{JA}$$

or, $(150°C - 70°C)/41°C/W$, which results in an allowable power of about 2W.

However, such a mode of operation falls short of the device's full power handling capacity. The AD815AVR's θ_{JC} is quite low at about 2°C/W, and if a heat sink of significantly less than 38°C/W is used with it, then it can dissipate much more power for a given junction temperature. A 20°C/W heat sink will allow almost twice the power to be dissipated by the same device, simply because of the lower net θ_{JA} only 22°C/W. This can be accomplished by a double-sided PCB copper plane area of 1k mm^2 [see Reference 1].

To illustrate, the general relationship of the AD815AVR and PCB heat sink net θ_{JA} is shown by Figure 7.51. In the first example cited above, full advantage of PCB heat sink area was not taken, and as the graph shows, the net θ_{JA} can be reduced to as low as $\cong 17°C/W$ by increasing the heat sink area further. The tradeoff is simply one of board area, and with a 2k mm^2 heat sink area, nearly 5W of power can be handled by the same device, assuming the same ΔT and max T_J. Of course, for the AD815 (and other devices) even more conservative operation is optionally possible by holding to a lower maximum T_J.

Note that for the data of Figure 7.51, these data assume that the AD815AVR is soldered directly to one of the dual copper PCB planes.

The power tab style package used with the AD815AVR can also be used with conventional PC mounted heat sinks, with θ_{JC} of 20°C/W and less. See Reference 2.

AD815AVR AND PCB HEAT SINK θ_{JA} VS. PCB HEAT SINK AREA

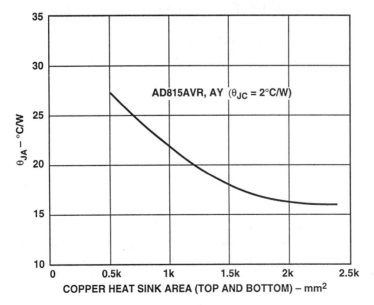

Figure 7.51

Calculating Power In Various Devices

In all instances of thermal calculations, a basic assumption is that the power is the total for a given package. With many modern devices now using more than one supply, the net total power dissipated will be the sum of all individual supply quiescent powers, plus any load dependent power. For many low output current op amps for example, total power will then be essentially the same as the quiescent. As long as this is safely less than the package can support, there is little worry. However, with some devices operable over a wide range of supply voltages, there are instances where high supply voltages and a medium to high quiescent current plus load current can be a problem.

The AD811 is such an example, being capable of operation from ±5V to ±15V, with a quiescent current of about 16mA. If operated at ±15V, the quiescent dissipation is nearly 500mW, which with a 90°C/W θ_{JA}, will push T_J to about 115°C in a 70°C ambient, high enough for concern. If the signal voltage output for such an amplifier doesn't require the ±15V supplies, then reducing the supplies will lower the quiescent power, and T_J.

To illustrate a general relationship of the power dissipated in an op amp and the power in a load for family of supply voltages, Figure 7.52 was prepared. This is a test simulation of a standard gain-of-2 non inverting amplifier driving a 150Ω load, with 1kΩ gain and feedback resistors. Assuming an input voltage of 1V DC, the 2V output across the net resistor load of 150Ω||2kΩ=140Ω will produce a power P_r of about 29mW. The AD817 amplifier operates over a supply range of ±5V to ±15V, which is the Vs sweep range for the test circuit. The op amp quiescent power P_q increases to 210mW at ±15V, while the signal power P_S dissipated by the op amp increases to 187mW at ±15V. The total power in the op amp is their sum, 397mW at ±15V. Clearly, operating relatively high current and low voltage loads from an op amp does waste considerable power, and lower voltage supplies will be much more efficient, where allowable.

AD817 OP AMP POWER DISSIPATION VS. SUPPLY VOLTAGE

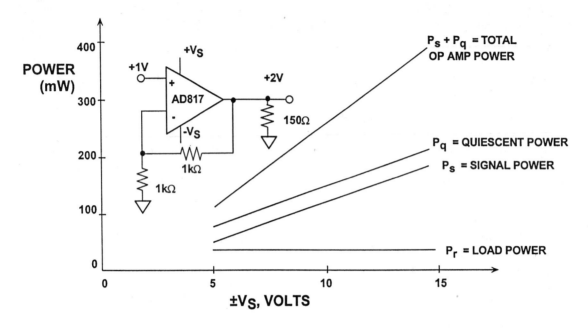

Figure 7.52

Where appropriate, a clip on DIP compatible heat sink such as the AAVID 580100 can be used [Reference 3]. This series has sinks compatible with ICs of 8 through 40 pin sizes, using a staggered fin design. Performance of these (and all) heat sinks is enhanced by air movement, either through forced convection, or as a minimum, by arranging PCB cards vertically to enhance natural convection.

A/D converters can consume considerable power, although the trend is towards lower voltage and lower power dissipation. Like op amps, they are generally analyzed by adding up the total power in the package, which can then be used with the package's θ_{JA} to compute junction temperature. In adding various

power totals, some care should be made to ascertain if any power is *clock dependent*. In some CMOS based designs, there can be appreciable differences in power as a function high/low clock speed as shown in Figure 7.53 for the AD9220 12-bit, 10MSPS ADC.

For example, the AD9042 12 bit A/D consumes about 600mW total on two 5V supplies, and its 28 pin DIP package has a θ_{JA} of 34°C/W. What will be the max T_J for this part in a T_A of 70°C? You should get a T_J of 90.4°C ($\Delta T = 0.6W \times 34°C/W = 20.4°C$, so T_J for T_A of 70°C, = 70°C + 20.4°C). This particular part is therefore in good shape for this T_A, assuming that there are no adjacent "hot spot" sources to increase the device's effective T_A.

AD9220 12-BIT, 10MSPS CMOS ADC POWER DISSIPATION VS. SAMPLING CLOCK FREQUENCY

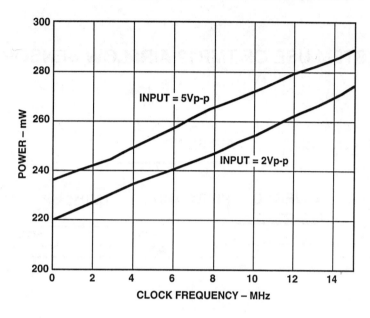

Figure 7.53

Airflow Control

For large power dissipations and/or to maintain low TJ's, forced air movement can be used to increase air flow and aid in heat removal. In its most simple form this can consist of a continuously or thermostatically operated fan, directed across high temperature, high wattage dissipation devices such as CPUs, DSP chips, etc.

Quite often however, more sophisticated temperature control is necessary. Recent temperature monitoring and control ICs such as the TMP12, an airflow temperature sensor IC, lend themselves to such applications.

The TMP12 includes on chip two comparators, a voltage reference, a temperature sensor and a heater. The heater is used to force a predictable internal temperature rise, to match a power IC such as a microprocessor. The temperature sensing and control portions of the IC can then be programmed to respond to the temperature changes and control an external fan, so as to maintain some range of temperature. Compared to a simple thermostat, this allows infinite resolution of user control for control points and ON/OFF hysteresis.

The device is placed in an airstream near the power IC, such that both see the same stream of air, and will thus have like temperature profiles, assuming proper control of the stream. This is shown in basic form by the layout diagram of Figure 7.54.

SYSTEM USE OF TMP12 AIRFLOW SENSOR

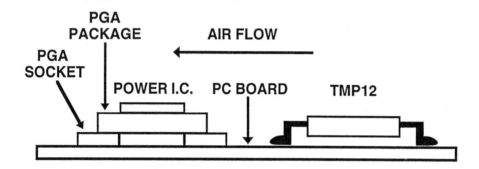

Figure 7.54

With the TMP12's internal 250mW heater ON and no airflow, the TMP12 thermal profile will look like the curve "A" of Figure 7.55, and will show a 20°C rise above T_A. When airflow is provided, this same dissipation results in a lower temperature, "D". In programming the device for airspeed control, the designer can set up to two switch points, shown here symbolically by "B" and "C", which are HIGH and LOW setpoints, respectively. The basic idea is that when the IC substrate reaches point B in temperature, the external fan will be turned on to create the airstream, and lower the temperature. If the overall system setup is reasonable in terms of thermal profiling, this small IC can thus be used to indirectly control another larger and independent power source with regard to its temperature. Note that the dual mode control need not necessarily be used, in all applications. An unused comparator is simply wired high or low.

TMP12 TEMPERATURE RELATIONSHIPS

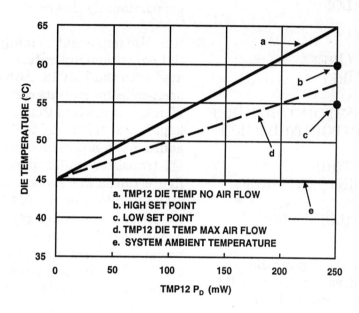

Figure 7.55

Figure 7.56 shows a circuit diagram using the TMP12 as a general purpose controller. The device is connected to a 5V supply, which is also used to power a control relay and the TMP12's internal heater at pin 5. Setpoint programming of the TMP12 is accomplished by the resistor string at pins 4 through 1, R1 - R3. These resistors establish a current drain from the internal reference source at pin 4, which sets up a reference current, I_{REF}, which is set as:

$$I_{REF} = (5\mu A/°C \times T_{HYS}) + 7\mu A$$

In this expression, T_{HYS} is the hysteresis temperature swing desired about the setpoint, in °C, and the 7μA is recommended minimum loading of the reference. For a 2°C hysteresis for example, I_{REF} is 17μA; for 5°C, it would be 32μA.

Given a desired setpoint temperature in °C, the setpoint can be converted to a corresponding voltage. Although not available externally, the internal temperature dependent voltage of the TMP12 is scaled at 5mV/°C, and is equal to 1.49V at 25°C.

To convert a setpoint temperature to a voltage $V_{SETPOINT}$,

$$V_{SETPOINT} = 1.49V + [5mV/°C \times (T_{SETPOINT} - T_{25})]$$

where $T_{SETPOINT}$ is the desired setpoint temperature, and T_{25} is 25°C. For a 50°C high setpoint, this works out to be $V_{SETPOINT(HI)} = 1.615V$. For a lower setpoint of 35°C, the voltage $V_{SETPOINT(LO)}$ would be 1.59V.

7

The divider resistors are then chosen to draw the required current I_{REF} while setting the two tap voltages corresponding to $V_{SETPOINT(HI)}$ and $V_{SETPOINT(LO)}$.

$$R_{TOTAL} = V_{REF} / I_{REF}$$
$$= 2.5V / I_{REF}$$

$$R1 = [V_{REF} - V_{SETPOINT(HI)}] / I_{REF}$$
$$= [2.5V - V_{SETPOINT(HI)}] / I_{REF}$$

$$R2 = [V_{SETPOINT(HI)} - V_{SETPOINT(LO)}] / I_{REF}$$

$$R3 = V_{SETPOINT(LO)} / I_{REF}$$

In the example of the figure, the resulting standard values for R1 - R3 correspond to the temperature/voltage setpoint examples noted above. Ideal 1% values shown give resistor related errors of only 0.1°C from ideal. Note that this is error is independent of the TMP12 temperature errors, which are ±2°C.

As noted above, both comparators of the device need not always be used, and in this case the lower comparator output is not used. For a single point 50°C controller, the 35°C setpoint is superfluous. One resistor can be eliminated by making R2 + R3 a single value of 95.3kΩ and connecting pin 3 to GND. Pin 6 should be left as a no-connect. If a greater hysteresis is desired, the resistor values will be proportionally lowered.

It is also important to minimize potential parasitic temperature errors associated with the TMP12. Although the open-collector outputs can sink up to 20mA, it is advised that currents be kept low at this node, to limit any additional temperature rise. The Q1 - Q2 transistor buffer shown in the figure raises the current drive to 100mA, allowing a 50Ω/5V coil to be driven. The relay type shown is general purpose, and many other power interfaces are possible with the TMP12. If used as shown, the relay contacts would be used to turn on a fan for airflow when the active low output at pin 7 changes, indicating the upper setpoint threshold.

A basic assumption of the TMP12's operation is that it will "mimic" another device in temperature rise. Therefore, a practical working system must be arranged and tested for proper airflow channeling, minimal disturbances from adjacent devices, etc. Some experimentation should be expected before a final setup will result.

TMP12 50° SETPOINT CONTROLLER

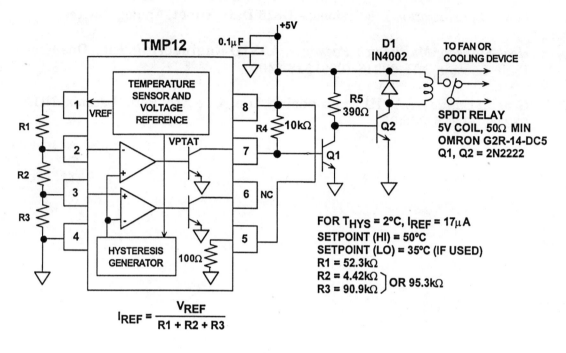

Figure 7.56

REFERENCES: THERMAL MANAGEMENT

1. *Power Consideration* Discussions, **AD815 Data Sheet**, Analog Devices.

2. *Heat Sinks for Multiwatt® Packages,* **AAVID Engineering, Inc.,** One Kool Path, Laconia, NH, 03246, (603) 528-3400.

3. *General Catalog*, **AAVID Engineering, Inc.**, One Kool Path, Laconia, NH, 03246, (603) 528-3400.

EMI/RFI CONSIDERATIONS
Adolfo A. Garcia

Electromagnetic interference (EMI) has become a hot topic in the last few years among circuit designers and systems engineers. Although the subject matter and prior art have been in existence for over the last 50 years or so, the advent of portable and high-frequency industrial and consumer electronics has provided a comfortable standard of living for many EMI testing engineers, consultants, and publishers. With the help of EDN Magazine and Kimmel Gerke Associates, this section will highlight general issues of EMC (electromagnetic compatibility) to familiarize the system/circuit designer with this subject and to illustrate proven techniques for protection against EMI.

A PRIMER ON EMI REGULATIONS

The intent of this section is to summarize the different types of electromagnetic compatibility (EMC) regulations imposed on equipment manufacturers, both voluntary and mandatory. Published EMC regulations apply at this time only to equipment and systems, and not to components. Thus, EMI *hardened* equipment does not necessarily imply that each of the components used (integrated circuits, especially) in the equipment must also be EMI *hardened*.

Commercial Equipment

The two driving forces behind commercial EMI regulations are the FCC (Federal Communications Commission) in the U. S. and the VDE (Verband Deutscher Electrotechniker) in Germany. VDE regulations are more restrictive than the FCC's with regard to emissions and radiation, but the European Community will be adding immunity to RF, electrostatic discharge, and power-line disturbances to the VDE regulations, and now requires mandatory compliance. In Japan, commercial EMC regulations are covered under the VCCI (Voluntary Control Council for Interference) standards and, implied by the name, are much looser than their FCC and VDE counterparts.

All commercial EMI regulations primarily focus on *radiated* emissions, specifically to protect nearby radio and television receivers, although both FCC and VDE standards are less stringent with respect to *conducted* interference (by a factor of 10 over radiated levels). The FCC Part 15 and VDE 0871 regulations group commercial equipment into two classes: Class A, for all products intended for business environments; and Class B, for all products used in residential applications. For example, Table 7.1 illustrates the electric-field emission limits of commercial computer equipment for both FCC Part 15 and VDE 0871 compliance.

7

Radiated Emission Limits for Commercial Computer Equipment

Frequency (MHz)	Class A (at 3 m)	Class B (at 3 m)
30 - 88	300 µV/m	100 µV/m
88 - 216	500 µV/m	150 µV/m
216 - 1000	700 µV/m	200 µV/m

Reprinted from EDN Magazine (January 20, 1994), © CAHNERS PUBLISHING COMPANY 1995, A Division of Reed Publishing USA.

Table 7.1

In addition to the already stringent VDE emission limits, the European Community EMC standards (IEC and IEEE) now requires mandatory compliance to these additional EMI threats: Immunity to RF fields, electrostatic discharge, and power-line disturbances. All equipment/systems marketed in Europe must exhibit an immunity to RF field strengths of 1-10V/m (IEC standard 801-3), electrostatic discharge (generated by human contact or through material movement) in the range of 10-15kV (IEC standard 801-2), and power-line disturbances of 4kV EFTs (extremely fast transients, IEC standard 801-4) and 6kV lightning surges (IEEE standard C62.41).

Military Equipment

The defining EMC specification for military equipment is MIL-STD-461 which applies to radiated equipment emissions and equipment susceptibility to interference. Radiated emission limits are very typically 10 to 100 times more stringent than the levels shown in Table 7.1. Required limits on immunity to RF fields are typically 200 times more stringent (RF field strengths of 5-50mV/m) than the limits for commercial equipment.

Medical Equipment

Although not yet mandatory, EMC regulations for medical equipment are presently being defined by the FDA (Food and Drug Administration) in the USA and the European Community. The primary focus of these EMC regulations will be on immunity to RF fields, electrostatic discharge, and power-line disturbances, and may very well be more stringent than the limits spelled out in MIL-STD-461. The primary objective of the medical EMC regulations is to guarantee safety to humans.

Industrial- and Process-Control Equipment

Presently, equipment designed and marketed for industrial- and process-control applications are not required to meet pre-existing mandatory EMC regulations. In fact, manufacturers are exempt from complying to any standard in the USA. However, since industrial environments are very much electrically *hostile*, all equipment manufacturers will be required to comply with all European Community EMC regulations in 1996.

Automotive Equipment

Perhaps the most difficult and hostile environment in which electrical circuits and systems must operate is that found in the automobile. All of the key EMI threats to electrical systems exist here. In addition, operating temperature extremes, moisture, dirt, and toxic chemicals further exacerbate the problem. To complicate matters further, standard techniques (ferrite beads, feed-through capacitors, inductors, resistors, shielded cables, wires, and connectors) used in other systems are not generally used in automotive applications because of the cost of the additional components.

Presently, automotive EMC regulations, defined by the very comprehensive SAE Standards J551 and J1113, are not yet mandatory. They are, however, very rigorous. SAE standard J551 applies to vehicle-level EMC specifications, and standard J1113 (functionally similar to MIL-STD-461) applies to all automotive electronic modules. For example, the J1113 specification requires that electronic modules cannot radiate electric fields greater than 300nV/m at a distance of 3 meters. This is roughly 1000 times more stringent than the FCC Part 15 Class A specification. In many applications, automotive manufacturers are imposing J1113 RF field immunity limits on *each of the active components* used in these modules. Thus, in the very near future, automotive manufacturers will require that IC products comply with existing EMC standards and regulations.

EMC Regulations' Impact on Design

In all these applications and many more, complying with mandatory EMC regulations will require careful design of individual circuits, modules, and systems using established techniques for cable shielding, signal and power-line filtering against both small- and large-scale disturbances, and sound multi-layer PCB layouts. The key to success is to incorporate sound EMC principles early in the design phase to avoid time-consuming and expensive redesign efforts.

7

A DIAGNOSTIC FRAMEWORK FOR EMI/RFI PROBLEM SOLVING

With any problem, a strategy should be developed before any effort is expended trying to solve it. This approach is similar to the scientific method: initial circuit misbehavior is noted, theories are postulated, experiments designed to test the theories are conducted, and results are again noted. This process continues until all theories have been tested and expected results achieved and recorded. With respect to EMI, a problem solving framework has been developed. As shown in Figure 7.57, the model suggested by Kimmel-Gerke in [Reference 1] illustrates that all three elements (a *source*, a *receptor* or *victim*, and a *path* between the two) must exist in order to be considered an EMI problem. The sources of electromagnetic interference can take on many forms, and the ever-increasing number of portable instrumentation and personal communications/computation equipment only adds the number of possible sources and receptors.

A DIAGNOSTIC FRAMEWORK FOR EMI

Reprinted from EDN Magazine (January 20,1994), © CAHNERS PUBLISHING COMPANY 1995, A Division of Reed Publishing USA

ANY INTERFERENCE PROBLEM CAN BE BROKEN DOWN INTO:

- ■ The SOURCE of interference

- ■ The RECEPTOR of interference

- ■ The PATH coupling the source to the receptor

SOURCES	PATHS	RECEPTORS

Microcontroller
◆ Analog
◆ Digital
	Radiated
	◆ EM Fields
	◆ Crosstalk
	  Capacitive
	  Inductive
		Microcontroller
		◆ Analog
		◆ Digital

ESD Communications Transmitters Power Disturbances Lightning	Conducted ◆ Signal ◆ Power ◆ Ground	Communications ◆ Receivers Other Electronic Systems

Figure 7.57

Interfering signals reach the receptor by *conduction* (the circuit or system interconnections) or *radiation* (parasitic mutual inductance and/or parasitic capacitance). In general, if the frequencies of the interference are less than 30MHz, the primary means by which interference is coupled is through the *interconnects*. Between 30MHz and 300MHz, the primary coupling mechanism is *cable radiation and connector leakage*. At frequencies greater than 300MHz, the primary mechanism is *slot and board radiation*. There are many cases where the interference is broadband, and the coupling mechanisms are combinations of the above.

When all three elements exist together, a framework for solving any EMI problem can be drawn from Figure 7.58. There are three types of interference with which the circuit or system designer must contend. The first type of interference is that generated by and emitted from an instrument; this is known as circuit/system *emission* and can be either *conducted* or *radiated*. An example of this would be the personal computer. Portable and desktop computers must pass the stringent FCC Part 15 specifications prior to general use.

THREE TYPES OF INTERFERENCE
EMISSIONS - IMMUNITY - INTERNAL

Reprinted from EDN Magazine (January 20,1994), © CAHNERS PUBLISHING COMPANY 1995, A Division of Reed Publishing USA

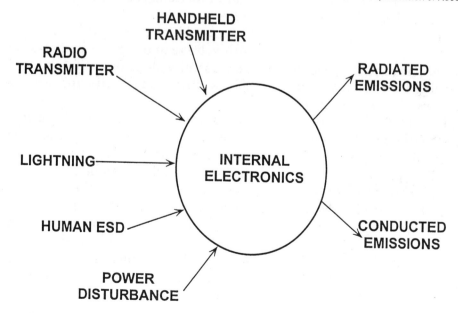

Figure 7.58

The second type of interference is circuit or system *immunity*. This describes the behavior of an instrument when it is exposed to large electromagnetic fields, primarily electric fields with an intensity in the range of 1 to 10V/m at a distance of 3 meters. Another term for immunity is *susceptibility*, and it describes circuit/system behavior against radiated or conducted interference.

The third type of interference is *internal*. Although not directly shown on the figure, internal interference can be high-speed digital circuitry within the equipment which affects sensitive analog (or other digital circuitry), or noisy power supplies which can contaminate both analog and digital circuits. Internal interference often occurs between digital and analog circuits, or between motors or relays and digital circuits. In mixed signal environments, the digital portion of the system often interferes with analog circuitry. In some systems, the internal interference reaches such high levels that even very high-speed digital circuitry can affect other low-speed digital circuitry as well as analog circuits.

In addition to the source-path-receptor model for analyzing EMI-related problems, Kimmel Gerke Associates have also introduced the FAT-ID concept [Reference 1]. FAT-ID is an acronym that describes the five key elements inherent in any EMI problem. These five key parameters are: *frequency, amplitude, time, impedance,* and *distance.*

The *frequency* of the offending signal suggests its path. For example, the path of low-frequency interference is often the circuit conductors. As the interference frequency increases, it will take the path of least impedance, usually stray capacitance. In this case,

the coupling mechanism is radiation.

Time and frequency in EMI problems are interchangeable. In fact, the physics of EMI have shows that the time response of signals contains all the necessary information to construct the spectral response of the interference. In digital systems, both the signal rise time and pulse repetition rate produce spectral components according to the following relationship:

$$f_{EMI} = \frac{1}{\pi \cdot t_{rise}} \qquad \text{Eq. 7.1}$$

For example, a pulse having a 1ns rise time is equivalent to an EMI frequency of over 300MHz. This time-frequency relationship can also be applied to high-speed analog circuits, where slew rates in excess of 1000V/μs and gain-bandwidth products greater than 500MHz are not uncommon.

When this concept is applied to instruments and systems, EMI emissions are again functions of signal rise time and pulse repetition rates. Spectrum analyzers and high speed oscilloscopes used with voltage and current probes are very useful tools in quantifying the effects of EMI on circuits and systems.

Another important parameter in the analysis of EMI problems is the physical dimensions of cables, wires, and enclosures. Cables can behave as either passive antennas (receptors) or very efficient transmitters (sources) of interference. Their physical length and their shield must be carefully examined where EMI is a concern. As previously mentioned, the behavior of simple conductors is a function of length, cross-sectional area, and frequency. Openings in equipment enclosures can behave as slot antennas, thereby allowing EMI energy to affect the internal electronics.

PASSIVE COMPONENTS: YOUR ARSENAL AGAINST EMI

Minimizing the effects of EMI requires that the circuit/system designer be completely aware of the primary arsenal in the battle against interference: *passive components*. To use successfully these components, the designer must understand their non-ideal behavior. For example, Figure 7.59 illustrates the *real* behavior of the passive components used in circuit design. At very high frequencies, wires become transmission lines, capacitors become inductors, inductors become capacitors, and resistors behave as resonant circuits.

A specific case in point is the frequency response of a simple wire compared to that of a ground plane. In many circuits, wires are used as either power or signal returns, and there is no ground plane. A wire will behave as a very low resistance (less than 0.02Ω/ft for 22-gauge wire) at low frequencies, but because of its parasitic inductance of approximately 20nH/inch, it becomes inductive at frequencies above 13kHz. Furthermore, depending on size and routing of the wire and the frequencies involved, it ultimately becomes a transmission line with an uncontrolled impedance. From our knowledge of RF, unterminated transmission lines become antennas with gain. On the other hand, large area ground planes are much more well-behaved, and maintain a low impedance over a wide range of frequencies. With a good understanding of the behavior of *real* components, a strategy can now be developed to find solutions to most EMI problems.

ALL PASSIVE COMPONENTS EXHIBIT "NON IDEAL" BEHAVIOR

Reprinted from EDN Magazine (January 20,1994), © CAHNERS PUBLISHING COMPANY 1995, A Division of Reed Publishing USA

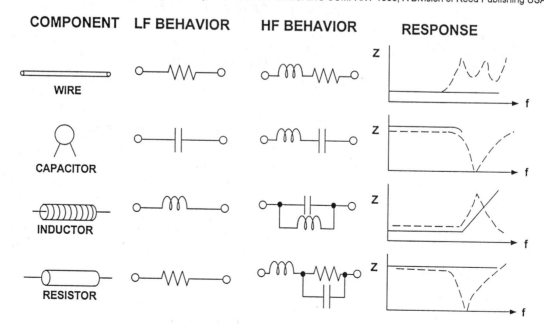

7

Figure 7.59

RADIO FREQUENCY INTERFERENCE

The world is rich in radio transmitters: radio and TV stations, mobile radios, computers, electric motors, garage door openers, electric jackhammers, and countless others. All this electrical activity can affect circuit/system performance and, in extreme cases, may render it inoperable. Regardless of the location and magnitude of the interference, circuits/systems must have a minimum level of immunity to radio frequency interference (RFI). The next section will cover two general means by which RFI can disrupt normal instrument operation: the direct effects of RFI sensitive analog circuits, and the effects of RFI on shielded cables.

Two terms are typically used in describing the sensitivity of an electronic system to RF fields. In communications, radio engineers define *immunity* to be an instrument's *susceptibility to the applied RFI power density at the unit.* In more general EMI analysis, the *electric-field intensity* is used to describe RFI stimulus. For comparative purposes, Equation 7.2 can be used to convert electric-field intensity to power density and vice-versa:

$$\vec{E}\left(\frac{V}{m}\right) = 61.4 \sqrt{P_T\left(\frac{mW}{cm^2}\right)} \quad \text{Eq. 7.2}$$

where E = Electric Field Strength, in volts per meter, and
P_T = Transmitted power, in milliwatts per cm^2.

From the standpoint of the source-path-receptor model, the *strength of the electric field*, E, surrounding the receptor is a function of *transmitted power*, *antenna gain*, and *distance* from the

source of the disturbance. An approximation for the electric-field intensity (for both near- and far-field sources) in these terms is given by Equation 7.3:

$$\vec{E}\left(\frac{V}{m}\right) = 5.5 \left(\frac{\sqrt{P_T \cdot G_A}}{d}\right) \quad \text{Eq. 7.3}$$

where E = Electric field intensity, in V/m;
P_T = Transmitted power, in mW/cm^2;
G_A = Antenna gain (numerical); and
d = distance from source, in meters

For example, a 1W hand-held radio at a distance of 1 meter can generate an electric-field of 5.5V/m, whereas a 10kW radio transmission station located 1km away generates a field smaller than 0.6V/m.

Analog circuits are generally more sensitive to RF fields than digital circuits because analog circuits, operating at high gains, must be able to resolve signals in the microvolt/millivolt region. Digital circuits, on the other hand, are more immune to RF fields because of their larger signal swings and noise margins. As shown in Figure 7.60, RF fields can use inductive and/or capacitive coupling paths to generate noise currents and voltages which are amplified by high-impedance analog instrumentation. In many cases, out-of-band noise signals are detected and rectified by these circuits. The result of the RFI rectification is usually unexplained offset voltage shifts in the circuit or in the system.

RFI CAN CAUSE RECTIFICATION IN SENSITIVE ANALOG CIRCUITS

Reprinted from EDN Magazine (January 20,1994), © CAHNERS PUBLISHING COMPANY 1995, A Division of Reed Publishing USA

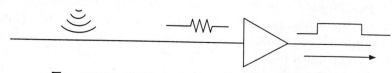

- INPUTS PICK UP HIGH FREQUENCY ENERGY ON SIGNAL LINE, WHICH IS DETECTED BY THE AMPLIFIER

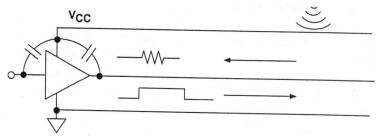

- OUTPUT DRIVERS CAN BE JAMMED, TOO: ENERGY COUPLES BACK TO INPUT VIA V_{CC} OR SIGNAL LINE AND THEN IS DETECTED OR AMPLIFIED

Figure 7.60

KEEPING RFI AWAY FROM ANALOG CIRCUITS

Reprinted from EDN Magazine (January 20,1994), © CAHNERS PUBLISHING COMPANY 1995, A Division of Reed Publishing USA

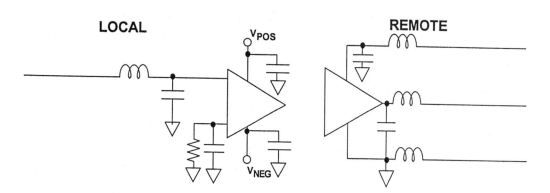

- Decouple all voltage supplies to analog chip with high-frequency capacitors
- Use high-frequency filters on all lines that leave the board
- Use high-frequency filters on the voltage reference if it is not grounded

Figure 7.61

There are techniques that can be used to protect analog circuits against interference from RF fields (see Figure 7.61). The three general points of RFI coupling are *signal inputs*, *signal outputs*, and *power supplies*. At a minimum, all power supply pin connections on analog and digital ICs should be decoupled with 0.1µF ceramic capacitors. As was shown in Reference 3, low-pass filters, whose cutoff frequencies are set no higher than 10 to 100 times the signal bandwidth, can be used at the inputs and the outputs of signal conditioning circuitry to filter noise.

Care must be taken to ensure that the low pass filters (LPFs) are effective at the highest RF interference frequency expected. As illustrated in Figure 7.62, real low-pass filters may exhibit *leakage* at high frequencies. Their inductors can lose their effectiveness due to parasitic capacitance, and capacitors can lose their effectiveness due to parasitic inductance. A rule of thumb is that a conventional low-pass filter (made up of a single capacitor and inductor) can begin to *leak* when the applied signal frequency is 100 to 1000 higher than the filter's cutoff frequency. For example, a 10kHz LPF would not be considered very efficient at filtering frequencies above 1MHz.

A SINGLE LOW PASS FILTER LOSES EFFECTIVENESS AT 100 - 1000 f_{3dB}

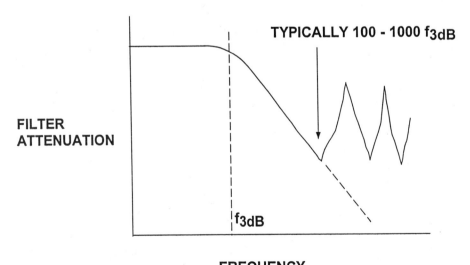

Figure 7.62

Rather than use one LPF stage, it is recommended that the interference frequency bands be separated into *low-band*, *mid-band*, and *high-band*, and then use individual filters for each band. Kimmel Gerke Associates use the stereo speaker analogy of *woofer-midrange-tweeter* for RFI low-pass filter design illustrated in Figure 7.63. In this approach, low frequencies are grouped from 10kHz to 1MHz, mid-band frequencies are grouped from 1MHz to 100MHz, and high frequencies grouped from 100MHz to 1GHz. In the case of a shielded cable input/output, the high frequency section should be located close to the shield to prevent high-frequency leakage at the shield boundary. This is commonly referred to as *feed-through* protection. For applications where shields are not required at

the inputs/outputs, then the preferred method is to locate the high frequency filter section as close the analog circuit as possible. This is to prevent the possibility of pickup from other parts of the circuit.

Another cause of filter failure is illustrated in Figure 7.64. If there is any impedance in the ground connection (for example, a long wire or narrow trace connected to the ground plane), then the high-frequency noise uses this impedance path to bypass the filter completely. Filter grounds must be broadband and tied to low-impedance points or planes for optimum performance. High frequency capacitor leads should be kept as short as possible, and low-inductance surface-mounted ceramic chip capacitors are preferable.

MULTISTAGE FILTERS ARE MORE EFFECTIVE

Reprinted from EDN Magazine (January 20,1994), © CAHNERS PUBLISHING COMPANY 1995, A Division of Reed Publishing USA

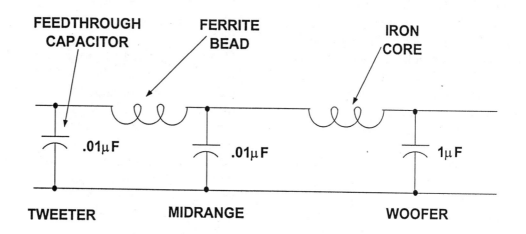

STEREO SPEAKER ANALOGY

Figure 7.63

NON-ZERO (INDUCTIVE AND/OR RESISTIVE) FILTER GROUND REDUCES EFFECTIVENESS

Reprinted from EDN Magazine (January 20,1994), © CAHNERS PUBLISHING COMPANY 1995, A Division of Reed Publishing USA

FILTER

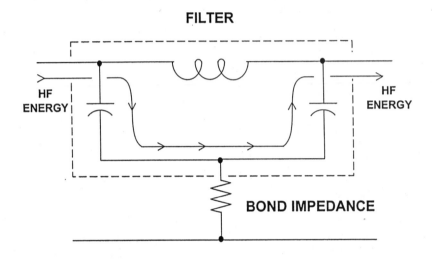

BOND IMPEDANCE

Figure 7.64

SOLUTIONS FOR POWER-LINE DISTURBANCES

The goal of this next section is not to describe in detail all the circuit/system failure mechanisms which can result from power-line disturbances or faults. Nor is it the intent of this section to describe methods by which power-line disturbances can be prevented. Instead, this section will describe techniques that allow circuits and systems to accommodate *transient* power-line disturbances.

Figure 7.65 is an example of a hybrid power transient protection network commonly used in many applications where lightning transients or other power-line disturbances are prevalent. These networks can be designed to provide protection against transients as high as 10kV and as fast as 10ns. Gas discharge tubes (crowbars) and large geometry zener diodes (clamps) are used to provide both differential and common-mode protection. Metal-oxide varistors (MOVs) can be substituted for the zener diodes in less critical, or in more compact designs. Chokes are used to limit the surge current until the gas discharge tubes fire.

Commercial EMI filters, as illustrated in Figure 7.66, can be used to filter less catastrophic transients or high-frequency interference. These EMI filters provide both common-mode and differential mode filtering as in Figure 7.66. An optional choke in the safety ground can provide additional protection against common-mode noise. The value of this choke cannot be too large, however, because its resistance may affect power-line fault clearing. These filters work in both directions: they are not only protect the equipment from surges on the power line but also prevent transients from the internal switching power supplies from corrupting the power line.

POWER LINE DISTURBANCES CAN GENERATE EMI

Reprinted from EDN Magazine (January 20,1994), © CAHNERS PUBLISHING COMPANY 1995, A Division of Reed Publishing USA

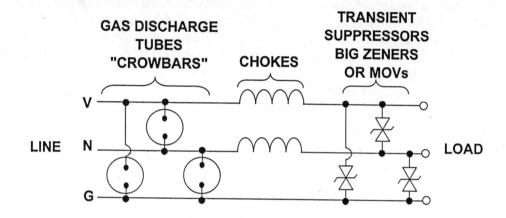

■ COMMON-MODE AND DIFFERENTIAL MODE PROTECTION

Figure 7.65

SCHEMATIC FOR A COMMERCIAL POWER LINE FILTER

Reprinted from EDN Magazine (January 20,1994), © CAHNERS PUBLISHING COMPANY 1995, A Division of Reed Publishing USA

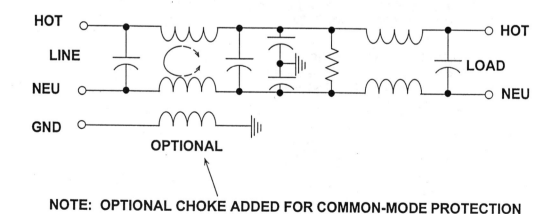

NOTE: OPTIONAL CHOKE ADDED FOR COMMON-MODE PROTECTION

Figure 7.66

7

Transformers provide the best common-mode power line isolation. They provide good protection at low frequencies (<1MHz), or for transients with rise and fall times greater than 300ns. Most motor noise and lightning transients are in this range, so isolation transformers work well for these types of disturbances. Although the isolation between input and output is galvanic, isolation transformers do not provide sufficient protection against extremely fast transients (<10ns) or those caused by high-amplitude electrostatic discharge (1 to 3ns). As illustrated in Figure 7.67, isolation transformers can be designed for various levels of differential- or common-mode protection. For differential-mode noise rejection, the Faraday shield is connected to the neutral, and for common-mode noise rejection, the shield is connected to the safety ground.

FARADAY SHIELDS IN ISOLATION TRANSFORMERS PROVIDE INCREASING LEVELS OF PROTECTION

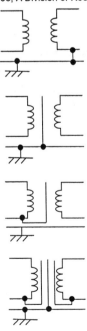

■ **STANDARD TRANSFORMER - NO SHIELD**
  ● NOTE CONNECTION FROM SECONDARY TO SAFETY GROUND TO ELIMINATE GROUND-TO-NEUTRAL VOLTAGE

■ **SINGLE FARADAY SHIELD**
  ● CONNECT TO SAFETY GROUND FOR COMMON-MODE PROTECTION

■ **SINGLE FARADAY SHIELD**
  ● CONNECT TO NOISY-SIDE NEUTRAL WIRE FOR DIFFERENTIAL-MODE PROTECTION

■ **TRIPLE FARADAY SHIELD**
  ● CONNECT TO SAFETY GROUND FOR COMMON MODE
  ● CONNECT TO NEUTRALS FOR DIFFERENTIAL MODE

Figure 7.67

PRINTED CIRCUIT BOARD DESIGN FOR EMI PROTECTION

This section will summarize general points regarding the most critical portion of the design phase: the printed circuit board layout. It is at this stage where the performance of the system is most often compromised. This is not only true for signal-path performance, but also for the system's susceptibility to electromagnetic interference and the amount of electromagnetic energy radiated by the system. Failure to implement sound PCB layout techniques will very likely lead to system/ instrument EMC failures.

Figure 7.68 is a real-world printed circuit board layout which shows all the paths through which high-frequency noise can couple/radiate into/out of the circuit. Although the diagram shows digital circuitry, the same points are applicable to precision analog, high-speed analog, or mixed analog/digital circuits. Identifying critical circuits and paths helps in designing the PCB layout for both low emissions and susceptibility to radiated and conducted external and internal noise sources.

METHODS BY WHICH HIGH FREQUENCY ENERGY COUPLED AND RADIATE INTO CIRCUITRY VIA PLACEMENT

Reprinted from EDN Magazine (January 20,1994), © CAHNERS PUBLISHING COMPANY 1995, A Division of Reed Publishing USA

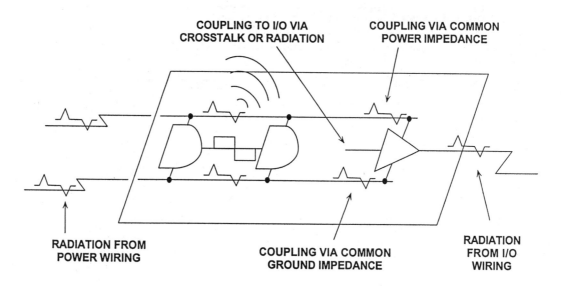

Figure 7.68

A key point in minimizing noise problems in a design is to *choose devices no faster than actually required by the application*. Many designers assume that faster is better: fast logic is better than slow, high bandwidth amplifiers are clearly better than low bandwidth ones, and fast DACs and ADCs are better, even if the speed is not required by the system. Unfortunately, faster is not better, but worse where EMI is concerned.

Many fast DACs and ADCs have digital inputs and outputs with rise and fall times in the nanosecond region. Because of their wide bandwidth, the sampling clock and the digital inputs and can respond to any form of high frequency noise, even glitches as narrow as 1 to 3ns. These high speed data converters and amplifiers are easy prey for the high frequency noise of microprocessors, digital signal processors, motors, switching regulators, hand-held radios, electric jackhammers, etc. With some of these high-speed devices, a small amount of input/output filtering may be required to desensitize the circuit from its EMI/RFI environment. Adding a small ferrite bead just before the decoupling capacitor as shown in Figure 7.69 is very effective in filtering high frequency noise on the supply lines. For those circuits that require bipolar supplies, this technique should be applied to both positive and negative supply lines.

To help reduce the emissions generated by extremely fast moving digital signals at DAC inputs or ADC outputs, a small resistor or ferrite bead may be required at each digital input/output.

POWER SUPPLY FILTERING AND SIGNAL LINE SNUBBING GREATLY REDUCES EMI EMISSIONS

Reprinted from EDN Magazine (January 20,1994), © CAHNERS PUBLISHING COMPANY 1995, A Division of Reed Publishing USA

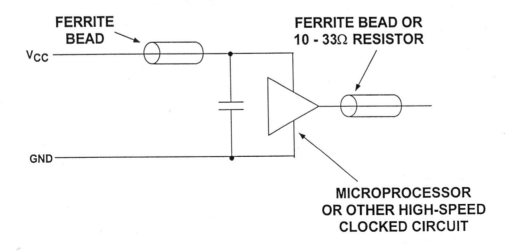

Figure 7.69

Once the system's critical paths and circuits have been identified, the next step in implementing sound PCB layout is to partition the printed circuit board according to circuit function. This involves the appropriate use of power, ground, and signal planes. Good PCB layouts also isolate critical analog paths from sources of high interference (I/O lines and connectors, for example). High frequency circuits (analog and digital) should be separated from low frequency ones. Furthermore, automatic signal routing CAD layout software should be used with extreme caution, and critical paths routed by hand.

Properly designed multilayer printed circuit boards can reduce EMI emissions and increase immunity to RF fields by a factor of 10 or more compared to double-sided boards. A multi-layer board allows a complete layer to be used for the ground plane, whereas the ground plane side of a double-sided board is often disrupted with signal crossovers, etc. If the system has sepa-

rate analog and digital ground and power planes, the analog ground plane should be underneath the analog power plane, and similarly, the digital ground plane should be underneath the digital power plane. There should be no overlap between analog and digital ground planes nor analog and digital power planes.

The preferred multi-layer board arrangement is to embed the signal traces between the power and ground planes, as shown in Figure 7.70. These low-impedance planes form very high-frequency *stripline* transmission lines with the signal traces. The return current path for a high frequency signal on a trace is located directly above and below the trace on the ground/power planes. The high frequency signal is thus contained inside the PCB, thereby minimizing emissions. The embedded signal trace approach has an obvious disadvantage: debugging circuit traces that are hidden from plain view is difficult.

"TO EMBED OR NOT TO EMBED" THAT IS THE QUESTION

Reprinted from EDN Magazine (January 20, 1994), © CAHNERS PUBLISHING COMPANY 1995, A Division of Reed Publishing USA

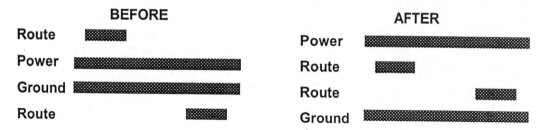

■ **Advantages of Embedding**

  ◆ Lower impedances, therefore lower emissions and crosstalk

  ◆ Reduction in emissions and crosstalk is significant above 50MHz

  ◆ Traces are protected

■ **Disadvantages of Embedding**

  ◆ Lower interboard capacitance, harder to decouple

  ◆ Impedances may be too low for matching

  ◆ Hard to prototype and troubleshoot buried traces

Figure 7.70

7

Much has been written about terminating printed circuit board traces in their characteristic impedance to avoid reflections. A good rule-of-thumb to determine when this is necessary is as follows: *Terminate the line in its characteristic impedance when the one-way propagation delay of the PCB track is equal to or greater than one-half the applied signal rise/fall time (whichever edge is faster).* A conservative approach is to use a 2 inch (PCB track length)/nanosecond (rise-, fall-time) criterion. For example, PCB tracks for high-speed logic with rise/fall time of 5ns should be terminated in their characteristic impedance and if the track length is equal to or greater than 10 inches (including any meanders). The 2 inch/nanosecond track length criterion is summarized in Figure 7.71 for a number of logic families.

This same 2 inch/nanosecond rule of thumb should be used with analog circuits in determining the need for transmission line techniques. For instance, if an amplifier must output a maximum frequency of f_{max}, then the equivalent risetime, t_r, can be calculated using the equation $t_r = 0.35/f_{max}$. The maximum PCB track length is then calculated by multiplying the risetime by 2 inch/nanosecond. For example, a maximum output frequency of 100MHz corresponds to a risetime of 3.5ns, and a track carrying this signal greater than 7 inches should be treated as a transmission line.

Equation 7.4 can be used to determine the characteristic impedance of a PCB

track separated from a power/ground plane by the board's dielectric (microstrip transmission line):

$$Z_0(\Omega) = \frac{87}{\sqrt{\varepsilon_r + 1.41}} \ln\left[\frac{5.98d}{0.89w + t}\right] \quad \text{Eq. 7.4}$$

where ε_r = dielectric constant of printed circuit board material;
d = thickness of the board between metal layers, in mils;
w = width of metal trace, in mils; and
t = thickness of metal trace, in mils.

The one-way transit time for a single metal trace over a power/ground plane can be determined from Eq. 7.5:

$$t_{pd}(ns/ft) = 1.017\sqrt{0.475\varepsilon_r + 0.67} \quad \text{Eq. 7.5}$$

For example, a standard 4-layer PCB board might use 8-mil wide, 1 ounce (1.4 mils) copper traces separated by 0.021" FR-4 (ε_r=4.7) dielectric material. The characteristic impedance and one-way transit time of such a signal trace would be 88Ω and 1.7ns/ft (7"/ns), respectively. Transmission lines can be effectively terminated in several ways depending on the application, as described in Section 2 of this book.

LINE TERMINATION SHOULD BE USED WHEN LENGTH OF PCB TRACK EXCEEDS 2 inches / ns

Reprinted from EDN Magazine (January 20,1994), © CAHNERS PUBLISHING COMPANY 1995, A Division of Reed Publishing USA

DIGITAL IC FAMILY	t_r, t_f (ns)	PCB TRACK LENGTH (inches)	PCB TRACK LENGTH (cm)
GaAs	0.1	0.2	0.5
ECL	0.75	1.5	3.8
Schottky	3	6	15
FAST	3	6	15
AS	3	6	15
AC	4	8	20
ALS	6	12	30
LS	8	16	40
TTL	10	20	50
HC	18	36	90

t_r = rise time of signal in ns
t_f = fall time of signal in ns

■ For analog signals @ f_{max}, calculate t_r = t_f = 0.35 / f_{max}

Figure 7.71

7

REFERENCES ON EMI/RFI

1. *EDN's Designer's Guide to Electromagnetic Compatibility*, **EDN**, January, 20, 1994, material reprinted by permission of Cahners Publishing Company, 1995.

2. *Designing for EMC (Workshop Notes)*, Kimmel Gerke Associates, Ltd., 1994.

3. **Systems Application Guide**, Chapter 1, pg. 21-55, Analog Devices, Incorporated, Norwood, MA, 1994.

4. Henry Ott, **Noise Reduction Techniques In Electronic Systems, Second Edition**, New York, John Wiley & Sons, 1988.

5. Ralph Morrison, **Grounding And Shielding Techniques In Instrumentation, Third Edition**, New York, John Wiley & Sons, 1986.

6. **Amplifier Applications Guide**, Chapter XI, pg. 61, Analog Devices, Incorporated, Norwood, MA, 1992.

7. B.Slattery and J.Wynne, *Design and Layout of a Video Graphics System for Reduced EMI*, **Analog Devices Application Note AN-333**.

8. Paul Brokaw, *An IC Amplifier User Guide To Decoupling, Grounding, And Making Things Go Right For A Change*, **Analog Devices Application Note**, Order Number E1393-5-590.

9. A. Rich, *Understanding Interference-Type Noise*, **Analog Dialogue**, 16-3, 1982, pp. 16-19.

10. A. Rich, *Shielding and Guarding*, **Analog Dialogue**, 17-1, 1983, pp. 8-13.

11. **EMC Test & Design**, Cardiff Publishing Company, Englewood, CO. An excellent, general purpose trade journal on issues of EMI and EMC.

SHIELDING CONCEPTS
Adolfo Garcia, John McDonald

The concepts of shielding effectiveness presented next are background material. Interested readers should consult References 1, 2, and 6 cited at the end of the section for more detailed information.

Applying the concepts of shielding requires an understanding of the source of the interference, the environment surrounding the source, and the distance between the source and point of observation (the receptor or victim). If the circuit is operating close to the source (in the near-, or induction-field), then the field characteristics are determined by the source. If the circuit is remotely located (in the far-, or radiation-field), then the field characteristics are determined by the transmission medium.

A circuit operates in a near-field if its distance from the source of the interference is less than the wavelength (λ) of the interference divided by 2π, or $\lambda/2\pi$. If the distance between the circuit and the source of the interference is larger than this quantity, then the circuit operates in the far field. For instance, the interference caused by a 1ns pulse edge has an upper bandwidth of approximately 350MHz. The wavelength of a 350MHz signal is approximately 32 inches (the speed of light is approximately 12"/ns). Dividing the wavelength by 2π yields a distance of approximately 5 inches, the boundary between near- and far-field. If a circuit is within 5 inches of a 350MHz interference source, then the circuit operates in the near-field of the interference. If the distance is greater than 5 inches, the circuit operates in the far-field of the interference.

Regardless of the type of interference, there is a characteristic impedance associated with it. The characteristic, or wave impedance of a field is determined by the ratio of its electric (or E-) field to its magnetic (or H-) field. In the far field, the ratio of the electric field to the magnetic field is the characteristic (wave impedance) of free space, given by $Z_0 = 377\Omega$. In the near field, the wave-impedance is determined by the nature of the interference and its distance from the source. If the interference source is high-current and low-voltage (for example, a loop antenna or a power-line transformer), the field is predominately magnetic and exhibits a wave impedance which is less than 377Ω. If the source is low-current and high-voltage (for example, a rod antenna or a high-speed digital switching circuit), then the field is predominately electric and exhibits a wave impedance which is greater than 377Ω.

Conductive enclosures can be used to shield sensitive circuits from the effects of these external fields. These materials present an impedance mismatch to the incident interference because the impedance of the shield is lower than the wave impedance of the incident field. The effectiveness of the conductive shield depends on two things: First is the loss due to the *reflection* of the incident wave off the shielding material. Second is the loss due to the *absorption* of the transmitted wave *within* the shielding material. Both concepts are illustrated in Figure 7.72. The amount of reflection loss depends upon the type of interference and its wave impedance. The amount of absorption loss, however, is independent of the type of interference. It is the same for near- and far-field radiation, as well as for electric or magnetic fields.

7

REFLECTION AND ABSORPTION ARE THE TWO PRINCIPAL SHIELDING MECHANISMS

Reprinted from EDN Magazine (January 20,1994), © CAHNERS PUBLISHING COMPANY 1995, A Division of Reed Publishing USA

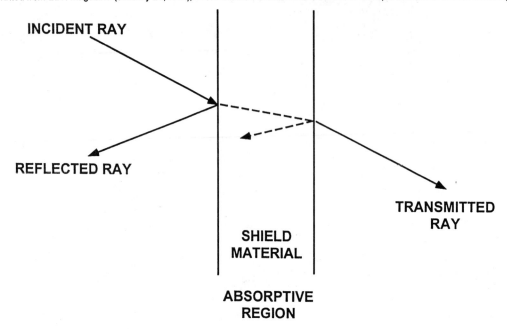

Figure 7.72

Reflection loss at the interface between two media depends on the difference in the characteristic impedances of the two media. For electric fields, reflection loss depends on the frequency of the interference and the shielding material. This loss can be expressed in dB, and is given by:

$$R_e(dB) = 322 + 10\log_{10}\left[\frac{\sigma_r}{\mu_r f^3 r^2}\right] \quad \text{Eq. 7.6}$$

where σ_r = relative conductivity of the shielding material, in Siemens per meter;
  μ_r = relative permeability of the shielding material, in Henries per meter;
  f = frequency of the interference, and
  r = distance from source of the interference, in meters

For magnetic fields, the loss depends also on the shielding material and the frequency of the interference. Reflection loss for magnetic fields is given by:

$$R_m(dB) = 14.6 + 10\log_{10}\left[\frac{fr^2\sigma_r}{\mu_r}\right] \quad \text{Eq. 7.7}$$

and, for plane waves ($r > \lambda/2\pi$), the reflection loss is given by:

$$R_{pw}(dB) = 168 + 10\log_{10}\left[\frac{\sigma_r}{\mu_r f}\right] \qquad \text{Eq. 7.8}$$

Absorption is the second loss mechanism in shielding materials. Wave attenuation due to absorption is given by:

$$A(dB) = 3.34 \ t\sqrt{\sigma_r \mu_r f} \qquad \text{Eq. 7.9}$$

where t = thickness of the shield material, in inches. This expression is valid for plane waves, electric and magnetic fields. Since the intensity of a transmitted field decreases exponentially relative to the thickness of the shielding material, the absorption loss in a shield one skin-depth (δ) thick is 9dB. Since absorption loss is proportional to thickness and inversely proportional to skin depth, increasing the thickness of the shielding material improves shielding effectiveness at high frequencies.

Reflection loss for plane waves in the far field decreases with increasing frequency because the shield impedance, Z_S, increases with frequency. Absorption loss, on the other hand, increases with frequency because skin depth decreases. For electric fields and plane waves, the primary shielding mechanism is reflection loss, and at high frequencies, the mechanism is absorption loss. For these types of interference, high conductivity materials, such as copper or aluminum, provide adequate shielding. At low frequencies, both reflection and absorption loss to magnetic fields is low; thus, it is very difficult to shield circuits from low-frequency magnetic fields. In these applications, high-permeability materials that exhibit low-reluctance provide the best protection. These low-reluctance materials provide a magnetic shunt path that diverts the magnetic field away from the protected circuit. Some characteristics of metallic materials commonly used for shielded enclosures are shown in Figure 7.73.

A properly shielded enclosure is very effective at preventing external interference from disrupting its contents as well as confining any internally-generated interference. However, in the real world, openings in the shield are often required to accommodate adjustment knobs, switches, connectors, or to provide ventilation (see Figure 7.74). Unfortunately, these openings may compromise shielding effectiveness by providing paths for high-frequency interference to enter the instrument.

7

IMPEDANCE AND SKIN DEPTHS
FOR VARIOUS SHIELDING MATERIALS

Material	Conductivity σ_r	Permeability μ_r	Shield Impedance $\lvert Z_s \rvert$	Skin Depth δ (inch)
Cu	1	1	$3.68\mathrm{E}\text{-}7 \cdot \sqrt{f}$	$\dfrac{2.6}{\sqrt{f}}$
Al	1	0.61	$4.71\mathrm{E}\text{-}7 \cdot \sqrt{f}$	$\dfrac{3.3}{\sqrt{f}}$
Steel	0.1	1,000	$3.68\mathrm{E}\text{-}5 \cdot \sqrt{f}$	$\dfrac{0.26}{\sqrt{f}}$
μ Metal	0.03	20,000	$3\mathrm{E}\text{-}4 \cdot \sqrt{f}$	$\dfrac{0.11}{\sqrt{f}}$

where $\sigma_o = 5.82 \times 10^7$ S/m

$\mu_o = 4\pi \times 10^{-7}$ H/m

$\varepsilon_o = 8.85 \times 10^{-12}$ F/m

Figure 7.73

ANY OPENING IN AN ENCLOSURE CAN ACT AS
AN EMI WAVEGUIDE BY COMPROMISING
SHIELDING EFFECTIVENESS

Reprinted from EDN Magazine (January 20,1994), © CAHNERS PUBLISHING COMPANY 1995, A Division of Reed Publishing USA

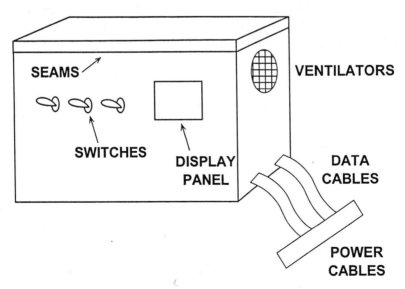

Figure 7.74

The longest dimension (not the total area) of an opening is used to evaluate the ability of external fields to enter the enclosure, because the openings behave as slot antennas. Equation 7.10 can be used to calculate the shielding effectiveness, or the susceptibility to EMI leakage or penetration, of an opening in an enclosure:

$$\text{Shielding Effectiveness (dB)} = 20\log_{10}\left(\frac{\lambda}{2\cdot L}\right) \quad \text{Eq. 7.10}$$

where λ = wavelength of the interference and
L = maximum dimension of the opening

Maximum radiation of EMI through an opening occurs when the longest dimension of the opening is equal to one half-wavelength of the interference frequency (0dB shielding effectiveness). A rule-of-thumb is to keep the longest dimension less than 1/20 wavelength of the interference signal, as this provides 20dB shielding effectiveness. Furthermore, a few small openings on each side of an enclosure is preferred over many openings on one side. This is because the openings on different sides radiate energy in different directions, and as a result, shielding effectiveness is not compromised. If openings and seams cannot be avoided, then conductive gaskets, screens, and paints alone or in combination should be used judiciously to limit the longest dimension of any opening to less than 1/20 wavelength. Any cables, wires, connectors, indicators, or control shafts penetrating the enclosure should have circumferential metallic shields physically bonded to the enclosure at the point of entry. In those applications where unshielded cables/wires are used, then filters are recommended at the point of shield entry.

Sensors and Cable Shielding

The improper use of cables and their shields is a significant contributor to both radiated and conducted interference. As illustrated in Figure 7.75, effective cable and enclosure shielding confines sensitive circuitry and signals within the entire shield without compromising shielding effectiveness.

Depending on the type of interference (pickup/radiated, low/high frequency), proper cable shielding is implemented differently and is very dependent on the length of the cable. The first step is to determine whether the length of the cable is *electrically short* or *electrically long* at the frequency of concern. A cable is considered *electrically short* if the length of the cable is less than 1/20 wavelength of the highest frequency of the interference, otherwise it is *electrically long*. For example, at 50/60Hz, an *electrically short* cable is any cable length less than 150 miles, where the primary coupling mechanism for these low frequency electric fields is capacitive. As such, for any cable length less than 150 miles, the amplitude of the interference will be the same over the entire length of the cable. To protect circuits against low-frequency electric-field pickup, only one end of the shield should be returned to a low-impedance point. A generalized example of this mechanism is illustrated in Figure 7.76.

LENGTH OF SHIELDED CABLES DETERMINES AN "ELECTRICALLY LONG" OR "ELECTRICALLY SHORT" APPLICATION

Reprinted from EDN Magazine (January 20,1994), © CAHNERS PUBLISHING COMPANY 1995, A Division of Reed Publishing USA

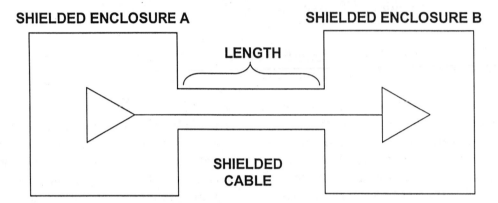

FULLY SHIELDED ENCLOSURES CONNECTED BY FULLY SHIELDED CABLE KEEP ALL INTERNAL CIRCUITS AND SIGNAL LINES INSIDE THE SHIELD.
● TRANSITION REGION: 1/20 WAVELENGTH

Figure 7.75

CONNECT THE SHIELD AT ONE POINT AT THE LOAD TO PROTECT AGAINST LOW FREQUENCY (50/60Hz) THREATS

Reprinted from EDN Magazine (January 20,1994), © CAHNERS PUBLISHING COMPANY 1995, A Division of Reed Publishing USA

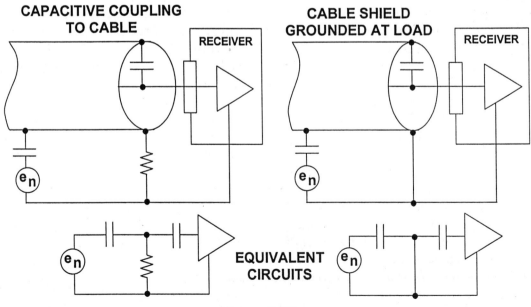

Figure 7.76

In this example, the shield is grounded at the receiver. An exception to this approach (which will be highlighted again later) is the case where line-level (>1Vrms) audio signals are transmitted over long distances using twisted pair, shielded cables. In these applications, the shield again offers protection against low-frequency interference, and an accepted approach is to ground the shield at the driver end (LF and HF ground) and ground it at the receiver with a capacitor (HF ground only).

In those applications where the length of the cable is *electrically long*, or protection against high-frequency interference is required, then the preferred method is to connect the cable shield to low-impedance points at both ends (direct connection at the driving end, and capacitive connection at the receiver). Otherwise, unterminated transmission lines effects can cause reflections and standing waves along the cable. At frequencies of 10MHz and above, circumferential (360°) shield bonds and metal connectors are required to main low-impedance connections to ground.

In summary, for protection against low-frequency (<1MHz), electric-field interference, grounding the shield at one end is acceptable. For high-frequency interference (>1MHz), the preferred method is grounding the shield at both ends, using 360° circumferential bonds between the shield and the connector, and maintaining metal-to-metal continuity between the connectors and the enclosure. Low-frequency ground loops can be eliminated by replacing one of the DC shield connections to ground with a low inductance 0.01µF capacitor. This capacitor prevents low frequency ground loops and shunts high frequency interference to ground.

Shielded Twisted Pair Cable Grounding Examples

The environments in which analog systems operate are often rich in sources of EMI. Common EMI noise sources include power lines, logic signals, switching power supplies, radio stations, electric lighting, and motors. Noise from these sources can easily couple into long analog signal paths, such as cables, which act as efficient antennas. Shielded cables protect signal conductors from electric field (E-field) interference by providing low impedance paths to ground at the offending frequencies. Aluminum foil, copper, and braided stainless steel are materials very commonly used for cable shields due to their low impedance properties.

Simply increasing the separation between the noise source and the cable will yield significant additional attenuation due to reduced coupling, but shielding is still required in most applications involving remote sensors.

There are two paths from an EMI source to a susceptible cable: capacitive (or E-field) and magnetic (or H-field) coupling. Capacitive coupling occurs when parasitic capacitance exists between a noise source and the cable. The amount of parasitic capacitance is determined by the separation, shape, orientation, and the medium between the source and the cable.

Magnetic coupling occurs through parasitic mutual inductance when a magnetic field is coupled from one conductor to another. Parasitic mutual inductance depends on the shape and relative orientation of the circuits in question, the magnetic properties of the medium, and is directly proportional to conductor loop area. Minimizing conductor loop area reduces magnetic coupling proportionally.

Shielded *twisted pair* cables offer further noise immunity to magnetic fields. Twisting the conductors together reduces the net loop area, which has the effect of canceling any magnetic field pickup, because the sum of positive and negative incremental loop areas is ideally equal to zero.

To study the shielding problem, a precision *RTD (Resistance Temperature Detector)* amplifier circuit was used as

the basis for a series of experiments. A remote 100Ω RTD was connected to the bridge, bridge driver, and the bridge amplifier circuit (Figure 7.77) using 10 feet of a shielded twisted pair cable. The RTD is one element of a 4-element bridge (the three other resistor elements are located in the bridge and bridge driver circuit). The gain of the instrumentation amplifier was adjusted so that the sensitivity at the output was 10mV/°C, with a 5V full scale. Measurements were made at the output of the instrumentation amplifier with the shield grounded in various ways. The experiments were conducted in lab standard environment where a considerable amount of electronic equipment was in operation.

UNGROUNDED SHIELDED CABLES ACT AS ANTENNAS

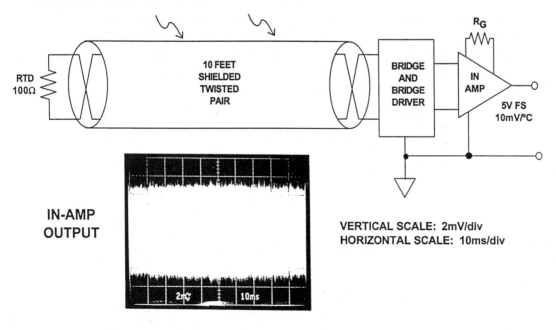

Figure 7.77

The first experiment was conducted with the shield ungrounded. As shown in Figure 7.77, shields left floating are not useful and offer no attenuation to EMI-induced noise, in fact, they act as antennas. Capacitive coupling is unaffected, because the floating shield provides a coupling path to the signal conductors. Most cables exhibit parasitic capacitances between 10-30pF/ft. Likewise, HF magnetically coupled noise is not attenuated because the floating cable shield does not alter either the geometry or the magnetic properties of the cable conductors. LF magnetic noise is not attenuated significantly, because most shield materials absorb very little magnetic energy.

To implement effective EMI/RFI shielding, the shield must be grounded. A grounded shield reduces the value of the impedance of the shield to ground to small values. Implementing this change will reduce the amplitude of the E-Field noise substantially.

Designers often ground both ends of a shield in an attempt to reduce shield impedance and gain further E-Field attenuation. Unfortunately, this approach can create a new set of potential problems. The AC and DC ground potentials are generally different at each end of the shield. Low-frequency ground loop current is created when both ends of a shield are grounded. This low frequency current flows through the large loop area of the shield and couples into the center conductors through the parasitic mutual inductance. If the twisted pairs are precisely balanced, the induced voltage will appear as a common-mode rather than a differential voltage. Unfortunately, the conductors may not be perfectly balanced, the sensor and excitation circuit may not be fully balanced, and the common mode rejection at the receiver may not be

sufficient. There will therefore be some differential noise voltage developed between the conductors at the output end, which is amplified and appears at the final output of the instrumentation amplifier. With the shields of the experimental circuit grounded at both ends, the results are shown in Figure 7.78.

Figure 7.79 illustrates a properly grounded system with good electric field shielding. Notice that the ground loop has been eliminated. The shield has a single point ground, located at the signal conditioning circuitry, and noise coupled into the shield is effectively shunted into the receiver ground and does not appear at the output of the instrumentation amplifier.

Figure 7.80 shows an example of a remotely located, ungrounded, passive sensor (ECG electrodes) which is connected to a high-gain, low power AD620 instrumentation amplifier through a shielded twisted pair cable. Note that the shield is properly grounded at the signal conditioning circuitry. The AD620 gain is 1000×, and the amplifier is operated on ±3V supplies. Notice the absence of 60Hz interference in the amplifier output.

Most high impedance sensors generate low-level current or voltage outputs, such as a photodiode responding to incident light. These low-level signals are especially susceptible to EMI, and often are of the same order of magnitude as the parasitic parameters of the cable and input amplifier.

Even properly shielded cables can degrade the signals by introducing parasitic capacitance that limits bandwidth, and leakage currents that limit sensitivity. An example is shown in Figure 7.81, where a high-impedance

GROUNDING BOTH ENDS OF A SHIELD PRODUCES LOW FREQUENCY GROUND LOOPS

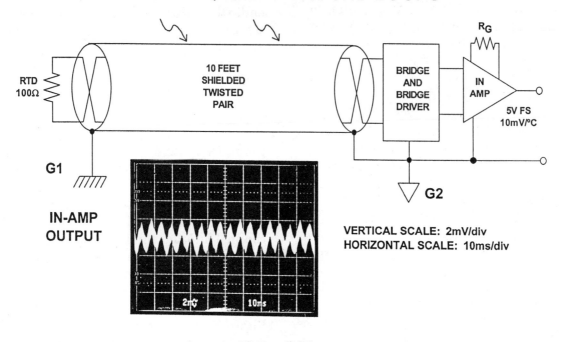

Figure 7.78

GROUNDING SHIELD AT RECEIVER END SHUNTS LOW AND HIGH-FREQUENCY NOISE INTO RECEIVER GROUND

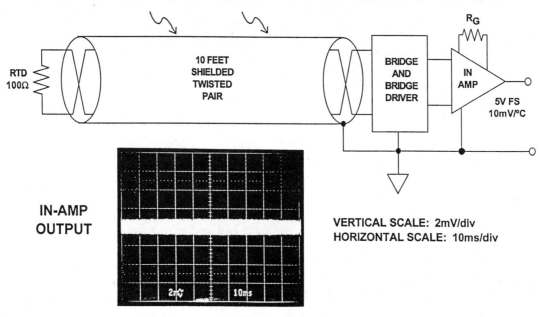

Figure 7.79

FOR UNGROUNDED PASSIVE SENSORS, GROUND SHIELD AT THE RECEIVING END

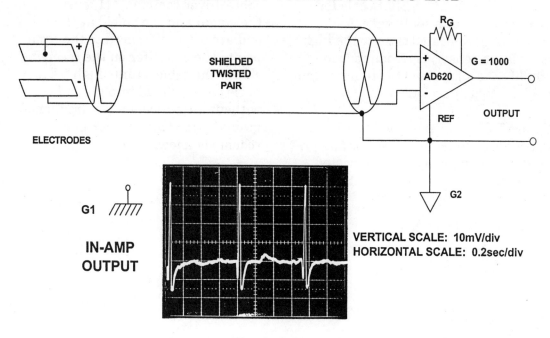

Figure 7.80

SHIELDS ARE NOT EFFECTIVE WITH HIGH IMPEDANCE REMOTE SENSORS

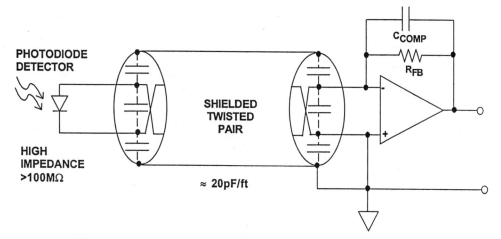

■ CABLE CAPACITANCE LIMITS BANDWIDTH

■ CABLE LEAKAGE CURRENT LIMITS SENSITIVITY

Figure 7.81

7

photodiode is connected to a preamp through a long shielded twisted pair cable. Not only will the cable capacitance limit bandwidth, but cable leakage current limits sensitivity. A pre-amplifier, located close to the high-impedance sensor, is recommended to amplify the signal and to minimize the effect of cable parasitics.

Figure 7.82 is an example of a high-impedance photodiode detector and pre-amplifier, driving a shielded twisted pair cable. Both the amplifier and the shield are grounded at a remote location. The shield is connected to the cable driver common, G1, ensuring that the signal and the shield at the driving end are both referenced to the same point. The capacitor on the receiving side of the cable shunts high frequency noise on the shield into ground G2 without introducing a low-frequency ground loop. This popular grounding scheme is known as *hybrid* grounding.

REMOTELY LOCATED HIGH IMPEDANCE SENSOR WITH PREAMP

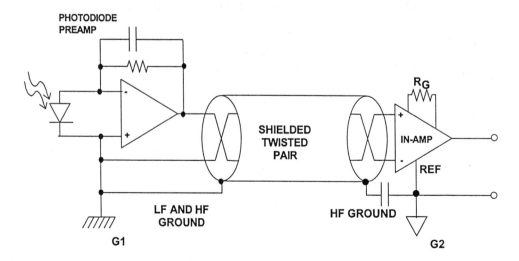

Figure 7.82

Figure 7.83 illustrates a balanced active line driver with a hybrid shield ground implementation. When a system's operation calls for a wide frequency range, the hybrid grounding technique often provides the best choice (Reference 8). The capacitor at the receiving end shunts high-frequency noise on the shield into G2 without introducing a low-frequency ground loop. At the receiver, a common-mode choke can be used to help prevent RF pickup entering the receiver, and subsequent RFI rectification (see References 9 and 10). Care should be taken that the shields are grounded to the chassis entry points to prevent contamination of the signal ground (Reference 11).

HYBRID (LF AND HF) GROUNDING WITH ACTIVE DRIVER

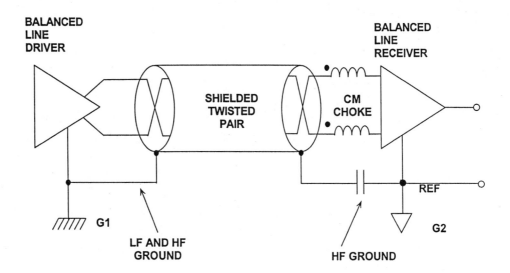

Figure 7.83

To summarize this discussion, shield grounding techniques must take into account the type and the configuration of the sensor as well as the nature of the interference. When a low-imped-ance passive sensor is used, grounding the shield to the receiving end is the best choice. Active sensor shields should generally be grounded at the source (direct connection to source ground) and at the receiver (connect to receiver ground using a capacitor). This hybrid approach minimizes high-frequency interference and prevents low-fre-quency ground loops. Shielded twisted conductors offer additional protection against shield noise because the coupled noise occurs as a common-mode, and not a differential signal.

The best shield can be compromised by poor connection techniques. Shields often use "pig-tail" connections to make the connection to ground. A "pig-tail" connection is a single wire connection from shield to either chassis or circuit ground. This type of connection is inexpensive, but at high frequency, it does not provide low impedance. Quality shields do not leave large gaps in the cable/instrument shielding system. Shield gaps provide paths for high frequency EMI to enter the system. The cable shielding system should include the cable end connectors. Ideally, cable shield connectors should make 360° contact with the chassis ground.

As shown in Figure 7.84, pigtail terminations on cables very often cause systems to fail radiated emissions tests because high-frequency noise has coupled into the cable shield, generally through stray capacitance. If the length of the cable is considered *electrically long* at the interference frequency, then it can behave as a very efficient quarter-wave antenna. The cable pigtail forms a matching network, as shown in the figure, to radiate the noise which coupled into the shield. In general, pigtails are only recommended for applications below 10kHz, such as 50/60Hz interference protection. For applications where the interference is greater than 10kHz, shielded connectors, electrically and physically connected to the chassis, should be used.

"SHIELDED" CABLE CAN CARRY HIGH FREQUENCY CURRENT AND BEHAVES AS AN ANTENNA

Reprinted from EDN Magazine (January 20,1994), © CAHNERS PUBLISHING COMPANY 1995, A Division of Reed Publishing USA

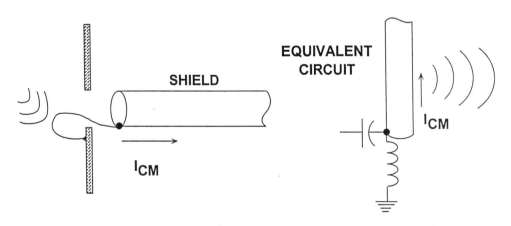

I_{CM} = COMMON-MODE CURRENT

Figure 7.84

REFERENCES: CABLE SHIELDING

1.   H.W. Ott, **Noise Reduction Techniques in Electronic Systems, Second Edition**, John Wiley & Sons, Inc., New York, 1988.

2.   Ralph Morrison, **Grounding and Shielding Techniques in Instrumentation, Third Edition**, John Wiley & Sons, Inc., New York, 1988.

3.   **Systems Application Guide**, Section 1, Analog Devices, Inc., Norwood, MA, 1993.

4.   AD620 Instrumentation Amplifier, Data Sheet, Analog Devices, Inc.

5.   A. Rich, *Understanding Interference-Type Noise*, **Analog Dialogue**, 16-3, 1982, pp. 16-19.

6.   A. Rich, *Shielding and Guarding*, **Analog Dialogue**, 17-1, 1983, pp. 8-13.

7.   *EDN's Designer's Guide to Electromagnetic Compatibility*, **EDN**, January, 20, 1994, material reprinted by permission of Cahners Publishing Company, 1995.

8.   *Designing for EMC (Workshop Notes)*, Kimmel Gerke Associates, Ltd., 1994.

9.   James Bryant and Herman Gelbach, *High Frequency Signal Contamination*, **Analog Dialogue**, Vol. 27-2, 1993.

10. Walt Jung, *System RF Interference Prevention*, **Analog Dialogue**, Vol. 28-2, 1994.

11. Neil Muncy, *Noise Susceptibility in Analog and Digital Signal Processing Systems*, presented at 97th **Audio Engineering Society Convention**, Nov. 1994.

7

GENERAL REFERENCES: HARDWARE DESIGN TECHNIQUES

1. **Linear Design Seminar**, Section 11, Analog Devices, Inc., 1995.

2. **E.S.D. Prevention Manual**
   Available free from Analog Devices, Inc.

3. B.I. & B. Bleaney, **Electricity & Magnetism**, OUP 1957, pp 23,24, & 52.

4. Paul Brokaw, *An I.C. Amplifier User's Guide to Decoupling, Grounding and Making Things Go Right for a Change*, **Analog Devices Application Note**, Available free of charge from Analog Devices, Inc.

5. Jeff Barrow, *Avoiding Ground Problems in High Speed Circuits*, **R.F. Design**, July 1989.

   AND

   Paul Brokaw & Jeff Barrow, *Grounding for Low- and High-Frequency Circuits*, **Analog Dialogue**, 23-3 1989.
   Free from Analog Devices.

6. International EMI Emission Regulations
   Canada   CSA C108.8-M1983   FDR   VDE 0871/VDE 0875
   Japan   CISPR (VCCI)/PUB 22   USA   FCC-15 Part J

7. Bill Slattery & John Wynne, *Design & Layout of a Video Graphics System for Reduced EMI*, Analog Devices Application Note (E1309-15-10/89)
   Free from Analog Devices.

8. William R. Blood, Jr., **MECL System Design Handbook** (HB205, Rev. 1), Motorola Semiconductor Products, Inc., 1988.

9. Wainwright Instruments Inc., 69 Madison Ave., Telford, PA, 18969-1829, Tel. 215-723-4333, Fax. 215-723-4620.

   Wainwright Instruments GmbH, Widdersberger Strasse 14, DW-8138 Andechs-Frieding, Germany. Tel: +49-8152-3162, Fax: +49-8152-40525.

10. Ralph Morrison, **Grounding and Shielding Techniques in Instrumentation, Third Edition**, John Wiley, Inc., 1986.

11. Henry W. Ott, **Noise Reduction Techniques in Electronic Systems, Second Edition**, John Wiley, Inc., 1988.

12. Robert A. Pease, **Troubleshooting Analog Circuits**, Butterworth-Heinemann, 1991.

13. Jim Williams, Editor, **Analog Circuit Design: Art, Science, and Personalities**, Butterworth-Heinemann, 1991.

14. Doug Grant and Scott Wurcer, *Avoiding Passive Component Pitfalls*, **The Best of Analog Dialogue**, pp. 143-148, Analog Devices, Inc., 1991.

15. Walt Jung and Richard Marsh, *Picking Capacitors, Part I.*, **Audio**, February, 1980.

16. Walt Jung and Richard Marsh, *Picking Capacitors, Part II.*, **Audio**, March, 1980.

17. Daryl Gerke and Bill Kimmel, *The Designer's Guide to Electromagnetic Compatibility*, **EDN Supplement**, January 20, 1994.

18. Walt Kester, *Basic Characteristics Distinguish Sampling A/D Converters*, **EDN**, September 3, 1992, pp.135-144.

19. Walt Kester, *Peripheral Circuits Can Make or Break Sampling ADC System*, **EDN**, October 1, 1992, pp. 97-105.

20. Walt Kester, *Layout, Grounding, and Filtering Complete Sampling ADC System*, **EDN**, October 15, 1992, pp. 127-134.

21. Howard W. Johnson and Martin Graham, **High-Speed Digital Design**, PTR Prentice Hall, 1993.

7

INDEX

■ **SUBJECT INDEX**

■ **ANALOG DEVICES PARTS INDEX**

I

SUBJECT INDEX

A

AAVID Engineering, Inc., 7.68
Absolute value amplifier, 4.42
AC-coupled single-ended-to-differential
    driver, single-supply, 2.50-51
AC-coupled single-supply circuit, head-
    room considerations, 2.48-50
Active and Passive Electrical Wave Filter
    Catalog, 4.48
AD538:
  Miller capacitance, 3.21
  monolithic analog computer, 3.21
AD600:
  op amp:
    voltage controlled:
      amplifier gain, 3.7, 5.45-46
      gain vs. differential control voltage,
        3.5-6
  X-AMP, key specifications, 3.8
AD602:
  gain vs. differential control voltage, 3.5-6
  signal-to-noise ratio, 3.7
  X-AMP, key specifications, 3.8
AD603:
  automatic gain control amplifier, 3.14-16
    circuit bandwidth, 3.16
  key specifications, 3.8
  low noise automatic gain control ampli-
    fier, 3.4
  X-AMP single version, 3.7
AD606:
  block diagram, 3.31
  key specifications, 3.31-32
  limiter output, 3.32
  logarithmic and limited outputs, 3.31
  monolithic log amp, 3.31
AD607:
  block diagram, 3.55-56
  IF subsystem, 3.55-57
    automatic gain control loop, 3.3.57
    inphase and quadrature demodulator,
      3.57
    linear amplifier, 3.57
    low noise/high intercept mixer, 3.57
    receiver, 3.57
  key specifications, 3.57
AD608:
  block diagram, 3.58
  IF subsystem, 3.57-59
    limiter, 3.59
    logarithmic amplifier/limiter, 3.59
    mixer, 3.59
    receiver, 3.59
  key specifications, 3.59

low pass filter, cutoff frequency, 3.59
AD636, RMS/DC converter, 3.9
AD641:
  block diagram, 3.28
  DC-coupling, 3.31
  error curve, 3.29
  gain, 3.31
  key features, 3.28
  log linearity, 3.27
  transfer function, 3.18, 3.29
AD645, photodiode preamplifier, 2.67
AD743, photodiode preamplifier, 2.67
AD744, photodiode preamplifier, 2.67
AD745, photodiode preamplifier, 2.67
AD780, Thevenin equivalent output
    voltage, 2.33
AD797, op amp, low noise, 5.45-46
AD813, programmable gain video ampli-
    fier, 2.54-55
AD815:
  applications, 2.60-61
  in asymmetric digital subscriber line
    system, 2.60-61
  THD vs. frequency, 2.61
AD817:
  capacitive loads, internal compensation
    scheme, 2.10-11
  high impedance compensation, 2.10
  power dissipation vs. supply voltage, 7.62
AD820, photodiode preamplifier, 2.67
AD823:
  photodiode preamplifier, 2.67-68
    dark current compensation, 2.68
AD831:
  block diagram, 3.47
  with external matching network, 3.50
  key specifications, 3.48
  low distortion active mixer, 3.36, 3.47-50,
    3.52-53
  noise figure, 3.49-50
AD831 Data Sheet, 3.61
AD834, as analog multiplier, 3.37
AD843, photodiode preamplifier, 2.67
AD845:
  BiFET op-amp, circuit, 1.10
  photodiode preamplifier, 2.67
AD847, op amp, ADSpice modeling, 7.5-6
AD847-family, folded cascode voltage
    feedback op-amp, circuit, 1.9
AD876:
  buffering by AD8011, 2.41
  DC-coupled single-supply driver, 2.40
  input, MOSFET switch, 2.41

sampling MOSFET, 2.41
AD976/977, 16-bit SAR ADC, 4.31
AD977X, 10-bit DAC, oversampling inter-
    polating, block diagram, 6.27
AD6461, quadrature demodulator/
    baseband filter, 5.52-53
AD6600:
    11-bit ADC:
        gain ranging:
            analog input and filter, 5.27
            block diagram, 5.25
            diversity, 5.27
            key specifications, 5.26
            with RSSI, 5.25
            SNR, 5.26
AD6620, dual channel decimating receiver,
    5.28
AD6640:
    architecture, 5.40
    key specifications, 5.40
    sampling, 5.41
AD6742:
    12-bit DAC:
        SHA deglitched:
            functional diagram, 6.24
            key specifications, 6.24
AD7882, 16-bit SAR ADC, 4.31
AD7892, 12-bit SAR ADC, 4.31
AD8001:
    cable driver, pulse response, 2.14-17
    input/output signal traces, 7.19-20
    resistors:
        DIP package, 2.2
        SOIC package, 2.2, 7.17-19
    three-capacitor decoupling, 7.19
AD8002, cross-coupled, frequency re-
    sponse, 2.24
AD8004, sensitivity to inverting input
    capacitance, 2.3
AD8011:
    frequency response, 1.15
    higher overall bandwidth, 1.17
    key specifications, 1.16
    output noise analysis, 1.31
    power supply rejection ratio, 1.35
    single-supply ADC direct-coupled driver,
        2.40-41
    two-stage gain configuration, 1.16-17
        advantages, 1.17
AD8013:
    differential voltage protected, 2.52
    triple current-feedback op amp, 2.51-53
AD8031, single-supply gain-of-two line
    driver, 2.46-47
AD8036:
    distortion near clamping region, 2.31

input vs. output clamping, 2.30
key specifications, 2.32
overdrive recovery, 2.32
performance, 2.30
unity gain voltage follower, equivalent
    circuit, 2.29
AD8037:
    distortion near clamping region, 2.31
    key specifications, 2.32
    overdrive recovery, 2.32
    performance, 2.30
    unity gain voltage follower, equivalent
        circuit, 2.29
AD8041:
    op amp:
        buffer for RGB signals, 2.43-44
        single-supply ADC driver, 2.42-43, 5.15
        AC-coupled composite video line
            driver, 2.49-50
            advantages, 2.50
            sync stripper, 2.44-45
AD8042:
    buffer for RGB signals, 2.43-44
    output saturation voltage vs. load cur-
        rent, 2.39
    single-supply AC-coupled differential
        driver, 2.50-51
AD8044, buffer for RGB signals, 2.43-44
AD8047, in video line driver, 2.18
AD8048:
    op amp:
        voltage feedback, in multiple feedback
            lowpass filter, 1.22-24
        voltage feedback in video line driver,
            2.18
AD8116:
    buffered video crosspoint switch:
        circuit, 2.59
        key specifications, 2.59
AD8170:
    bipolar video multiplexer:
        block diagram, 2.56
        key specifications, 2.56
AD8174:
    bipolar video multiplexer:
        block diagram, 2.56
        key specifications, 2.56
AD8180:
    bipolar video multiplexer:
        block diagram, 2.56
        key specifications, 2.56
AD8182:
    bipolar video multiplexer:
        block diagram, 2.56
        key specifications, 2.56
AD9002, flash converter, 2.33

AD9042:
  12-bit subranging ADC:
    in AMPS cellular system, 5.33-34
    block diagram, 5.11
    digital error correction, 5.43-44
      scheme, 4.37
    dithering effects, 5.45-48
    evaluation board:
      block diagram, 7.21
      FIFO memory, 7.23
    fabrication, 5.11
    FFT outputs, 5.36-38, 5.47-48
    key specifications, 4.39, 5.12
    MagAmp architecture, 4.37
    noise power ratio, 4.27
    performance, 5.12
    process gain, 4.22
    SFDR, 4.21-22, 4.24, 5.12, 5.36-39, 5.43, 5.47
      limitations, 5.43
    subranging point DNL errors, 5.44
AD9050:
  10-bit single-supply ADC:
    AC input coupling, 5.15
    block diagram, 5.13
    fabrication, 5.12
    FFT output, 2.43
    input circuit, 5.12-14
    key specifications, 5.14
    op amp single-supply driver, 2.42-43
    SINAD, 5.15
AD9059:
  8-bit dual ADC:
    functional diagram, 4.46
    key specifications, 4.47
AD9066:
  6-bit ADC, 4.33, 5.50-51
    flash converter:
      basic interpolation circuit, 4.34
      BiCMOS process, 4.33
      ENOB vs. analog input frequency, 4.34
      key specifications, 4.35
    IF sampling, 5.50-51
AD9220:
  12-bit pipelined CMOS ADC:
    block diagram, 4.39, 5.3
    input circuit with SHA, 5.4
    key specifications, 4.40, 5.3
    latency delay, 4.39
    SFDR and SNR, 5.10
    THD vs. input frequency, 5.5, 5.7
AD9221:
  12-bit pipelined CMOS ADC:
    block diagram, 5.3
    input circuit with SHA, 5.4

    key specifications, 4.40, 5.3
    latency delay, 4.40
AD9223:
  12-bit pipelined CMOS ADC:
    block diagram, 5.3
    input circuit with SHA, 5.4
    key specifications, 4.40, 5.3
    latency delay, 4.40
AD9721:
  10-bit DAC:
    midscale glitch impulse, 6.14-15
    SFDR plot, 6.17
AD9760:
  100MSPS DAC:
    applications, 6.22
    key specifications, 6.22
AD9762:
  100MSPS DAC:
    applications, 6.22
    key specifications, 6.22
AD9764:
  100MSPS DAC:
    applications, 6.22
    key specifications, 6.22
AD9805, 10-bit ADC, 5.20
AD9807, 12-bit ADC, CCD imaging decoder/signal processor, schematic, 5.20
AD9830/9831 CMOS DDS system, key specifications, 6.11
AD9850:
  10-bit CMOS:
    current switch DAC core, 6.20-21
      SFDR, 6.21
  125MSPS DDS/DAC synthesizer, 6.7-8
    frequency tuning, 6.8
    key specifications, 6.8
    serial loading, 6.8
AD9853:
  digital QPSK modulator:
    in CATV setup, 6.28
    key specifications, 6.29
AD620 Instrumentation Amplifier, 7.103
AD815 Data Sheet, 7.68
ADC, 5.1-54
  3-bit MagAmp folding, 4.44
    block diagram, 4.44
    equivalent circuit, 4.44
    input, 4.45
    residue waveforms, 4.45
  3-bit serial binary:
    residue outputs, 4.42-43
    simplified scheme, 4.42
  8-bit, subranging, block diagram, 4.36
  8-bit MagAmp folding, 4.45
  10-bit, distortion and noise, noise power ratio, theoretical curve,

4.26
11-bit, distortion and noise, noise power
ratio, theoretical curve,
4.26
12-bit:
    distortion and noise:
        noise power ratio, theoretical curve,
    4.26
        SINAD and ENOB, 4.19
    SAR, sampling rates, 4.31
    subranging, digitally corrected, block
    diagram, 4.37
    wideband, high SFDR, 4.21-22
16-bit, SAR, sampling rates, 4.31
applications, 5.1-54
    CCD imaging, 5.17-20
    digital receivers, 5.21-53
    low distortion/wide dynamic range
    inputs, 5.1-16
architectures, 4.30-47
bipolar input, uses, 5.11
bit-per-stage, 4.41-47
    folding converter, 4.42
    MagAmp architecture, 4.42
    scheme, 4.41
    serial-Gray architecture, 4.42
    single binary bit conversion stage, 4.41-
    42
    see also ADC, serial; ADC, ripple
CCD imaging, 5.17-20
    charge detector readout, 5.18
    correlated double sampling, 5.18-19
    linear CCD array scheme, 5.17
    output waveform, 5.19
    pixel charge, 5.18
    SHA, 5.18-19
digital receivers, 5.21-53
direct-coupled driver, single-supply, 2.40-
41
distortion mechanisms, 4.1
distortion and noise, 4.14-29
    analog bandwidth, 4.20-21
        definition, 4.20
    aperture jitter and delay, 4.27-29
        effects, 4.27-28
        SNR, 4.29
    differential non-linearity:
        distortion products, 4.16-17
        encoding process, 4.16
    effective aperture delay time, 4.28, 4.29
    ENOB, 4.18-21
        gain vs. frequency, 4.21
    equivalent number of bits, 4.19
    harmonic distortion, 4.17
    integral and differential non-linearity,
    4.16-17

noise power ratio, 4.24-27
    measurements, 4.25
    summary, 4.26
    theoretical curves, 4.26
sampling clock jitter, 4.28
    SNR, 4.29
SFDR, 4.21-22
SHA, aperture jitter, 4.28
SINAD ratio, 4.18-19
SNR, 4.18-19
    phase jitter, 4.27
sources:
    equivalent input referred noise, 4.15
    grounded-input histogram, 4.15
    model, 4.14
    thermal noise, 4.15
THD+N, 4.17
THD, 4.17
two tone IMD, 4.22-24
    measurement, 4.22
    second- and third-order
    intermodulation products, 4.23
    worst harmonic, 4.17
dither, and SFDR, 5.41
DNL errors, correction by dither, 5.43
dynamic performance quantification, 4.16
evaluation board:
    buffer memory design, 7.22
    DAC, 7.20-21
    FFT, 7.20-21
    FIFO memory, 7.22-23
fabrication:
    CMOS, 4.1-2
    XFCB process, 4.2
FFT processing gain, 4.14
flash converter, 4.31-35
gain-of-two MagAmp folding stage, 4.46
grounding, 7.28
half-flash, 4.36
high speed, 4.1-47
    evaluation board, 7.20-21
    maximizing SFDR, limitations, 5.41
ideal 12-bit:
    FFT testing, noise floor, 4.13
    input frequency vs. sampling clock
    ratio, SFDR, 4.12
ideal N-bit:
    distortion and noise, 4.10-13
        over Nyquist bandwidth, 4.10
    dynamic performance analysis, 4.12
    input, 4.11
    oversampling, 4.10
        FFT processing gain, 4.10, 4.13
    quantization noise, 4.11
    sampling, dither signal, 4.13
    sampling and quantization errors, 4.10

testing, FFT, 4.13
with integral sample-and-hold, 4.14
low distortion/wide dynamic range
    inputs, 5.1-16
    bipolar input, 5.11-16
        AC coupling, 5.15
        DC coupling, 5.15-16
        drive circuit, 5.16
    input /output common-mode range, 5.1
    switched-capacitor input, 5.2-10
        buffered AC-coupled input drive
    circuit, 5.7-8
        direct-coupled level shifter, 5.8
        input voltage range options, 5.4
        output impedance, 5.6
        output voltage span, 5.6
        SFDR, 5.4
        single-ended AC coupling circuit, 5.6-7
        THD vs. input frequency, 5.5, 5.7
        track-and-hold, 5.4
        transformer coupling, 5.9-10
lower power and voltage, 4.1
parallel, 4.31-35
    diagram, 4.32
    see also ADC, flash converter
pipelined, 4.36-40
real-time DSP signal processing, 4.1
    advantages, 4.1
ripple, 4.41-47
sampling, 4.1
    characteristics, 4.2
    integral SHA, jitter elimination, 4.28
    Nyquist zones, 4.8
SAR, 4.30-31
    accuracy, 4.31
    block diagram, 4.30
    with calibration DAC, 4.31
    as quantizer, 4.31
serial, 4.41-47
SHA, 4.14
single-supply low-distortion ADC driver,
    2.42-43
subranging, 4.36-40
    block diagram, 4.36
    digital correction, 4.36
    see also ADC, pipelined
ADP3367:
    load current vs. input/output voltage,
        7.54
    low dropout fixed/variable regulator, 7.53
    shutdown mode, 7.53
ADP3367 Data Sheet, 7.55
ADSL; See: Asymmetric digital subscriber
    line
ADSpice model:

feature summary, 7.7-8
input and gain stage model, 7.3-4
open architecture, 7.3
other features, 7.7-8
output stage, 7.5
pole and zero stage, 7.4
Advanced mobile phone service; See:
    AMPS
AGC; See: Automatic gain control loop
Aliases, 4.2-3
Amplifier, voltage controlled, 3.1
Amplifier Applications Guide (1992), 1.36,
    2.71, 3.60, 4.49, 7.26, 7.88
Amplifier input bias current, and common-
    mode voltage, 2.37
AMPS:
    analog cellular phone system, 5.21, 5.33
        process gain, 5.35
    vs. GSM, 5.34
Analog bandwidth, fundamental swept
    frequency, 4.20
Analog circuit:
    ADSpice model, 7.3-6
        input and gain stage model, 7.3-4
        open architecture, 7.3
        other features, 7.7-8
        output stage, 7.5
        pole and zero stage, 7.4
    Boyle model, 7.3
    definition, 7.1
    evaluation boards, 7.17-26
    mixed-signal, high-speed vs. high-
        precision, 7.8
    prototyping, 7.8-17
    sensitivity to RFI, 7.76
    simulation, 7.1-7
    Spice micromodel, 7.1
    Spice simulations, comparison, 7.2
Analog ground, separated from digital
    ground, 7.28-29
Analog ground plane, for decoupling, 7.29
Analog multiplier, as voltage-controlled
    amplifier, 3.4
Analog superheterodyne, receiver, 3.33,
    5.21
Antialiasing filter, in undersampling, 4.8-10
Antognetti, Paolo, 7.26
Aperture jitter, 4.28
Armstrong, Major Edwin H., 3.33, 5.21
The ARRL Handbook for Radio Amateurs,
    6.30
Asymmetric digital subscriber line:
    and high power line drivers, 2.60-61
    low-distortion differential drive ampli-
        fier, 2.60

Automatic gain control, 3.2-9
  nonlinear filtering, 3.3
  received signal strength indicator, 3.3
  system schematic, 3.3

B

Baines, Rupert, 5.54
Bandpass sampling, 4.4-10
Barber, William L., 3.60
Barrow, Jeff, 7.104
Bennett, W.R., 4.48
Best, R.E., 6.30
BiFET process, 1.1-2
Blackman, R.B., 4.49
Bleaney, B., 7.104
Bleaney, B.I., 7.104
Blood, William R. Jr., 2.71, 7.104
Bode plot, 1.4, 1.14, 1.20, 1.21, 1.25
Boltzmann's constant, 1.30
Boyle, —, 7.26
Brannon, Brad, 5.1, 5.54
Broadband Amplifier Applications, 3.60
Brokaw, Paul, 7.88, 7.104
Brown, Edmund R., 3.60
Bryant, James M., 3.1, 3.60, 7.1, 7.8, 7.27,
  7.103
Buffer:
  single-supply:
    gain-of-two, 2.43-44
      diagram, 2.44
      output, 2.45
Buffer latch:
  decoupling, 7.30
  grounding, 7.30
Butterworth filter, 4.5, 6.25
Buxton, Joe, 1.36, 2.71, 7.1

C

Cable drivers, 2.12-17
  characteristics, 2.13
  coaxial cable:
    bandwidth flatness loss, 2.14
    pulse response, 2.15
    skin effect, 2.13
Cable radiation and connector leakage,
  EMI/RFI coupling, 7.73
Cable receivers, 2.12-17
Cage jacks, 7.16
Capacitive loading:
  compensation:
    active, limitations, 2.9
    drawbacks, 2.12
    forced-high loop noise gain, 2.4
    in-the-loop, 2.8-9
    overcompensation, 2.4

  passive, 2.6
  driving, amplifier stability, 2.4
  high speed op amp:
    effects, 2.3, 2.5
    open-loop series resistance, 2.6
Capacitor:
  ceramic, 7.34-35
    multilayer ceramic "chip caps", 7.37
    NP0 types, 7.37
  characteristics, 7.34-35
  classes, 7.34-35
  electrolytic, 7.34-35
    aluminum, 7.36
      OS-CON, 7.36
      ESR, 7.38
      switching, 7.36
    ESR degradation, 7.37
    high frequency impedance, 7.38
    tantalum, 7.36
  ESL, 7.35
  film, 7.34-35
    inductive, 7.37
    low dielectric loss, 7.36-37
    noninductive, 7.37
    stacked-film, noninductive, 7.37
  finite ESR, 7.37
  real, parasitics, 7.38
CB bipolar process, 1.1-2, 2.34
CB process, 1.1-2
CCD systems, using programmable gain
  video amplifier, 2.54
Chadwick, P.E., 3.60
Channelizer, with numerically controlled
  oscillator (NCO), 5.31
Checkovich, Peter, 2.71
Clamping amplifiers, 2.28-34
  input and output compared, 2.30
Clarke, Bob, 3.1, 3.33-34, 3.54
Clelland, Ian, 7.46
CMOS switch:
  disadvantages, 2.55
  "on" resistance, 2.55
CMR; see: Common-mode rejection
CMRR; see: Common-mode rejection-ratio
Coaxial cable:
  skin effect, 2.13
  wire resistance, 2.13
Coleman, Brendan, 4.49
Colotti, James J., 4.49
Common-mode rejection-ratio instrumen-
  tation amplifiers, 2.18-19
Communications, high speed integrated
  circuits, chipset solutions, P.2
Compandor, 3.1
Complementary bipolar process, 1.1
Compression:

linear dynamic range, 3.1
  variable-gain amplifiers, 3.1
  magnetic recording, 3.1
Counts, Lew, 3.60
Coupling, EMI/RFI, 7.73
Current feedback (CFB) process, 1.2
Current noise gain, op amp, definition,
  1.21-22
Current-output DACs, 1.12
Current-to-voltage converter, input capaci-
  tance compensation, 1.24

D

DAC:
  5-bit binary, architectures, 6.19
  5-bit thermometer:
    architecture, 6.19
      disadvantage, 6.18
  10-bit, CMOS current switch core,
    scheme, 6.20
  10-bit segmented:
    PMOS transistor current switches, 6.21
    scheme, 6.20
  12-bit:
    SFDR, clock vs. output frequency, 6.13
    SHA deglitched, XFCB fabricated, 6.23-
      24
  and DDS systems, 6.1-30
  deglitching, 6.23-24
    using SHA, 6.23
  fully decoded, architecture, 6.19
  glitch impulse area, 6.14
  grounding, 7.28
  interpolating, 6.25-27
  low distortion, architecture, 6.18-22
  performance:
    measurement, spectrum analyzer, 6.15
    SFDR measurement, 6.16
  SFDR, improvement, using SHA
    deglitchers, 6.23-24
  triple video, 2.43, 2.46
  TTL-compatible, 6.15, 6.17
Data transmission:
  asymmetric digital subscriber line, 2.60-
    61
  discrete multi tone modulation, 2.60
DDS:
  125MSPS system, 6.7-8
    frequency tuning, 6.8
    phase modulation, 6.8
    serial loading, 6.8
  AD9830/9831 CMOS system, 6.10-11
    key specifications, 6.11
    structure, 6.10-11
  as ADC clock drivers, 6.9

  comparator, 6.9
  complementary DAC, 6.9
  filter, 6.9
  scheme, 6.9
aliasing, 6.5-6
  DAC output, 6.5-6
  graph, 6.6
  higher-order harmonics, 6.6
  Nyquist bandwidth, 6.6
  Nyquist criteria, 6.5
  Nyquist frequency, 6.5
amplitude modulation:
  by digital multiplier, 6.10
  scheme, 6.10
basic architecture:
  differing from PLL, 6.2
  flexible system, scheme, 6.3
  numerically controlled oscillator, 6.3
    block diagram, 6.3
    flexibility, 6.4
    output spectrum, 6.4-5
  PROM-driven clock, 6.2
  scheme, 6.2
digital audio CD player, interpolation,
  6.25
filter:
  analog, requirements, 6.26
  antialiasing, 6.25
  Butterworth, 6.25
  low pass, 6.25
interpolation, 6.25
QPSK signal generation, 6.28-29
  constellation, 6.29
  modulator, 6.28
  scheme, 6.28
SFDR considerations, 6.12-17
  clock selection, 6.12
  DAC glitch impulse area, 6.14
  DAC output spectral purity, 6.12
  digital dither, and quantization noise,
    6.13
  harmonic distortion, 6.14
  harmonics, 6.12
    even, location, 6.16
    odd, location, 6.17
  non-ideal DAC, distortion, 6.14
  Nyquist bandwidth, 6.12
  output glitches, 6.14
  specifications, 6.15
  tuning equation, 6.4
Deadbug prototyping, 7.9-10
Designing for EMC (Workshop Notes),
  7.88, 7.103
Differential line drivers and receivers,
  2.18-28
  active feedback receiver, 2.26-28

I

video, 2.26-27
approaches, 2.19-20
cross-coupled driver, 2.22-24
  cell bandwidth, 2.23
  circuit benefits, 2.23
  gain calculations, 2.22-23
  high common-mode rejection, 2.22
four-resistor receiver, 2.24-26
  video:
    diagram, 2.25
    drawback, 2.26
    gain/phase performance, 2.26
high common-mode rejection-ratio
  instrumentation amps, 2.18-19
inverter-follower driver, 2.20-21
  diagram, 2.20
  input impedance, 2.21
  open-loop bandwidth matching, 2.21
  resistor gain error effects, 2.21
single-ended driver, source-terminated
  coaxial cable, 2.20
Digital communication systems, 16-QAM
  modulation, 5.50
Digital communications system, QPSK
  modulation, 5.49
Digital ground, separated from analog
  ground, 7.28-29
Digital mobile radio, IF stages, schematic,
  3.33
Digital receivers:
  AMPS analog cellular phone system,
    5.21, 5.33
    image frequency at receiver, 5.21
    one receiver per channel, 5.22
  digital communication systems, 5.49-53
    16-QAM modulation system, 5.50
    modulation systems, 5.49-50
    QPSK modulation system, 5.49-50
  digital processing at baseband, 5.22-24
    schematic, 5.23
    software radios, 5.22-23
  direct broadcast satellite set-top boxes,
    5.49-53
  direct IF-to-digital, 5.38-41
    FFT output, 5.39
    SFDR, 5.38-39
  narrowband IF-sampling, 5.24-30
    advantages, 5.24
    comparison with wideband, 5.31
    DSP functions, 5.28
    GSM system, 5.24, 5.27-28
      Bandpass sampling, 5.29
      digital filtering and decimation, 5.29
      diversity, 5.27-28
    GSM vs. AMPS, 5.34
    Nyquist frequency, 5.28

Nyquist zones, 5.28
oversampling, 5.28
processing gain, 5.30
RSSI peak detector function, 5.27
SINAD, 5.30
SNR, Nyquist bandwidth, 5.30
wide dynamic range using dither, 5.41-48
  ADC transfer function randomizing,
    5.42
  dither noise generator, scheme, 5.46
  effect on SFDR, 5.41-43
wideband IF-sampling, 5.31-38
  AMPS cellular system, 5.33-34
    process gain, 5.35
  AMPS vs. GSM, 5.34
  comparison with narrowband, 5.31
  digital radio Channelizer, 5.31-32
    scheme, 5.32
  GSM:
    disadvantages, 5.35-36
    two-tone intermodulation distortion,
  5.36
  Nyquist zones, 5.35
  SFDR, 5.33
Direct broadcast satellite set-top boxes:
  IF signal processing, 5.52-53
  modulation, 5.52-53
Direct broadcast satellite system:
  ADC sampling rate, 5.50
  bandwidth smears, 5.50
  baud rate, 5.49
  bit-error-rate, 5.49
  block diagram, 5.52
  constellation, 5.49
  downlink frequency, Kuband, 5.52
  eye patterns, 5.50
  low noise block converter (LNBC), 5.52
  MPEG encoding/decoding, 5.51
  symbols, 5.49
Direct digital synthesis; See: DDS
Direct IF to digital conversion, 4.4-10
Discrete multi tone, modulation scheme,
  2.60
Dostal, J., 1.36
Dual conversion superhet receiver, 3.33

E
EDN (Jan. 20, 1994), 7.88, 7.103
Edson, J.O., 4.48
Electric field, strength, definition, 7.76
Electric-field intensity, in RFI, 7.76
Electromagnetic compatibility; See: EMC
Electromagnetic interference; See: EMI
Elliptic filter, 4.5
EMC Design Workshop Notes, 7.46

EMC Test & Design, 7.88
EMI:
  cable:
    capacitive coupling, 7.95
    magnetic coupling, 7.95-96
    twisted pair, for noise immunity, 7.96
    unshielded as antenna, 7.96
  paths, 7.34, 7.72
  printed circuit board design, 7.83-87
    device speed, 7.84
    embedding, 7.85
    multi-layer arrangement, striplines, 7.85
    noise filter, 7.84
    planes, 7.85
    power supply filter, 7.84
    signal line snubbing, 7.84
    trace termination, 7.86
    transmission lines, 7.86-87
  protection, printed circuit board design, 7.83-87
  receptors, 7.34, 7.72
  regulations, 7.69-71
    automotive equipment, SAE standards, 7.71
    commercial equipment:
      conducted interference, 7.69
      emission limits, 7.70
      FCC and VDE, 7.69-70
      radiated emissions, 7.69
    impact on design, 7.71
    industrial- and process-control equipment, 7.71
    medical equipment, 7.70
    military equipment, MIL-STD-461, 7.70
  sources, 7.34, 7.72
    power-line transients, 7.80-81
  see also entries under EMI/RFI and RFI
EMI/RFI, 7.69-87
  coupling:
    cable radiation and connector leakage, 7.73
    slot and board radiation, 7.73
    via interconnects, 7.73
  diagnostics, source, path, and receptor, 7.72-74
  emission:
    conduction, 7.73
    radiation, 7.73
  immunity, 7.74
  internal, 7.74
  passive components, 7.75
  path:
    conduction, 7.73
    radiation, 7.73
  shielding, 7.89-102

    ground loops, 7.97-98
    grounded, 7.97
  signal amplitude, 7.74
  signal distance, 7.74
  signal frequency, 7.74
  signal impedance, 7.74
  signal time, 7.74
  source-path-receptor model, 7.72-74
  susceptibility, 7.74
  see also separate entries under EMI, RFI
Emitter degeneration:
  voltage feedback op-amp, 1.6
    effects on equipment, 1.6
ENOB, 4.18-21
Equivalent number of bits; See: ENOB
Equivalent series inductance; See: ESL
E.S.D. Prevention Manual, 7.104
European digital cellular system; See: GSM system
Evaluation board, 7.17-26
  buffer memory design, 7.22
  DAC, 7.20-21
  FFT, 7.20-21
  FIFO memory, 7.22-23
  IC performance verification, 7.24
  for op amp, 7.17-19
  power supply decoupling, 7.19
  transient currents, 7.19
  Windows software:
    DNL histogram, 7.25
    FFT output, 7.25
    time-domain data, 7.24
Exponential amplifier, 3.4
Extra fast complementary bipolar (XFCB) process, 1.1

F

Faraday shields, 7.82
Federal Communications Commission; See: FCC
Ferrite:
  bead, 7.39
  characteristics, 7.39
  choice, 7.40
  impedance, 7.39-40
  leaded bead, 7.39
  low-pass filter, 7.39
  nonconductive ceramics, 7.39
  PSpice models, 7.40
Filter:
  antialiasing:
    effects on system dynamic range, 4.4
    and Nyquist frequency, 4.5
    requirements:
      and increasing sampling frequency,

4.6
  relaxed, 4.6
  specifications, 4.4
  transition band:
    determination, 4.5
    sharpness vs. ADC sampling frequency, 4.6
  undersampling, 4.8-10
    Bandpass specifications, 4.9
    centering signal in Nyquist zones, 4.9
    equations, 4.8-10
band, 7.40
baseband antialiasing, 4.4-6
Butterworth, 4.5
elliptic, 4.5
low pass:
  ferrite, 7.39
  and RFI effects, 7.78-79
multiple feedback lowpass, design calculations, 1.24
multistage, for RFI effects, 7.79
RFI effects:
  band filters, 7.79
  feed-through protection, 7.79
Fixed-gain amplifier, in X-AMP, 3.4
Flash converter:
  3 clock cycle latency, 4.38-39
  basic interpolation circuit, 4.34
  clamp amplifier driven, 2.33
  diagram, 4.32
  input, 4.33
  input capacitance, high frequency distortion, 4.33
  latency cycles, 4.38
  multi-pass subranging pipelined, 4.38
  multi-stage conversion technique (pipelining), 4.37
  pipeline delay, 4.38
  pipelining, 4.37
  preamplifiers, 4.35
  sampling device, 4.32
  thermometer code output, 4.31
Folded cascode:
  voltage feedback op-amp architecture, 1.8-9
  single-stage, 1.8-9
FPBW; See: Full-power bandwidth
Franco, Sergio, 1.36
Fredericksen, Thomas M., 1.36
Frequency division multiplexed communications, noise power ratio testing, 4.24
Frequency synthesis, using oscillators and PLLs, 6.1
Frequency synthesizer, 6.1
Full power bandwidth (FPBW), 4.20

G

Garcia, Adolfo A., 7.1, 7.69, 7.89
Gardner, F.M., 6.30
Gay, M.S., 3.60
Gelbach, Herman, 7.103
Gerke, Daryl, 7.105
Ghausi, M.S., 4.50
Gilbert cell, mixer, 3.57
Gilbert, Barrie, 1.36, 3.1, 3.34, 3.60-61
Glitch impulse area, 6.14
Gold, Bernard, 4.50
Gosser, Roy, 1.36, 4.48
Graeme, Jerald G., 1.36, 2.71
Graham, Martin, 7.26, 7.105
Grant, Doug, 7.105
Gray code, 4.42, 4.46
Gray, G.A., 4.48
Gray, Paul R., 1.36
Ground impedance, multicard system, 7.27
Ground loops, 7.97-98
Ground plane, EMI/RFI emissions, minimizing, 7.27
Grounding:
  buffer latch, 7.30
  and decoupling, 7.28-30
  EMI/RFI emissions, minimizing, 7.27-33
  high speed systems, 7.27-33
  multiple ground pins, 7.33
  power supply, 7.30
  sampling clock, 7.31
  star ground, 7.27-28
GSM system, 5.24, 5.27-29, 5.33

H

Hageman, Steve, 7.46
Harmonic distortion, 4.17
  definition, 4.17
  location of distortion products, graph, 4.18
Harmonic sampling, 4.4-10
Harris, Frederick J., 4.49
Hendricks, Paul, 5.1
Henning, H.H., 4.48
Higgins, Richard J., 4.50
High speed hardware, design techniques, 7.1-105
High speed systems:
  analog components, separation, 7.27-28
  ground plane, low impedance, 7.27
  grounding, 7.27-33
Hilton, Howard E., 4.50
Hodges, David A., 4.49
Homodyne architecture, and advantage of superheterodyne, 3.33, 5.21

HP Journal (Apr. 1988), 4.49
HP Journal (June 1988), 4.50
HP Journal (Nov. 1982), 4.49
HP Product Note 5180A-2, 4.49
Hughes, Richard Smith, 3.60

I
IEEE Standard 746-1984, 2.71
IEEE Trial-Use Standard for Digitizing
    Waveform Recorders, 4.50
IF sampling, 4.4-10
Imaging, high speed integrated circuits,
    chipset solutions, P.2
Immunity, 7.76
Instrumentation, high speed integrated
    circuits, chipset solutions, P.2
Integrated circuits:
    chipset solutions, P.2
    core competencies, P.3
    markets, P.2
Interconnects, EMI/RFI coupling, 7.73
Intermodulation distortion; See: IMD
International EMI Emission Regulations,
    7.104
An Introduction to the Imaging CCD
    Array, 5.54

J
Johnson noise, 1.29
Johnson, Howard W., 7.26, 7.105
Jung, Walter G., 1.36, 2.1, 2.71, 7.1, 7.34,
    7.46-47, 7.55-56, 7.103,
    7.105

K
Kaufman, M., 1.36
Keate, Chris, 5.54
Kerr, Richard J., 6.30
Kester, Walter A., 1.1, 2.1, 2.71, 3.1, 3.33-
    34, 3.54, 4.1, 4.49, 5.1,
    6.1, 7.1, 7.8, 7.17, 7.27, 7.105
Kimmel, Bill, 7.105
Kitchen, Charles, 3.60
Koernberg, Joey, 4.49

L
Laker, K.R., 4.50
Lane, Chuck, 4.48
LE1182 11-pole elliptic antialiasing filter,
    characteristics, 4.5
Lee, Hae-Seung, 4.49
Line driver, high speed op amp, single-
    supply, 2.47
Linear Design Seminar (1995), 3.61, 4.48,
    7.104

Log amp; See: Logarithmic amplifier
Log video, 3.19-20
Logarithmic amplifier, 3.17-32
    basic architectures:
        basic diode log amp, 3.21
        successive detection log amp, 3.21
        true log amp, 3.21
    basic graph, 3.19
    as converter, 3.17
    detecting, 3.19-20, 3.23
    diode/op-amp log amp, 3.21-22
        disadvantages, 3.21
    filter, internal low pass, cutoff frequency,
        3.59
    graph, 3.17
    high frequency applications, preferred
        architectures, 3.23
    intercept voltage, 3.18
    key parameters, 3.27
    monolithic, successive detection stages,
        3.31-32
    multi-stage architecture, 3.23
    multi-stage response, unipolar, 3.24
    noise in dynamic range, 3.18
    nonlinear dynamic range compression,
        3.1
    slope voltage, 3.19
    specifications, 3.26-27
        dynamic range, 3.26-27
        frequency response, 3.26-27
        intercept point, 3.26-27
            waveform effect, 3.29-30
        log linearity, 3.26-27
            graph, 3.27
            waveform effect, 3.30
        noise, 3.26-27
        slope of transfer characteristic, 3.26-27
    successive detection:
        cascaded limiting stages, 3.26
        log and limiter outputs, 3.25-26
    summing, 3.25
    transfer characteristic, 3.18
    transistor/op-amp log amp, 3.22
    true, 3.19-20, 3.23
        in summing amplifier, 3.25
    in video display, 3.19
    volts per decade factor, 3.19
Logarithmic video amplifier, 3.19

M
McDonald, John, 7.1, 7.34, 7.89
MagAmp, 4.42
    3-bit folding ADC, 4.44
        block diagram, 4.44
        equivalent circuit, 4.44
        input, 4.45

residue waveforms, 4.45
6- and 7-bit ADCs, 4.37
8-bit folding ADC, 4.45
architecture, 4.36
gain-of-two folding stage, 4.46
Magnitude amplifier, 4.42
architecture, 4.36
Mahoney, Matthew, 4.50
Marsh, Richard, 7.46, 7.105
Massobrio, Guiseppi, 7.26
Mathcad 4.0 Software Package, 4.50
Mayo, J.S., 4.48
Meehan, Pat, 4.49
Melsa, James L., 1.36
Meyer, Robert G., 1.36
Mil-STD-461, 7.70
Miller capacitance, in logarithmic ampli-
fier, 3.21
Miller integrator, voltage feedback op-amp,
CB process, 1.7
Mini-Circuits LRMS-1H mixer, 3.44
Mitola, Joe, 5.54
Mixed-signal circuit, definition, 7.1
Mixed-signal IC, grounding, 7.28
Mixer:
active, 3.36
1dB gain compression level, 3.50-53
basic operation, 3.46-47
BJT form, 3.45-46
classic, 3.45-46
design objectives, 3.50
different from diode-ring, 3.46
gain, 3.47
IMD, 3.50
spur chart, 3.52-53
third-order, plot, 3.51
third-order intercept, 3.50-53
noise figure, 3.49
poor dynamic range, 3.53
scheme, 3.45
various uses, 3.47
as analog multiplier, optimized for
frequency translation, 3.53
conversion gain, 3.36
definition, 3.36
diode-ring, 3.43-44
circuit non-linearity, 3.52
diagram, 3.43
gallium-arsenide diodes, 3.43
passive, noise figure, 3.49
silicon junction diodes, 3.43
silicon Schottky-barrier diodes, 3.43
diodes, nonlinearity, impedances, 3.43
downconverter, 3.35
FET, 3.44-45
diode burnout prevention, 3.44

dual-gate MOS-FET, 3.44-45
insertion losses, 3.44
high level, 3.35
high-side downconverter, 3.35
ideal, 3.40-42
idealized, scheme, 3.34
low-side downconverter, 3.35
modulator optimized for frequency
translation, 3.36
multiplying:
inputs and outputs, 3.37
mathematics, 3.38
output spectrum, 3.38
noise and matching, 3.36
port:
intermediate frequency output, 3.34
local oscillator input, 3.34
RF input, 3.34
RF, scheme, 3.37
summary, 3.53
switching:
harmonic components, 3.42
image response, 3.42
inputs and outputs, 3.41
mathematics, 3.41-42
output spectrum, 3.42
scheme, 3.40
upconverter, 3.35
Mobile phone, RF signal, mixing, demodulation, 3.59
Modulator:
balanced, 3.35
doubly-balanced, 3.35
high level mixer, 3.35
response, 3.36
as sign-changer, 3.35
Moreland, Carl, 4.48
Morrison, Ralph, 7.88, 7.103, 7.104
Motion Picture Experts Group; See: MPEG
Motorola 5082-4204 PIN Photodiode, 2.64
characteristics, 2.64-65
Motorola MC1496 mixer, 3.45
Multiplexer:
expanding two 4:1 into 8:1, 2.58
video circuit, op amps using disable
function, 2.51-53
Multiplier:
analog, 3.35
for mixing, 3.36-38
four-quadrant, 3.35
linear, devices, 3.35
mathematical, 3.35
response, 3.36
single-quadrant, 3.35
two-quadrant, 3.35
Muncy, Neil, 7.103

Murden, Frank, 4.48
Mux; See: Video multiplexer

N

N-channel JFET pair input stage, negative
    rail, 2.36
Nash, Eamon, 2.46
Nicholas, Henry T., III, 6.30
Noise:
    Boltzmann's constant, 1.30
    calculation, principles, 1.30-31
    equivalent noise bandwidth, calculation,
      1.28
    Johnson, 1.29
    minimizing, by signal separation, 7.31
    photodiode preamplifier, analysis, 2.69-70
    power supply, reduction and filtering,
      7.34-46
    reduction tools, 7.35
    shot-noise voltage, 1.30
    sources, output, 1.29
    voltage, 1.30
Noise analysis, photodiode preamplifier,
    2.69-70
Noise figure:
    calculation, 3.49
    definition, 3.49
    op amp, 1.32
      calculation, 1.32
Noise gain:
    circuit, 1.22
    definition, 1.21-22
    high, 2.4-5
      follower stability, 2.5
      inverter stability, 2.5
    source, 1.21-22
Noise power ratio, 4.24-27
    peak, 4.26
Non-saturating emitter-coupled logic, 1.12
Numerically controlled oscillator:
    32-bit phase accumulator, output spec-
      trum, 6.4-5
    delta phase register, 6.3
    n-bit phase accumulator, 6.4
    part of DDS system, 6.4
    phase accumulator, 6.3
Nyquist bandwidth, 4.3, 4.10, 5.30, 6.2, 6.6,
    6.12
Nyquist criteria, 4.7-8, 6.5
Nyquist frequency, 5.28, 6.5
Nyquist zones, 4.3, 4.8, 5.28, 5.35, 5.40

O

O'Brien, Mark, 5.54
Ohmtek (firm), 2.71

Op amp:
    amplifier bandwidth vs. supply current,
      1.1
      diagram, 1.2
    applications, 2.1-71
      gain/phase matched signals, 2.18
    bias currents, 1.34
    cable driver:
      pulse response, 2.14-17
      source-end termination, 2.15-16
    cable drivers and receivers, 2.12-17
    capacitive load compensation:
      active, 2.8-9
      damping resistor, 2.7-8
      and frequency response, 2.7
      in-the-loop, 2.8-9
      internal, 2.9-10
    CFB; See: Op amp, current feedback
    clamping, 2.28-34
    classical noise model, 1.28-29
    closed-loop output impedance, 2.16
    current feedback, 1.12-18
      active filter, 1.22-23
      bandwidth, 1.17, 1.18
      Bode plot, 1.14
      closed-loop bandwidth, 1.14-15
        determination, 1.17
      current-to-voltage converter:
        advantages, 1.26-27
        input capacitance compensation, 1.25
        low inverting input impedance, 1.27
      distortion, 1.18
      family characteristics, 1.18
      feature summary, 1.18
      feedback capacitance effects, noise gain,
      1.20-21
      full-power bandwidth, 1.17
      input bias currents, 1.34
      input capacitance compensation,
      current-to-voltage converter, 1.25
      input current noise, 1.30
      input voltage noise, 1.30
      inverting impedance level, 1.12-13
      inverting input impedance, 1.17, 1.27
      inverting mode, advantages, 1.27
      key features, 1.17
      low impedance, 1.27
      model, 1.14
      simplified diagram, 1.13
      slew rate, 1.13, 1.18
      suitability, configurations, 1.22
      triple, 2.51-53
        in video programmable gain ampli-
      fier, 2.54-55
      wideband:
        capacitive loads, 2.3-12

forced-high loop noise gain, 2.4
    overcompensation, 2.4
    stability, 2.4
  linear drivers, design, 2.3
    optimum bandwidth flatness, 2.1-12
    feedback resistors, 2.1-2
  zero slew-rate limitation, 1.13
current feedback vs. voltage feedback,
  noise comparisons, 1.28-33
current-to-voltage converter, 1.24-27
  compensation calculations, 1.25
  inverting input capacitance effects,
  1.24-27
DC characteristics, 1.33-35
  output offset voltage, summary, 1.34
differential line drivers and receivers,
  2.18-28
evaluation board, schematic, 7.17-18
feedback capacitance effects, 1.19-24
  Bode plot, 1.20-21
  closed loop bandwidth, 1.20
  noise gain, 1.19-20
  signal bandwidth, 1.20
  signal gain, 1.19-20
feedforward/feedback resistors, 1.31
input bias current, and common-mode
  voltage, 2.37
Johnson noise, 1.29-30
N-channel JFET pairs, 2.36
noise, summary, 1.33
noise comparisons, 1.28-33
  model, 1.28-29
noise figure, 1.32
  calculation, 1.32
noise sources, 1.29, 1.31
  closed-loop gain, 1.31
output stage:
  common emitter, 2.39
  emitter follower, 2.39
output voltage offset, model, 1.33
PNP input, negative rail, 2.36
power pins, decoupling, 1.35
power supply rejection ratio, characteristics, 1.35
rail-to-rail input, 2.34
rail-to-rail output, in low dropout references, 17.48
review, 1.1-36
single-supply, 2.34
  AC-coupled, headroom considerations,
  2.48-50
  AC-coupled single-ended-to-differential
  driver, 2.50-51
  ADC direct-coupled driver, 2.40-41
  ADC low-distortion ADC driver, 2.42-43
  applications, 2.40-51

    AC-coupled, headroom consider-
ations, 2.48-50
    AC-coupled single-ended-to-differen-
tial driver, 2.50-51
    ADC low-distortion ADC driver, 2.42-
43
    direct-coupled driver, 2.40-41
    RGB buffer, 2.43-44
    sync stripper, 2.44-46
    video line driver with zero-volt
output, 2.46-47
  characteristics, 2.35
  design tradeoffs, 2.35
  rail-to-rail input, 2.35
  RGB buffer, 2.43-44
  sync stripper, 2.44-46
  video line driver with zero-volt output,
  2.46-47
terminated cable, resistive load, 2.12
total output RMS noise, 1.28
VFB; See: Op amp, voltage feedback
video, 2.51
video line driver, 2.17
video line receiver, 2.25
voltage feedback, 1.2-12
  active filter, 1.22-23
  amplifier unity gain-bandwidth product, 1.3
  bandwidth calculation, 1.6
  bipolar:
    inefficiency, 1.6
    slew rates, 1.6
  Bode plot, 1.4
  capacitive load compensation, in-the-
  loop, 2.9
  capacitor in feedback loop, 1.20
    noise gain, 1.20-21
  circuit topology, 1.2
  closed-loop bandwidth vs. closed-loop
  gain, 1.5
  complementary bipolar process, 1.1,
  1.7-10
    BiFET, circuit, 1.10
    components, 1.7
    input differential pair, 1.7
    JFETs, 1.9
      tail currents, 1.9
    Miller integrator, 1.7
    model, 1.8
    two gain stages, diagram, 1.7
  current-on-demand architecture, 1.10-
12
    quad-core structure, diagram, 1.11
  current-to-voltage converter:
    input capacitance compensation, 1.24
    in photodiode, 2.65-66

de-compensated, 1.5
emitter degeneration, 1.6
feedback capacitance effects, noise gain
  stability, 1.20-21
folded cascode architecture, 1.8-9
  circuit, 1.9
  stability, 1.9
  unity-gain compensated, 1.9
full-power bandwidth, 1.6
  calculation, 1.5
fundamental property, 1.5
gain-bandwidth product, 1.5
in high-speed ADC applications, 5.16
model, 1.4
NPN process, 1.2-3
  diagram, 1.3
quad-core structure, diagram, 1.11
rail-to-voltage, single-supply, performance, 2.46
slew rate calculation, 1.6
structure, 1.3-4
  equations, 1.4-5
  input stage, 1.3
  tail current, 1.3
  transconductance stage, 1.3
voltage feedback vs. current feedback,
  noise comparisons, 1.28-33
OS-CON capacitor, 7.36
Ott, Henry W., 1.36, 7.46, 7.88, 7.103, 7.104
Overcompensation, op amp bandwidth
  reduction, 2.4
Oversampling; See: Sampling,
  oversampling

P
PCRR; See: Power supply rejection ratio
Pease, Robert A., 7.10, 7.26, 7.104
Personal communications systems, 5.31
PGA; See: Programmable gain video
  amplifier
Phase jitter, 4.27
Phase-Locked Loop Design Fundamentals,
  6.30
Phase-locked loops, 6.1
Photoconductive photodiode mode, 2.63
Photodiode:
  circuit sensitivity, 2.64
  dark current, 2.63
  equivalent circuit, 2.62
  frequency response and stability analy-
    sis, 2.65-66
  high bandwidth preamplifier, equivalent
    circuit, 2.64
  Motorola 5082-4204 PIN:
    characteristics, 2.64-65

Photoconductive mode, 2.64-65
operating bias, 2.63
operating modes, 2.63
preamplifier:
  comparisons, 2.67
  dark current compensation, 2.68
  equivalent noise bandwidth, 2.69
  key parameters, 2.64
  noise analysis, 2.69-70
  optimizing, 2.63-64
  output noise analysis, 2.69-70
    equivalent circuit, 2.70
  selection, 2.67-68
preamps, 2.62-70
second-order current-to-voltage converter:
  input capacitance compensation, 2.66
  using voltage-feedback op-amp, 2.65-66
  shunt resistance, 2.62-63
Photovoltaic photodiode mode, 2.63
Pin sockets, 7.16
PMOS transistor current switches, 6.21
PNP input stage, negative rail, 2.36
Power:
  dissipation:
    A/D converters, 7.62
    calculation, 7.61-62
    clock dependent, 7.62
Power supply:
  analog ready filters, 7.34
  decoupling, 7.30
  filter, ferrites, 7.39
  grounding, 7.30
  noise reduction and filtering, 7.34-46
  power line filter, 7.44-45
  regulation/conditioning, 7.47-54
    basic references, 7.47-48
    low dropout references, 7.47-54
      linear IC regulators, 7.52-53
      rail-to-rail output op amp, 7.48
    low dropout regulators, 7.50-54
      boosted output with current limiting,
      7.51
      controlled gain bipolar power transis-
      tor, 7.50
    scaled references, 7.49-50
      low voltage rail-rail, 7.49
  separate for analog/digital circuits, 7.31
  switcher:
    band filter, 7.40
    "card-entry" filter, 7.41
      disadvantages, 7.43
      output response testing, 7.42
      SPICE simulation, 7.42
    filter layout/construction, guidelines,
    7.44

high frequency localized decoupling, 7.43
output noise, 7.34
   capacitor as filter, 7.34
Practical Analog Design Techniques (1995), 2.71, 4.48, 7.26
Printed circuit board design, EMI protection, 7.83-87
Programmable gain video amplifier, using triple current-feedback op amp, 2.54-55
Prototyping, 7.8-17
   CAD techniques:
      Gerber file, 7.14
      pattern-generation tape, 7.14
   commercial breadboarding, 7.11
   "Deadbug", 7.9-10
   "Deadbug" with predrilled copper-clad board, 7.10-11
   gold-plated contacts, 7.16
   IC sockets:
      cage jacks, 7.16
      cautions, 7.16
      pin sockets, 7.16
   large-area ground-plane, 7.8
   "milled" technique, 7.14-15
   multilayer PC boards, disadvantages, 7.16
   point-to-point wiring, "bird's nest", 7.10
   Solder-Mount, 7.11-14
      advantages, 7.11-13
      components, 7.12
PSpice Simulation Software, 7.26

Q

QPSK modulation, in digital communication systems, 5.49-50
Quadrature phase shift keying; See: QPSK
Quantization noise, 4.11

R

Rabiner, Lawrence, 4.50
Radio frequency interference; See: RFI
Rail-to-rail:
   high speed op amp:
      application considerations, 2.38
      characteristics, 2.34
      input stage:
         topology, 2.37
         two long-tailed pairs, 2.36
      output stage, 2.38-39
      implications, 2.34-39
Ramierez, Robert W., 4.49
Received signal strength indicator; See: RSSI

Receiver:
   demodulation:
      architecture, 3.57
         linear, 3.55
      inphase/quadrature, 3.56
      polar, 3.57-58
   design overview, 3.33-34
   high-side injection, 3.35
   image frequency, 3.39
   image response, 3.39-40
      filter, 3.40
      scheme, 3.39
   low-side injection, 3.35
   modulation, 3.54-57
      amplitude, 3.54
         rectangular and polar representations, 3.54
      phase, 3.54
         rectangular and polar representations, 3.54
   subsystem, 3.54-59
Rectification, analog circuits, 7.77
Reidy, John, 4.49
RF/IF subsystems, 3.1-61
   automatic gain control, 3.2-9
   dynamic range compression, 3.1-2
   logarithmic amplifiers, 3.17-32
   modulation/demodulation, 3.2
   multipliers, modulators, and mixers, 3.34-53
   receivers, 3.54-59
      overview, 3.33-34
   RMS-linear-dB measurement system, 3.9-16
   RMS/DC converters, 3.9-16
   signal dynamic range compression techniques, 3.2
   voltage-controlled amplifiers, 3.4-9
RFI, 7.76-80
   analog circuits:
      coupling:
         power supplies, 7.78
         signal inputs, 7.78
         signal outputs, 7.78
      filter failure, 7.79-80
      low pass filters, leakage, 7.78
      multistage filters, 7.79
      protection, 7.77-80
      rectification, 7.77
   disruption:
      shielded cables, 7.76
      to analog circuits, 7.76
   electric-field intensity, 7.76
   immunity, definition, 7.76
   power-line disturbances, 7.80-82
      Faraday shields, 7.82

filters, 7.81
  transformers, 7.82
  transient protection, 7.80-81
rectification, analog circuits, 7.77
  see also entries under EMI/RFI and EMI
RGB buffer, single-supply, 2.43-44
RGB multiplexer, dual source, with three
  2:1 multiplexers, 2.57
RGB signal, digitizer, with ADC and 4:1
  multiplexer, 2.57
Rich, A., 7.88, 7.103
RMS-linear-dB measurement system:
  deviation from ideal logarithmic output,
  3.12
  logarithmic output vs. input signal level,
  3.12
  signal output vs. input level, 3.11
RMS/DC converter, as detector element in
  automatic gain control loop, 3.9
Roberge, J.K., 1.36
Ruscak, Steve, 4.48
Ruthroff, C.L., 3.60

S
S/N+D; See: Signal to noise and distortion
Sallen-Key filter, 1.22-23
Sampling, 4.1-47
  and analog demodulation, 4.8
  bandpass, 4.7-10
  baseband, Nyquist zones, 4.4
  direct IF to digital conversion, 4.4-10
  filters, 4.3
    baseband antialiasing, 4.4-6
  frequency vs. antialiasing filter require-
    ments, 4.6
  fundamentals, 4.2-3
    aliases, 4.2-3
    Nyquist bandwidth, 4.3-4
    Nyquist zones, 4.3-4, 4.7-8
    signal images, 4.2
  harmonic, 4.7-10
  IF, 4.7-10
  oversampling, 4.10
  undersampling, 4.7-10
    antialiasing filters, 4.8-10
    Nyquist criteria, 4.7-8
    Nyquist zones, 4.7-8
    scheme, 4.7
Sampling clock:
  distribution, digital to ground plane, 7.32
  generator, grounded to analog ground
    plane, 7.31
  grounding, 7.31
  jitter, 4.28
    SNR degradation, 7.31
Samueli, Henry, 6.30

Schmid, Hermann, 4.48
Schottky diode, 1.27, 2.33, 7.28
Schultz, Donald G., 1.36
Schweber, Bill, 5.54
Semiconductor:
  ambient temperature, 7.58
  device junction, 7.58
  junction temperature upper limit, 7.56
  standard package thermal resistance,
    7.59
  thermal management, 7.56-68
SFDR, 4.21-22
SHA, deglitcher for DAC, 6.23-24
Sheingold, Daniel H., 1.36, 3.60, 4.50
Shielding:
  cable, 7.93-95
    electrically short/long application, 7.93-
    95
    low frequency interference, 7.95
    pigtail terminations, 7.102
    twisted-pair, grounding, 7.95-102
  circuit:
    characteristics, 7.89
    conductive enclosures, 7.89
      absorption, 7.89-91
      effectiveness, 7.89-90
      reflection, 7.89-90
    materials, impedance and skin depths,
      7.92
    openings as EMI waveguides, 7.92-93
  effectiveness, equation, 7.93
  EMI/RFI emissions, 7.89-102
  ground loops, 7.97-98
  grounding, 7.97-98
    proper techniques, 7.97-98
  interference:
    distance, 7.89
    impedance, 7.89
    source, 7.89
    surrounding environment, 7.89
  line driver, hybrid grounding, 7.101
  sensor, 7.93-95, 7.97-100
    hybrid grounding, 7.100
    type and configuration, 7.101-102
Shot-noise voltage, 1.30
Signal routing, in PC board layout,
  scheme, 7.32
Signal-to-noise and distortion ratio; See:
  SINAD
Signal-to-noise ratio; See: SNR
SINAD, 4.18-19
Singer, Larry, 4.48
Single-supply:
  high speed op amp:
    applications, 2.40-51
    characteristics, 2.35

rail-to-rail input, 2.35
  implications, 2.34-39
  signal swing maximization, 2.34
Single-supply AC-coupled circuits, head-
    room considerations, 2.48-50
Single-supply AC-coupled single-ended-to-
    differential driver, 2.50-51
Single-supply ADC direct-coupled driver,
    2.40-41
Single-supply ADC low-distortion ADC
    driver, 2.42-43
Single-supply RGB buffer, 2.43-44
Single-supply sync stripper, 2.44-46
  output, 2.46
Single-supply video line driver with zero-
    volt output, 2.46-47
Slattery, B., 7.88
Slattery, Bill, 7.104
Slot and board radiation, EMI/RFI, 7.73
Small signal bandwidth (SSBW), 4.20
Smith, Lewis, 1.36
SNR, 4.18-19
Source-path-receptor model, EMI/RFI,
    7.72-74
Spurious free dynamic range; See: SFDR
Stout, D., 1.36
Successive approximation; See: SAR
Superheterodyne, receiver, 3.33, 5.21
Sync stripper, single-supply, 2.44-46
Systems Application Guide (1993), 4.48,
    4.49, 7.103
Systems Application Guide (1994), 7.88

T
Tail current, voltage feedback, 1.3
Tant, M.J., 4.48
THD+N, 4.17
THD, 4.17
Thermal management:
  airflow control, 7.63-68
    on-chip temperature control, 7.63
  calculating power in various devices,
    7.61-63
    power dissipation, 7.61-62
  semiconductors, 7.56-68
  thermal basics, 7.56-60
  thermal resistance, 7.56-57
    power dissipation vs. temperature, 7.57
TMP12:
  airflow sensor, 7.64
  parasitic temperature errors, minimiza-
    tion, 7.66
  setpoint controller, scheme, 7.67
  temperature relationships, 7.65
Total harmonic distortion; See: THD

Total harmonic distortion plus noise; See:
    THD+N
Transconductance, voltage feedback, small-
    signal, formula, 1.3
Transmission line:
  driving, preferred method, 2.15
  parasitics, 2.3
True log amplifier, 3.19-20, 3.26
Tukey, J.W., 4.49

U
Ultrasound systems, using programmable
    gain video amplifier, 2.54
Undersampling:
  Nyquist criteria, 4.7-8
  Nyquist zones, 4.7-8
  scheme, 4.7

V
VCA; See: Voltage controlled amplifier
Vector Electronic Company, 7.26
Verband Deutscher Electrotechniker; See:
    VDE
VFB; See: Voltage feedback
Video:
  composite, single-supply AC-coupled line
    driver, 2.49-50
  high speed integrated circuits, chipset
    solutions, P.2
Video amplifier, programmable gain, 2.54-
    55
Video crosspoint switch, buffered, 2.59
Video line driver, 2.18
  single-supply:
    AC-coupled, 2.49
    zero-volt output, 2.46-47
Video line receiver, 2.25
  gain-scaling, 2.26
  loop-through connection, 2.27-28
  NTSC performance, 2.28
  overvoltage protection, 2.25-26
Video log amplifier, 3.26
Video multiplexer:
  2:1:
    diagram, 2.53
    off-channel isolation, 2.53
  3:1, diagram, 2.52
  bipolar, diagrams, 2.56
  crosspoint switches, 2.55-59
  disable function, 2.51-53
Video op amps, 2.51
Video programmable gain amplifier, with
    triple current-feedback op amp,
    2.54-55
Video signals, terminated coaxial cable,

2.12
Voltage controlled amplifier, 3.1-2, 3.4-9
    using analog multiplier, 3.4
        gain linear in volts, 3.4
Voltage feedback (VFB) process, 1.2
Voltage noise, 1.30
Voltage-controlled oscillator (VCO), 6.1
Voluntary Control Council for Interfer-
        ence; See: VCCI

W

Wainwright Instruments GmbH, 7.104
Wainwright Instruments Inc., 7.11, 7.26,
        7.104
Waldhauer, F.D., 4.42, 4.48
Waveform duty cycle, headroom, 2.48
Weaver, Lindsay A., 6.30
Weeks, Pat, 4.49
Wepman, Jeffery, 5.54
Whitney, Dave, 2.71
Williams, Jim, 7.26, 7.105
Witte, Robert A., 4.49
Worst harmonic, 4.17
Wurcer, Scott, 2.71, 7.105
Wynne, John, 7.88, 7.104

X

X-AMP:
    attenuator, 3.6
    bias current, Gaussian distribution, 3.7
    bias current transfer, 3.7
    dual op amp:
        gain, 3.5
        single channel, schematic, 3.5
    effective gain, 3.7
    gain ripple, 3.13
    key specifications, 3.8
    logarithmic error, output vs. input signal,
        3.13-14
    low distortion, 3.7
    operational diagram, 3.6
    total input-referred noise, 3.7
XFCB, bipolar process, 1.1-2, 2.34

Z

Zener, low voltage, 7.47
Zeoli, G.W., 4.48

ANALOG DEVICES PARTS INDEX

A

AD524, 7.59
AD534, 3.35
AD538, 3.21, 3.35
AD539, 3.21, 3.35
AD582, 7.59
AD585, 7.59
AD589, 7.48, 7.50
AD600, 3.4-7, 3.9-11, 3.13, 3.15, 5.45-46
AD602, 3.4-7, 3.15
AD603, 3.4, 3.14-15
AD606, 3.31-32, 3.59
AD607, 3.36, 3.55-57
AD608, 3.36, 3.57-59
AD620, 7.97-98
AD633, 3.35
AD636, 3.9-11, 3.13
AD641, 3.26, 3.28-31, 3.59
AD645, 2.67
AD712, 1.1-2, 3.9, 7.59
AD713, 7.59
AD734, 3.35
AD743, 2.67
AD744, 2.67
AD745, 2.67
AD780, 2.33, 5.8
AD797, 5.45-46
AD810, 2.51
AD811, 1.1-2, 2.6-7, 7.59, 7.61
AD812, 2.20-21
AD813, 2.21, 2.51, 2.54-55, 7.59-60
AD815, 2.60-61
AD815AVR, 7.59-60
AD817, 1.1-2, 2.10-12, 7.61-62
AD818, 2.25
AD820, 2.36, 2.42, 2.67, 5.16, 7.49-51
AD822, 2.36, 2.40, 7.49
AD823, 2.36, 2.67-68, 2.70, 7.56, 7.59
AD824, 2.36, 7.49
AD826, 2.11, 2.21
AD827, 2.11
AD828, 2.21, 2.26
AD829, 2.4
AD830, 2.26-28
AD831, 3.36, 3.47-50, 3.52-53
AD834, 3.35, 3.37
AD835, 3.35
AD841, 7.59
AD843, 2.67
AD845, 1.9-10, 2.9, 2.67
AD847, 1.1-2, 1.9-10, 2.11-12, 7.5
AD876, 2.40-41
AD976, 4.31
AD977, 4.31

AD1580, 7.48-49
AD6461, 5.52-53
AD6462, 5.52-53
AD6600, 5.25-28
AD6620, 5.28
AD6640, 5.40-41
AD6742, 6.23-24
AD7013, 3.57
AD7015, 3.57
AD7547, 7.59
AD7575, 7.59
AD7892, 4.31
AD8001, 1.2, 1.16, 1.18, 2.1-2, 2.14-17, 7.17-19
AD8002, 1.16, 1.18, 2.22-24
AD8004, 1.16, 1.18, 2.2-3
AD8005, 1.16, 1.18
AD8009, 1.16, 1.18
AD8011, 1.1-2, 1.15-16, 1.18, 1.31-32, 1.35, 2.7-8, 2.40-41, 5.7-8
AD8013, 1.16, 1.18, 2.51-53
AD8031, 1.12, 2.37-38, 2.46-47
AD8032, 1.12, 2.37-38
AD8036, 1.11-12, 2.28-32
AD8037, 1.11-12, 2.28-33
AD8041, 1.11-12, 2.36, 2.38, 2.42-46, 2.49-50, 5.8, 5.15-16
AD8042, 1.11-12, 2.36, 2.38-39, 2.43, 2.50-51
AD8044, 1.11-12, 2.36, 2.38, 2.43
AD8047, 1.11-12, 2.18
AD8048, 1.11-12, 1.22-24, 2.18, 5.45
AD8072, 1.16, 1.18
AD8073, 1.16, 1.18
AD8116, 2.58
AD8170, 2.56-57
AD8174, 2.56, 2.58
AD8180, 2.56
AD8182, 2.56
AD9002, 2.33
AD9042, 4.21-23, 4.27, 4.36-38, 5.1, 5.27, 5.33-34, 5.36-40, 5.43-48, 7.20-21, 7.23, 7.62
AD9050, 2.42-43, 5.12-16
AD9059, 4.46-47
AD9066, 4.33, 5.50-51
AD9100, 6.23
AD9101, 6.23
AD9220, 4.18-19, 4.38-40, 5.1-10, 7.62-63
AD9221, 4.38-40, 5.1-10
AD9223, 4.38-40, 5.1-10
AD9631, 1.11-12
AD9632, 1.11-12

AD9720, 6.15
AD9721, 6.14-15, 6.17
AD9760, 6.22
AD9762, 6.22
AD9764, 6.22
AD9805, 5.20
AD9807, 5.20
AD9830, 6.10-11
AD9831, 6.10-11
AD9850, 6.7-10, 6.20-22
AD9853, 6.28-29
ADP3367, 7.52-54, 7.59
ADSP-2181, 5.22, 5.28, 5.32
ADSP-21062, 5.22, 5.28, 5.32
ADV7120, 2.43, 2.46
ADV7121, 2.43
ADV7122, 2.43

O
OP07, 7.59
OP27, 1.33
OP184, 7.49
OP191, 7.49
OP193, 7.49-50
OP196, 7.49
OP249, 1.1-2
OP279, 7.49-50
OP282, 2.36
OP284, 7.49
OP291, 7.49
OP293, 7.49-50
OP295, 7.49
OP296, 7.49
OP482, 1.2, 2.36
OP484, 7.49
OP491, 7.49
OP493, 7.49-50
OP495, 7.49
OP496, 7.49

R
REF19X-family, 7.47, 7.51-52
REF191, 7.48
REF192, 7.48, 7.51
REF193, 7.48, 7.51
REF194, 7.48, 7.51
REF195, 7.47-48, 7.51
REF196, 7.48, 7.51-52
REF198, 2.40, 7.48

S-X
SSM-2141, 2.19
SSM-2142, 2.19
SSM-2143, 2.19
TMP12, 7.63-67